ANNUAL EDITIONS

Educating Exceptional Children

06/07

Eighteenth Edition

EDITOR

Karen L. Freiberg

University of Maryland, Baltimore County

Dr. Karen Freiberg has an interdisciplinary educational and employment background in nursing, education, and developmental psychology. She received her B.S. from the State University of New York at Plattsburgh, her M.S. from Cornell University, and her Ph.D. from Syracuse University. She has worked as a school nurse, a pediatric nurse, a public health nurse for the Navajo Indians, an associate project director for a child development clinic, a researcher in several areas of child development, and a university professor. Dr. Freiberg is the author of an award-winning textbook, *Human Development: A Life-Span Approach*, which is now in its fourth edition. She is currently on the faculty at the University of Maryland, Baltimore County.

McGraw Hill

Contemporary Learning Series

2460 Kerper Blvd., Dubuque, IA 52001

Visit us on the Internet
http://www.mhcls.com

Credits

1. **Inclusive Education**
   Unit photo—© PunchStock/Punchstock/Digital Vision
2. **Early Childhood**
   Unit photo—© Getty Images/Ryan McVay
3. **Learning Disabilities**
   Unit photo—© Punchstock/Digital Vision
4. **Speech and Language Impairments**
   Unit photo—© Getty Images/Photodisc Collection
5. **Developmental Disabilities/Autistic Spectrum Disorders**
   Unit photo—© PunchStock/Punchstock/Digital Vision
6. **Emotional and Behavioral Disorders**
   Unit photo—© image100 Ltd
7. **Vision and Hearing Impairments**
   Unit photo—© Getty Images/Scott T. Baxter
8. **Multiple Disabilities**
   Unit photo—© PunchStock/Punchstock/Digital Vision
9. **Orthopedic and Health Impairments**
   Unit photo—© Getty Images/EyeWire, Inc. 1998
10. **Giftedness**
    Unit photo—© CORBIS/Royalty-Free
11. **Transition**
    Unit photo— © Getty Images/David Buffington

Copyright

Cataloging in Publication Data
Main entry under title: Annual Editions: Educating Exceptional Children. 2006/2007.
1. Educating Exceptional Children—Periodicals. I. Freiberg, Karen L., *comp.* II. Title: Educating Exceptional Children.
ISBN-13: 978–0–07–354581–3   ISBN-10: 0–07–354581–3   658'.05   ISSN 0198–7518

Eighteenth Edition

Cover image © Photodisc Collection/Getty Images and SW Productions/BrandX Pictures/Getty Images
Printed in the United States of America   1234567890QPDQPD9876   Printed on Recycled Paper

Editors/Advisory Board

Members of the Advisory Board are instrumental in the final selection of articles for each edition of ANNUAL EDITIONS. Their review of articles for content, level, currentness, and appropriateness provides critical direction to the editor and staff. We think that you will find their careful consideration well reflected in this volume.

Preface

In publishing ANNUAL EDITIONS we recognize the enormous role played by the magazines, newspapers, and journals of the public press in providing current, first-rate educational information in a broad spectrum of interest areas. Many of these articles are appropriate for students, researchers, and professionals seeking accurate, current material to help bridge the gap between principles and theories and the real world. These articles, however, become more useful for study when those of lasting value are carefully collected, organized, indexed, and reproduced in a low-cost format, which provides easy and permanent access when the material is needed. That is the role played by ANNUAL EDITIONS.

President George W. Bush signed into law the No Child Left Behind Act (NCLB) in 2002. The Individuals with Disabilities Education Act (IDEA) was amended by Congress in 2004 to be aligned with NCLB. Both NCLB and IDEA relate to two other civil rights laws of the United States, the Rehabilitation Act Amendment (Section 504), and the Americans with Disabilities Act (ADA). The latter two laws prohibit disability discrimination while the NCLB and the IDEA authorize funding to educate students with disabilities.

Under current law all children with disabilities are entitled to supportive educational services from diagnosis until age 21, and to reasonable accommodations and freedom from discrimination for life. Disability advocacy groups are continually alert to signs of exclusion of people with disabilities. Despite diverse attitudes, Congress set out four goals for them: equal opportunity, full participation, independent living, and economic self-sufficiency. IDEA, as amended in 2004, stated that a disability is a natural part of the human experience and in no way diminishes the right of individuals to participate in or contribute to society.

No Child Left Behind (NCLB) has generated controversy for its emphasis on accountability and proficiency testing in several core academic subjects (eg. English, math, reading, science). Congress believed that assessing all students would enable them to maximize their self-sufficiency and achieve more life skills, rather than slipping through the cracks. Students with disabilities may have alternate assessments geared to their special educational goals. This compendium of articles includes several discussions of such testing.

The U.S. Congress and the legislative bodies of many other countries, have offered several educational goals for all schools. These include high expectations for students, high qualifications for teachers, safety in schools, flexible curricula to meet specific needs, parental participation, and evidence-based instructional methods and intervention. The use of twenty-first century technology is also a priority.

Scientific researchers have recently completed the mapping of the human genome. This means that we have knowledge of the sequencing of CATG (cytosine, adenine, thymine, and guanine), the chemicals that form DNA. It means that we can replace strands of DNA (genes) with altered CATG sequences. It means that we can alter human development if we so choose, and possibly eliminate many conditions of disability. Should twenty-first century scientists be allowed to alter genes? Who will pay for resequencing of CATG to bring about new behaviors? Should human cloning be allowed to prevent the birth of any human with a disability? Will test tube fertilization, genome inspection, and genetic correction be used as an alternative means of preventing the birth of so-called "imperfect" beings? These and other questions are likely to lead to contentious debates for many years to come.

This compendium of articles about children who need—and benefit from—special educational services, focuses on the six principles of The Individuals with Disabilities Education Act (IDEA). These are zero reject, non-discriminatory evaluation free and appropriate public education, least restrictive environment, parental participation, and the right to due process.

Annual Editions: Educating Exceptional Children 06/07 includes many interesting articles discussing the current status and suggested reforms for special education. It explains how the new U.S. laws (NCLB, IDEA) are being implemented in all areas of special education. Selections have been made with an eye to conveying information, giving personal experiences, offering suggestions for implementation, and stimulating meaningful discussions among future parents and teachers.

To help us improve future editions of this anthology, please complete and return the postage-paid article rating form on the last page. Your suggestions are valued and appreciated..

Karen Freiberg

Karen Freiberg
Editor

Contents

Preface   **iv**

Topic Guide   **xii**

Internet References   **xv**

UNIT 1
Inclusive Education

Unit Overview   **xviii**

1. **An Interview With Dr. Marilyn Friend,** Mary T. Brownell and Chriss Walther-Thomas, *Intervention in School and Clinic,* March 2002
   Dr. Marilyn Friend is a leading expert in *inclusive education* for students with disabilities. By answering questions about special education today, she addresses what it takes to make it work, the importance of *collaboration,* and how to help administrators support inclusion and *socialization* of all children.   **3**

2. **Rethinking Inclusion: Schoolwide Applications,** Wayne Sailor and Blair Roger, *Phi Delta Kappan,* March 2005
   The *legalities* of No Child Left Behind (NCLB) have promoted *inclusion* and accountability in education to enhance learning *schoolwide*. The authors describe a *collaborative* model, tested at nine schools, which helps integrate general and special education by six guiding principles.   **7**

3. **Assessment That Drives Instruction,** Pokey Stanford and Stacy Reeves, *Teaching Exceptional Children,* March/April 2005
   Appropriate *assessment* can maximize learning for students with special needs in *inclusion* classrooms. *Individualized education programs (IEPs)* should include alternate strategies for assessing *learners with disabilities.* The authors give examples of creative ways for special and general education *collaboration* in *school* progress reports.   **14**

4. **Meaningful Inclusion of All Students in Team Sports,** Yoshihisa Ohtake, *Teaching Exceptional Children,* November/December 2004
   The author tells how and why physical education boosts *self-esteem* in students with *health, developmental, and multiple disabilities. Creative* adaptations can make *inclusion* possible in team sports. Conversion stategies allow *IEP* goals to be achieved with the assistance of *peer* or *parent* volunteers.   **17**

UNIT 2
Early Childhood

Unit Overview   **22**

5. **Making the Case for Early Identification and Intervention for Young Children at Risk for Learning Disabilities,** Marcee M. Steele, *Early Childhood Education Journal,* October 2004
   Preschoolers with *Learning Disabilities (LD)* can be *assessed* in *early childhood.* Strategies for LD identification are given in this article as well as suggestions for teachers. Early intervention makes *IEPs, inclusion, and socialization* easier in *elementary school.*   **25**

The concepts in bold italics are developed in the article. For further expansion, please refer to the Topic Guide and the Index.

6. **Music in the Inclusive Environment,** Marcia Earl Humpal and Jan Wolf, *Young Children,* March 2003

Music is valuable in **early childhood education** because it speaks to the emotions. It helps children with special needs relax and make the **transition** from special class to **inclusion** class. It also organizes brain activity and enhances perception, **speech, socialization,** and **creativity.**

29

7. **Building Relationships With Challenging Children,** Philip S. Hall and Nancy D. Hall, *Educational Leadership,* September 2003

Early childhood is an opportune time to **socialize** more appropriate behaviors in students with **emotional and behavioral disorders** in **inclusion** classrooms. Philip and Nancy Hall illustrate **conflict resolution** without punishment. They recommend gentle intervention, bonding, support, and targeted instruction for at-risk students.

33

UNIT 3
Learning Disabilities

Unit Overview

36

8. **Providing Support for Student Independence Through Scaffolded Instruction,** Martha J. Larkin, *Teaching Exceptional Children,* September/October 2001

Studies of adults who are successful and **learning disabled** show past supportive **elementary education.** Scaffolded instruction, as described in this article, fosters independence, provides support, and leads to success. **Assessment** of the needs of the learner and engagement, goals, feedback, and generalization are illustrated.

39

9. **Celebrating Diverse Minds,** Mel Levine, *Educational Leadership,* October 2003

Students with **learning disabilities** may be brilliant (eg. Einstein, Edison) but their specialized minds may earn disappointing school grades. Dr. Levine reviews variations in **brain development** and reasons why schools are ill-equipped to support learning in diverse minds. He suggests different **assessments,** curriculum, and teacher preparation for the future.

45

10. **No More Friday Spelling Tests? An Alternative Spelling Assessment for Students With Learning Disabilities,** Kelly A. Loeffler, *Teaching Exceptional Children,* March/April 2005

Students with **learning disabilites** benefit from a spelling rubric, which teaches complex cognitive, **linguistic** aspects of the task, rather than using rote memorization. The author reviews LD literature and explains how rubrics are used both to **assess** and teach writing skills to **elementary, middle, and high school** students.

50

11. **Group Intervention: Improving Social Skills of Adolescents with Learning Disabilities,** Deborah Court and Sarah Givon, *Teaching Exceptional Children,* November/December 2003

Students with **learning disabilities** often suffer low **self-esteem. Middle and high school** programs which teach social skills can improve their **conflict resolution** and confidence in groups. **Assessments** by parents reflect more **family involvement** after social skills training. Teachers in **inclusion** classrooms should also help students with LD form friendships with other students.

53

The concepts in bold italics are developed in the article. For further expansion, please refer to the Topic Guide and the Index.

UNIT 4
Speech and Language Impairments

Unit Overview 58

12. **Language Differences or Learning Difficulties,** Spencer J. Salend and AltaGracia Salinas, *Teaching Exceptional Children,* March/April 2003

    Students with limited English proficiency should not be labeled *language impaired* or *learning disabled* unless they are significantly disabled in their first language as well. *Family involvement* and multi-disciplinary *collaboration* are vital. *Cultural diversity* and alternative *assessment* procedures must be heeded. 61

13. **A Speech-Language Approach to Early Reading Success,** Adele Gerber and Evelyn R. Klein, *Teaching Exceptional Children,* July/August 2004

    Drs. Gerber and Klein, *speech-language* pathologists, address many issues involved in communication and reading skills: articulation, phonetic awareness, decoding, hearing the sounds of speech, and discriminating defective production of sounds. A two-stage program with *assessment* and remediation is described. 69

UNIT 5
Developmental Disabilities/Autistic Spectrum Disorders

Unit Overview 74

14. **When Does Autism Start?,** Claudia Kalb, *Newsweek,* February 28, 2005

    The *autistic spectrum disorders (ASD)* have spiked tenfold in 20 years. Attempts are being made to *assess* ASDs in *early childhood* and provide more appropriate *family involvement* and therapy. This article explains current knowledge about *brain development*, early signs of ASDs, and new treatments and trends. Early treatment may be able to improve cognition and *social skills.* 77

15. **Service-Learning Opportunities That Include Students With Moderate and Severe Disabilities,** Harold Kleinert, et al., *Teaching Exceptional Children,* November/December 2004

    Public law 107-110 (No Child Left Behind Act) of 2001 requires alternative *assessments* for students with *developmental disabilities.* *High school* service-learning projects provide excellent vehicles for assessing *language,* reading, math, science and other skills. *Family involvement and peer tutoring* in the service-learning projects provides benefits for those with and without disabilities. 80

16. **Inscrutable or Meaningful? Understanding and Supporting Your Inarticulate Students,** Robin M. Smith, *Teaching Exceptional Children,* March/April 2002

    Children with *developmental disabilities* or *autism* often have atypical *language processes and speech.* Their skills and strengths are missed if they are *assessed* as inscrutable. This article gives competence-oriented strategies to find meanings in both *emotions and behaviors.* Supporting such students aids in their *socialization, self-esteem,* and *creativity.* 87

The concepts in bold italics are developed in the article. For further expansion, please refer to the Topic Guide and the Index.

UNIT 6
Emotional and Behavioral Disorders

Unit Overview   92

17. **Psychiatric Disorders and Treatments: A Primer for Teachers,** Steven R. Forness, Hill M. Walker, and Kenneth A. Kavale, *Teaching Exceptional Children,* November/December 2003

Severe *emotional and behavioral disorders* are difficult to *assess*. They are often treated with both drugs and behavioral therapy. *Parent participation* and *collaboration* with teachers are essential. Social skills training is also helpful, especially for *conflict resolution*. This article describes the more common psychiatric disorders with symptoms and psychopharmacological treatments.   95

18. **I Want to Go Back to Jail,** Lynn Olcott, *Phi Delta Kappan,* December 2004

Teaching *culturally diverse* students with *emotional and behavioral disorders*—arrested for assaults, selling drugs, and other crimes—is not easy. Lynn Olcott is an inspiration for all teachers. She not only taught GED (general education) to jailed adolescent women, but also taught self-advocacy. Her instruction succeeded!   104

19. **The Importance of Teacher Self-Awareness in Working With Students With Emotional and Behavioral Disorders,** Brent G. Richardson and Margery J. Shupe, *Teaching Exceptional Children,* November/December 2003

Helping students with *emotional and behavioral disorders* requires self-awareness. Good natured humor helps in *conflict resolution*. Making a difference for even one child is important. This article identifies questions and strategies to help teachers become more self-aware regarding their interactions with difficult students.   106

20. **Classroom Problems That Don't Go Away,** Laverne Warner and Sharon Lynch, *Childhood Education,* Winter 2002–2003

Educators have all experienced children with chronic *emotional and behavioral disorders.* This article suggests exploring the ABCs of difficulties (antecedents, behaviors, consequences). The authors give many suggestions for prevention of behaviors. Teaching the child alternatives can bring much *conflict resolution* and improved *socialization.*   112

UNIT 7
Vision and Hearing Impairments

Unit Overview   116

21. **A Half-Century of Progress for Deaf Individuals,** McCay Vernon, *CSD Spectrum,* Summer 2002

In 50 years, individuals with *hearing impairments* have made amazing progress: acceptance of ASL as a *language,* bilingual-*bicultural communication, legal mandates* for *individualized education transition* and employment, mental health services, *technology* in audiology and telecommunications, and medical reductions in deafness. Educators still have a long way to go.   119

22. **Using Tactile Strategies With Students Who Are Blind and Have Severe Disabilities,** June E. Downing and Deborah Chen, *Teaching Exceptional Children,* November/December 2003

This article describes tactile strategies to support instruction of students who have *multiple disabilities* and *visual impairments*. Teachers need *creative* ways to bypass tactile defensiveness. *Collaboration* with specialists, *family,* and *peer-tutors* can provide ideas. Plans for teaching the use of touch should be written into *individualized education programs* in *schools*.   123

The concepts in bold italics are developed in the article. For further expansion, please refer to the Topic Guide and the Index.

UNIT 8
Multiple Disabilities

Unit Overview   128

23. **Making Inclusion a Reality for Students With Severe Disabilities,**
Pamela S. Wolfe and Tracey E. Hall, *Teaching Exceptional Children,*
March/April 2003
Students with **multiple disabilities,** often mainstreamed only for **socialization**
activities in **public schools,** can benefit from **inclusion** in instruction as well. The
Cascade of Integration Options, described in this article, explains how. **Collaboration** and careful **IEP** planning are essential. Different goals will be set for the
individual with severe disabilities.   131

24. **Choice Making: A Strategy for Students With Severe Disabilities,**
Alison M. Stafford, *Teaching Exceptional Children,* July/August 2005
Students with **multiple disabilities** often become dependent on others to make
decisions for them. Choice-making is a fundamental human right which can be
afforded to even those with severe disabilities. Alison Stafford explains how to
assess preferences and student response models. This choice-making ability benefits **family, school,** and student.   137

25. **Empowering Students With Severe Disabilities to Actualize Communication Skills,** Paul W. Cascella and Kevin M. McNamara, *Teaching Exceptional Children,* January/February 2005
Students with **mental retardation** and **multiple disabilites** often find **language**
especially problematic. Their **individualized education programs (IEPs)** focus
on functional communication. This article describes realistic goals such as gestures, augmentative **technology,** sign language, and interpretation of vocalizations
and sounds.   144

UNIT 9
Orthopedic and Health Impairments

Unit Overview   150

26. **Savior Parents,** Elizabeth Weill, *Time,* May 2004
There is new hope for some **orthopedic and health impairments** which in the
recent past were incurable. **Genetic** understanding, **family advocacy,** and advanced therapies are working miracles. Elizabeth Weill describes progress made
in chromosome syndromes, progeria, and ataxia-telangiectasia (A-T). **Computers
and biotechnology,** plus a refusal to give up, have made this possible.   153

27. **Accommodations for Students With Disabilities: Removing Barriers
to Learning,** MaryAnn Byrnes, *NASSP Bulletin,* February 2000
Legal processes mandate accommodations for students with disabilities (such
as 504 plans), even if they do not require **individualized education plans** (IEPs)
and special education. This article explains what kinds of accommodations are
appropriate, where to have them, when, who decides, and why.   156

28. **Trick Question,** Michael Fumento, *The New Republic,* February 3,
2003
The **assessment** of attention-deficit hyperactive disorder (ADHD) as a **health
impairment, learning disability, or emotional/behavioral disorder** has been
criticized. Using the drug Ritalin is condemned for making boys like girls and
reducing **creativity**. This article argues that ADHD is a real **brain disorder**. Ritalin
helps students wherever they are in school; **elementary, middle, or high school**. 160

The concepts in bold italics are developed in the article. For further expansion, please refer to the Topic Guide and the Index.

29. **Finding What Works,** Peg Tyre, *Newsweek,* April 25, 2005
Medications help many students with **orthopedic and health impairments,** such as attention deficit hyperactive disorder and Asperger Syndrome (an **autistic spectrum disorder**). Physicians find it hard to know how much and what, to prescribe. **Collaboration** between parents, school, and specialists is essential. Behavior therapy can reduce medication dosages. 164

UNIT 10
Giftedness

Unit Overview 166

30. **Understanding the Young Gifted Child: Guidelines for Parents, Families, and Educators,** Jennifer V. Rotigel, *Early Childhood Education Journal,* Summer 2003
Gifted children need **early childhood** enrichment. Their **language** proficiency is an **assessment** "heads-up." While they benefit from **socialization** in mixed-ability groups, **peer tutoring,** used excessively, leads to problems. Their **self-esteem** is enhanced by challenging them in their area of **creativity** and allowing self-acceleration. 169

31. **Read All About It,** Bruce Bower, *Science News,* April 30, 2005
A precociousness in reading, called hyperlexia, has been **assessed** with **technology** called functional magnetic resonance imaging (FMRI). This reveals **brain development** with intense activity in the superior temporal cortex. Other special **gifts and talents**, and **learning disorders**, may soon be better understood using FMRI. 174

32. **Teaching Strategies for Twice-Exceptional Students,** Susan Winebrenner, *Intervention in School and Clinic,* January 2003
Students who are **gifted** may also be students with **learning disabilities**. Assessment typically focuses on their deficits rather than their gifts. Their **self-esteem** suffers when they are given praise for easy, unchallenging work. **Inclusion** classes need differentiation, more assistance in deficiency areas, and compacted learning with challenges in strength areas. Many ideas for empowering twice-exceptional students are offered in this article. 177

UNIT 11
Transition

Unit Overview 184

33. **Moving From Elementary to Middle School: Supporting a Smooth Transition for Students With Severe Disabilities,** Erik W. Carter, et al., *Teaching Exceptional Children,* January/February 2005
The **legal processes** of IDEA mandate **transition** supports for students with disabilites. This article focuses on the needs of students with **severe disabilities** as they move from **elementary** to **middle school**. Several strategies are presented to assist students and their **families**, including a timeline, nine practical steps, and recommended resources. 187

34. **The Transition from Middle School to High School,** Theresa M. Letrello and Dorothy D. Miles, *The Clearing House,* March/April 2003
The **transition** from **middle to high school** requires adjusting to a larger school size, new social interactions, and different academic demands at a time when adolescents are also dealing with puberty and identity issues. This is problematic for students with **learning disabilities** and other exceptionalities. They need more support from teachers and **peers**. Extra curricular activity involvement makes moving easier. 193

The concepts in bold italics are developed in the article. For further expansion, please refer to the Topic Guide and the Index.

35. Navigating the College Transition Maze: A Guide for Students with Learning Disabilities, Joseph W. Madaus, *Teaching Exceptional Children,* January/February 2005

Negotiating the **transition** from **high school** to college when special services for **learning disabilities** are required can be tricky. Not all colleges provide the same support. IDEA mandates support services until age 21, and the ADA requires equal access for Americans with Disabilities at all ages. This article reviews the **legal** requirements of students and colleges.   195

Index   200
Test Your Knowledge Form   204
Article Rating Form   205

The concepts in bold italics are developed in the article. For further expansion, please refer to the Topic Guide and the Index.

Topic Guide

This topic guide suggests how the selections in this book relate to the subjects covered in your course. You may want to use the topics listed on these pages to search the Web more easily.

On the following pages a number of Web sites have been gathered specifically for this book. They are arranged to reflect the units of this *Annual Edition*. You can link to these sites by going to the student online support site at *http://www.mhcls.com/online/*.

ALL THE ARTICLES THAT RELATE TO EACH TOPIC ARE LISTED BELOW THE BOLD-FACED TERM.

Assessment

2. Rethinking Inclusion: Schoolwide Applications
3. Assessment That Drives Instruction
5. Making the Case for Early Identification and Intervention for Young Children at Risk for Learning Disabilities
8. Providing Support for Student Independence Through Scaffolded Instruction
9. Celebrating Diverse Minds
10. No More Friday Spelling Tests? An Alternative Spelling Assessment for Students With Learning Disabilities
11. Group Intervention: Improving Social Skills of Adolescents with Learning Disabilities
12. Language Differences or Learning Difficulties
13. A Speech-Language Approach to Early Reading Success
14. When Does Autism Start?
15. Service-Learning Opportunities That Include Students With Moderate and Severe Disabilities
16. Inscrutable or Meaningful? Understanding and Supporting Your Inarticulate Students
17. Psychiatric Disorders and Treatments: A Primer for Teachers
24. Choice Making: A Strategy for Students With Severe Disabilities
28. Trick Question
30. Understanding the Young Gifted Child: Guidelines for Parents, Families, and Educators
31. Read All About It
32. Teaching Strategies for Twice-Exceptional Students
35. Navigating the College Transition Maze: A Guide for Students with Learning Disabilities

Autism

16. Inscrutable or Meaningful? Understanding and Supporting Your Inarticulate Students

Brain development

9. Celebrating Diverse Minds
14. When Does Autism Start?

Collaboration

1. An Interview With Dr. Marilyn Friend
3. Assessment That Drives Instruction
12. Language Differences or Learning Difficulties
17. Psychiatric Disorders and Treatments: A Primer for Teachers
22. Using Tactile Strategies With Students Who Are Blind and Have Severe Disabilities
23. Making Inclusion a Reality for Students With Severe Disabilities

Computers

20. Classroom Problems That Don't Go Away
26. Savior Parents

Conflict

20. Classroom Problems That Don't Go Away

Conflict resolution

7. Building Relationships With Challenging Children
11. Group Intervention: Improving Social Skills of Adolescents with Learning Disabilities
17. Psychiatric Disorders and Treatments: A Primer for Teachers
19. The Importance of Teacher Self-Awareness in Working With Students With Emotional and Behavioral Disorders

Creativity

4. Meaningful Inclusion of All Students in Team Sports
6. Music in the Inclusive Environment
16. Inscrutable or Meaningful? Understanding and Supporting Your Inarticulate Students
28. Trick Question
30. Understanding the Young Gifted Child: Guidelines for Parents, Families, and Educators

Cultural diversity

12. Language Differences or Learning Difficulties
18. I Want to Go Back to Jail
21. A Half-Century of Progress for Deaf Individuals
35. Navigating the College Transition Maze: A Guide for Students with Learning Disabilities

Developmental disabilities

4. Meaningful Inclusion of All Students in Team Sports
15. Service-Learning Opportunities That Include Students With Moderate and Severe Disabilities
16. Inscrutable or Meaningful? Understanding and Supporting Your Inarticulate Students

Early childhood education

5. Making the Case for Early Identification and Intervention for Young Children at Risk for Learning Disabilities
6. Music in the Inclusive Environment
7. Building Relationships With Challenging Children
14. When Does Autism Start?
30. Understanding the Young Gifted Child: Guidelines for Parents, Families, and Educators

Elementary school

2. Rethinking Inclusion: Schoolwide Applications
5. Making the Case for Early Identification and Intervention for Young Children at Risk for Learning Disabilities
8. Providing Support for Student Independence Through Scaffolded Instruction
10. No More Friday Spelling Tests? An Alternative Spelling Assessment for Students With Learning Disabilities
28. Trick Question
33. Moving From Elementary to Middle School: Supporting a Smooth Transition for Students With Severe Disabilities

Emotional and behavioral disorders

7. Building Relationships With Challenging Children
16. Inscrutable or Meaningful? Understanding and Supporting Your Inarticulate Students
17. Psychiatric Disorders and Treatments: A Primer for Teachers
18. I Want to Go Back to Jail
19. The Importance of Teacher Self-Awareness in Working With Students With Emotional and Behavioral Disorders
20. Classroom Problems That Don't Go Away
28. Trick Question

Family involvement

4. Meaningful Inclusion of All Students in Team Sports
11. Group Intervention: Improving Social Skills of Adolescents with Learning Disabilities
12. Language Differences or Learning Difficulties

14. When Does Autism Start?
15. Service-Learning Opportunities That Include Students With Moderate and Severe Disabilities
17. Psychiatric Disorders and Treatments: A Primer for Teachers
24. Choice Making: A Strategy for Students With Severe Disabilities
26. Savior Parents
33. Moving From Elementary to Middle School: Supporting a Smooth Transition for Students With Severe Disabilities

Genetics

21. A Half-Century of Progress for Deaf Individuals
23. Making Inclusion a Reality for Students With Severe Disabilities
26. Savior Parents
28. Trick Question

Gifted children and youth

30. Understanding the Young Gifted Child: Guidelines for Parents, Families, and Educators
31. Read All About It
32. Teaching Strategies for Twice-Exceptional Students

Health impairments

4. Meaningful Inclusion of All Students in Team Sports
26. Savior Parents
28. Trick Question

Hearing impairments

21. A Half-Century of Progress for Deaf Individuals

High school

2. Rethinking Inclusion: Schoolwide Applications
10. No More Friday Spelling Tests? An Alternative Spelling Assessment for Students With Learning Disabilities
11. Group Intervention: Improving Social Skills of Adolescents with Learning Disabilities
15. Service-Learning Opportunities That Include Students With Moderate and Severe Disabilities
18. I Want to Go Back to Jail
27. Accommodations for Students With Disabilities: Removing Barriers to Learning
28. Trick Question
29. Finding What Works
34. The Transition from Middle School to High School

Inclusive education

1. An Interview With Dr. Marilyn Friend
2. Rethinking Inclusion: Schoolwide Applications
3. Assessment That Drives Instruction
4. Meaningful Inclusion of All Students in Team Sports
5. Making the Case for Early Identification and Intervention for Young Children at Risk for Learning Disabilities
6. Music in the Inclusive Environment
7. Building Relationships With Challenging Children
11. Group Intervention: Improving Social Skills of Adolescents with Learning Disabilities
23. Making Inclusion a Reality for Students With Severe Disabilities
32. Teaching Strategies for Twice-Exceptional Students

Individualized education programs

3. Assessment That Drives Instruction
4. Meaningful Inclusion of All Students in Team Sports
5. Making the Case for Early Identification and Intervention for Young Children at Risk for Learning Disabilities
21. A Half-Century of Progress for Deaf Individuals
22. Using Tactile Strategies With Students Who Are Blind and Have Severe Disabilities
23. Making Inclusion a Reality for Students With Severe Disabilities
25. Empowering Students With Severe Disabilities to Actualize Communication Skills
27. Accommodations for Students With Disabilities: Removing Barriers to Learning
29. Finding What Works

Language

10. No More Friday Spelling Tests? An Alternative Spelling Assessment for Students With Learning Disabilities
12. Language Differences or Learning Difficulties
13. A Speech-Language Approach to Early Reading Success
15. Service-Learning Opportunities That Include Students With Moderate and Severe Disabilities
21. A Half-Century of Progress for Deaf Individuals
25. Empowering Students With Severe Disabilities to Actualize Communication Skills
30. Understanding the Young Gifted Child: Guidelines for Parents, Families, and Educators

Learning disabilities

3. Assessment That Drives Instruction
8. Providing Support for Student Independence Through Scaffolded Instruction
9. Celebrating Diverse Minds
11. Group Intervention: Improving Social Skills of Adolescents with Learning Disabilities
12. Language Differences or Learning Difficulties
28. Trick Question
32. Teaching Strategies for Twice-Exceptional Students
34. The Transition from Middle School to High School
35. Navigating the College Transition Maze: A Guide for Students with Learning Disabilities

Legal processes

2. Rethinking Inclusion: Schoolwide Applications
15. Service-Learning Opportunities That Include Students With Moderate and Severe Disabilities
21. A Half-Century of Progress for Deaf Individuals
33. Moving From Elementary to Middle School: Supporting a Smooth Transition for Students With Severe Disabilities
35. Navigating the College Transition Maze: A Guide for Students with Learning Disabilities

Middle school

2. Rethinking Inclusion: Schoolwide Applications
10. No More Friday Spelling Tests? An Alternative Spelling Assessment for Students With Learning Disabilities
11. Group Intervention: Improving Social Skills of Adolescents with Learning Disabilities
28. Trick Question
33. Moving From Elementary to Middle School: Supporting a Smooth Transition for Students With Severe Disabilities
34. The Transition from Middle School to High School

Multiple disabilities

4. Meaningful Inclusion of All Students in Team Sports
15. Service-Learning Opportunities That Include Students With Moderate and Severe Disabilities
22. Using Tactile Strategies With Students Who Are Blind and Have Severe Disabilities
23. Making Inclusion a Reality for Students With Severe Disabilities
24. Choice Making: A Strategy for Students With Severe Disabilities
25. Empowering Students With Severe Disabilities to Actualize Communication Skills
33. Moving From Elementary to Middle School: Supporting a Smooth Transition for Students With Severe Disabilities

Orthopedic and health impairments

4. Meaningful Inclusion of All Students in Team Sports
26. Savior Parents
27. Accommodations for Students With Disabilities: Removing Barriers to Learning
28. Trick Question
29. Finding What Works

Parent participation

4. Meaningful Inclusion of All Students in Team Sports
11. Group Intervention: Improving Social Skills of Adolescents with Learning Disabilities
12. Language Differences or Learning Difficulties
14. When Does Autism Start?
17. Psychiatric Disorders and Treatments: A Primer for Teachers
24. Choice Making: A Strategy for Students With Severe Disabilities
33. Moving From Elementary to Middle School: Supporting a Smooth Transition for Students With Severe Disabilities

Peer tutoring

4. Meaningful Inclusion of All Students in Team Sports
15. Service-Learning Opportunities That Include Students With Moderate and Severe Disabilities
22. Using Tactile Strategies With Students Who Are Blind and Have Severe Disabilities
30. Understanding the Young Gifted Child: Guidelines for Parents, Families, and Educators
34. The Transition from Middle School to High School

Schools

3. Assessment That Drives Instruction
18. I Want to Go Back to Jail
22. Using Tactile Strategies With Students Who Are Blind and Have Severe Disabilities
23. Making Inclusion a Reality for Students With Severe Disabilities
24. Choice Making: A Strategy for Students With Severe Disabilities
28. Trick Question
32. Teaching Strategies for Twice-Exceptional Students

Self-esteem

4. Meaningful Inclusion of All Students in Team Sports
11. Group Intervention: Improving Social Skills of Adolescents with Learning Disabilities
16. Inscrutable or Meaningful? Understanding and Supporting Your Inarticulate Students
30. Understanding the Young Gifted Child: Guidelines for Parents, Families, and Educators

Socialization

1. An Interview With Dr. Marilyn Friend
5. Making the Case for Early Identification and Intervention for Young Children at Risk for Learning Disabilities
6. Music in the Inclusive Environment
7. Building Relationships With Challenging Children
14. When Does Autism Start?
16. Inscrutable or Meaningful? Understanding and Supporting Your Inarticulate Students
20. Classroom Problems That Don't Go Away
23. Making Inclusion a Reality for Students With Severe Disabilities
30. Understanding the Young Gifted Child: Guidelines for Parents, Families, and Educators

Speech and language impairments

6. Music in the Inclusive Environment
13. A Speech-Language Approach to Early Reading Success
15. Service-Learning Opportunities That Include Students With Moderate and Severe Disabilities
16. Inscrutable or Meaningful? Understanding and Supporting Your Inarticulate Students
21. A Half-Century of Progress for Deaf Individuals

Talented children and youth

30. Understanding the Young Gifted Child: Guidelines for Parents, Families, and Educators
31. Read All About It
32. Teaching Strategies for Twice-Exceptional Students

Technology

21. A Half-Century of Progress for Deaf Individuals
25. Empowering Students With Severe Disabilities to Actualize Communication Skills
26. Savior Parents
31. Read All About It

Transition

6. Music in the Inclusive Environment
21. A Half-Century of Progress for Deaf Individuals
33. Moving From Elementary to Middle School: Supporting a Smooth Transition for Students With Severe Disabilities
34. The Transition from Middle School to High School
35. Navigating the College Transition Maze: A Guide for Students with Learning Disabilities

Visual impairments

22. Using Tactile Strategies With Students Who Are Blind and Have Severe Disabilities

Internet References

The following internet sites have been carefully researched and selected to support the articles found in this reader. The easiest way to access these selected sites is to go to our student online support site at *http://www.mhcls.com/online/*.

AE: Educating Exceptional Children 06/07

The following sites were available at the time of publication. Visit our Web site—we update our student online support site regularly to reflect any changes.

General Sources

Consortium for Citizens With Disabilities
http://www.c-c-d.org

Included in this coalition organization is an Education Task Force that follows issues of early childhood special education, the president's commission on excellence in special education, issues of rethinking special education, 2001 IDEA principles, and many other related issues.

Family Village
http://www.familyvillage.wisc.edu/index.htmlx

Here is a global community of disability-related resources that is set up under such headings as library, shopping mall, school, community center, and others.

National Information Center for Children and Youth With Disabilities (NICHCY)
http://www.nichcy.org/index.html

NICHCY provides information and makes referrals in areas related to specific disabilities, early intervention, special education and related services, individualized education programs, and much more. The site also connects to a listing of Parent's Guides to resources for children and youth with disabilities.

National Rehabilitation Information Center (NARIC)
http://www.naric.com

A series of databases that can be keyword-searched on subjects including physical, mental, and psychiatric disabilities, vocational rehabilitation, special education, assistive technology, and more can be found on this site.

President's Commission on Excellence in Special Education (PCESE)
http://www.ed.gov/inits/commissionsboards/whspecialeducation/

The report stemming from the work of the PCESE, *A New Era: Revitalizing Special Education for Children and Their Families,* can be downloaded in full at this site.

School Psychology Resources Online
http://www.schoolpsychology.net

Numerous sites on special conditions, disorders, and disabilities, as well as other data ranging from assertiveness/evaluation to research, are available on this resource page for psychologists, parents, and educators.

Special Education Exchange
http://www.spedex.com/main_graphics.htm

SpEdEx, as this site is more commonly known, offers a wealth of information, links, and resources to everyone interested in special education.

Special Education News
http://www.specialednews.com/disabilities/disabnews/povanddisab031200.html

This particular section of this site discusses the problems of coping with both poverty and disability. Explore the rest of the site also for information for educators on behavior management, conflict resolution, early intervention, specific disabilities, and much more.

UNIT 1: Inclusive Education

Institute on Disability/University of New Hampshire
http://iod.unh.edu

This site includes Early Childhood, Inclusive Education, High School and Post-Secondary School, Community Living and Adult Life, Related Links, both state and national, and information on technology, health care, public policy, as well as leadership training and professional development.

Kids Together, Inc.
http://www.kidstogether.org

Based on the IDEA law about teaching children with disabilties in regular classrooms, this site contains all the information on inclusion you might need to know.

New Horizons for Learning
http://www.newhorizons.org

Based on the theory of inclusion, this site is filled with information on special needs inclusion, technology and learning, a brain lab, and much more, presented as floors in a building.

UNIT 2: Early Childhood

Division for Early Childhood
http://www.dec-sped.org

A division of the Council for Exceptional Children, the DEC advocates for the improvement of conditions of young children with special needs. Child development theory, programming data, parenting data, research, and links to other sites can be found on this site.

Institute on Community Integration Projects
http://ici.umn.edu/projectscenters/

Research projects related to early childhood and early intervention services for special education are described here.

National Academy for Child Development (NACD)
http://www.nacd.org

The NACD, an international organization, is dedicated to helping children and adults reach their full potential. Its home page presents links to various programs, research, and resources into such topics as learning disabilities, ADD/ADHD, brain injuries, autism, accelerated and gifted, and other similar topic areas.

Special Education Resources on the Internet (SERI)
http://seriweb.com

SERI offers helpful sites in all phases of special education in early childhood, including disabilities, mental retardation, behavior disorders, and autism.

UNIT 3: Learning Disabilities

Children and Adults With Attention Deficit/Hyperactivity Disorder (CHADD)
http://www.chadd.org

CHADD works to improve the lives of people with AD/HD through education, advocacy, and support, offering information that can be trusted. The site includes fact sheets, legislative information, research studies, and links.

The Instant Access Treasure Chest
http://www.fln.vcu.edu/ld/ld.html

Billed as the Foreign Language Teacher's Guide to Learning Disabilities, this site contains a very thorough list of resources for anyone interested in LD education issues.

Learning Disabilities Association of America (LDA)
http://www.ldanatl.org

The purpose of the LDA is to advance the education and general welfare of children of normal and potentially normal intelligence who show handicaps of a perceptual, conceptual, or coordinative nature.

Learning Disabilities Online
http://www.ldonline.org

This is a good source for information about all kinds of learning disabilities with links to other related material.

Teaching Children With Attention Deficit Disorder
http://www.kidsource.com/kidsource/content2/add.html

This in-depth site defines both types of ADD and discusses establishing the proper learning environment.

UNIT 4: Speech and Language Impairments

Issues in Emergent Literacy for Children With Language Impairments
http://www.ciera.org/library/reports/inquiry-2/2-002/2-002.html

This article explores the relationship between oral language impairment and reading disabilities in children. The article suggests that language impairment may be a basic deficit that affects language function in both its oral and written forms.

Speech Disorders WWW Sites
http://www.socialnet.lu/handitel/wwwlinks/dumb.html

A thorough collection of Web sites, plus an article on the relationship between form and function in the speech of specifically language-impaired children, may be accessed here.

UNIT 5: Developmental Disabilities/Autistic Spectrum Disorders

Arc of the United States
http://www.thearc.org

Here is the Web site of the national organization of and for people with mental retardation and related disabilities and their families. It includes governmental affairs, services, position statements, FAQs, publications, and related links.

Disability-Related Sources on the Web
http://www.arcarizona.org/dislnkin.html

This resource's many links include grant resources, federally funded projects and federal agencies, assistive technology, national and international organizations, and educational resources and directories.

Gentle Teaching
http://www.gentleteaching.nl

Maintained by the foundation for Gentle Teaching in the Netherlands, this page explains a nonviolent approach for helping children and adults with special needs.

UNIT 6: Emotional and Behavioral Disorders

Educating Students With Emotional/Behavioral Disorders
http://www.nichcy.org/pubs/bibliog/bib10txt.htm

Excellent bibliographical and video information dealing with the education of children with emotional and/or behavioral disorders is available at this site.

Pacer Center: Emotional Behavioral Disorders
http://www.pacer.org/ebd/

Active in Minnesota for 8 years in helping parents become advocates for their EBD children, PACER has gone on to present workshops for parents on how to access aid for their child, explain what a parent should look for in a child they suspect of EBD, prepare a behavioral intervention guide, and link to resources, including IDEA's Parnership in Education site, and much more./

UNIT 7: Vision and Hearing Impairments

Info to Go: Laurent Clerc National Deaf Education Center
http://clerccenter.gallaudet.edu/InfoToGo/index.html

Important for parents and educators, this Web site from Gallaudet University offers information on audiology, communication, education, legal, and health issues of deaf people.

The New York Institute for Special Education
http://www.nyise.org/index.html

This school is an educational facility that serves children who are blind or visually impaired. The site includes program descriptions and resources for the blind.

UNIT 8: Multiple Disabilities

Activity Ideas for Students With Severe, Profound, or Multiple Disabilities
http://www.palaestra.com/featurestory.html

The Fall 1997 issue of the *Palaestra* contains this interesting article on teaching students who have multiple disabilities. The complete text is offered here online.

Severe and/or Multiple Disabilities
http://www.nichcy.org/pubs/factshe/fs10txt.htm

This fact sheet offers a definition of multiple disabilities, discusses incidence, characteristics, medical, and educational implications, and suggests resources and organizations that might be of help to parents and educators of children with severe impairments.

UNIT 9: Orthopedic and Health Impairments

Association to Benefit Children (ABC)
http://www.a-b-c.org

ABC presents a network of programs that includes child advocacy, education for disabled children, care for HIV-positive children, employment, housing, foster care, and day care.

An Idea Whose Time Has Come
http://www.boggscenter.org/mich3899.htm

The purpose of community-based education is to help students in special education to become more independent. Here is an excellent description of how it is being done in at least one community.

www.mhcls.com/online/

Resources for VE Teachers
http://www.cpt.fsu.edu/tree//ve/tofc.html
  Effective practices for teachers of varying exceptionalities (VE) classes are listed here.

UNIT 10: Giftedness

The Council for Exceptional Children
http://www.cec.sped.org/index.html
  This page will give you access to information on identifying and teaching gifted children, attention-deficit disorders, and other topics in gifted education.

UNIT 11: Transition

National Center on Secondary Education and Transition
http://www.ncset.org
  This site coordinates national resources, offers technical assistance, and disseminates information related to secondary education and transition for youth with disabilities in order to create opportunities for youth to achieve successful futures.

We highly recommend that you review our Web site for expanded information and our other product lines. We are continually updating and adding links to our Web site in order to offer you the most usable and useful information that will support and expand the value of your Annual Editions. You can reach us at: *http://www.mhcls.com/annualeditions/.*

UNIT 1

Inclusive Education

Unit Selections

1. **An Interview With Dr. Marilyn Friend**, Mary T. Brownell and Chriss Walther-Thomas
2. **Rethinking Inclusion: Schoolwide Applications**, Wayne Sailor and Blair Roger
3. **Assessment That Drives Instruction**, Pokey Stanford and Stacy Reeves
4. **Meaningful Inclusion of All Students in Team Sports**, Yoshihisa Ohtake

Key Points to Consider

- How important is collaboration between regular education and special education teachers?

- What pedagogical models exist to make collaboration more successful?

- How does appropriate assessment serve the goals of the NCLB Act?

- Will inclusion in team sports benefit all students: both those with and those without disabilities? Why?

Student Website

www.mhcls.com/online

Internet References

Further information regarding these websites may be found in this book's preface or online.

Institute on Disability/University of New Hampshire
http://iod.unh.edu

Kids Together, Inc.
http://www.kidstogether.org

New Horizons for Learning
http://www.newhorizons.org

A huge strength of American schools is the dedication and motivation of its professional teachers. Weaknesses include inadequate social, emotional, and financial support, provision of more inservice education, and the wherewithal for continuing education. Teachers need all the help they can get to be the best they can possibly be, and to feel appreciated!

This unit on Inclusive Education highlights what's good in special education, and includes some suggestions for ways it can be improved.

Regular education teachers are expected to know how to provide special educational services to every child with an exceptional condition in their classroom, despite not having had course work in special education. The numbers of students with exceptionalities who are being educated in regular education classes are increasing annually. The Individuals with Disabilities Education Act (IDEA) has reduced the numbers of special needs students being educated in residential centers, hospitals, homes, or special schools to less than 5 percent. Children who once would have been turned away from public schools are now being admitted in enormous numbers. The No Child Left Behind Act (NCLB) has increased the emphases on high expectations for all students from highly qualified teachers who do frequent proficiency assessments.

The trend toward inclusive education necessitates more knowledge and expertise on the part of the regular education teachers. Educating children with exceptionalities can no longer be viewed as the job of special-education teachers. This trend also mandates knowledge about collaboration and advisory activities on the part of all special educators. Teamwork is essential as special education and regular education are becoming more and more intertwined.

Public schools have an obligation to provide free educational services in the least restrictive environment possible to all children who have diagnosed conditions of exceptionality. Although laws in Canada and the United States differ slightly, all public schools have an obligation to serve children with exceptional conditions in as normal an educational environment as possible. Inclusive education is difficult. It works very well for some students with exceptionalities in some situations and marginally or not at all for other students with exceptionalities in other situations.

For inclusion to succeed within a school, everyone must be committed to be part of the solution: superintendent, principal, teachers, coaches, aides, ancillary staff, students, parents, and families. Special education teachers often find their jobs involving much more than instructing students with special needs. They serve as consultants to regular education teachers to assure that inclusion is meaningful for their students. They collaborate with parents, administrators, support personnel, and community agencies as well as with regular education teachers. They plan curriculum and oversee the writing of Individualized Family Service Plans (IFSPs), Individualized Education Plans (IEPs), and Individualized Transition Plans (ITPs). They schedule and make sure that services are provided by all team-involved persons. They keep up with enormous amounts of paperwork. They update parents even when parents are too involved, or not involved enough. They keep abreast of new resources, new legal processes, and new instructional techniques. They make projections for the futures of their students and set out ways to make good things happen. They also struggle to be accountable, both educationally and financially, for all they do.

The term "least restrictive environment" is often mistakenly understood as the need for all children to be educated in a regular education classroom. If students can learn and achieve better in inclusive programs, then they belong there. If students can succeed only marginally in inclusive education classrooms, some alternate solutions are necessary. A continuum of placement options exists to maximize the goal of educating every child. For some children, a separate class, or even a separate school, is still optimal.

Every child with an exceptional condition is different from every other child in symptoms, needs, and teachability. Each child is, therefore, provided with a unique individualized education plan. This plan consists of both long- and short-term goals for education, specially designed instructional procedures with related services, and methods to evaluate the child's progress. The IEP is updated and revised annually. Special education teachers, parents, and all applicable service providers must collaborate at least this often to make recommendations for goals and teaching strategies. The IEPs should always be outcomes-oriented with functional curricula.

The first selection in this unit is an interview with an expert on inclusive education for students with disabilities. Dr. Marilyn

Friend discusses what it takes to make collaboration of regular education and special education work. She answers questions about the challenges as well as the resources for success.

The second selection "Rethinking Inclusion: Schoolwide Applications" describes a pedagogical strategy which helps make regular and special educational collaboration succeed.

The third article reports on "Assessment That Drives Instruction." The No Child Left Behind Act (NCLB) set forth 6 major principles for education: accountability, highly qualified teachers, scientifically based intervention, local flexibility, safe schools, and parental participation and choice. These principles make it necessary for special and general education teachers to collaborate. The author suggests that appropriate assessment is an important key to making inclusion work.

The last article in this unit discusses "Meaningful Inclusion of All Students in Team Sports." Teaching students with disabilities to feel good about themselves can be enhanced with lessons on physical fitness, team work, and fair play. Peers and parents can also participate and benefit in inclusive sports.

An Interview With... **Dr. Marilyn Friend**

Mary T. Brownell and Chriss Walther-Thomas, Dept. Editors

Dr. Marilyn Friend is a leading expert in the areas of professional collaboration, coteaching, and inclusive education for students with disabilities. She began her educational career with a dual degree in special education and general education. Her first teaching job was as a fifth-grade teacher in a large urban school district where many tensions existed within the school among the teachers and between the teachers and principal. The disagreements extended to the community, and several lawsuits had been filed by parents naming the principal and the school district. Because of the problems, teachers tended to keep to themselves. It was a hostile environment for a beginning teacher, and Dr. Friend felt very isolated there, reluctant to ask colleagues for much-needed advice.

In contrast, she spent her last year of public school teaching working as a special education teacher in a highly collaborative, small urban school. The teachers worked well together in both formal (e.g., curriculum committee) and informal (e.g., problem solving about students at risk for failure) situations to maximize their limited resources. At this school, Dr. Friend collaborated in a variety of instructional activities, including coteaching with a sixth-grade teacher at a time when such an arrangement was not even considered an option for delivering services to students with disabilities. Students with disabilities and typical learners succeeded in this setting, and the teachers supported and learned from each other. Because of these dramatically different experiences, Dr. Friend recognized the critical importance of collaboration in public school environments.

She decided to pursue the study of collaboration as a doctoral student at Indiana University, and in addition to special education, she included study in psychology because of its rich history of theory, literature, and practice related to collaboration. After graduating, she served as a faculty member at the University of Oklahoma, Northern Illinois University, and Indiana University–Purdue University at Indianapolis. Currently, she is the chairperson of the Department of Specialized Education Services at the University of North Carolina at Greensboro. Throughout her academic career, Dr. Friend has focused on effective collaboration, inclusive practices, and related areas such as teaming and consultation. She has written numerous articles and produced several videotapes on these topics that are widely used by teachers, teacher educators, and staff developers. She is the co-author of two best-selling texts on these topics, Including Students with Special Needs: A Practical Guide for Classroom Teachers (2002, authored with Dr. William Bursuck) and Interactions: Collaboration Skills for School Professionals (2000, authored with Dr. Lynne Cook). Additionally, Dr. Friend has been active in teacher education efforts, serving in a variety of national leadership positions in

the Council for Exceptional Children (CEC), including president of the Teacher Education Division (TED). Through her writing, research, teaching, staff development, and advocacy efforts, Dr. Friend has been a leading voice on the importance of preparing preservice and inservice teachers as well as administrators and related services personnel for roles as effective collaborators.

Q: Why is collaboration important in schools?

At the broadest level, collaboration is important in schools because it has become a defining characteristic of society in the 21st century. If you examine publications in business, health, social services, technology, and other major disciplines, you will find that collaboration is a unifying theme. In fact, Bennis and Biederman (1997) proposed that all the most societally defining inventions of the 20th century were the result of collaboration. Lisbeth Schorr's (1997) book about creating healthy communities and overcoming poverty is another example: The overriding theme is collaboration. Collaboration has become the primary contemporary strategy to foster innovation, create effective programs, and sustain them over time. Since schools reflect the society in which they exist, it is becoming a tenet that they must, too, rely on collaboration.

The importance of collaboration for schools is also a pragmatic matter: In this day and age there is simply too much for any one educator to know in order to effectively meet the needs of all his or her students. If in schools we would act in the understanding that some professionals should be experts in instructional strategies, some in the use of cooperative learning approaches, some in responding to troubling student behavior, some in assessment practices, and some in building students' self-esteem and social skills, we could draw on each others' knowledge and skills and collectively create more effective schools for our students. Too often, though, educators seem uncomfortable with this type of culture of sharing expertise. While we talk a lot about collaboration in education, in many schools each teacher seems to feel responsible for addressing academic and behavior concerns until the problems are so serious that the teacher is convinced that someone else should assume responsibility for solving them. We use the word *collaboration*, and some shared efforts do occur, but the culture of schools still fosters isolated, individual professional problem solving.

One other reason that collaboration is important for today's schools comes from a legislative and legal impetus. The expectation in the Individuals with Disabilities Education Act of 1997 concerning the least restrictive environment and the assumption that the general education classroom is that environment for many students with disabilities leads almost inevitably to increased attention on collaboration. Likewise, the law's provision for participation by parents in their children's education and by general education teachers sets the stage for the growing centrality of collaboration in schools.

But even beyond law concerning special education services, collaboration is being recommended as a way for schools to operate—in middle school teams, in site-based leadership teams, in collegial staff development, and so on. Collaboration is a means to accomplish the complex goals of schools, a way to build community while responding to the many pressures of the contemporary education system. We need collaboration to ensure that schools are positive, supportive, and effective places for students to learn and teachers to teach. Classroom teachers and other educators (e.g., special education teachers, reading specialists, Title I teachers) are working with increasingly diverse students; all school personnel are under tremendous pressure to ensure that all students achieve higher academic standards. In this context, collaboration is not a luxury; it is a necessity.

Q: What does it take to make collaboration work effectively in schools?

Although I could make many recommendations about specific ideas and strategies for promoting collaborative practices in schools, the very first and most fundamental one would be to raise teachers' and administrators' understanding of and commitment to collaboration as a critical part of school functioning, and then to extend that understanding to the general community. A disposition for collegiality is essential because of the elusive nature of collaboration: Unlike some trends in education, collaboration is a sum of subtleties and thus more difficult to build support for and give attention to. Maybe an example would help. If you asked any group of citizens about important trends in schools, technology would probably be mentioned. Many initiatives exist to ensure that all schools have adequate computer resources and that access to the Internet is available. Significant funding is committed to technology goals, and the private sector is helping schools become technologically up-to-date. However, if you asked that same group of citizens about collaboration in schools, it is likely that you would receive little response or support or possibly an assertion that teachers certainly should learn to work together. Without the concrete evidence of hardware and software and with the dilemma that collaboration requires time away from students for educators to interact, it is more difficult for collaboration to become a prominent issue in terms of public support, funding, or private sector attention. How common is it for a business to offer schools funding to build teams or opportunities to participate in staff development to become more effective at interpersonal communication skills? Collaboration is unlikely to receive the attention it deserves without increased understanding.

After that general notion of a commitment to collaboration, I would say that the most important factor in making collaboration a reality in schools is the principal. An expectation set at the district level certainly is helpful, but it seems that collabora-

tion can be accomplished without such a central mandate if the principal not only desires a collaborative culture but also is willing to express that expectation and devote resources to reaching it. This moves collaboration far beyond a laudable approach that some teachers use informally because they see its value as a standard for a school. One outstanding principal I know worked in a school in which teachers tended to stay in their classrooms, where small cliques existed but little collaboration occurred. He decided a change was in order, and he took specific steps to recreate the school culture. He created lunch-hour study groups where teachers read about and debated various issues related to collaboration. He created working committees assigned to make important decisions concerning the school, and he taught committee members strategies for working effectively during meetings and for group problem solving. He asked an external consultant to meet with staff to identify concerns and resolve them, including interpersonal issues. After 2 years, teachers and other professionals in the school worked closely together, and they saw collaboration as an essential element of all aspects of their jobs. This all happened because someone in the school set the standard and led staff to it; the someone who can do this is the principal.

Q: What do teachers need to learn about working with others?

After the disposition supportive of collaboration that I mentioned before, all preservice and inservice teachers should have knowledge and skills that contribute to effective collaboration. For example, preservice teachers should learn and experience in their initial training the concept that "effective teachers work together." Thus, they should work with partners and in small groups in their methods classes, and they should reflect on the advantages and potential problems of working with colleagues. In field experiences and student teaching, they should have opportunities to watch effective collaboration among experienced educators, and they should discuss what makes the interactions effective and how they could do the same. For example, they might observe planning meetings in which coteachers set priorities and make decisions for the upcoming week. They might also participate in intervention assistance meetings during which professionals problem solve for students experiencing persistent serious academic or behavior problems. A third example would be to observe teacher interactions with parents. Experiences such as these can assist preservice teachers in developing an appreciation for the value of collaboration and in building a knowledge base for successful professional interactions. This approach also recognizes the importance of identifying collaboration skills. Expecting preservice teachers to learn about collaboration simply by being together in schools is not enough; proximity is a necessary but insufficient condition for collaboration.

Both preservice and inservice teachers should also learn and practice specific skills, especially communication skills. Here is one small example: Sometimes I hear teachers interacting in ways that are not particularly respectful of others' perspectives. If a teacher says, "Don't you think it would be better if we…," that professional is actually expressing his or her own opinion but trying to assign it to the other person in the interaction. That type of comment doesn't encourage colleagues to voice their opinions and may be perceived as a tactic to avoid hearing anyone else's opinion. A better way to interact might be to say, "My preference is that we…. What do you think?" In this case the speaker has owned and offered an opinion, not assigned it to the other person, and has invited the other person to express an opinion, too. In addition to appropriate communication skills, educators need to understand how to complete a process of working together. Most importantly, they need skills for engaging in a problem-solving process with others to reach a shared goal.

Third, teachers need to demonstrate through their actions that collaboration is not about working with best friends or, necessarily, with like-minded people. Collaboration is about trust and respect. It's about working together to create better outcomes for all students. If teachers learn to like each other in the process, that is a bonus, but it is not a prerequisite. I mention this because in some schools, the professionals who collaborate are those who are most comfortable with each other; others are not part of the culture. Educators collaborate because doing so benefits students. They sometimes work together, even if they would not socialize and sometimes even if they have rather opposing views of teaching and learning. Collaboration is not a personal preference; it is a strategy to do what is best for students.

Finally, experienced teachers need to understand how to work effectively with new teachers and with new partners who may have less experience in collaboration. When veteran teachers have built a strong background of interacting with others in consultative, teaming, or co-teaching relationships, they sometimes, consciously or unconsciously, think that their own experiences comprise the best way to collaborate. When their partners change, they are tempted to keep doing things the old way without allowing the new partnership to develop a character of its own. In addition, they may not understand that inexperienced colleagues do not have the same level of skills, experience, or confidence in the process. Effective collaboration is always about lifelong learning. Successful collaborators believe that there is still more to know, and they are respectful of their colleagues' level of understanding and comfort in working together.

Q: What are the biggest challenges that collaborators face?

Principals and teachers must first address pragmatic barriers in order to make collaboration work. By far, the biggest such barrier is time, not just time to work together but time for constructive communication. Time is such a precious resource in school environments. Teachers need time for planning and preparation, they need time for joint teaching, they need time to share their perspectives on the success of their efforts. Given the amount of time that professionals typically are expected to work alone with students and to spend on preparing reports and completing other responsibilities, not much time is left for collaborating with colleagues unless collaboration is viewed as a priority. In both large and small schools, in urban, suburban, and rural schools, teachers often find it nearly impossible to arrange common planning

time. Overcoming this barrier requires creative thinking. In one high school where I recently worked, teachers regularly used technology to facilitate their collaboration. This school was so large that finding common planning time was not realistic. As a result, teachers used e-mail to share ideas, plan lessons, communicate concerns, and jointly problem solve. For them, e-mail is an efficient communication approach, and although the teachers would like more opportunities for face-to-face interactions, they decided to be constructive about the constraints instead of succumbing to the temptation to complain about it.

Some institutional barriers to collaboration also seem to be emerging, possibly because of reform and accountability initiatives. Some teachers fear that collaborating to meet the needs of a diverse group of students may result in slowing the progress of typical learners. Some also fear that students with disabilities will not achieve high enough outcomes and that teachers will unjustly be held accountable for this. Additionally, some principals are hesitant to support adults working together when it appears that such time is taken away from instruction. They mistakenly see collaboration as less important than direct teaching, forgetting that teaching could be significantly more effective as the result of the collaboration. It is interesting that in schools that overcome this kind of thinking, many students who struggle to learn are making significant educational progress, and other students are not being held back.

As I noted earlier, some teachers and principals also have mindsets that can work against collaboration. For example, some teachers are territorial about classroom space and teaching procedures. They resent any indication that alternatives to their practices could also be effective. I hear from special education teachers that their role in some classrooms is that of assistant; it is such a waste of valuable teaching resources. But I am also upset when classroom teachers describe special educators who are reluctant to do anything other than work with small groups. Again, so many teaching and learning options are being overlooked.

Another "mindset" challenge has to do with administrators and their understanding of collaboration. Administrators sometimes do not understand the complexities of collaboration, and consequently, they are not sure how to nurture it, assess it, and determine the type of professional development needed to make it happen. Even when administrators are well intentioned, they do things that create hurdles for collaboration. For instance, a set of coteachers recently explained with frustration that their principal told them that coteaching was a great idea but that each teacher was to teach only her "own" students in the shared classroom! Principals need to know how to create a vision for collaboration as well as how to create structures and processes for collaboration.

Q : In addition to the strategies we've already discussed, what else can effective school leaders do to facilitate collaboration in their schools?

Principals can help their faculty members develop technical skills involved in collaboration. They need to know what the skills are, model them appropriately, and provide professional development opportunities that will enable people to develop new skills and enhance existing ones. It is also important for school leaders to stay involved in collaborative efforts to ensure that participants have the support they need to address challenging issues that are bound to arise. As teachers become more comfortable working with one another, tensions often develop as they become aware of differences in their philosophies and approaches to instruction. Principals can point out commonalties that exist and help teachers keep thinking about the main goals for their students. Effective principals serve as facilitators and problem solvers by sending the message that they are not afraid of difficult issues and that they don't give up when conflicts arise. They work effectively to bring people together to problem solve and get past the rough spots. For example, on one intervention team, members agreed with a highly vocal reading specialist to complete an extensive assessment of a student's skills. Outside the specialist's presence, though, other team members expressed regret at the decision and grumbled that they had gone along with the specialist just so that she would quit repeating her preference for the assessment. The principal called the team to a meeting to discuss how members were participating in decision making, how disagreements were being addressed, and how to express dissatisfaction during team interactions. The somewhat painful but tremendously honest conversation resulted in a huge improvement in the team's functioning, and it was the principal's ability to facilitate the breakthrough to a new level of collaborative skill that made the difference. I believe that collaboration is not about how big the school budget is or the size of classrooms or the number of personnel. Once you have healthy safe schools, it is more about people, expectations, and ways to work together.

Q: What if an administrator is not a strong supporter of collaboration?

Teachers can help administrators understand the importance of collaboration by providing information, discussing its importance, undertaking collaborative initiatives that are a result of their own efforts. They also can participate in collaborative endeavors if they are personally satisfying. However, having said that, I also want to make it clear that individual teachers can only go so far. It is not realistic to think that an individual teacher can be expected to set the standard for the entire school. Teachers can be a strong positive influence and enthusiastic participants and spokespeople for collaboration; principals are the ones who have to create the standard for it. If a principal is not supportive or is actively opposed to collaborative efforts, teachers may have to adjust their own expectations, at least temporarily. I have a cartoon that explains it well: One character explains to the other, "They say the secret of success is to be in the right place at the right time... But since you never know when the right time is going to be... I figure the best strategy is to find the right place and just hang out!" For teachers anxious to collaborate in nonsupportive atmospheres, the advice seems apt.

Q: What are some resources that teachers, teacher educators, and administrators can use to improve their knowledge of collaboration?

Many authors are now addressing the topic of collaboration. Here are some of the materials that teachers and administrators may find useful:

Bennis, W., & Biederman, P. W. (1997). *Organizing genius: The secrets of creative collaboration*. Reading, MA: Addison-Wesley.

Brownell, M. T., Yeager, E., Rennells, M. S., & Riley, T. (1997). Teachers working together: What teacher educators and researchers should know. *Teacher Education and Special Education, 20*, 340-359.

Burrello, L. C., Lashley, C. L., & Beatty, E. E. (2001). *Educating all students together: How school leaders create unified systems*. Thousand Oaks, CA: Corwin.

Daane, C. J., Beirne-Smith, M., & Latham, D. (2001). Administrators' and teachers' perceptions of the collaborative efforts of inclusion in the elementary grades. *Education, 121*, 331-338.

Fishbaugh, M. S. E. (2000). *The collaboration guide for early career educators*. Baltimore: Brookes.

Friend, M. (2000). Perspectives: Collaboration in the twenty-first century. *Remedial and Special Education, 20*, 130-132, 160.

Friend, M., Burrello, L., & Burrello, J. (Co-Producers). (2001). *Leading a district to scale: Access to the general education curriculum for every student* [videotape]. Bloomington: Indiana University, Elephant Rock Productions.

Friend, M., Burrello, L., & Burrello, J. (Co-Producers). (2001). *Successful high school inclusion: Making access a reality for all students* [videotape]. Bloomington: Indiana University, Elephant Rock Productions.

Friend, M., Burrello, L., & Burrello, J. (2000). *Complexities of collaboration* [videotape]. Bloomington: Indiana University, Elephant Rock Productions.

Friend, M., & Bursuck, W. (2002). *Including students with special needs: A practical guide for classroom teachers* (3rd ed.). Needham Heights, MA: Allyn & Bacon.

Friend, M., & Cook, L. (2000). *Interactions: Collaboration skills for school professionals* (3rd ed.). White Plains, NY: Longman.

Friend, M. (Co-Producer with L. Burrello & J. Burrello). (1995). *The power of two: Including students through coteaching* [videotape]. Bloomington, IN: Elephant Rock Productions. (Distributed by the Council for Exceptional Children, Reston, VA)

Martin, A. K., & Hutchinson, N. L. (1999). *Two communities of practice: Learning the limits to collaboration*. Paper presented at the annual meeting of the Educational Research Association (Montreal, Quebec, Canada). (ERIC Document Reproduction No. ED 435 732)

Schorr, L. B. (1997). *Common purpose: Strengthening families and neighborhoods to rebuild America*. New York: Anchor Books/Random House.

Walther-Thomas, C., Korinek, L., & McLaughlin, V. L. (2000). Collaboration to support students' success. *Focus on Exceptional Children, 32*(3), 1-18.

Walther-Thomas, C., Korinek, L., McLaughlin, V. L., & Williams, B. T. (2000). *Collaboration for inclusive education: Developing successful programs*. Boston: Allyn & Bacon.

From *Intervention in School and Clinic*, March 2002, pp. 223-228. © 2002 by Pro-Ed Inc. Reprinted by permission.

Rethinking Inclusion:

Schoolwide Applications

"Inclusion" is usually regarded as the placement of special education students in general education settings. But Mr. Sailor and Ms. Roger present a new vision of integrated education, in which previously specialized adaptations and strategies are used to enhance the learning of all students.

WAYNE SAILOR AND BLAIR ROGER

As A FIELD, special education presents an excellent case study of the paradox of differentiation and integration, wherein we seek solutions through increased specialization but, in so doing, we redefine a problem in terms of discrete parts at the expense of the whole. As Thomas Skrtic pointed out more than a decade ago, a large and ever-widening gap exists between the purpose of special education—to provide needed supports, services, adaptations, and accommodations to students with disabilities in order to preserve and enhance their educational participation in the least restrictive environment—and its practice.[1] And that practice has evolved over three decades into a parallel and highly differentiated educational structure, often with only loosely organized connections to the general education system.[2]

Having disengaged from general education early on, special education began to undergo a process that, at times, has seemed to mimic cell division. At one point in its ontogeny, the field could list some 30 distinct eligibility categories for special education services (e.g., learning disabilities, behavioral disorders, severe disabilities, autism, and so on).[3] Many of these early categories further subdivided, with autism, for example, splitting into a host of subcategories lumped under "autism spectrum disorders."[4]

How has all of this come about? The paradox of differentiation and integration—with its tensions in practice and contradictions in policy—offers a reasonable hypothesis. In our efforts to better meet the educational needs of

specific identifiable groups, we have promoted differentiation at the expense of integration. If such a policy produced exemplary outcomes, the only remaining questions would concern how to direct scarce resources to meet the needs of a few individuals, and the values underlying special education would no doubt resolve the tension in favor of customization and differentiation. But the positive outcomes don't seem to be there.[5]

In its early days, special education embraced the diagnostic/prescriptive model characteristic of modern medicine, and disability was viewed as pathology. Psychology, with its partner the test industry, became the "gatekeeper" for special education. Students referred by teachers and parents were diagnosed in one of the categories of disability and tagged for separate (highly differentiated) treatment. Indeed, special education policy handbooks at the district level came to resemble the *Diagnostic and Statistical Manual* of the American Psychiatric Association.

Then in the 1980s, the U.S. Department of Education began to advance policy reforms designed to slow the growth in the number of special education categorical placements and practices. These initiatives occurred against a backdrop of publications citing positive outcomes from integrated practices and a corresponding barrage of studies associating separate classrooms and pullout practices with negative outcomes.[6]

The first of these reforms was called the Regular Education Initiative and was designed to stimulate the provision of special education supports and services in general education classrooms. It generated enormous controversy within special education. Indeed, a special issue of the *Journal of Learning Disabilities* was devoted entirely to an attempt to refute the research underlying the policy.[7] Framing the reform of special education policy as general education policy ("regular" education initiative) failed completely within the community of special education.

More recently, federal policy has advanced "inclusion" as recommended practice and has expended significant funds for training, research, and demonstration purposes. This initiative, too, has failed to significantly change special education placement and service configurations, over about a 15-year period. Again, the policy has drawn fire from within special education and has failed to attract interest and enthusiasm from general education.[8]

The No Child Left Behind (NCLB) legislation, for all its problems, does offer special education an opportunity to pursue once again the pathway to integration. First, NCLB makes clear that *all children* in public education are general education students. Second, the law is firmly anchored in accountability, even going so far as to define "evidence" and to restrict scientific inquiry to approved methodologies. If students identified for special education are placed in general education settings and provided with specialized services and supports, and if evidence for academic and social outcomes is to be evaluated according to approved methodologies, then there is an opportunity to achieve a measure of integrated education policy. And the sum of available evidence overwhelmingly supports integrated instructional approaches over those that are categorically segregated,[9] regardless of the categorical label or severity of the disability.[10]

A SCHOOLWIDE APPROACH

That inclusion policy has failed to garner much support from general education can be partially attributed to the way "inclusion" has been defined. Virtually all definitions begin with a general education classroom as the unit of interest and analysis for the provision of supports and services. The problem with a general-classroom-based model is that it doesn't seem credible to the general education teacher, whose job is usually seen as moving students as uniformly as possible through the curriculum. Students whose disabilities impede them from progressing at the expected rate and who, as a result, fall whole grade levels behind their classmates on various components of the curriculum seem to belong elsewhere. Special education has usually been there to oblige with separate categorical placements, particularly when "inclusion" has been tried and has "failed."

Alternatively, when inclusion is a core value of the school program, students with IEPs (individualized education programs) who cannot function in various components of the classroom curriculum often find themselves at tables, usually in the back of the classroom, with paraprofessionals who, in a one-on-one approach, work with them on "something else." This practice not only segregates special education students within the general education classroom but also creates a distraction that has a detrimental effect on general and special education students alike.[11]

But does inclusion need to be tied to a classroom-based model? If the objective is to avoid separate, categorical placements as the chief alternative to general education placements, then can we shift the unit of analysis from the classroom to the school? So if Joey is a student who, because of his disabilities, cannot progress at grade level in the third grade, then we can ask, For those portions of the third-grade curriculum that Joey cannot successfully engage, even with support, where should he be? With whom? And doing what? The problem then becomes one of scheduling, personnel deployment, and the use of space, not one of alternative placement.

A schoolwide approach is not a variation on the older "pull-out" model. Under emerging schoolwide models, students with IEPs are not removed from general education classrooms to receive one-on-one therapies and tutorials or to go to "resource rooms." Following the logic of integration, all services and supports are provided in such a way as to benefit the maximum number of students, including those not identified for special education. Indeed, in recent years, special education has developed evidence-based practices that have been shown to work for general education students as well. Learning strategies, positive behavior support, and transition planning are three excellent examples.[12] Here's a good summary of this new kind of thinking:

> In a transformed urban school, then, learning and other educational supports are organized to meet the needs of all students rather than historical conventions or the way the rooms are arranged in the building. Creative reallocation of even limited resources and innovative reorganization of teachers into partnerships and teams offer ways to break old molds and create the flexibilities needed to focus on student learning and achievement. Previously separate "programs," like special education, Title I, or bilingual education, come together to form a new educational system that delivers necessary additional supports and instruction in the same spaces to diverse groups of students. The new system anchors both organizational and professional effort in student content, performance, and skill standards that are owned by local communities and families while informed by national and state standards, curriculum frameworks, and effective assessment strategies.[13]

The Individuals with Disabilities Education Act (IDEA) contains language in its "incidental benefits" section that encourages applications of special education that hold promise for general education students. This approach enables special educators to support students with special needs by means of integrated arrangements.

Three decades of comprehensive special education have produced an extraordinary wealth of pedagogical adaptations and strategies to enhance learning. This unique set of conditions came about through the provision of set-aside funds for research under IDEA, and much of that research has focused on problem-solving strategies that can benefit any hard-to-teach students. Today, NCLB exhorts us to teach all students to the highest attainable standards. Special education has designed instructional enhancements that can facilitate this outcome, but for these research-based enhancements to benefit all students, special education needs to be integrated with general education. Emerging schoolwide approaches and the call for a "universal design for learning"[14] represent early efforts in this direction.

When a schoolwide approach is applied to "lower-performing" schools, such as those sometimes found in isolated rural settings or in inner-city areas affected by conditions of extreme poverty, mounting evidence suggests that integrated applications of special education practices can yield positive outcomes for all students. For example, when fully integrated applications of learning strategies designed originally for students with specific learning disabilities have been implemented, scores on NCLB-sanctioned accountability measures for all students have increased. Where social development is at issue, the use of schoolwide positive behavior support has led to higher standardized test scores for general education students in low-performing schools.[15]

SAM

To illustrate how an integrated model works in practice, we describe below our own version of such an approach, called SAM for Schoolwide Applications Model, which is being implemented and evaluated in eight California elementary and middle schools and in one elementary school in Kansas City, Kansas. We describe this model in terms of six "guiding principles," which can be broken down into 15 "critical features." Each feature can be evaluated over time using SAMAN (Schoolwide Applications Model Analysis System), an assessment instrument designed to enable schools themselves to link specific interventions to academic and social outcomes for all students. While this approach can appear to mimic comprehensive school reform in some ways, it is specifically designed to be integrated into the existing values and culture of each individual school. In other words, under SAM, a school that wishes to unify its programs and resources is presented with the 15 critical features and instructed to use team processes to implement them according to its own culture and time lines. Across our nine research sites, we are seeing great diversity and creativity on the part of school teams.

GUIDING PRINCIPLES AND CRITICAL FEATURES

Guiding Principle 1. General education guides all student learning. As a fully integrated and unified model, SAM proceeds on the key assumption that all student learning is guided by a district's framework for curriculum, instruction, and assessment and is thus aligned with state standards. Four critical features support this principle: 1) all students attend their regularly assigned school; 2) all students are considered general education students; 3) general education teachers are responsible for all students; and 4) all students are instructed in accordance with the general education curriculum.

Most teacher training programs today continue to encourage general education teachers to expect special education teachers to assume primary responsibility for students with IEPs. Special education departments at colleges and universities reinforce this notion by training special education teachers in self-contained classrooms and by having little overlap with general education departments, such as departments of curriculum and instruction.[16] An integrated schoolwide model, on the other hand, essentially requires teachers to see their role differently. At SAM schools, the general education teacher is the chief agent of each child's educational program, with support from a variety of others. Using SAM, general education teachers have primary responsibility for all students, consider themselves responsible for implementing IEPs, and collaborate with special education professionals to educate students with disabilities.

Furthermore, this guiding principle encourages schools to avoid such alternative placements as special schools for students who need extensive services and supports. Through SAM, schools welcome these students and configure any funding that comes with them to benefit a variety of students through integrated applications.

At our research sites, it is school policy to encourage parent participation and involvement, and parents are given extensive information about the schoolwide model. In those rare cases when parents feel strongly that their child requires a separate, self-contained placement —and the district concurs—the student may be referred to a comparable non-SAM school that offers self-contained classes for students with disabilities.

SAM does not allow for separate classes for students with disabilities at the school site, so the challenge is to focus on how such students can be supported in the general education classroom, how they can be supported in other environments, and how specialized therapies and services can be provided. The use of space, the deployment of support personnel, and scheduling issues become significant. At SAM schools, very little attention is focused on the existence of disabilities among some students. Every effort is made to foster friendships and positive relationships among students with and without disabilities.

SAM differs from traditional inclusion models by ensuring that students with IEPs are pursuing goals and objectives matched to and integrated with the curriculum being implemented in the general education classroom. Under SAM, no student with disabilities would be found at the rear of a classroom, engaged with a paraprofessional on some task that is unrelated to what the rest of the class is doing. If the class is engaged in a higher level curricular activity, say, algebra, and a student with disabilities cannot engage that material with measurable benefit, then that student might be assigned to an integrated grouping outside of the classroom for that period. In that case, instruction in remedial math would take place with general education students who are also operating at the same curricular level.

There are times, of course, when one-on-one instruction is appropriate in the general education classroom, but this option would be available to any student who could benefit rather than restricted solely to students identified for special education. For example, any child who needs intensive instruction in reading might receive a 30-minute tutorial session in the school's learning center while the rest of the class is engaged in a reading exercise.

Guiding Principle 2. All school resources are configured to benefit all students. Three critical features support this principle: 1) all students are included in all activities; 2) all resources benefit all students; and 3) the school effectively incorporates general education students in the instructional process.

In traditional schools, students in special education often do not accompany general education students on field trips; attend sporting events, assemblies, performances, and after-school programs; or take part in specialized reading, math, and science programs or enrichment programs in the arts. SAM schools seek to overcome such barriers to inclusion in all regular school events. All students with IEPs are members of age-appropriate, grade-level classrooms, and they attend all non-classroom functions with their classmates.

The trick is to enable all school personnel to contribute to the mission of the school.

Large SAM schools, particularly secondary schools, also make use of small-group arrangements at the classroom level and small learning communities at the school level. Cooperative learning groups, student-directed learning, peer tutorials, peer-mediated instructional arrangements, and so on can greatly enhance outcomes for all students in integrated instructional settings. In addition, particularly in large middle schools and high schools, teams of general and support teachers skilled in math or literacy can use learning centers to support any student's needs. The learning center becomes flexible space for tutorial services offered by teachers or volunteer members of the National Honor Society, as well as a place to make up tests, complete homework with assistance, see a missed film, find resources for a paper or project, and so forth.

Guiding Principle 3. Schools address social development and citizenship forthrightly. A single critical feature undergirds this principle: the school incorporates positive behavior support (PBS) at the individual, group, and schoolwide levels. PBS was originally developed as specialized instruction in social development for students with behavioral disabilities. But it has demonstrated its efficacy for all students, particularly those in schools challenged by urban blight and poverty.[17] SAM schools incorporate schoolwide PBS as a comprehensive intervention package to help meet the social development needs of all students.

Guiding Principle 4. Schools are democratically organized, data-driven, problem-solving systems. Four critical features support this principle: 1) the school is data-driven and uses team processes; 2) all personnel take part in the teaching/learning process; 3) the school employs a noncategorical lexicon; and 4) the school is governed by a site leadership team.

SAM schools are encouraged to upgrade district software to enable the leadership team to make use of all available databases that affect the social and academic performance of students. Through a process called schoolcentered planning, SAM schools use a variety of performance data fields, disaggregated at the district level, to make decisions regarding priorities related to school improvement.

SAM schools recognize that all salaried personnel at a school can contribute to the teaching/learning process. A custodian may have hidden talents for vocational training, or a speech therapist may be skilled in musical composition. The trick is to enable all school personnel to contribute to the primary mission of the school and not to be completely constrained by bureaucratic specifications of roles. SAM schools also seek to move away from such categorical descriptors as "learning disabilities," "inclusion," "specials," and so on. There are just two kinds of teachers in a SAM school: classroom teachers and support teachers.

A site leadership team is established at each SAM school. It represents all school personnel and may include parents and members of the local community. This team undertakes the process of school-centered planning to evaluate data related to student academic and social performance, to prioritize specific interventions to improve outcomes, and to advance the mission of the school through full implementation of SAM.

Guiding Principle 5. Schools have open boundaries in relation to their families and communities. Two critical features support this guiding principle: 1) schools have working partnerships with their students' families; and 2) schools have working partnerships with local businesses and service providers.

SAM schools go beyond the traditional structure of parent/teacher organizations and solicit the active participation of family members in the teaching/learning process. Some SAM sites have made the establishment of a family resource center at the school a top priority. Some have even created a "parent liaison" position.

SAM schools also reach beyond the "business partnership" relationship that has characterized some school reform efforts. Schools undertake a "community mapping" process to understand their respective communities. Under many circumstances, the school community may not be geographically defined. But the point is to engage the school's constituents in the life of the school.

Furthermore, effective community partnerships set the stage for meaningful service-learning opportunities and open up possibilities for community-based instruction for any student. Students with IEPs, for example, who cannot engage a secondary-level, classroom-based math curriculum, might take part in "community math" in real-life applied settings such as banks and stores. Other students who are chronically unmotivated by school may reconnect with the learning process through community-based learning opportunities.

Guiding Principle 6. Schools enjoy district support for undertaking an extensive systems-change effort. Just one critical feature is necessary here: schoolwide models such as SAM that offer a significant departure from traditional bureaucratic management and communication processes must have district support . One way to garner such support is to set up pilot projects with the understanding that expansion to additional sites is contingent on documented gains in measured student academic and social outcomes. District-level support may be expected to increase following successful demonstrations and sharing results across schools over time.

MEASUREMENT STRATEGIES

Each SAM school employs a package of psychometrically established instruments with which to assess progress related to the priorities that were established through the school-centered planning process. These instruments include a schoolwide evaluation tool to assess support for positive behavior,[18] SAMAN to assess the 15 critical features of SAM, and EVOLVE to assess the training of paraprofessionals and the ways they are deployed.[19]

Districts are encouraged to use the COMPASS Data Analyzer[20] as an adjunct to the districtwide data system to enable each SAM school to receive feedback about its own priorities and specific data of interest. The program also facilitates reporting to the other teams and committees at the school.

STRUCTURAL ELEMENTS OF SAM

SAM is a fully integrated and unified approach to the education of all students. As a process, it is intended to enable schools to engage in collaborative, team-driven decision making that is focused on interventions de-signed to enhance academic and social outcomes for students. The process of educating all students together presents both challenges and opportunities. The SAM approach requires certain structural elements to be in place. As touched upon earlier, two elements, a site leadership team and school-centered planning, must be present at the school level. And two more elements, a district leadership team and a district resource team, must be present at the district level.

Site leadership team. The SLT, usually with between eight and 12 members, evaluates schoolwide data on student progress; sets priorities, goals, and objectives for each school term; and networks with and reports to the other teams and committees that function at the school. The principal is usually a member of the SLT but does not need to be its chair. Membership on SLTs is usually determined by a combination of internal teacher nominations, with elections for one-year renewable terms; principal appointments; and invitations to specific parents and community members. Expenses incurred by parent and community participants, the cost of substitutes for participating teachers who attend out-of-class meetings, the cost of supplies, and so on, can become budget items for SLTs. SLTs follow strict team procedures with regard to agenda, floor time, minutes, and so on, so that precious time is not wasted. SLTs meet at least biweekly and undergo full-day "retreats" at least twice a ye a r, prior to the beginning of each new term. The school-centered-planning process takes place during these retreats.

School-centered planning. The SCP process is patterned after empowerment evaluation.[21] Using this process, a facilitator, supplied by the district or arranged through a university partnership, assists the SLT to begin with a vision for why the school decided to become a SAM school. A set of goals is derived to make the vision real, and a set of specific objectives for the coming term is spelled out for the various school/community personnel. Measurement strategies are identified for each objective so that subsequent planning and objective setting can take account of data on pupil performance that are linked to specific measurable processes. The SLT holds interim meetings to review progress in the implementation of each SCP action plan for the term.

District leadership team. The DLT consists of district personnel with an interest in implementing SAM. The superintendent may well be a member but usually will not be the chair. DLTs are frequently chaired by the head of curriculum and instruction, since SAM processes are driven primarily by general education. Other members of the DLT typically include the head of pupil support services, the special education director, the Title I director, and the director of programs for second-language learners. The superintendent may appoint other members as needed. The DLT usually meets three or four times a year to review SAM school-site plans and to consider requests for approval of policy and budget items arising from these plans.

District resource team. The final structural component is the DRT. This team is usually made up of district-level staff members who work closely with the schools, such as regional special education personnel, grade-level specialists, the parent support coordinator, and transportation officials. The function of the DRT is to help the DLT consider requests for resources from each school site for the coming term. If, for example, a SAM site requests two additional paraprofessionals to implement one or more objectives on its plan for the coming term, the DRT will consider the request, balance the needs of that site against the collective needs of all district schools, and make recommendations to the DLT. Typically, DRTs with several SAM sites in the district will meet on a fairly frequent basis to help the district stay ahead of the curve of systems change.

The Schoolwide Applications Model is a work in progress. It represents an effort to integrate all aspects of comprehensive school reform with a new and innovative approach to the delivery of special education supports and services. Research must continue if we are to determine whether the premise of SAM holds: namely, that de-differentiated educational practices can support personalized learning—in and outside of classrooms—while creating a sense of unity and a culture of belonging in the school.

Notes

1. Thomas M. Skrtic, *Behind Special Education: A Critical Analysis of Professional Culture and School Organization* (Denver: Love Publishing, 1991).

2. Steven J. Taylor, "Caught in the Continuum: A Critical Analysis of the Principle of the Least Restrictive Environment," *Journal of the Association for Persons with Severe Handicaps*, vol. 13, 1988, pp. 41-53.

3. Wayne Sailor and Doug Guess, *Severely Handicapped Students: An Instructional Design* (Boston: Houghton Mifflin, 1983).

4. Johnny L. Matson, *Autism in Children and Adults: Etiology, Assessment, and Intervention* (Pacific Grove, Calif.: Brookes/Cole, 1994).

5. See for example, Wayne Sailor, testimony before the Research Agenda Task Force of the President's Commission on Excellence in Special Education, 18 April 2002.

6. See, for example, Diane Lea Ryndak and Douglas Fisher, eds., *The Foundations of Inclusive Education: A Compendium of Articles on Effective Strategies to Achieve Inclusive Education*, 2nd ed. (Baltimore: TASH, 2003), available at www.tash.org; and Margaret Wang, Maynard C. Reynolds, and Herbert J. Wahlberg, eds., *Handbook of Special Education: Research and Practice Vol. 1: Learner Characteristics and Adaptive Education* (Oxford: Pergamon Press, 1987).

7. See *Journal of Learning Disabilities*, vol. 21, 1988.

8. James M. Kauffman, Kathleen McGee, and Michele Brigham, "Enabling or Disabling? Observations on Changes in Special Education," *Phi Delta Kappan*, April 2004, pp. 613-20; and Larry M. Lieberman, "Special Education and Regular Education: A Merger Made in Heaven?," *Exceptional Children*, vol. 51, 1985, pp. 513-16.

9. An exception can be made for students with a hearing problem. Some recent research suggests that instruction delivered in American Sign Language results in better academic outcomes than interpreted instruction in general education classrooms.

10. Wayne Sailor and Kathy Gee, "Progress in Educating Students with the Most Severe Disabilities: Is There Any?," *Journal of the Association for Persons with Severe Handicaps*, vol. 13, 1988, pp. 87-99.

11. Michael F. Giangreco and M. B. Doyle, "Students with Disabilities and Paraprofessional Supports: Benefits, Balance, and Band-Aids," *Exceptional Children*, vol. 68, 2002, pp. 1-12.

12. Sailor and Gee, op. cit.; George Sugai and Rob H. Homer, "Including Students with Severe Behavior Problems in General Education Settings: Assumptions, Challenges, and Solutions," in Alice J. Marr, George Sugai, and Gerald A. Tindal, eds., *The Oregon Conference Monograph 6* (Baltimore: Paul H. Brookes, 1994), pp. 102-20; and Mary Morningstar, Jeannie Kleinhammer-Tramill, and Dana Lattin, "Using Successful Models of Student-Centered Transition Planning and Sevices for Adolescents with Disabilities," *Focus on Exceptional Children*, vol. 31, no. 9, 1999, pp. 1-19.

13. Dianne L. Ferguson, Elizabeth B. Kozleski, and Anne Smith, "Transformed, Inclusive Schools: A Framework to Guide Fundamental Change in Urban Schools," National Institute for Urban School Improvement: The Office of Special Education Programs, August 2001, available from www.inclusiveschools.org/publicat.htm#transformed.

14. Cynthia Curry, "Universal Design: Accessibility for All Learners," *Educational Leadership*, October 2003, pp. 55-60; "Principles of Universal Design," Center for Universal Design, North Carolina State University, 1997, available at www.design.ncsu.edu/cud; James Rydeen, "Universal Design," available at http://industryclick.com//magazinearticle.asp?magazinearticleid=33035&mode=print; and David H. Rose, Sheela Sethuraman, and Grace J. Meo, "Universal Design for Learning," *Journal of Special Education Technology*, vol. 15, no. 2, 2000, pp. 56-60.

15. Steve R. Lassen, Michael M. Steele, and Wayne Sailor, "The Relationship of School-wide Positive Behavior Support to Academic Achievement in an Urban Middle School," manuscript in preparation.

16. Claude Goldenberg, "School-University Links: Settings for Joint Work," in *Successful School Change* (New York: Teachers College Press, 2004), pp. 138-62.

17. Cheryl Utley and Wayne Sailor, eds., *Journal of Positive Behavior Interventions*, vol. 4, 2002.

18. Robert H. Horner et al., "The School-wide Evaluation Tool (SET): A Research Instrument for Assessing School-wide Positive Behavior Support," *Journal of Positive Behavior Interventions*, vol. 6, 2004, pp. 3-12.

19. Giangreco and Doyle, op. cit.

20. Robert Harsh, "COMPASS Data Management System," available at http://sbiweb.kckps.org:2388/common/default.asp.

21. David M. Fetterman, "Empowerment Evaluation: An Introduction to Theory and Practice," in idem, Sakeh J. Kafterian, and Abraham Wandersman, eds., *Empowerment Evaluation: Knowledge and Tools for Self-Assessment and Accountability* (Thousand Oaks, Calif.: Sage, 1997), pp. 1-46.

WAYNE SAILOR is a clinical psychologist, a professor of special education, and an associate director of the Beach Center on Disability, University of Kansas, Lawrence. **BLAIR ROGER** is an educational consultant based in Oakland, Calif. They wish to thank the administrators, teachers, staff, students, and families of the Ravenswood (Calif.) School District, East Palo Alto, and of USD 500, Wyandotte County, Kansas City, Kan. The authors also thank Leonard Burrello of Indiana University, Bloomington, and the Forum on Education (www.forumon-education.org) for initiating a forum on the paradox of differentiation, which led to this article. Preparation of this article was supported, in part, by the National Center on Positive Behavior Interventions and Supports (Grant no. 113265980003).

Assessment That Drives Instruction

Pokey Stanford • Stacy Reeves

Two challenging aspects of inclusive education are knowing what to teach children with learning disabilities and knowing how to teach the material. Instructional decision making is confounded by variability in instructors' personal teaching philosophies and interventions. However, a fundamental truth in effective teaching is that assessment strategies, both formal and informal, must help the teacher determine the most appropriate instruction, in addition to assessing progress. The question for teachers becomes, How do we maximize instruction for students with special needs in general education classrooms? The answer may lie in effective and appropriate assessment, including rubrics, T-charts, and checklists for students.

Why Change How We Assess?

For generations, assessment and its focus on standards and accountability have controlled the public discourse regarding the improvement of education. Discussions about balancing achievement within the curriculum, making the goals of the individualized education program (IEP) compatible with high standards, and determining what constitutes a thoughtfully directed curricular focus are common. These concerns focus attention on the performance and progress of all learners (Pugach & Warger, 2001). Assessment drives instruction, but assessments often lack the primary goal of guiding instructional decisions (Olson, 2003).

In meeting IEP goals, the assessment used—which is often a pencil-and-paper test—should match the instruction given. In many instances, "the test" is not an assessment that guides instructional decisions; it is, instead, just another assignment that will become a grade in the grade book. Matching IEP goals to performance tasks and designing assessments that offer guidance for teachers, parents, and learners will result in better individualized learning. A comprehensive assessment tool furnishes an academic or behavioral growth measure that aligns with IEP goals, content-area objectives, and national standards; and it enables teachers to identify trends toward meeting these expectations and monitor them (Olson, 2003).

> **Assessment drives instruction, but assessments often lock the primary goal of guiding instructional decisions.**

According to the Individuals With Disabilities Education Act (IDEA) 1997 regulations and amendments from the U. S. Department of Education (1999), educators must assess learners with disabilities in the general education curriculum, and they must show progress. Educators must develop instruction that is specifically designed to meet the needs of learners with disabilities. Also, the IEP requires that educators consider how a learner will participate in statewide and districtwide assessments of achievement. The IDEA amendments indicate that instruction designed to meet the individual needs of learners with disabilities must include instructional access to the general education curriculum so that learners can meet educational standards.

However, the pencil-and-paper assessments used for today's learners are often not relevant to the content being taught. Expanding the repertoire of assessment strategies will help teachers meet the needs of every learner in the classroom. The most important criterion is making sure that the assessment tool selected allows the teacher to focus appropriately on the learner (Olson, 2003). Such alternative assessments as rubrics, T-charts, and checklists focus on individualized instruction while meeting the instructional needs of the class.

Design a Rubric

A rubric, which is a set of criteria that outlines expectations for a completed product, can serve as an effective basis for assessment and consequently, for instructional decision making (Erickson, 1995). Rubrics require a Likert-type scale to quantify decisions about performance and a semantic scale to describe different levels of learning for a particular activity. A rubric also identifies performance competencies that separate student performance into a number of interrelated instructional concerns. For instance, Criteria 1 of the rubric in Figure 1 refers to meaning. The scales, or semantic descriptors, provide details about the concept of conveying meaning for the learner, the teacher, and all members of the class. Every participant understands the desired learning outcomes.

The time spent designing the scale proves its worth, because all students gain a common focus of instruction and the teacher maintains a basis for relating progress and performance within the context of metacognition. The teacher must remember to discuss the rubric standards with the learners before giving the assignment. A clear understanding of what will be assessed is fundamental to obtaining an accurate understanding of what the learner may need.

Rubrics are useful in characterizing a learner's strengths and weaknesses with respect to instructional design.

- One useful outcome of using a rubric is a graph that allows a learner to see his or her progress—or stagnation—in a particular aspect of learning. Educators can tailor outcomes to a specific objective, which may naturally emerge from the IEP. For example, if basic writing is an IEP goal for the year, the short-term objective may be to use sight words in context. The rubric given in Figure 1 includes spelling and punctuation as one of six criteria for evaluating a learner's journal. The spelling and punctuation criterion can be tailored to focus on a particular spelling or punctuation strategy, such as spelling sight words correctly in context. As progress is monitored, data can link daily instruction with the IEP. More specifically, the data generated can help the teacher make daily instructional decisions.

Figure 1. Rubric for Creative Writing

Rubric for Creative Writing

Date_____

Teacher _____ Self _____ Peer _____

Meaning

0---------------------1---------------------2---------------------3   **Comments:**

Unclear intent of writer	Vague or weak expla-nation of writer	Writer's intent some-what clear, few details	Writer's intent is easy to follow and understand, numerous details

Editing

0---------------------1---------------------2---------------------3   **Comments:**

No evidence of editing	Little evidence of editing	Editorial marks used, few corrections made	Proficient use of edito-rial marks, appropriate corrections made

Organization

0---------------------1---------------------2---------------------3   **Comments:**

No organization	Difficult to follow, few transitions	Organization evident, transitions used	Well organized, ideas easy to follow, logical sequence and clear transitions

Creativity

0---------------------1---------------------2---------------------3   **Comments:**

No imagination used	Few creative details, but unrelated to topic, some imagination	Creative details evi-denced, imagination used for the reader's enjoyment	Many creative details, imagination used for the reader's enjoyment

Spelling and Punctuation

0---------------------1---------------------2---------------------3   **Comments:**

Final draft has more than 3 spelling and punctuation errors	2-3 spelling and punctuation errors in the final draft	1 spelling or punctuation error in the final draft	No spelling or punctuation errors in the final draft

The pencil-and-paper assessments used for today's learners are often not relevant to the content being taught.

- Accurate development of the rubric links instruction and learning through assessment in a continuous feedback loop. The learning process becomes more concrete with the narration and feedback inherent in the rubric. Sources of input to the rubric for a student include the teacher, the student, and his or her peers.

- A learner's use of a rubric paces the student through an internal review of a learning task. Using writing to reflect on the learning task may encourage self-assessment and self-directed instruction (Erickson, 1995). A student's written metacognitive reflections are helpful for the teacher because committing the learning processes to paper can illustrate a student's metacognitive processing. For example, if a learner comments after reading his or her own work that she or he does not understand why he or she received an editing score of 1, the teacher then knows that the learner does not understand how to edit or has not generalized editing to his or her journal. If the learner still continues to make 1s on editing after more instruction from the teacher, the learner may need to question himself or herself about why he or she continues to make the mistakes repeatedly. Focused corrective feedback from the teacher becomes more individualized and specific.

- Rubrics often make feedback easier to share because the student knows what will be evaluated and how the work will be evaluated before the teacher gives the assignment. Feedback may be one of the most neglected aspects of teaching special-needs students because of the perceived time involved in this level of decision making. The rubric makes the decision process more direct and less time-consuming for a teacher and a learner. Peer feedback, within the framework of the classroom environment, can provide a structured social context and often a less threatening, yet inclusive, response to the special learner and to his or her instructional and assessment needs.

Every participant understands the desired learning outcomes.

Developing a T-Chart

A T-chart (see Figure 2) is an assessment tool that easily indicates behavioral goals or objectives. The T-chart is designed to ask the learner what appropriate behavior looks and sounds like.

Talking with the learner and clearly articulating what is meant by appropriate behavior results in clearer communication and a better understanding of what is expected from the learner. The teacher and the learner have defined expectations within the vocabulary of the learner.

The teacher may often find that giving examples of what is not appropriate is beneficial. Such examples indicate and model what the expected behavior does not look like and does not sound like. Learners often understand what is expected of them more clearly when given a nonexample. Fully describing behavioral goals or objectives ensures that the learner has a clear understanding of what is expected because she or he has participated in defining the behavior or objective.

Devising a Checklist

After developing and monitoring the T-chart, educators can derive a more concrete assessment from it. A checklist (see Figure 3) that is based on a T-chart can help facilitate the growth and development of instructional and behavioral expectations, all of which lead to clearly defined assessments.

Figure 3 shows how key behaviors can be exhibited in varying degrees. The teacher should clearly define the terms "almost always," "sometimes," and "never" in a way that is appropriate to the age and needs of the individual. As in developing the T-chart, the teacher will find that showing models and examples of what is and what is not appropriate for the behaviors and actions contained on the checklist is helpful.

Final Thoughts

Assessment must be derived from instruction. After meeting the basic requirements of the assessment needs, the teacher should consider these final aspects of the decision-making process:

- Provide information on how a learner is performing on a unit of instruction.
- Set long-term goals and note achievements as they are reached.
- Show the learner his or her performance on individualized, district-, and statewide assessments.
- Design and build instructional decisions on the basis of assessment results.
- Inform learners, parents, and other relevant decisionmakers about the learner's progress (Olson, 2003).

The assessment process must move to learner-centered methods, because learners need to clearly understand the task and understand how the teacher will assess the task.

Figure 2. Sample T-Chart

What Does Appropriate Cafeteria Behavior Look Like and Sound Like?

👁	👂
1. Looks like using table manners • Napkin in lap • Eating with appropriate utensils • Chewing with mouth closed 2. Looks like sitting in your seat 3. Looks like walking while in line 4. Looks like feet on the floor or under table 5. Looks like carrying tray or lunchbox correctly	1. Sounds like using *please* and *thank you* 2. Sounds like eating with your mouth closed (no smacking) 3. Sounds like appropriate language (excuse me, would you please pass the...) 4. Sounds like using an inside voice when speaking to someone next to you 5. Sounds like using appropriate voice while waiting in line

The greatest advantage to using more authentic assessments is that they are concrete and establish an understanding of expectations for learners, teachers, and parents. Rubrics can also be individually tailored to meet specific objectives or needs of learners with disabilities. Furthermore, T-charts provide clarity of expectations within a context of mutual understanding. When the learner understands what is expected, the likelihood becomes greater that she or he will master the goal. A checklist provides learners, teachers, and parents with more structure and a better understanding of the assessment being used. When the learners and their parents ask precise questions about assessment and instructional decisions, all learners can receive the most accurate individualized education available.

References

Erickson, H. L. (1995). *Stirring the head, heart and soul: Redefining curriculum and instruction.* Thousand Oaks, CA: Corwin Press.

Individuals with Disabilities Act Amendments of 1997, 20 U.S.C. 1415.

Olson, A. (2003). The answer to getting better test data: Ask the right questions. *Multimedia Schools, 10,* 28–31.

Pugach, M. C. & Warger, C. L. (2001). Curriculum matters: Raising expectations for students with disabilities. *Remedial and Special Education, 22,* 194–200.

U.S. Department of Education. (1999). Assistance to States for the Education of Children With Disabilities; Final Rule. Federal Register [online]. Retrieved February 7, 2005 from http://www.ed.gov/legislation/FedRegister/finrule/19992/062499a.html

Pokey Stanford (CEC MS Federation), *Assistant Professor, and Stacy Reeves, Assistant Professor, Department of Education, William Carey College, Hattiesburg, Mississippi.*

Address correspondence to Dr. Pokey Stanford. Department of Education, William Carey College, 498 "Tuscan Avenue, WCC Box 3, Hattiesburg, MS 39401. (e-mail: barbarastanford@wmcarey.edu.)

From *Teaching Exceptional Children,* Vol. 37, No. 4, March/April 2005, pp. 18-20, 22. Copyright © 2005 by Council for Exceptional Children. Reprinted by permission.

Meaningful Inclusion of *All* Students in Team Sports

Yoshihisa Ohtake

• Jesse, a second grader with cerebral palsy, assists his T-ball team in scoring by maintaining his attention and his upright posture.

• Maki, a sixth grader with severe multiple disabilities, meets her goal of walking steadily and thus influences the yardage gained by her team in flag football.

• David, a tenth grader with severe mental retardation, assists his basketball team to make baskets when he meets his goal of making adapted "shots" from his wheelchair.

These students, at various grade levels, are actively participating in team sports, thanks to the creative adaptations their teachers have made so as to include the students in meaningful ways. In fact, teams clamor to have these students on their side, because of the opportunities to make more points in the game, no matter what the sport.

This article shows how to take what we know about adapted physical education and boost students' capabilities and self-esteem in innovative, fulfilling ways (for background information about adaptive physical education, see box, "What Does the Literature Say?").

Four Standard Plus One

Here, I describe five standards that any game modifications should meet to ensure participation of students with severe multiple disabilities in team sport games.

• First, let's examine four widely accepted standards proposed by Block (2000).

• Second, I propose a fifth standard.

• Finally, let's explore new strategies for developing game modifications that meet all five standards.

Block's Four Standards

Block (2000) proposed four standards for evaluating the appropriateness of game modifications, as follows:

• *Challenging*. This standard recommends that modifications should promote the maximum use of physical, cognitive, and social skills possessed by the student with disabilities. Too much or too little support deprives students of opportunities to practice these skills.

• *Safety*. Any modifications need to contribute to making an injury-free environment. If the modification allows team players without disabilities to bump into a student who uses a wheelchair, that should be discarded.

• *Integrity*. Substantial changes in rules and materials might undermine the integrity of the game, leading students without disabilities to having fewer opportunities to enjoy the original format of the game. Therefore, we need to develop modifications that allow *all* students to maximize their potentials in the game.

• *Implementation*. Because both human and material resources tend to be in short supply, the modifications should not cause undue burden on practitioners. Table 1 lists the four standards with a brief description of each.

When adhering to these standards, we are more likely to develop modifications that ensure that students with severe multiple disabilities are able to participate in team sport games according to their ability. Block (2000) provided an excellent example of a game modification that meets the four criteria. In the case example, a student who has advanced muscular dystrophy and uses an electric wheelchair assumes a permanent throw-in role in soccer games. That is, every time the ball is out of bounds, the student pushes the ball off his lap. Given the student's disability, this is a challenging achievement (Challenging Standard). The student plays along the sideline of the field. This off-contact strategy ensures a safe environment for

Table 1. Four Standards for Ensuring Appropriate Involvement of Students With Disabilities In Team Sports

Standard	Description
Challenging	The game modification should allow the student with disabilities to use individualized education program (IEP) skills so that the participation is meaningful and challenging.
Safety	The game modification should not allow players without disabilities to physically contact the student with disabilities.
Integrity	The game modification should minimize the deviation from the original format of the game so that students without disabilities can enjoy and maximize their potential in the game.
Implementation	The game modification should not cause undue burden (e.g., money, time, skills) on the practitioners.

all players (Safety Standard). Yet at the same time, this way of participating does not restrict the movement of the peers without disabilities or the flow of the game (Integrity Standard). Finally, the modification is neither time-consuming nor expensive to implement. In addition, no assistants art' needed (Implementation Standard).

Proposed Fifth "Essential" Standard

The four standards proposed by Block (2000) are useful in developing modifications that ensure students with severe multiple disabilities participate in team sport games. These standards, however, do not ensure that the student participates in the *essential part* of the game. The term *essential part* refers to the core meaning of a sport and contributes to getting scores or defending one's team from being scored on. For example, shooting a ball, assisting a shot, or blocking a pass are all examples of the essential part of soccer games or basketball games.

In contrast, a nonessential part does not characterize the sport and does not have any direct influence on the scoring process. The throw-in role in soccer or basketball games illustrated in the previous example is considered a nonessential part.

A student with a disability would especially value being involved offensively or defensively in a scoring process—making a direct contribution to the game's outcome.

For example, the play preventing an opponent from making a shot is more valued than the throw-in ball play. Just as a direct contribution to a group project is more likely to help build a sense of group membership (Williams & Downing, 1998), direct contribution to the game's outcome is more likely to enhance a sense of team membership of the students. Students with severe multiple disabilities are often marginalized in social activities (Williams & Downing); thus, being involved in an essential part of the sport contributes to students' sense of "belonging." We need to add the "essential" standard to the four proposed by Block (2000).

What Does the Literature Say About Adapted Team Sports?

Team sports and games are ubiquitous in most students' lives. In free time, after-school programs, and physical education programs, students are engaged in a variety of team sports like T-ball, basketball, and soccer. Engaging in team sports offers many benefits by allowing students to develop physical, cognitive, and social skills; improve their health; and build friendships (Block, 2000; Schleien, Ray, & Green, 1997). Among these benefits, enhancing social skills and building friendships are more expected in team sports than in individually based sports (e.g., aerobics, walking, bowling) because the former includes ample opportunities to interact and collaborate with peers.

The social aspect of team sports (i.e., opportunities to interact and collaborate with peers) is especially important to students with severe mental retardation and physical disabilities. Promoting social interactions and building friendships are frequently mentioned by families of students as a valued life outcome (Giangreco, Cloninger, Dennis, & Edelman, 1993). If students with severe multiple disabilities are provided opportunities to participate meaningfully in team sports, they are more likely to increase social interactions and enhance social relationships with peers without disabilities.

Because of the frequently observed extreme gap between skills possessed by students with severe multiple disabilities and the skills required to participate in team sports, modifications are necessary. Such modifications include, but are not limited to, providing an assistant, changing rules, developing adaptive devices, and providing alternative activities (Block, 2000). To help practitioners develop appropriate game modifications, standards are needed to guide them.

Challenging Issues

We might ask, "Are there practical ways to modify a game that will meet all of the five standards?" Practitioners of physical education or community recreation programs must first ensure student safety; and the Essential Standard presents a challenge in this area. Physical contact is unavoidable in popular team sports like basketball, soccer, and flag football. But such contact may be too dangerous to risk for a student who is physically fragile and uses assistive tools (e.g., wheelchair, trunk or neck stabilizer).

For safely reasons, therefore, students with severe multiple disabilities are often required to play in a special zone. This practice, however, is incompatible with ensuring that they are involved in the scoring process, as required by the Essential Standard. For example, if a student with severe multiple disabilities plays along the sideline of the court or field, how can he or she join the scoring process that occurs inside of the sideline? The next section answers this question.

Effort Conversion Strategy

The effort conversion strategy I propose (see Table 2) offers a way to meet two requirements: playing in a special "safe" zone and being involved in an essential part of the sport. *Effort conversion* means changing the *capacity of the equipment, momentarily*

Jesse and T-Ball

Jesse is a second-grade student who has cerebral palsy and severe mental retardation. He uses a wheelchair, but needs full physical support to move. According to one of his IEP goals, he will keep an upright position toward classmates as long as possible during an interaction.

In a softball game, efforts to keep an upright position may be converted into the capacity of the special equipment that is used to stop a hit ball. The equipment in this case is a circle drawn around the student on the ground. When a hit ball reaches the circle, a whistle is blown and the runner has to stop. In advance, a few concentric circles are drawn around the student. For the student's protection, a portable net screen needs to be placed in front of him or her as well.

When a new player is at the batter's box, his team players call him, "Hey, Jesse, look up and watch the ball." if Jesse maintains his upright position one second longer, a larger concentric circle is applied as a line of the catching zone. Thus, his catching zone becomes momentarily and proportionally larger on the basis of the duration of his target behavior.

This procedure is repeated each time a new player is at the batter's box. For safety reasons, outfield players are told not to enter Jesse's catching zone. By showing the target behavior in a timely manner, Jesse can help his team stop the runner.

Table 2. Effort Conversion Strategy

Key Word	Definition
Effort conversion	A process whereby the *capacity of the equipment is changed momentarily and proportionally* to the degree of *effort* made by a student with severe multiple disabilities.
Effort	A measurable change made by the student in the targeted physical, social, or cognitive behaviors written in the individualized education program.
Changed momentarily	Initiating a changing process each time the student starts showing a target behavior.
Changed proportionally	Changing the capacity of the equipment being used, depending totally on the student's effort.
Capacity of equipment	The potential of the equipment in terms of facilitating an involvement in the scoring process.

and proportionally, to match the degree of *effort* made by a student with severe multiple disabilities, as follows:

- *Effort* refers to a measurable change made by the student in the targeted physical, social, or cognitive behaviors written in the individualized education program (IEP). For example, the duration of keeping an upright position may be used as a measure of the effort a student with severe multiple disabilities is making.

- *Changed momentarily* means that each time the student starts showing a target behavior, the changing process is initiated.

- *Changed proportionally* means that the capacity of the equipment being used depends totally on the student's effort.

Resources on Sports Adaptations

Print

Auxter, D., Pyfer, J., & Huettig, C. (2000). *Principles and methods of adapted physical education and recreation.* Madison, WI: McGraw-Hill.
Dunn, J. (1997). *Special physical education* (7th ed.). Madison, WI: Brown & Benchmark.
Sherrill, C. (2002). *Adapted physical activity, recreation and sport.* Madison, WI: McGraw-Hill.
Winnick. J. P. (2000). *Adapted physical education and sport* (3rd ed.). Champaign, IL: Human Kinetics.

On the Web

http://www.pecentral.com/adapted/adaptedmenu.html
This Web site is designed for teachers and parents who are involved in adapted physical education. The site describes assessment and implementation strategies, laws, rescues, and feedback for those having specific questions about implementation of adapted physical education.

Maki and Flag Football

Maki is a sixth grader with cerebral palsy and severe mental retardation. She moves using a walker, but does so in an unstable manner when the surface is rough, bumpy, or slanting. One of her IEP goals is to walk without falling with her walker regardless of the condition of the surface.

Maki shows interest in flag football. When blocking practice begins, she actively practices pushing a dummy.

Her preference and IEP skills can be infused into flag football games. For safety reasons, she plays out of bounds. On offense, she is positioned along the intersection between the sideline and the first-down marker. Her role is to start pushing a dummy toward the line of scrimmage each time her team players start playing. She continues pushing until her team stops playing.

As part of the modification, the first-down marker for her team is moved to the point she reached at the end of the play. Thus, the more she pushes the dummy, the closer her team is to a first down. This procedure is repeated each time the team on offense starts playing.

Maki's efforts to push a dummy are converted momentarily and proportionally into the position of the first-down marker and therefore allows her to help her team gain yardage.

The term *essential* part refers to the core meaning of a sport—getting scores or defending one's team from being scored on.

- *Capacity of equipment* refers to the potential of the actual game equipment in terms of facilitating an involvement in the scoring process. For example, a larger goal is more likely to facilitate a successful shot than a smaller goal as in basketball, soccer, and hockey games.

Table 3. Three Determination Steps In the Three Vignettes

Step	Jesse: T-Ball	Maki: Flag Football	David: Basketball
Step 1 (target behavior)	Control head.	Walk steadily.	Pick up and throw a ball
Step 2 (equipment)	A circle drawn around the student on the ground (functioning as a catching glove).	First down marker.	Basket: Two types of baskets are placed side by side: one has a higher rim, the other has a lower rim.
Step 3 (exchange rate)	If Jesse maintains his upright position one second longer, a larger concentric circle is applied as a line of the catching zone.	The first down marker for Maki's team is moved to the point she reached at the end of the play.	Each time David successfully makes an adapted shot, his team is allowed to use a lower basket.

David and Basketball

David is a tenth-grade student with cerebral palsy and severe mental retardation. He moves around in his wheelchair with full support from others. One of David's IEP objectives addresses participation in recreational activities that include a movement of picking up and throwing a ball.

In basketball games, two types of baskets are placed side by side: one has a higher rim, the other has a lower rim. To ensure David's essential involvement in the game, which basket his team can use depends totally on the degree of effort David makes. During a basketball game, David engages in picking up and throwing a basketball to make an adapted shot outside of the basket court. Each time he successfully makes an adapted shot, his team is allowed to use the lower basket.

Thus, David's efforts to throw a ball are converted momentarily and proportionally into the height of a basket. In this way, he can assist team players without disabilities, who are not good at shooting, in making more successful shots. Therefore, David is considered an active participant in an essential part of the basketball game.

Accordingly, in effort conversion, practitioners develop a modification by which engaging in a better practice by the student immediately results in better capacity of equipment, which in turn results in a better outcome for the team.

A student with a disability would especially value being involved offensively or defensively in a scoring process—making a direct contribution to the game's outcome.

When developing a game modification on the basis of the effort conversion strategy, take at least the following three steps:

1. Determine a target behavior (i.e., IEP skill) for the student to engage in during the game.
2. Determine which equipment is targeted to be changed and how the capacity of the equipment can be made changeable.
3. Determine the exchange rate between effort to engage in a target behavior and the capacity of the equipment.

To get a clear idea of how the effort conversion strategy works, take a look at Jesse, Maki, and David playing T-ball, flag football, and basketball, respectively (see boxes). Table 3 indicates the content of each step applied for the three students.

Table 4 shows how the modifications meet the five standards (i.e., Block's four standards and the fifth "essential" standard).

Special Issues Related to the Effort Conversion Strategy

The effort conversion strategy is useful in helping students with severe multiple disabilities participate in an essential part of team sports. In addition, the strategy meets the four standards previously mentioned as essential for involving students with severe multiple disabilities in team sports. But let's take a look at issues that arise when we involve students with severe disabilities as equally as possible in team sports with students without disabilities.

First, the strategy may break the balance between teams, which would be a threat to the Integrity Standard (Bernabe & Block, 1994). One solution would be that both teams include a player with severe multiple disabilities so that the same advantage is available to both teams. As an alternative, if only one student with severe multiple disabilities is available, practitioners may create rules to provide the team without a student with disabilities opportunities to change capacity of equipment. For example, in a basketball game, the team might be allowed to choose a student as "the special player of the day." If the player makes a successful play (e.g., pass interception), the team can use a larger and lower ring to shoot in the next offense.

Second, the effort conversion strategy requires an assistant to be responsible for helping the student with disabilities practice IEP skills and change the capacity of the equipment. If only one teacher is in charge of the game, this requirement could be a threat to the Implementation Standard. This problem may be solved relatively easily by asking peers or parent volunteers to serve as a special assistant to the student with disabilities.

Final Thoughts

Physical education and community recreation programs do not consist of only team sport games. In addition, team sports do not exclusively consist of game activities. Activities other than team sports, such as aerobics, walking, and bowling, and individual or small-group activities such as swimming in team sport programs may provide students with severe multiple disabilities opportunities to practice important targeted skills.

Table 4. The Evaluation of the Game Modifications Described In the Three Vignettes

Standard	Jesse: T-Ball	Maki: Flag Football	David: Basketball
Challenging	Jesse needs to maintain his upright position.	Maki needs to start pushing a dummy toward the line of scrimmage.	David engages in picking up and throwing a basketball to make an adapted shot out of the basketball court.
Safety	Outfield players are told not to enter Jesse's catching zone.	Maki plays out of bounds.	David is placed out of the court.
Integrity	Students without disabilities play as usual.	Students without disabilities play as usual.	Students without disabilities play as usual with an exception that they need to change the target rim.
Implementation	A few concentric circles are drawn around Jesse.	The first down marker for her team is moved to the point Maki reached at the end of the play.	Two types of baskets are placed side by side: one has a higher rim, the other has a lower rim.
Essential	Jesse's catching zone becomes momentarily and proportionately larger on the basis of the duration of his target behavior. By showing the target behavior in a timely manner, Jesse can help his team stop the runner.	Maki's efforts to push a dummy are converted momentarily and proportionally into the position of the first down marker and therefore allow her to help her team gain yardage.	Each time David successfully makes an adapted shot, his team is allowed to use a lower basket. In this way, he can assist team players without disabilities, who are not good at shooting, in making more successful shots.

Nevertheless, participating in an essential part of team sport games seems to have a special meaning by allowing students with severe multiple disabilities to contribute to their team and build a sense of membership.

We need to give students with severe multiple disabilities new opportunities to participate in an essential part of team sport games. We can thus improve the students' targeted skills, enhance their sense of belonging, and ultimately build friendships with their peers.

References

Bernabe, E. A., & Block, M. E. (1994). Modifying rules of a regular girls softball league to facilitate the inclusion of a child with severe disabilities. *Journal of the Association for Persons with Severe Handicaps, 19,* 24–31.

Block, M. E. (2000). *A teacher's guide to including students with disabilities in general physical education.* Baltimore: Paul H. Brookes.

Giangreco, M. F., Cloninger, C. J., Dennis, R., & Edelman, S. W. (1993). National expert validation of COACH: Congruence with exemplary practice and suggestions for improvement. *Journal of the Association for Persons with Severe Handicaps, 18,* 109–120.

Schleien, S. J., Ray, M. T., & Green, F. P. (1997). *Community recreation and people with disabilities: Strategies for inclusion.* Baltimore: Paul H. Brookes

Williams, L. J., & Downing. J. E. (1998). Membership and belonging in inclusive classrooms: What do middle school students have to say? *Journal of the Association for Persons with Severe Handicaps, 23,* 98–110.

Yoshihisa Ohtake, Associate Professor, Department of Special Education, University of Okayama, Japan.

Address correspondence to the author at the University of Okayama, Department of Special Education, 3-1-1 Tsushina-naka, Okayama, Japan 700-8530, (e-mail: ohtake@cc.okayama-u.ac.jp).

From *Teaching Exceptional Children,* Vol. 37, No. 2, November/December 2004, pp. 22-27. Copyright © 2004 by Council for Exceptional Children. Reprinted by permission.

UNIT 2
Early Childhood

Unit Selections

5. **Making the Case for Early Identification and Intervention for Young Children at Risk for Learning Disabilities**, Marcee M. Steele
6. **Music in the Inclusive Environment**, Marcia Earl Humpal and Jan Wolf
7. **Building Relationships With Challenging Children**, Philip S. Hall and Nancy D. Hall

Key Points to Consider

- Can early childhood special services identify learning disabilities before public school? How?
- How does music benefit preschoolers with special needs in inclusive settings?
- Can teachers bond with sullen, angry, aggressive young children without punishing them? How?

Student Website
www.mhcls.com/online

Internet References
Further information regarding these websites may be found in this book's preface or online.

Division for Early Childhood
http://www.dec-sped.org
Institute on Community Integration Projects
http://ici.umn.edu/projectscenters/
National Academy for Child Development (NACD)
http://www.nacd.org
Special Education Resources on the Internet (SERI)
http://seriweb.com

Public law 99-457 has been called one of the most important educational decisions of the United States. It was a 1986 amendment (Part H) to PL94-142 (the Education for All Handicapped Children Act), which the U.S. Congress established as a grant incentive aimed at providing services for young children at risk of disability beginning at the age of 3. By 1991 this amendment to the now-renamed Individuals with Disabilities Education Act (IDEA) was reauthorized. It operates through "Child Find," which are organizational groups that look for babies, toddlers, and preschoolers with conditions of obvious disability (such as blindness, deafness, or orthopedic handicap). These young children can receive special educational services according to IDEA's mandate, "a free and appropriate education for all in the least restrictive environment." Many infants and young children are being found who are at "high risk" of developing educational disabilities (for example, low vision, hearing impairments, developmental delays) unless education begins before the age of 6. This outreach is having a profound impact on the care of families and children.

The United States is faced with multiple questions about the education of its future citizens—its young children. Many American babies are born preterm, small for gestational age, or with extremely low birth weight. This is a direct result of the United States' high rate of teenage pregnancy (nearly double that of most European countries and Canada) and its low rate of providing adequate prenatal care, especially for the young, the poor, or recent immigrant mothers. These infants are at high risk for developing disabilities and conditions of educational exceptionality. Early intervention can help these babies.

All services to be provided for any infant, toddler, or preschooler with a disability, and for his or her family, are to be articulated in an Individualized Family Service Plan (IFSP). The IFSP is to be written and implemented as soon as the infant or young child is determined to be at risk. IFSPs specify what services will be provided for the parents, for the diagnosed child, for siblings, and for all significant caregivers. Children with pervasive disabilities (such as autism, traumatic brain injuries, blindness, deafness, orthopedic impairments, severe health impairments, or multiple disabilities) may require extensive and very expensive early childhood interventions.

IFSPs are written in collaboration with parents, experts in the area of the child's exceptional condition, teachers, home-service providers, and other significant providers. They are updated every 6 months until the child turns 3 and receives an individualized Education Plan (IEP). A case manager is assigned to oversee each individual child with an IFSP to ensure high-quality and continuous intervention services.

In the United States, Child Find locates and identifies infants, toddlers, and young children who qualify for early childhood special education and family services. An actual diagnosis, or label of condition of exceptionality, is not required. Assessment is usually accomplished in a multidisciplinary fashion. It can be very difficult, but as much as possible, it is conducted in the child's home in a nonthreatening fashion. Diagnosis of exceptionalities in children who cannot yet answer questions is complicated. Personal observations are used as well as parent reports. Most of the experts involved in the multidisciplinary assessment want to see the child more than once to help compensate for the fact that all children have good days and bad days. In cases where the parents are non-English speakers and a translator is required, assessment may take several days.

Despite the care taken, many children who qualify for, and would benefit from, early intervention services are missed. Child Find associations are not well funded. There are constant shortages of time, materials, and multidisciplinary professionals to do assessments. Finding translators for parents who speak uncommon foreign languages adds to the problems. Occasionally the availability of funds for early childhood interventions encourages the overdiagnosis of risk factors in infants from low-income, minority, immigrant, or rural families.

A challenge to all professionals providing early childhood special services is how to work with diverse parents. Some parents welcome any and all intervention, even if it is not merited. Other parents resist any labeling of their child as "disabled" and refuse services. Professionals must make allowances for cultural, economic, and educational diversity, multiple caregivers, and single parents. Regardless of the situation, parental participation is the sine qua non of early childhood intervention.

At-home services may include instruction in the educational goals of the IFSP, and in skills such as discipline, behavior management, nutrition, and health maintenance. At-home services also include counseling for parents, siblings, and significant others to help them deal with their fears and to help them accept, love, and challenge their special child to become all he or she is capable of being. A case manager helps ensure that there is cooperation and coordination of services by all team members.

Most children receiving early childhood services have some center-based or combined center- and home-based special education. Center care introduces children to peers and introduces the family to other families with similar concerns. It is easier to ensure quality education and evaluate progress when a child spends at least a part of his or her time in a well-equipped educational center.

The first article in Unit 2 discusses the benefits of early identification of young children with learning disabilities. The author suggests ways in which this can be accomplished. When intervention is started with IFSPs before elementary school, late school progress is greatly enhanced.

The second article in this unit addresses the importance of rhythm and music in early childhood. New research suggests that music and math stimulate development of neurons in the same brain areas. Music not only helps organize and promote neuronal growth, it also enhances socialization between children and stimulates language and creative production.

The last article, "Building Relationships With Challenging Children" presents positive ways to help at-risk students. The authors, Philip and Nancy Hall eschew punishment. They recommend gentle intervention and bonding. They describe the components of these practices which help ensure that the student will become a good learner and achieve educational success.

Making the Case for Early Identification and Intervention for Young Children at Risk for Learning Disabilities

The early identification of children with learning disabilities (LD) is difficult but can be accomplished. Observation of key behaviors which are indicators of LD by preschool and kindergarten teachers can assist in this process. This early identification facilitates the use of intervention strategies to provide a positive early experience for children at risk for academic difficulties.

Marcee M. Steele[1,2]

INTRODUCTION

Early identification and intervention for children with special needs has been strongly recommended. Professionals in psychological, medical, scientific, and educational fields have documented the importance of the years between birth and five for learning. If there is any risk of disability, these early years become even more critical (Lerner, Lowenthal, & Egan, 2003). There is a history of research documenting the value of early identification and intervention; however, in the field of learning disabilities (LD) specifically, the literature is not as definite. There is still controversy over whether very early identification for LD is possible. A child is considered to have a LD if he/she is not working to potential in at least one academic area, has trouble processing information, and does not have any other primary disability (Lerner, 2003). The cause is generally considered neurological. The author of this article will review related literature suggesting that early LD identification is difficult but feasible, and in fact beneficial. She will make suggestions to help with early LD identification and then recommend some early intervention strategies for preschool and kindergarten teachers.

CONTROVERSY OVER EARLY IDENTIFICATION OF LEARNING DISABILITIES

Although there is still much debate concerning the identification of LD prior to grade two, there is overwhelming research to support this timing and practice. Survey results of Snyder, Bailey, and Auer (1994), for example, reflected agreement that early LD identification is important despite confusion indicated about the LD label and diagnosis for young children.

One value of early identification and intervention is that it provides a foundation for later learning and could thereby foster later academic success experiences for children at risk (Peltzman, 1992; Soyfer, 1998). If children with LD are identified in the early childhood years, it is much more likely that they will have the opportunity to develop to potential (Peltzman, 1992).

In addition, early identification can prevent secondary problems from occurring. Unless children with potential reading and LD are identified early, they will have a greater chance of developing secondary problems such as frustration and anxiety (Catts, 1991; Lowenthal, 1998). Taylor and others, in their review of related literature, indicated that if children with LD are not identified early, the learning problems continue and could lead to more students dropping out of school, exhibiting behavior problems, and developing greater academic deficiencies. The early identification, in contrast, prevents the need for more extensive special education services in the future and leads to more inclusive programming (2000).

Reading problems, in particular, if not identified early lead to subsequent motivational problems. When children are not motivated, they have fewer opportunities to practice reading skills and therefore get even further behind academically (Catts, 1997). Vandervelden and Siegel (1997) suggest that early phonics instruction, for example, prevents later reading deficits and enhances early reading and writing experiences.

Even though these benefits support early identification of LD, there are also many concerns that should be addressed. Probably one of the biggest fears relates to the potential stigma and unnecessary labeling of young children (Snyder et al., 1994; Taylor, Anselmo, Foreman, Schatschneider, & Angelopoulos, 2000). It is not, however, necessary to use the term LD at a young age as it is for older students when determining eligibility for special education classes in public schools. Therefore, the stigma and labeling can be avoided.

In addition, there are problems with the tests that are used, especially for identification of young children with LD. The readiness tests that are normed for young children are not always accurate for prediction purposes, and they are generally

[1]University of North Carolina at Wilmington.
[2]Correspondence should be directed to Marcee M. Steele, Watson School of Education, University of North Carolina, Wilmington, NC 28403; e-mail: steelem@uncw.edu

very expensive (Taylor et al., 2000). A survey of states and their procedures indicated that many states are concerned with LD eligibility determination especially because of testing concerns with young children and reliability and validity issues with the tests themselves (Snyder et al., 1994). Informal assessment procedures, discussed in the next section, can be considered a viable alternative especially with young children.

Another problem with early identification is that the LD definition requires a discrepancy in an academic area, in other words, a child not working to potential. Early identification of LD is difficult with preschool children because the required underachievement does not clearly relate to young children. They would not necessarily have been exposed to academics in the formal sense so it would be difficult to determine if preschool or kindergarten children have a significant discrepancy between ability (measured by IQ tests) and achievement (based on academic test results). There are not always clear academic expectations at such an early age (Snyder et al., 1994), and therefore some schools delay the process until there is a significant discrepancy. Of course, then teachers will have wasted significant teaching time (Taylor et al., 2000). If the discrepancy cannot be determined at an early age, it is often suggested that the schools should wait until there is a discrepancy to label a child. In other words, wait until children fail and then give them the help they need! (Catts, 1991). In addition, discrepancy determination involves measures of intelligence (Lowenthal, 1998), and the intelligence tests are controversial at best. They have been highly criticized for bias, reliability, and other related issues. Instead of delaying the identification and intervention until the child is in even more trouble, it is important to realize that the technical definition is not required for young children with LD to receive services. More general labels such as developmental delay or at risk can be used instead, avoiding some of the above concerns.

Some people even suggest that because of these difficulties and criticisms, it is not possible to identify LD at such an early age (Snyder et al., 1994). Furthermore, it is very possible that children could appear to have LD at a young age, but then the problems could disappear a little later on if it is just a lag or delay in development. (Lowenthal, 1998). Many of the LD characteristics look like typical preschool characteristics, and it is therefore difficult to make an early determination. However, if children are identified early and later outgrow their problems, there really is no harm done. The label and services can be discontinued.

STRATEGIES FOR LD IDENTIFICATION AND INTERVENTION IN PRESCHOOL AND KINDERGARTEN

In order to address many of these potential problems, early childhood teachers can implement observation strategies. Systematic observation of behaviors and search for patterns can be very useful in determining potential learning problems. Taylor et al., (2000), suggested that an alternative to discrepancy determination, teacher judgments of progress, be used especially with young children who are at risk. Mantzicopoulus and Morrison (1994) similarly concluded from their study of various prediction tools that teacher prediction is an accurate part of the process to determine early reading failure and success. Using observation as a diagnostic tool then is one way to get the benefits of early identification without the potential for stigma, unnecessary labeling, and use of questionable testing procedures. The LD label would not be necessary; instead teachers can determine that a particular child is at risk and implement appropriate interventions.

Language is one of the skill areas that teachers can observe for early identification purposes. Catts (1991), for example, suggests that it would be wise to look for some of the developmental characteristics like oral language difficulties as early as preschool to avoid some of the problems with LD identification. Because early language problems are often indicative of later reading problems, Catts (1997) suggests that observations of these language problems be used diagnostically. Difficulties with morphology, syntax, understanding words and sentences orally, awareness of speech sounds, word retrieval, verbal memory, and speech production correlate with later problems in word recognition and phonics. These problems can be observed prior to formal reading instruction and therefore are indicators of potential reading problems. He designed a list of behaviors to help with the observation of these deficits and to refer children for comprehensive evaluation. The list includes behaviors such as trouble with rhyming, difficulty remembering the alphabet, difficulty following directions, frequent mispronunciations, trouble understanding stories, small vocabulary, and short disorganized sentences when talking.

Other observable behaviors that indicate potential learning problems in preschool include hyperactivity, incoordination, perseveration, impulsivity, processing deficits, distractibility, and memory problems (Lowenthal, 1998; Peltzman, 1992). In kindergarten, readiness skills such as listening, following directions, dressing, appropriate attention span; and prerequisite academics such as alphabet skills, rhyming, colors, counting, and copying can be observed (Lowenthal, 1998).

Once identified as having possible delays and potential learning disabilities, there are several recommended strategies for early childhood teachers. The environment and focus of the program can be modified to enhance development. Peltzman (1992) recommends that the focus of an early intervention program should be to build a strong foundation rather than remediate a problem. Practice on skills in all of the developmental areas with opportunities for guidance and success is helpful. In arranging preacademic activities, Allen and Schwartz (2001) recommend short tasks with familiar materials, individual workspaces, choice of activities, clear organization and preparation, and clear transitions. In addition, consistency, repetition, and regularity in routines benefit children at risk for LD. Tasks are generally mastered more efficiently if broken down into small segments, especially for children with special needs (Klein, Cook, & Richardson-Gibbs, 2001).

In addition, early literacy interventions help prevent later reading deficits in some cases (Catts, 1996). Emerging Literacy and preacademics can be taught in a "developmentally appropriate" way. All children need to be taught skills to help them with later academic success, but if there is a disability it is even

Table I. Indicators of Learning Disabilities

Difficulty with the following behaviors could indicate risk for LD if the behaviors are noticeably different from that of most peers:

Talking with words in correct order
Understanding words said aloud
Understanding sentences said aloud
Remembering specific words when talking
Remembering what they hear
Participating in rhyming games and activities
Remembering the alphabet
Following directions
Pronouncing many words correctly when speaking spontaneously
Understanding stories read aloud
Using words properly when speaking
Talking with organized sentences and thoughts
Sitting still for appropriate periods of time
Changing from one activity to another
Attending to tasks
Remembering what they see
Thinking before talking or acting
Staying focused on a topic
Listening to stories and songs for extended periods of time
Dressing
Identifying colors
Counting
Copying

Table II. Suggestions for Teachers

The following types of activities would be helpful when teaching children who are at risk for LD:

Use materials that are familiar to the children
Have individual workspaces
Allow some choice in activities
Organize and prepare tasks
Plan for clear transitions between activities
Expand children's words into sentences
Provide good language models
Teach beginning phonics skills
Label objects around the classroom
Clap out syllables
Use rhyming activities
Play alphabet and vocabulary games
Use topics of particular interest to children
Have children dictate stories and ideas
Practice with sounds
Read aloud to children from books suited to their levels and interests
Use finger plays
Incorporate songs in lessons
Use puzzles, blocks, and pegboard activities
Incorporate arts and crafts
Play memory games
Have children count objects
Develop behavior plan
Be consistent with routines and rules
Incorporate group activities
Break down tasks into small steps
Repeat new learnings frequently

more important to start at their own level and then progress. Children's interests and related questions could be used to help guide this type of instruction. For example, oral language activities that are natural and involve typical routines and activities are most effective. Teachers can assist by expanding children's own words into complete sentences, describing their own activities, and providing models of language that describe what children are doing. (Lowenthal, 1998).

Some direct teaching can also be included in the instructional plan for preschool children with potential LD. Sensory activities can be used to enhance curiosity; students at this age need freedom to explore. Some examples of activities that can be used to help prepare children for later academic learning include: writing down what children say and then reading it back, and writing their questions down and helping them find answers (Allen & Schwartz, 2001). Catts (1996) suggests including practice in sounds and words, rhyming activities, numerous experiences with books including oral reading, discussion, and vocabulary activities. Other literacy activities for kindergarten children include phonics practice to improve later reading and writing skills for children with mild disabilities. Activities such as labeling, syllable clapping, children's dictation of words, rhyming activities, and letter games all provide practice in prerequisite skills in a motivating and enjoyable way (O'Connor & others, 1996). To help prepare children for later literacy instruction, it is important that they are exposed to reading, writing, and oral language activities.

Cognitive or processing skills can be practiced through directions, listening activities, games, and multisensory activities (using the sense of touch, movement, sight, and hearing), finger plays, songs, stories, puzzles, blocks, pegboards and matching games (Lowenthal, 1998). Allen and Schwartz (2001) suggest using colorful manipulatives, imitation with models and mirrors, water play, arts and crafts, housekeeping, copying patterns, memory games, following directions, coloring, cutting, counting, and grouping objects as appropriate processing and pre-academic practice.

Practice developing social emotional skills, such as getting along with others and sharing, is also important for young children, especially children who are impulsive. Self-esteem needs to be addressed as well as social skills. Examples of behavioral intervention strategies for young children include taking away toys and activities for misbehavior, maintaining attention through novelty, structuring transition times, keeping consistency in routine, using short activities, structuring the environment, using token economies, shaping, timeout, and reinforcement for appropriate behaviors. It is also helpful to use group tasks and activities which integrate typically and atypically developing children (Lowenthal, 1998). In addition, it is important to establish clear rules, review rules frequently for prevention, and use consequences consistently (Klein et al., 2001).

CONCLUSION

It is clear from reviewing the related literature that early identification and intervention for young children with potential LD is valuable. A summary of key ideas for early identification and intervention by preschool and kindergarten teachers is included in Tables I and II. These suggestions can help early childhood teachers make every child's first school experience a success.

REFERENCES

Allen, K. E., & Schwartz, I. S. (2001). *The exceptional child: Inclusion in early childhood education.* Albany, NY: Delmar.

Catts, H. W. (1991). Early identification of reading disabilities. *Topics in Language Disorders, 12*(1), 1–16.

Catts, H. W. (1996). Defining dyslexia as a developmental language disorder: An expanded view. *Topics in Language Disorders, 16*(2), 14–29.

Catts, H. W. (1997). The early identification of language based reading disabilities. *Language, Speech, and Hearing Services in Schools, 28*(1), 86–89.

Klein, M. D., Cook, R. E., & Richardson-Gibbs, A. M. (2001). *Strategies for including children with special needs in early childhood settings.* Albany, NY: Delmar.

Lerner, J. W. (2003). *Learning disabilities: Theories, diagnosis, and teaching strategies.* Boston: Houghton Mifflin.

Lerner, J. W., Lowenthal, B., & Egan, R. W. (2003). *Preschool children with special needs.* Boston: Allyn and Bacon.

Lowenthal B. (1998). Precursors of learning disabilities in the inclusive preschool. *Learning Disabilities: A Multidisciplinary Journal, 9*(2), 25–31.

Mantzicopoulos, P. Y., & Morrison D. (1994). Early prediction of reading achievement: Exploring the relationship of cognitive and noncognitive measures to inaccurate classifications of at-risk status. *Remedial and Special Education, 15*(4), 244–251.

O'Connor, R. E., & others. (1996). The effect of kindergarten phonological intervention on the first grade reading and writing of children with mild disabilities (ERIC Document Reproduction Service No. 394129).

Peltzman, B. R. (1992). Guidelines for early identification and strategies for early intervention of at-risk learning disabled children. (ERIC Document Reproduction Service No. 351111).

Snyder, P., Bailey, D. B., & Auer, C. (1994). Preschool eligibility determination for children with known or suspected learning disabilities under IDEA. *Journal of Early Intervention, 18*(4), 380–390.

Soyfer, V. (1998) Parents promoting school success for young children with learning disabilities (ERIC Document Reproduction Service No. 428488)

Taylor, H. G., Anselmo, M., Foreman, A. L., Schatschneider, C., & Angelopoulos J. (2000). Utility of kindergarten teacher judgments in identifying early learning problems. *Journal of Learning Disabilities, 33*(2), 200–210.

Vandervelden, M. C., & Siegel, L. S. (1997). Teaching phonological processing skills in early literacy: A developmental approach. *Learning Disability Quarterly, 20*(2), 63–81.

Marcee M. Steele, PhD, *University of South Florida is a professor of special education at the University of North Carolina at Wilmington. She teaches undergraduate and graduate courses in learning disabilities, diagnostic techniques, exceptional students, and current issues in special education. She has also taught individuals with learning disabilities from pre-school to graduate school level in public and private settings for over 30 years.*

From *Early Childhood Education Journal,* Vol. 32, No. 2, October 2004, pp. 75-79. Copyright © 2004 by Springer Science and Business Media. Reprinted by permission.

Music in the Inclusive Environment

Five-year-old Sam uses a wheelchair. Due to a difficult birth, he has little motor development or control and no spoken language. He understands but can't speak.

Twice a week, I [Jan] am the music teacher for 22 kindergartners, including Sam. His level of participation is that of an observer, and at times I am not sure what he feels about our time together. The children accept his level of ability and when we put his wheelchair in the center of the circle for "Ring around the Rosy," his squeals of delight give it all away. He laughs and bobs his head back and forth, eyes sparkling all the while as we circle his chair, fall down, and bounce back up only to play the game one more time.

Marcia Earl Humpal and Jan Wolf

What did Sam gain from this musical experience? Pure joy! At first I felt I was slighting him. Wasn't there a way to make his experience more active and inclusive? We tried pushing the wheelchair in the circle, but Sam's response was not the same. He became withdrawn. The experience of sharing the joy from his pivotal center position evoked the most expression.

Music in the early childhood environment offers varying levels of engagement ranging from simply listening or observing to joining in as an active participant.

To onlookers Sam may appear passive, but all of us who know him well are aware of his participation. The music reaches him, as it does all of us, in his way and at his time and place. His squeals and screeches, sparkling eyes, and smiling face communicate his delight to everyone in the room.

Music in the early childhood environment does not depend on specific skills or competence. It offers varying levels of engagement ranging from simply listening or observing to joining in as an active participant. Music stimulates the senses and involves children at many levels, reaching them aesthetically and appealing to their emotional sense. It is playful, soothing, and joyful! It promotes literacy growth by engaging children in experiences involving language; new vocabulary in an engaging context; print; and rhymes, chants, and songs that may inspire higher-level thinking concepts. It con-

Music lets everyone participate

Six-year-old Anthony has a diagnosis of autism. He has little tolerance for musical sounds. Every time we sing, he moans as though in pain from the sound. I [Jan] try to remember that maybe for Anthony our music is too loud.

One day the other children and I gather in the front of the room with drums, triangles, shakers, and sand blocks. I play my guitar. Anthony crawls under his desk and makes every effort to stay there. At the end of each repetition of our song, we switch instruments so everyone can have a chance to play something new.

As we near the end of the song, I nod to Emily, the teaching assistant. Emily understands my unspoken suggestion. She gets up and quietly offers Anthony her drum. As we continue singing and playing, Emily and I peek over to see Anthony playing the drum. He is still under the desk and perhaps is still somewhat bothered by the sounds, but he has found his own sense of pleasure in playing the instrument with us.

Anthony has found a way to join us, on his own time and his own terms. The music that so upset him has become an ally. He is now willing to play with the class, just from a distance.

tributes to a feeling of community as children come together through shared songs, rhymes, chants, and singing games.

Music enhances an inclusive classroom by leveling the playing field so everyone can be a participant. Whether a

Music calms and focuses the mind

I hurry into the school to get to my assigned first grade classroom. The children love music, and I [Jan] look forward to working with them. I crash nose-to-nose with a teaching assistant who works with the youngest children in the school district who have severe behavioral disabilities—the children in my assigned class. Many of them come to school with concerns that would make most of us stagger.

This is a particularly difficult Monday. The assistant quickly summarizes the turmoil. George has had a horrible weekend at home. Alexis has not taken her medication. Justin has spent the weekend away from the consistency of home with Mom and is in a spin as a result. Perhaps, I think, I can find a way to help.

In the classroom I find the teacher sitting in the rocking chair humming, rocking, and holding a child. Two other children are listening through headsets to Baroque music. Soft music comes from the CD player on the shelf. The music's power of relaxation fills the room. The teacher has found solutions on her own. It had been an overwhelming 90-minute beginning to the day, but now, with understanding and change of mood, the atmosphere is calm. The music speaks to the children's emotions. They can now leave their homeroom, go to their inclusive environments, and learn and play with their friends. Music has met the children's need for peace. It has elicited a sense of calm in all of them.

child is a listener or a player, music is accessible and partial participation does not detract from its positive effects.

The essence of music is joyful, nonjudgmental, noncompetitive, and predictable.

For all aspects of music making, children can respond in a range of ways. Some children may be able to sing complete songs with the group or make up their own songs while playing. For others, imitating vocal sounds or playing with their voices is "singing" (Johnson 1996). As an aesthetic expression, the essence of music is joyful, nonjudgmental, noncompetitive, and predictable. Everyone joins in at his or her own level of comfort.

Music activities can encourage interaction among all children in nonthreatening and enjoyable ways.

Musical activities can include all children in meaningful ways when they are designed to offer varied levels of participation. Music can engage all children as collaborators, participants, and community members in activities ranging from group singing and instrument playing to movement games. Individually, music allows children to personalize experiences through listening and bonding with recorded music, moving in expressive ways, entering into song dialogues with a friend, or creating sound segments on drums.

Music teaches social skills

Ariel has difficulty adjusting to the social demands of the classroom. She screams when her mother leaves in the morning and refuses to sit with the group during circle time. Sometimes she throws instruments against the wall or hits children who approach her. Because of this behavior, the children no longer try to be her friend. She plays and works alone. Within her established routine, she seems to be happy.

I [Marcia] come to Ariel's preschool class for 30 minutes each week to conduct music sessions. As a music specialist who is also a music therapist, I not only teach music concepts, but also help the classroom staff and specialists adapt activities and use music to reinforce goals such as sharing, learning concepts, and refining fine and gross motor movements. Often I suggest songs and strategies staff can use throughout the day to meet a variety of needs.

The classroom teachers and I have noticed that Ariel stops and looks when anyone sings a cleanup song. We discover that if we keep the song going and guide her to the toy shelves, Ariel will help with the cleanup. Barney's ditty, "Clean up, clean up, everybody everywhere, clean up, clean up, everybody do your share" really works if we keep singing it over and over until all the children complete the task.

Because music works to encourage Ariel to put toys away, we decide to try it for other tasks. I write simple messages to accompany familiar tunes. The teachers post these throughout the classroom and use them regularly during transitions. After cleaning up, it is time for snacks. "Mmmmm, good, mmmmm, good. Now it's time to have our snack, mmmmm good." When sung to the Campbell's Soup theme, these words round up the children, including Ariel.

As time passes Ariel learns to say good-bye to her mother and join the group for a short time when she hears specific songs. Near the end of the year, she begins to share instruments with a friend when the instructions are given in the context of music: "I'll pass the sticks from me to you; I'll pass the sticks, and you can do it too." Music helps Ariel be an involved member of the class.

Research supports the value of music in learning. Music releases endorphins that provide feelings of happiness and energy. It helps to organize the firing patterns in the cerebral cortex, strengthening creativity and spatial-temporal reasoning (Campbell 1997). A study by Colwell (1994) indicates that using music with a whole language approach to reading facilitates greater text accuracy. Music can also enhance print concepts and prewriting skills (Standley & Hughes 1997) as well as receptive and expressive language (Harding & Ballard 1983; Hoskins 1988; Birkenshaw-Fleming 1997). Music acts as a catalyst to calm listeners, improve special perceptions, and encourage focused, clear thinking (Campbell 1997).

Music can open doors and allow children to join in classroom routines with their friends. Music activities can encourage interaction among all children in nonthreaten-

Start the Music

In 2000 the National Association for Music Education (MENC), Texaco Foundation, NAEYC, and the U.S. Department of Education developed Start the Music, a series of projects and events designed to help bring age-appropriate music education to every child in America. These organizations solicited the expertise of early childhood music educators, music therapists, education association administrators, early childhood educators, and health care providers to identify best practices for early childhood music education and to develop strategies to implement those practices.

Developmentally and individually appropriate musical experiences are guided by these beliefs (MENC 1995):

- All children have music potential. They
  —bring their own unique interests and abilities to the music learning environment;
  —can develop critical thinking skills through musical ideas;
  —come to early childhood music experiences from diverse backgrounds;
  —should experience exemplary musical sounds, activities, and materials.
- Young children should not be expected to meet *performance* goals.
  —Their play is their work.

—They learn best in pleasant physical and social environments.
—They need diverse learning environments.
—They need effective adult models.

Start the Music recognizes the role adults play in assisting young children in their musical development. Families, caregivers, and teachers can all help children grow musically (Neelly, Kenney, & Wolf 2000, 1) by

- **immersing children in musical conversations** while singing, speaking rhythmically, moving expressively, and playing musical instruments. By doing these things, we stimulate children's initial awareness of the beauty and the structure of musical sound.

- **encouraging children's musical responses** by smiling, nodding, and responding with expressive sounds and movements. We thus show children that music making is valuable and important.

- **finding ways to encourage and motivate children's playful exploration,** interpretation, and understanding of musical sound.

Start the Music recognizes that all children are individuals and that music experiences should be a part of *every* child's world.

---

ing and enjoyable ways. In fact, music can actually teach social skills.

Inclusion has become the norm in preschool classrooms throughout the United States, and in some cases has been facilitated by early childhood inclusive music pilot programs (Davis 1990; Hughes et al. 1990; Humpal 1991; Furman & Furman 1996; Humpal & Dimmick 1996). Hughes and colleagues (1990) note that peer acceptance is often viewed as the most serious obstacle to successful inclusive programming and that acceptance can be successfully reached through structured musical interactions. Further, since the brain processes music in both hemispheres, music can stimulate cognitive functioning and may allow for understanding when the spoken word fails (Campbell 1997). Music may provide a cue for an upcoming event or may act as a gentle reminder of what is expected in a group situation.

Conclusion

Music should be a part of *every* young child's day (see "Start the Music"). Music's power to reach *all* children is driven by the sense of community originating from shared songs, rhymes, chants, singing games, and musical books. These activities serve as gateways to involving

individuals and groups of young children. Music creates joy through aesthetics. Music creates inspirational moments and opportunities to make sense out of chaos. Music *belongs* in the inclusive classroom.

References

Birkenshaw-Fleming, L. 1997. Music for young children: Teaching for the fullest development of every child. *Early Childhood Connections* 3 (2): 6–13.

Campbell, D. 1997. *The Mozart effect.* New York: Avon.

Colwell, C. 1994. Therapeutic application of music in the whole language kindergarten. *Journal of Music Therapy* 31 (4): 238–47.

Davis, R. 1990. A model for the integration of music therapy within the preschool classrooms for children with physical disabilities or language delays. *Music Therapy Perspectives* 8: 82–84.

Furman, A., & C. Furman. 1996. Music therapy for learners in a public school early education center. In *Models of music therapy interventions in school settings: From institution to inclusion,* ed. B. Wilson, 258–76. Silver Spring, MD: American Music Therapy Association. [Monograph]

Harding, C., & K. Ballard. 1983. The effectiveness of music as a stimulus and as a contingent reward in promoting the spontaneous speech of three physically handicapped preschoolers. *Journal of Music Therapy* 20 (2): 86–101.

Hoskins, C. 1988. Use of music to increase verbal response and improve expressive language abilities of preschool language-delayed children. *Journal of Music Therapy* 25 (2): 73–83.

Hughes, J., B. Robbins, B. MacKenzie, & S. Robb. 1990. Integrating exceptional and nonexceptional young children through music play: A pilot program. *Music Therapy Perspectives* 8: 52–56.

Humpal, M. 1991. The effects of an integrated early childhood program on social interaction among children with handicaps and their typical peers. *Journal of Music Therapy* 28 (3): 161–77.

Humpal, M., & J. Dimmick. 1996. Music therapy for learners in an early childhood community interagency setting. In *Models of music therapy interventions in school settings: From institution to inclusion*, ed. B. Wilson, 271–311. Silver Spring, MD: American Music Therapy Association. [Monograph]

Johnson, F. 1996. Models of service delivery. In *Models of music therapy interventions in school settings: From institution to inclusion*, ed. B. Wilson, 48–77. Silver Spring, MD: American Music Therapy Association.

MENC (National Association for Music Education). 1995. *Prekindergarten music education standards*. Reston, VA: MENC.

Neely, L., S. Kenney, & J. Wolf. 2000. *Start the Music strategies*. Reston, VA: MENC.

Standley, J., & J. Hughes. 1997. Evaluation of an early intervention music curriculum for enhancing prereading/writing skills. *Music Therapy Perspectives* 15 (2): 79–86.

For further reading

American Music Therapy Association. 1999. Music therapy and the young child fact sheet. Silver Spring, MD: AMTA.

Boston, B.O. 2000. Start the Music: A report from the Early Childhood Music Summit. Online: http://www.menc.org/guides/startmusic/stmreport.htm

Campbell, D. 2000. *The Mozart effect for children*. New York: HarperCollins.

Miranda, L., A. Arthur, T. Milan, O. Mahoney, & B. Perry. 1998. The art of healing: The CIVITAS Healing Arts Project. *Early Childhood Connections* 4 (4): 35–39.

A Special Book for Children Ages 4–8

Millman, I. 1998. *Moses goes to a concert*. New York: Frances Foster.

Moses and his school friends are deaf. They communicate through American Sign Language (ASL). Today Moses and his classmates are going to a concert. Their teacher, Mr. Samuels, has two surprises in store for them to make this particular concert a special event. At the end of the book are two full conversations in sign language and a page showing the hand alphabet.

Marcia Earl Humpal, M.Ed., MT-BC, is a music therapist in the early childhood division of the Cuyahoga County Board of Mental Retardation and Developmental Disabilities in Cleveland, Ohio. Her model for early childhood inclusive music programs has been the topic of published research and numerous conference presentations.

Jan Wolf, M.S.Ed., is an adjunct instructor in early childhood education at Kent State University and music teacher at The Kindergarten Center, Medina City Schools, Ohio. Jan is a frequent presenter at conferences and is the author of articles on music and young children and the book *Teaching Music*.

Building Relationships with Challenging Children

Teachers who intervene gently, forego punishment, work at bonding, and ensure student success can help at-risk students make positive changes in their lives and in the classroom.

Philip S. Hall and Nancy D. Hall

In their classic study, *400 Losers*, Ahlstrom and Havighurst (1971) were chagrined to discover that their six-year-long, intensive intervention program did not help a group of at-risk youth find success. But, to their surprise, a handful of the participants did turn their lives around. The adolescents who "made it" all had one experience in common: Each had developed a special relationship with either a teacher or a work supervisor during the treatment program. These adults valued the students, treated them as individuals, and expressed faith in their ability to succeed.

A strong relationship with an adult enables an at-risk youth to make life-altering changes. Educators can use specific strategies to develop these nurturing relationships, as one teacher's story demonstrates.

The Chocolate Milk Incident

When the 1st graders came into Ms. Hubble's room from recess, they were rambunctious and hard to settle. "Take your seats," Ms. Hubble told them, "and my two helpers for the week will come by with milk." That helped. At least, it helped everyone except Andreen. As the other students finished their milk and the helpers collected the empty cartons, Andreen got up from her desk. Taking her milk with her, she went to the salamander cage at the back of the room. She peered into the cage and began poking at the salamanders with her straw.

"Please take your seat, Andreen," Ms. Hubble said quietly, walking up to the girl and gently putting a hand on her shoulder. Lurching away, Andreen threw her milk carton into the air. The carton hit Ms. Hubble on the

chest, and chocolate milk gushed out, staining the teacher's white blouse.

Andreen was a new student in Ms. Hubble's class. A week ago, her mother had brought her to school but stayed only long enough to complete the necessary paperwork. Officially, Ms. Hubble knew little about Andreen, but the girl's appearance and behavior told the big picture. The facts that emerged when Andreen's records arrived from her previous school only filled in the blanks.

On her first day, Andreen came into the classroom disheveled and unkempt. Her long auburn hair, tangled and unwashed, coursed down her back over her faded brown dress. Seeing Andreen's appearance and downcast demeanor, the other 1st graders instantly shunned the little girl as if her plight were contagious.

But Andreen's appearance was not her only problem. Andreen had an attitude, and that attitude was not endearing. She was a sullen, angry little girl, hypersensitive about her space and possessions. She pushed or kicked students who walked close to her desk. At recess, her classmates quickly learned to exclude her because she played to win, even if it meant bullying and inventing new rules. In the classroom, Andreen seldom complied with Ms. Hubble's requests. Just that morning, Ms. Hubble had asked Andreen to put her math paper away and finish it later, and the girl had ripped up her paper and defiantly thrown it into her desk.

For a week, Ms. Hubble had been hoping that Andreen's attitude would improve with her adjustment to the new school. But now Ms. Hubble realized that if the little girl was ever going to be successful in school, she, as her teacher, needed to immediately put time and energy into building a relationship with her.

Gentle Intervention

As chocolate milk seeped into her blouse, Ms. Hubble reminded herself that her response to this incident would set the tone for their relationship. She must let Andreen know that she was physically and emotionally safe in her teacher's presence despite this behavior. The situation required a gentle intervention.

The principle of this key relationship-building technique is that when a child engages in behavior that threatens health, safety, property, and basic rights, educators do only what is necessary to protect themselves and others (Hall, 1989). This approach reduces the number of behaviors requiring intervention, so the educator can ignore a lot of students' inappropriate behaviors for the moment and deal with them later if necessary. A gentle intervention defuses rather than detonates the situation and allows the student to maintain a sense of dignity.

After Andreen threw the milk, she turned her back on Ms. Hubble and walked quickly toward another learning center, looking as if she were about to shove the first available thing off the table. "Students," the teacher announced to the class, "it's time for reading. Everyone take out your reading book." Andreen stopped. Turning, she looked at Ms. Hubble. Stepping to her left, so as to give Andreen an unobstructed path to her desk, Ms. Hubble whispered to Andreen, "We're on page 80." For a moment, Andreen thought about what to do. Then she abruptly went to her desk and got out her reading book. As Ms. Hubble walked to the front of the room, she caught Andreen's eye and nodded her approval.

Ms. Hubble's gentle intervention had five important components:

- She unobtrusively interrupted behavior that might have resulted in property destruction.
- She preserved Andreen's dignity.
- She directed Andreen toward a positive response.
- Her directive led Andreen to an appropriate response that could be praised.
- Her directive was, at that moment, the easiest response for Andreen to make. After all, the other students were getting out their reading books, and the most unobstructed path was to her desk.

What Ms. Hubble didn't do as the chocolate milk ran down her blouse was as important as what she did. To her credit, the teacher resisted the emotion-driven impulse to reprimand Andreen. At the very least, Ms. Hubble might have said, "Look at what you've done! You've stained my blouse. You should be ashamed of yourself." That would have felt good! Certainly Andreen had it coming. And the teacher might have added, "And for that little shenanigan, Andreen, you'll stay in from recess for the rest of the week!"

In the heat of the moment, any or all of those actions would have been understandable. But what would have been their effect? In all likelihood, either the admonition or the consequence would have spurred Andreen to sweep her arm across the table, knocking something to the floor. In response, Ms. Hubble would have had to move quickly to restrain Andreen before she broke more things; and if Andreen resisted, Ms. Hubble might have had to drag her down to the principal's office where, by golly, she would have learned her lesson!

Or would she have? Actually, all Andreen would have learned is that Ms. Hubble is, in her opinion, a mean person. An hour later, Andreen would have returned to the classroom temporarily subdued but full of resentment and mistrust.

No Punishment

Had Ms. Hubble made those comments to Andreen or restricted her recess, the teacher would have punished Andreen. Punishment, we believe, is anything an educator says or does to make a student feel guilty, humiliated, or remorseful so that the student will never behave that way again (Hall & Braun, 1988).

A key to building a relationship, however, is not punishing the student—ever. Why not? Because punishment strains or even breaks the bond between teacher and student. Punishment may temporarily control behavior, but it does nothing to teach the student an appropriate response. Worse, punishing a student often instills a desire for revenge. An effective response to behavior that threatens health, safety, property, or basic rights does not include doling out punishment.

That evening, Ms. Hubble phoned Andreen's mother. She did not phone to report the chocolate milk incident. Instead, she asked permission to spend some special time with Andreen. Ms. Hubble said,

> Many of the girls in class are coming to school with their hair in braids. It's the in thing. I would love to help Andreen put her hair in braids, if she wants. Would the two of us have your permission to do that?

The mother, of course, granted permission. "Please share our conversation with Andreen," Ms. Hubble concluded.

Bonding

The next day, Ms. Hubble devoted time to another key principle of relationship building—some call it *bonding* (McGee, Menolascino, Hobbs, & Menousek, 1987). To bond, we value the student for the socially appropriate behaviors that the student can demonstrate and then provide the structure, support, and recognition that the student needs to demonstrate these behaviors. During this bonding time, the adult does not place any expectations on the student for doing the activity the "right" way.

The activity provides opportunities for the adult to value the student, which enhances the student's sense of self-worth and encourages the development of internal standards for behavior. Moreover, when a teacher values a student, the student seems to be biologically inhibited from acting aggressively against that teacher. While the student is in this zone of positive regard, she is disposed to attend to the teacher. Expanding the zone of positive regard mitigates noncompliance and defiance.

That morning, Ms. Hubble talked privately to Andreen:

We can wash and comb your hair during the lunch break and then braid it during afternoon recess. Is that something you'd like to do?

And that is what they did. As they ate lunch privately in the classroom, the two of them chatted up a storm. They talked about anything that the little girl had on her mind, even for a fleeting instant. Ms. Hubble used the conversation not to pry, but rather to enter, by invitation only, into Andreen's world of interests, experiences, and thoughts. Some might call their student-driven conversation trite and meaningless. It wasn't. The conversation and the hair washing were a vehicle for Ms. Hubble to bond with Andreen.

The relationship that Ms. Hubble and Andreen developed that day had immediate results. When the other students saw that Ms. Hubble valued the new girl, they shifted their attitude. Several girls complimented Andreen on her braids and slowly began to take the new girl into their fold.

Ensuring Success

Ensuring success means providing the student with the structure and support for becoming a good learner. When students, especially those with difficult temperaments, fail at learning tasks, they often explode into defiant behaviors. On the day of the chocolate milk incident, Ms. Hubble retrieved the math assignment that Andreen had torn to pieces, carefully taped the paper together, identified the specific math skill that Andreen was missing, and began to address the problem with targeted instruction.

The New Paradigm

By implementing these relationship-building principles, Ms. Hubble enabled Andreen to change her behavior and attitude. When Andreen came into the classroom each morning, she no longer hung her head and scowled. She did not push or kick students who passed by her desk; rather, she smiled at them. When Ms. Hubble made a request, Andreen usually complied. Rather than tearing up her papers, Andreen took them home to show her mother. In Ms. Hubble's classroom, the relationship building with Andreen paid dividends.

Building relationships with students who have challenging behaviors is consistent with an emerging paradigm in education. In the old paradigm, educators developed behavior programs designed to squelch students' inappropriate behaviors, a process that focused on what the student was doing wrong. Educators assumed that when they had brought the inappropriate behaviors under control, the student would automatically demonstrate socially appropriate behaviors. Behavior programming typically contained objectives like "Andrew will decrease (or increase) this behavior," an approach that put most of the responsibility for behavior change on the student—the least capable person in the classroom.

The relationship-building approach more often leads to success.

In contrast, a relationship-building approach helps the student develop positive, socially appropriate behaviors by focusing on what the student is doing right. In the new paradigm, behavior programming puts the initial responsibility for behavior change on the teacher, the most capable and only professionally trained person in the classroom. The relationship-building approach more often leads to success.

References

Ahlstrom, W. M., & Havighurst, R. J. (1971). *400 losers*. San Francisco: Jossey-Bass.

Hall, P. S. (1989, Fall). Teaching for behavior change. *Counterpoint*, 3.

Hall, P. S., & Braun, V. R. (1988, June). Punishment: A consumer's perspective. *TASH Newsletter*, 9.

McGee, J. J., Menolascino, F. J., Hobbs, D. C., & Menousek, P. E. (1987). *Gentle teaching: A nonaversive approach for helping persons with mental retardation*. New York: Human Science Press.

Philip S. Hall (hallps@minotstateu.edu) is a professor in the school psychology program at Minot State University.

Nancy D. Hall (halln@minotstateu.edu), a former elementary school principal, is Vice President for Academic Affairs at Minot State University, 500 University Ave. West, Minot, ND 58707. Their most recent book is *Educating Oppositional and Defiant Children* (ASCD, 2003).

UNIT 3

Learning Disabilities

Unit Selections

8. **Providing Support for Student Independence Through Scaffolded Instruction**, Martha J. Larkin
9. **Celebrating Diverse Minds**, Mel Levine
10. **No More Friday Spelling Tests? An Alternative Spelling Assessment for Students With Learning Disabilities**, Kelly A. Loeffler
11. **Group Intervention: Improving Social Skills of Adolescents with Learning Disabilities**, Deborah Court and Sarah Givon

Key Points to Consider

- Describe scaffolded instruction. What is the goal of scaffolding for students with LDs?

- How can diversities in the ways our brains operate be beneficial to our society? Can spelling rubrics replace spelling tests? What are their advantages?

- What can be done to reduce the social isolation of students with learning disabilities?

Student Website

www.mhcls.com/online

Internet References

Further information regarding these websites may be found in this book's preface or online.

Children and Adults With Attention Deficit/Hyperactivity Disorder (CHADD)
http://www.chadd.org

The Instant Access Treasure Chest
http://www.fln.vcu.edu/ld/ld.html

Learning Disabilities Association of America (LDA)
http://www.ldanatl.org

Learning Disabilities Online
http://www.ldonline.org

Teaching Children With Attention Deficit Disorder
http://www.kidsource.com/kidsource/content2/add.html

Learning how to learn is one of life's most important tasks. For students with disabilities of learning it is a most critical lesson. Today general education teachers and special educators must seriously attend to the growing numbers of students who have a wide range of different learning disabilities (LDs). LD enrollments in inclusive, regular education classes have skyrocketed. They are the fastest growing and largest category of exceptionalities in elementary, middle, and high schools. Children with LDs now make up over 50 percent of those receiving special educational services.

The ways in which students with LDs are identified and served have been radically transformed with IDEA (Individuals with Disabilities Education Act). New assessment methods have made the identification of students with LDs easier and far more common. Many lawmakers and educators, however, feel that students who have other problems (for example, behavior disorders, poor learning histories, or dysfunctional families) are erroneously being diagnosed with LDs. IDEA requires states to place students with disabilities in regular classrooms as much as possible or lose their federal funding. A landmark U.S. Supreme Court case in November of 1993 (*Carter v. Florence Co. , S. C.*) ruled that public schools must give appropriate educational services to students with LDs or pay the tuition for private schools to do so. This ruling opened a floodgate of new litigation by parents. IDEA has turned out to be much more expensive than Congress envisioned when it enacted this education bill 26 years ago. The recent passage of No Child Left Behind (2002) requires that schools be held accountable for appropriate education of all students.

Is the rapid increase in students assessed to have learning disabilities an artifact of misdiagnoses, exaggeration, and a duping of the system that makes funding available for special needs? Neonatal medical technology and achievements in preventive medicine and health maintenance have greatly reduced the numbers of children who are born deaf, blind, severely physically disabled, or with multiple exceptional conditions. The very same medical technology has greatly increased the numbers of children kept alive who are born prematurely, small for gestational age, with low birth weight, and at-risk for less severe disabilities such as LDs.

A learning disability is usually defined by the lay public as difficulty reading or calculating. IDEA defines it as a disorder in the processes involved in understanding or in using language, spoken or written, that may manifest itself in an imperfect ability to listen, speak, read, write, spell, or do mathematical calculations. Learning disabilities are identified differently outside of education. *The Diagnostic and Statistical Manual of Mental Disorders* (4th edition) divides LDs into academic skills disorders (reading, mathematics, written expression) and attention deficit hyperactive disorder (ADHD). The National Joint Committee for Learning Disabilities (NJCLD) separates LDs into specific problems related to the acquisition and use of listening, speaking, reading, writing, reasoning, or mathematical abilities. Attention deficit hyperactive disorder, if not accompanied by any specific learning problem or any specific behavioral/emotional disorder, can be assessed as a health disability by both IDEA and NJCLD espe-

cially if it can be ameliorated with medication. Due to parental pressures, the IDEA definition of LDs has been amended administratively to include ADHD if the deficit in attention leads to difficulty in learning. In this compendium, ADHD is treated as a health disability.

The rest of the definition of an LD is an exclusionary definition. It helps clarify the nature of LDs. They are not developmental disabilities. They are not deficiencies in any of the sensory systems (vision, hearing, taste, touch, smell, kinesthetics, vestibular sensation). They are not problems associated with health or physical mobility. They are not emotional or behavioral disorders. They are not disabilities of speech or language. They can be assessed as true LDs only if there is a discrepancy between the child's ability to learn and his or her actual learning.

IDEA's and No Child Left Behind's strong emphases on a free and appropriate educational placement for every child with a disability has forced schools to be more cautious about all assessments and labeling. Increasing numbers of children are now being assessed as LD who once might have been labeled developmentally disabled or disabled by speech, language, emotions, behavior, or one of the senses. A child with an LD may concurrently have a disability in any of these other areas, but if this occurs, both the LD and any other disabilities must be addressed in an individualized Education Plan (IEP) designed especially for that unique child.

Recent research suggests that reading disabilities may affect about 15 percent of elementary school-aged children. If this is accurate, many LD children are not yet being identified and serviced. The causes of LDs are unknown. Usually some central nervous system glitches are believed to underlie the disabilities, even if their existence cannot be demonstrated. Other suspected causes include genetic inheritance, poor nutrition, or exposure to toxic agents. The NJCLD definition of LD presumes biological causation and lifetime chronicity.

This unit on learning disabilities addresses both the successes and the frustrations of educating children with LDs. The first article in the section discusses the importance of a supportive environment. It describes scaffolded instruction, the systematic sequencing of prompted content, materials, tasks, and teacher and peer support to optimize learning. The goal of scaffolding is to support students until they can carry out tasks or skills independently. The careful sequencing helps control frustration and assists students to clear their minds of the word can't. Guidelines for effective scaffolding are given by Martha Larkin.

The second article, "Celebrating Diverse Minds," helps the reader understand that the central nervous system glitches which may be responsible for LDs, may also be advantageous outside the educational system. Many persons with LDs have made significant creative contributions to our world.

In the third selection, Kelly Loeffler asks, "No More Friday Spelling Tests?" Spelling rubrics which can replace spelling tests are described. These rubrics teach students how to spell with knowledge of the cognitive-linguistic aspects of language. They also improve writing skills and can be used as assessment tools.

The last selection depicts the problems of social skills in students with LDs. Deborah Court and Sarah Givon suggest ways to improve these skills.

Providing Support for Student Independence Through Scaffolded Instruction

Martha J. Larkin

Students with learning disabilities need a supportive environment to function successfully in school—and later in the workplace. A supportive environment enables them to capitalize on their strengths and minimize or cope effectively with their weaknesses. Gerber, Ginsberg, and Reiff (1992) noted characteristics of successful adults with learning disabilities:

- Having the desire to excel.
- Reframing their disability in a positive manner.
- Setting explicit personal goals.
- Being willing to take risks.
- Taking advantage of strengths.

If students with learning and other disabilities are to exhibit characteristics of successful adults, they need appropriate support in school. Such support includes "scaffolding," or providing steps that lead to achievement (see box, "What Is Scaffolded Instruction?").

In this article, we visit a special education teacher who practiced effective scaffolding. This teacher shares her thoughts about the challenges she faced in assisting a student to achieve independence. Several other teachers provide guidelines for effective scaffolding.

Breaking the Failure Cycle

Many students who receive special education services as early as second and third grades already have become well immersed in a "failure cycle." These students are not identified to receive special educational services until the number of their failures well exceeds the number of their successful experiences. Melanie (not her real name), a third grader identified with a learning disability, lost all hope that she could be successful in school until Anna Davis (again, not her real name), a special education teacher, provided her a supportive environment (see box, "Meet Melanie").

Through scaffolded instruction, Anna Davis provided Melanie with the support she needed to become a successful reader and to begin developing confidence in her abilities. As Anna's comments indicated, ensuring a supportive environment for Melanie and her peers with disabilities is a substantial challenge. It is labor intensive and time consuming, and success is measured in small increments. As Melanie performs tasks with less teacher assistance, she gains more self-confidence and is more likely to take risks (e.g., attempting to perform a portion or even entire tasks independently). A measure of success for Melanie and many of her peers with learning disabilities is achieving the independence in at least some academic areas.

Educators can learn much from teachers like Anna who facilitate a caring, supportive environment for their students—to help them strive for independence.

How Can Teachers Provide Effective Scaffolded Instruction?

In a summary of the literature, Hogan and Pressley (1997) listed eight essential elements of scaffolded instruction: pre-engagement; establishing a shared goal; actively diagnosing the understandings and needs of the learners; providing tailored assistance; maintaining pursuit of the goal; giving feedback; controlling for frustration and risk; and assisting internationalization, independence, and generalization to other contexts. Teachers need not follow these elements in lockstep succession, but use them as general guidelines for dynamic, flexible scaffolding. Let's examine each, as it applies to the example of Melanie.

Pre-engagement with the Learner and Curriculum. During pre-engagement, the teacher considers curriculum goals and student needs to select an appropriate task (Hogan & Pressley, 1997). Anna Davis selected appropri-

What Is Scaffolded Instruction?

Scaffolded instruction is "the systematic sequencing of prompted content, materials, tasks, and teacher and peer support to optimize learning" (Dickson, Chard, & Simmons, 1993, p. 12). Scaffolding provides students with the help they need and allows them to complete a task with assistance before they are able to complete it independently (Pearson, 1996). The goal of scaffolding is to support students until they can apply the new skills and strategies independently. This means a gradual decrease in supports and a gradual increase in student responsibility with the responsibility for learning shifting from the teacher to the student (Rosenshine & Meister, 1992). In other words, scaffolded instruction means that teachers make sure that their students have the necessary support to complete a task successfully. When learning something new or difficult, students may need more assistance; and as they begin to demonstrate task mastery, the support is removed gradually. Through appropriately scaffolded instruction, students accept more responsibility for their learning and become more independent learners.

Dixon (1994) provided an example of scaffolded instruction as it might be used to teach a child with physical disabilities or a young child how to use a playground slide. An adult might begin by carrying the child up the steps to the slide and holding the child while both adult and child slide together. After a few times of sliding together, some of the scaffolding or adult support may be removed by placing the child low on the slide, allowing him or her to slide independently for a short distance. Gradually the scaffolding would be removed as the child assumed more responsibility toward sliding the entire distance independently.

Dixon (1994) cautioned against removing the scaffolding all at once or prematurely. Doing so—on a playground slide—could cause serious physical injury to the child. Likewise, removing scaffolding prematurely or never providing students with any supports in academic subjects could result in "serious intellectual injury." Physical injuries can heal, but achievement injuries may be difficult to rehabilitate (Dixon).

Ensuring a supportive environment for students with disabilities is a substantial challenge.

Establishing a Shared Goal. Mutual goal setting for Melanie and Anna was not difficult. Unlike some students who say that they don't want to learn to read, Melanie did want to read. Like many teachers of third-grade students with disabilities, Anna devoted a large portion of the day to teaching her students to read. As noted by Hogan and Pressley (1997), motivating students toward establishing a shared goal is providing a delicate balance between allowing the student to lead and following the traditional path of teacher-directed instruction.

Actively Diagnosing the Understandings and Needs of the Learners. The teacher must be sensitive to the learner and be knowledgeable of content matter to compare student performance to external standards for growth (Hogan & Pressley, 1997). Anna was sensitive to Melanie's need to feel successful and comfortable with the reading process. Anna reminded Melanie of her recent successful reading experiences when Melanie was convinced that she could not perform a similar reading task. In addition, Anna frequently questioned her students to determine their understanding of a task.

Providing Tailored Assistance. Hogan and Pressley (1997) suggested that assistance could take the form of cueing or prompting, questioning, modeling, telling, or discussing. Although Anna used all these forms of assistance, most of the examples provided will focus on cueing. The following illustrates how she used cueing to help Melanie with letter reversals.

> In reading, we used the rabbits [small plastic counters] for phonemic awareness. We were practicing spelling words. When you have *b* and *d*, if you turn the rabbits in that direction [the stomach of one rabbit counter points in the direction of the round part of the letter *b*, and another points in the opposite direction for the letter *d*], they're getting a pictorial cue again of which way [the letter should be turned]. I noticed that when Melanie wrote *bud*, she reversed her *b*s and *d*s. I said to her, "Remember the rabbits." She looked down and said, "Oh yeah," erased it, and put it the correct way. I think it's better to use little clues rather than saying, "Oh, you reversed that letter, or that letter is wrong." All I had to do is say, "Remember the rabbits," because I think that is a far more positive way of saying it.

Maintaining Pursuit of the Goal. Students who have been immersed in the "failure cycle" may have trouble maintaining pursuit of the goal. Particularly for compli-

ate reading tasks for Melanie, as guided by Melanie's individualized education program (IEP) goals. Anna was aware of the difficulties that Melanie had with reading and her lack of self-confidence in her reading ability.

Meet Melanie

Melanie said she wanted to be able to read. She didn't realize that she could read and that was a goal she desired. She said, "If I can only read like everyone else."

Then I said, "Well, you can."

She said, "No, I can't. I don't know how."

I said, "Yes, you do; but you don't know you do." I basically showed her that she could read. She is one of the stronger readers of the group.

I showed her that she knew how to do word-attack skills because she didn't think that she did. I showed her how to look for the small word in the big word and how to leave out a word she didn't know by reading the whole sentence and then figuring out the word. She learned to understand what she read just by asking the *who, what, where,* and *why* questions. She never asked herself those questions before because she never knew that was something you did. So she feels pretty good about herself.

Melanie attempts to pass over areas in which she is uncertain, rather than shut down and say she can't do it. I say, "Now, look how well you did there. Look how well you read and understood what you read. Now, let's try this. It is a little bit harder, but let's try it."

I will keep saying, "Look, remember what you did before? Think about how you used the techniques that you were using at that time to read that passage. Now let's try this one." If you don't make her feel that she has succeeded in one place, Melanie would tend to shut down and not want to try.

—*Anna Davis*

cated tasks, teachers may need to provide more support for students to be persistent and focused (Hogan & Pressley, 1997). Anna gave Melanie extra praise and encouragement to increase her level of motivation. Notice how Anna bolstered Melanie's confidence at the slightest indication that Melanie was slipping into failure.

Giving Feedback. Hogan and Pressley (1997) noted that the teacher who uses scaffolding summarizes student progress and highlights behaviors that lead to success in anticipation that students eventually will self-monitor their own learning. Anna provided feedback appropriately to Melanie by summarizing the progress that she had made in reading; Anna mentioned particular behaviors (i.e., Anna called them "techniques") that led to Melanie's success. Anna was keen on giving immediate feedback (i.e., as soon as possible following a behavior or task completion, usually within the same class period) to

her students and giving feedback in a way that students could have opportunities to correct their errors.

As a student performs tasks with less and less teacher assistance, she gains more self-confidence and is more likely to take risks.

Controlling for Frustration and Risk. The teacher needs to create an environment in which students are free to try alternatives without being penalized and in which mistakes are considered part of learning (Hogan & Pressley, 1997). Anna's classroom environment was one in which students could feel safe in taking risks with their learning. Students like Melanie knew that errors were part of the learning process. Anna described her classroom as

> easy-going, relaxed, a place where learning is fun, where success if far more important than failure. Feedback is positive, so that there is no negativism. These kids have come from classes where they've been put down all of their life, three years of school.... They have been just miserable, and they hurt. They think they are dumb and can never learn. My job is to tell them, "Yes, you can learn, and you will, and this is how we are going to do it. It's easy. It's fun. Let's get on with it." I teach to make them succeed.

Assisting Internalization, Independence, and Generalization to Other Contexts. This means helping students to become less dependent on the teacher's extrinsic signals for what to do next and providing students with the opportunity to practice the skills in different contexts (Hogan & Pressley, 1997). Successful instruction is defined by the degree to which the student uses the information learned to meet the demands of natural settings (Ellis & Larkin, 1998). Anna wanted her students to become independent learners; she recognized that once the students left her classroom and the elementary school, there would be fewer opportunities for teacher assistance. Students would have to become more independent, or run the risk of failure. Anna valued student independence but realized that it would have to occur gradually for some:

> I'm hoping I can find some small tiles where I can put letters on the tiles instead of using the rabbits. We are going to start moving the tiles so that I can see where there's awareness of the vowel sounds. Now we have done vowels for two years and [mastery] is still not there. I'll have to use the tiles where they [the students] place them. They're going to get a visual as well as a kinesthetic [cue], so when they write the word, I'm hoping it transfers.

Guidelines for Effective Scaffolding

- *Identify what students know.* Effective scaffolding requires that teachers are cognizant of what a student already knows (background or prior knowledge), the student's misconceptions, and the student's current zone of proximal development (i.e., which competencies are developing and which are beyond the student's current level of functioning; Pressley, Hogan, Wharton-McDonald, Mistretta, & Ettenberger, 1996). For example, Anna was aware that some of her students "think in terms of money." When she taught "rounding" to those students, Anna used the familiar concept of money.

- *Begin with what students can do.* Laura (not her real name), another special education teacher, was aware of individual student ability levels. When Laura began reading lessons, she gave the students with learning disabilities an opportunity to read something that could be read independently or with little teacher assistance. This enabled students to begin the reading lesson successfully.

- *Help students achieve success quickly.* Laura found that writing and penmanship tasks were laborious for some of her students with written expression disabilities. When she assisted her special education students in the general education classroom for a lesson on storytelling, Laura asked the students to dictate their ideas while she wrote them on paper. This accommodation enabled the students who had difficulty with written expression to generate ideas without worrying how to convey them on paper. Also, Laura served as an adult listener to reinforce the notion that storytelling and written expression is an act of communication and shared experience.

- *Help students to "be" like everyone else.* Miller and Fritz (1998) interviewed a successful adult with learning disabilities about his school history and found that a major theme was the individual's desire to be regarded like other students. These researchers suggested that as much as possible, teachers orient classroom tasks for students' work to be perceived as being like that of their peers. For example, Anna suggested that Mark (not his real name), a struggling student, be moved into a third-grade text like that of his peers. She informed Mark of his responsibility to work hard, but also let him know that she would be there to give him the assistance he needed. Anna noted that when Mark was placed in the third-grade math book with her assistance, he was still struggling with math, but was holding his own. She was confident that she made the right decision to place him in a more difficult math book, with assistance, because Mark felt good about using the same book as his third-grade peers.

- *Know when it's time to stop.* Anna learned from experience that continued drill and practice may not always be effective. She stated, "Overkill erases." Anna found that once her students had demonstrated mastery of a skill, continued practice may result in the students' refusing to work or students' producing work with numerous errors. For example, when some of Anna's students with learning disabilities were asked to complete a general education math assignment with 50 problems, she noticed that the students completed the first three rows of problems without an error. Students began making numerous errors on the final three rows. Anna found that employing systematic review and purposeful practice with a limited number of math problems was effective. She also noted that a just a few written or spoken questions regarding reading or language arts assignments provided needed review without overkill.

- *Help students be independent when they have command of the activity.* Effective scaffolding means that teachers need to listen and watch for clues from their students as to when teacher assistance is or is not needed. Obviously, teachers do not want students to fail, but they should not allow students to become too dependent on the teacher. As special education teacher Beverly (not her real name) noted, achieving independence is different for individual students. Some students may be at identical skill levels, but emotionally may be at different levels regarding the amount of frustration they can tolerate. Students may not be able "to be weaned" from teacher assistance at the same time. In other words, some students will need more teacher support while learning to perform a task; others will demonstrate task mastery more quickly. Like the mother bird that helps her chicks leave the nest to become independent birds, teachers need to help their students gradually move from teacher assistance to student independence as students demonstrate command of the task or activity.

By expressing that she hopes the visual and kinesthetic cues from the use of the tiles will aid transfer, Anna recognized how difficult the generalization of learned skills may be for some students with learning disabilities. Students first must acquire and maintain skills at a proficient level before they can be generalized to other contexts. Although much of her instructional time was spent helping students with skill acquisition and maintenance, Anna fostered independence and generalization in the area of student self-monitoring for errors. Just like she cued her students when they made letter reversals in reading, Anna also used cues to call students' attention to number reversals in math

> For number reversals like 5, 3, 6, and 7, I usually will say something like, "You really have to discipline your 3. It keeps jumping around on you." The kids laugh and they go, "Oh, yeah!"

Students who have been immersed in the "failure cycle" may have trouble maintaining pursuit of the goal.

Anna's sense of humor not only made the students feel at ease with error monitoring and correction, but also gave them opportunities to practice these skills when the teacher made a error.

> I usually tell them it is safe to make mistakes in here, because your teacher makes them every day.... I allow them to catch me on mistakes.... Yesterday, I couldn't get that word spelling right, s-c-r-a-t-c-h. The students were laughing and having a wonderful time, but I turned that into learning. "You tell me how to spell it, because I'm having a terrible time with this word."

Anna tried to provide cues only when students needed them (e.g., struggling with a familiar task in a new context, or making an error). To lessen teacher dependence gradually, Anna cued students to use "error monitoring" strategies when she gave the directions for an assignment. "When you do your sentences on page 86, please read them to yourself. Sometimes, when you read them to yourself, you find what you left out." Another way Anna used cues was to help students to verbalize how they recognized their own errors (e.g., "How did you recognize your mistake, Randy?"). Anna seized this opportunity to help Randy (not his real name) identify the naturally occurring events that alerted him to his error. Although Anna's students needed more assistance with generalization of skills, they were making progress on the road to independence.

In addition to the eight essential elements of scaffolded instruction, teachers like Anna have developed their own guidelines for effective scaffolding (see box, "Guidelines").

Final Thoughts

Students with learning disabilities need a supportive classroom environment that can help them recognize

their strengths and feel confident about their abilities in order to achieve at least some degree of independent functioning. Through carefully scaffolded instruction, special education and general education teachers can take proactive paths of moving their students towards independence and achieving success. This path will be challenging for teachers and students. To provide effective scaffolding for some or all students in the classroom across several content areas may require an enormous amount of time and energy from the teacher (Pressley et al., 1996). Teachers must tailor scaffolding to meet individual student needs. Also, effective scaffolding requires the provision of "calibrated assistance" (Wong, 1998). Teachers must be cognizant of the kinds and degrees of assistance provided to individual students (for more about scaffolded instruction, see box, "Resources"). Support or assistance must be removed gradually (Rosenshine & Meister, 1992).

Finally, teachers need to pay attention to clues from their students as to when teacher support is or is not needed. As noted by Beed, Hawkins, and Roller (1991). "Independence must somehow be achieved through the daily interaction between teachers and children" (p. 648).

Although the examples in this article have focused on elementary school students and teachers, scaffolding principles and techniques can guide teachers to assist students on any grade level to become more independent learners.

References

Beed, P. L., Hawkins, E. M., & Roller, C. M. (1991). Moving learners toward independence: The power of scaffolded instruction. *The Reading Teacher, 44*, 648–655.

Dickson, S. V., Chard, D. J., & Simmons, D. C. (1993). An integrated reading/writing curriculum: A focus on scaffolding. *LD Forum, 18* (4), 12–16.

Dixon, R. (1994). Research-based guidelines for selecting a mathematics curriculum. *Effective School Practices, 13* (2), 47–61.

Ellis, E. S., & Larkin, M. J. (1998). Strategic instruction for adolescents with learning disabilities. In B. Y. L. Wong (Ed.), *Learning about learning disabilities* (2nd ed.; pp. 585–656). San Diego, CA: Academic Press.

Gerber, P. J., Ginsberg, R., & Reiff, H. B. (1992). Identifying alterable patterns in employment success for highly successful adults with learning disabilities. *Journal of Learning Disabilities, 25*, 474–487.

Hogan, K., & Pressley, M. (1997). Scaffolding scientific competencies within classroom communities of inquiry. In K. Hogan & M. Pressley (Eds.), *Scaffolding student learning: Instructional approaches & issues* (pp. 74–107). Cambridge, MA: Brookline Books.

Miller, M., & Fritz, M. F. (1998). A demonstration of resilience. *Intervention in School and Clinic, 35*, 265–271.

Pearson, P. D. (1996). Reclaiming the center, *The first R: Every child's right to read* (pp. 259–274). New York: Teachers College Columbia University.

Pressley, M., Hogan, K., Wharton-McDonald, R., Mistretta, J., & Ettenberger, S. (1996). The challenges of instructional scaffolding: The challenges of instruction that supports student

Resources for Scaffolded Instruction

Beed, P. L., Hawkins, E. M., & Roller, C. M. (1991). Moving learners toward independence: The power of scaffolded instruction. *The Reading Teacher, 44*, 648–655.

Dickson, S. V., Chard, D. J., & Simmons, D. C. (1993). An integrated reading/writing curriculum: A focus on scaffolding. *LD Forum, 18* (4), 12–16.

Dixon, R. C., & Carnine, D. (1993). Using scaffolding to teach writing. *Educational Leadership, 51* (3), 100–102.

Gambrell, L. B., Morrow, L. M., Neuman, S. B., & Pressley, M. (Eds.). (1999). *Best practices in literacy instruction.* New York: The Guilford Press.

Graves, M. F., & Braaten, S. (1996). Scaffolded reading experiences: Bridges to success. *Preventing School Failure, 40* (4), 169–173.

Graves, M. F., Graves, B. B., & Braaten, S. (1996). Scaffolded reading experiences for inclusive classes. *Educational Leadership, 53* (5), 14–16.

Hiebert, E. H., & Raphael, T. E. (1998). *Early literacy instruction.* Fort Worth, TX: Harcourt Brace College Publishers.

Hogan, K., & Pressley, M. (Eds). (1997). *Scaffolding student learning: Instructional approaches & issues.* Cambridge, MA: Brookline Books.

Kameenui, E. J., & Carnine, D. W. (1998). *Effective teaching strategies that accommodate diverse learners.* Upper Saddle River, NJ: Merrill.

Meichenbaum, D., & Biemiller, A. (1998). *Nurturing independent learners: Helping students take charge of their learning.* Cambridge, MA: Brookline Books.

Palincsar, A. S. (1991). Scaffolded instruction of listening comprehension with first graders at risk for academic difficulty. In A. McKeough & J. L. Lupart (Eds.), *Toward the practice of theory-based instruction* (pp. 50–65). Hillsdale, NJ: Erlbaum.

Pressley, M., Hogan, K., Wharton-McDonald, R., Mistretta, J., & Ettenberger, S. (1996). The challenges of instructional scaffolding: The challenges of instruction that supports student thinking. *Learning Disabilities Research & Practice, 11* (3), 138–146.

Rosenshine, B., & Meister, C. (1992). The use of scaffolds for teaching higher-level cognitive strategies. *Educational Leadership, 49* (7), 26–33.

Soderman, A. K., Gregory, K. M., & O'Neill, L. T. (1999). *Scaffolding emergent literacy: A child-centered approach for preschool through grade 5.* Boston: Allyn & Bacon.

Wollman-Bonilla, J. E., & Werchadlo, B. (199). Teacher and peer roles in scaffolding first graders' responses to literature. *Reading Teacher, 52*, 598–608.

Wong, B. Y. L. (Ed.). (1998). Scaffolding. (Special issue). *Journal of Learning Disabilities, 31* (4).

thinking. *Learning Disabilities Research & Practice, 11* (3), 138–146.

Rosenshine, B., & Meister, C. (1992). The use of scaffolds for teaching higher-level cognitive strategies. *Educational Leadership, 49* (7), 26–33.

Wong, B. Y. L. (1998). Analyses of intrinsic and extrinsic problems in the use of the scaffolding metaphor in learning disabilities intervention research: An introduction. *Journal of Learning Disabilities, 31*, 340–343.

Martha J. Larkin (CEC Chapter #356), Assistant Professor of Special Education, State University of West Georgia, Carrollton, Georgia.

Address correspondence to the author at Department of Special Education and Speech Language Pathology, 1600 Maple Street, State University of West Georgia, Carrollton, GA 30118 (e-mail: mlarkin@westga.edu).

This research was supported by a grant from the Donald D. Hammill Foundation. The author would like to thank the special education teachers in Alabama and Virginia who opened the doors to their classrooms and gave so willingly of their time, expertise, and perspectives.

Celebrating Diverse Minds

Many faltering students have specialized minds—brains exquisitely wired to perform certain kinds of tasks masterfully.

Mel Levine

A distraught mother recently sent me this e-mail: *Every morning when I send Michael off to school, I feel as if I'm sending him to jail. He can't spell, he forgets his math facts even after we study them together, his handwriting is hard to decipher, and he is hopelessly absent-minded. The other kids see his papers and say that he "writes like a mental case." All day, he faces nonstop criticism from his teacher. She scolds him in front of his classmates for not trying. And you know, his teacher's right. He's not trying—he's scared to try. He's decided that if you're going to fail, it's better to fail without trying.*

He can fix absolutely anything that's broken and he is brilliant when he plays with his Legos. I can't believe the complicated things he makes. He is convinced that he is hopelessly dumb, and he worries about school all the time. A lot of nights, Michael cries himself to sleep. We are losing this darling boy and he is such a beautiful child, such a decent kid. Please help us.

We have all heard the success stories of Albert Einstein, Thomas Edison, Steve Jobs, and Charles Schwab—accomplished adults whose minds failed to fit in school. But what becomes of those whom we never hear about—students like Michael, who give up on themselves because they lack the kinds of minds needed to satisfy existing criteria for school success?

For more than 30 years, my work as a pediatrician has been dedicated to such out-of-step children and adolescents. Although some of them have officially acknowledged collisions with word decoding or attention, many contend with more elusive differences in learning. These students may have trouble organizing time and prioritizing activities, communicating effectively, grasping verbal or nonverbal concepts, retrieving data precisely and quickly from long-term memory, recognizing and responding to recurring patterns, or assimilating fine detail.

Such insidious dysfunctions can constitute daunting barriers, especially when they are not recognized and managed. Most important, these breakdowns can mislead us into undervaluing, unfairly accusing, and even undereducating students, thereby stifling their chances for success in school and life.

The Challenge of Disappointing School Performance

Many faltering students have specialized minds—brains exquisitely wired to perform certain kinds of tasks masterfully, but decidedly miswired when it comes to meeting other expectations. A student may be brilliant at visualizing, but embarrassingly inept at verbalizing. Her classmate may reveal a remarkable understanding of people, but exhibit no insight about sentence structure.

Within every student contending with learning differences, an area invariably exists in which her or his mind has been amply equipped to thrive. In the e-mail from Michael's mother, the clue to his mind's early specialization practically jumps out at you: "He can fix absolutely anything that's broken." Michael's mechanical brilliance gets eclipsed by our focus on what he can't do.

I love to spend time explaining his strengths and their possibilities to a student like Michael who feels depleted and diminished (and perhaps even demolished) by the experience of school. I talk to him about the different careers in which he could readily succeed given the abilities he already possesses. I feel as if I have stepped inside a shadowy passageway suddenly illuminated, as revealed by a newly radiant facial expression. I can't help but conclude that the real challenge for schools rests more with identifying and fortifying individuals' strengths than with caulking academic crevices.

My long-term experience working at the interface between pediatrics and education has allowed me to synthesize the body of research on neurodevelopmental function and variation (Levine & Reed, 1999) and to construct a framework for understanding the enigma of disappointing school performance. Three factors play major roles:

• The traditional paradigms for understanding learning differences focus on exposing and fixing deficits, often neglecting the latent or blatant talents within struggling learners.

- Instructional practices and curricular choices fail to provide educational opportunities for diverse learners and to prepare them for a successful life.

- Because knowledge about learning emanating from the explosion of insights from brain research is not yet part of teacher preparation and professional development, most educators lack the expertise to understand and support their students' diverse minds.

To stem the tide of needless and wasteful failure facing thousands of kids, we need to take robust action on three fronts: broadened student assessment, curriculum reexamination, and professional development for educators.

Broadened Student Assessment

The methods that schools typically deploy to assess students with learning problems are not up to the task. The discrepancy formulas used to determine eligibility for specialized assistance have been shown repeatedly to have serious flaws (Kavale & Forness, 2000).

Moreover, testing that merely generates a label, such as LD or ADD, accomplishes little. These vague labels do not suggest specific approaches to remediation; instead, they pessimistically imply a relatively permanent pathological condition. What a colossal self-fulfilling prophecy! Most important, diagnosis spawned from a deficit model fails to take into account the most important feature of a student—his strengths.

Smokescreen Labels

Phillip's parents reported that he seemed to generate about two highly original and unorthodox ideas per minute. His teacher described this irrepressible 4th grader as a brilliant conceptualizer, always coming up with creative analogies. When the class studied terrorism, Phillip compared suicide bombers to strep germs that make you sick and then die in your throat.

But Phillip's day-to-day performance in school was disappointing. When he listened or read, Phillip missed or forgot much of the information he was expected to absorb. He would tune out and become fidgety during extended explanations or directions. His parents sought help from their son's pediatrician, who diagnosed ADD and prescribed a stimulant medication. This treatment helped, but not much.

It turns out that Phillip owned the kind of mind that becomes enthralled with the big picture and rejects fine detail. Consequently, in math he mastered the concepts readily but couldn't be bothered to notice the difference between a plus sign and a minus sign (a mere detail). His writing was creative and amusing but sparse on specific information. In subject after subject, Phillip's overall understanding far exceeded his handling of the details.

Like Phillip, many kids with problems don't ooze easily into categories. Students with his kind of detail intolerance often get diagnosed with ADD or accused of not really trying. In Phillip's case, the label ADD was a smokescreen that obscured people's view of his remarkable strengths and stopped them short of managing his specific weakness in detail assimilation. Phillip improved markedly after his teacher began encouraging him to make detail thinking a separate step in any activity he undertook—scan first, get the big picture, have some great ideas, and then revisit the material to vacuum up the important details.

Incidentally, society desperately needs big-picture people who can collaborate meaningfully with administrators who thrive on detail. So let's take care not to disparage or discourage the flourishing of Phillip's kind of mind.

Assessment for Diverse Minds

In addition to rethinking the assessments used to diagnose learning problems, schools need to design regular tests and quizzes so that different kinds of minds can show what they know in different ways. Teachers should be careful not to tap exclusively rote memory or straight regurgitation of skills and knowledge. They should often allow students to use notes and encourage them to take as much time as they need to respond to questions. It makes more sense to limit space than time—for instance, telling students, "You can't write more than two pages, but you can take as long as you want to do so."

High-stakes testing can pulverize many mismatched students. How commonly does end-of-grade testing discriminate against certain kinds of minds? Frequently. As a clinician, I encounter many students who have difficulty performing on multiple-choice tests or operating under timed conditions. These students' dysfunctions in certain skill areas are more than out-weighed by their assets in other domains, but standardized testing never gives them the opportunity to exhibit their strengths.

> ## I look forward to the day when our schools offer every student the opportunity to become a leading expert on a chosen topic.

On entering the medical profession, we take an oath that in our practice we will first of all "do no harm." I offer five suggestions (see "Do No Harm" Testing Practices, p. 17) to my professional colleagues in education so that they may strive for testing practices that do no harm to students with different kinds of minds. We need to advocate for the elimination of testing practices that inflict needless damage and unfair humiliation on so many students.

Curriculum Reexamination

It's ironic that at the same time that neuroscience is telling us so much about differences in learning, we are imposing curriculum standards that offer our students fewer learning alternatives than ever before. If we aspire to meet the challenge of leaving no child behind, we must provide diverse learners with diverging pathways that lead to their success. Such roads should maintain rigorous performance standards, while permitting innovation and creativity in curricular choices and allowing early, highly specialized minds to envision and prepare for productive adulthood.

For example, children like Michael, with his impressive mechanical aptitude, should not be sentenced to wait until adulthood to experience success. We should encourage, not constrain, the development of magnet schools and vocational education opportunities. I look forward to the day when thousands of students pursue a vocationally oriented curriculum that does not put a ceiling on their aspirations.

> ### If we aspire to meet the challenge of leaving no child behind, we must provide diverse learners with diverging pathways that lead to their success.

While studying auto mechanics (and the physics that is a part of it), a teenager should learn the ins and outs of various related careers. She or he should see the possibility of someday climbing the corporate ladder at Ford Motor Company, owning a repair business franchise, designing solar-powered engines, or managing the service department of a dealership. In this way, no one gets written off or limited because of the nature of his passions or the specialized apparatus of her mind.

Many schools have worked against odds to provide educational experiences that involve all students in conducting independent study projects in their area of personal affinity and ability. One school, for example, asked all 3rd grade students to pick a country and become the school's leading expert on that nation. The projects carried over from 3rd through 5th grade, and the students traversed content areas as they studied their country's culture, history, language, animal life, government, and music. They did art projects and wrote reports on their country.

Students learned how it feels to know more about something than anyone around, including their teachers and parents. They became valued consultants on particular countries; when the newspaper reported a current event in their country, they were asked to provide some commentary in class—a great vitamin for intellectual self-esteem!

Another school pursued a similar strategy during students' three years in middle school. Students selected any topic from a list for long-term pursuit across disciplines. They found experts in the community to assist them with their topics. Any student who did not want to claim one of the listed topics could submit one of his or her own choosing.

I look forward to the day when our schools offer every student the opportunity to become a leading expert on a chosen topic—one that harmonizes with his or her kind of mind—and to share that expertise with the community through Web sites, community-based projects, and other venues. Such a practice would give students a powerful experience of success, as well as cultivate their appetite for systematic research and focused, in-depth knowledge.

While advocating ardently for flexibility in achieving the educational aims of schooling, we can still preserve student accountability. No student should be permitted to work, study, or produce less than his or her peers. But we should never insist that everyone put forth identical output.

Professional Development for Educators

In medical practice, highly specific knowledge of the individual needs of a patient is indispensable when selecting the best treatment. This holds true in all "helping" professions—especially in education.

Teachers are in an excellent position to observe, interpret, and celebrate all kinds of minds on a daily basis. Newly acquired knowledge emanating from neuroscientific and education research can empower educators to observe and understand students' minds. Most of the phenomena that determine a student's individual strengths, shortcomings, and preferred ways of learning and producing cannot be found on any test that a clinician gives. Classroom teachers enjoy exclusive screenings—if they pay attention and know what to look for.

Becky

Eight-year-old Becky is an accomplished origami creator, a deft modern dancer, and a gifted mathematician. She thrives on science and computers. Yet in school, this girl appears shy, passive, and eternally anguished. Becky has accurate spelling, but she dislikes writing and avoids it. Becky's teacher, Mrs. Sorenson, having been educated to observe neurodevelopmental phenomena, has noticed that Becky seems to struggle and falter when called on in class. Recently, the teacher led a discussion on whether animals have feelings as people do. She called on Becky and the following dialogue ensued:

Becky: My puppy feels, uh, things like happy and, um, sad.

Mrs. Sorenson: Becky, what makes her happy or sad?

Becky (after a long pause): Different things.

Mrs. Sorenson: Such as?

Becky: Like a dog, uh, basket.

Mrs. Sorenson: Do you mean a dog biscuit?

Becky: Yeah, like that.

Becky's reading comprehension is more than a year above grade level. Yet she has trouble with word finding, shows pronounced verbal hesitancy, puts forth only simple or incomplete sentences, and fails to use verbal elaboration. The same phenomena are conspicuous in her

"Do No Harm" Testing Practices

1. Testing can help elevate education standards, but not if it creates larger numbers of students who are written off as unsuccessful. When a student does poorly, determine which link in the learning chain is uncoupled. Always have constructive, nonpunitive contingency plans for students who perform poorly on a test. Testing should not be an end in itself, but rather a call to action.

2. Not all students can demonstrate their strengths in the same manner. Allow different students to demonstrate their learning differently, using the means of their choice (portfolios, expert papers, oral presentations, and projects, as well as multiple-choice tests).

3. Never use testing as justification for retaining a student in a grade. Retention is ineffective and seriously damaging to students. How can you retain a child while claiming you are not leaving anyone behind?

4. Some students who excel on tests might develop a false sense of security and confidence, failing to realize that adult careers tap many abilities that no test can elicit. Take care to nurture vital capacities that are not testable.

5. Avoid the hazard of teachers' teaching to the tests because your work or school is being judged solely on the basis of examination scores. Teachers should never have their students rehearse or explicitly prepare for tests. Testing should be unannounced. Good results on such tests should be the product of the regular, undisturbed curriculum.

—Mel Levine

writing. Becky has strong receptive language but markedly weak expressive language—she understands better than she talks. No wonder she's so shy, self-conscious, and passive! Language output plays a vital role in school success. Verbal communication affects writing, class participation, social success, and the control of emotions and behavior.

Becky could fall through the cracks because we do not have valid tests of language production. For example, the WISC (the commonly used IQ test in her age group) does little to capture expressive language fluency. In fact, by far the best test of expressive language is a classroom teacher who knows what to listen for in gauging the adequacy of a student's verbal output, and who understands the everyday classroom phenomena associated with breakdowns in language production.

Bruce

Here's another example of the role that teachers can play in detecting learning differences. Bruce was disruptive in most of his 7th grade classes. He fashioned himself as an entertainer and often disengaged from classroom activities. Mr. Jackson, a social studies teacher knowledgeable about early adolescent development and learning, made the astute observation that Bruce often appeared confused about dates and about the sequences of events in the various historical periods that they studied. Mr. Jackson also noted that Bruce often looked distressed when given directions.

On one occasion, Mr. Jackson told the class:

> This morning I want you all to open your books to page 47, read the first three paragraphs, and study the diagram at the top of the page. And when you're finished doing that, read and think about the first two questions at the end of the chapter. I'm going to give you 10 minutes, and then I'll be calling on you to discuss the questions.

Bruce seemed to hear only something about page 47 (or was it 57?). His teacher suspected rightly that this boy was having problems processing sequences—sequential directions, chains of events in history, and multi-step explanations. His weak temporal-sequential ordering accounted for his problems in social studies and in math. This insight enabled teachers to give Bruce strategies to manage his sequencing problems: taking notes, whispering sequences under his breath, and picturing sequences in his mind. His behavior and demeanor in class improved dramatically.

Although continuing education programs abound to help teachers stay abreast of their content, we have found few comprehensive programs devoted to helping educators deepen their expertise in the science of learning. Our not-for-profit institute, All Kinds of Minds, has developed a professional development and school service model called Schools Attuned to help experienced classroom educators become knowledgeable about neurodevelopmental function and variation.[1] Participating teachers learn to analyze how their own instructional delivery and content taps specific aspects of memory, attention, motor function, language, and other areas of brain function. They are guided to observe everyday classroom phenomena that open windows on relevant learning processes (Levine, 1994).

Equipped with their Schools Attuned training, teachers lead a coalition involving the student, parents, and other adults in the school to unmask the specific learning profile of a struggling student. With help from professionals trained as neurodevelopmental consultants, whom we call profile advisors (usually school psychologists or special educators), teachers become the primary detectors of student strengths, weaknesses, and content affinities. The teachers then infuse their insights into their daily group instructional strategies and lesson designs. Frequently, a strategy that they develop to help a particular struggling student benefits the entire class. It's called excellent pedagogy.

Testing that merely generates a label, such as LD or ADD, accomplishes little.

Schools Attuned teachers are also committed to making sure that all of their students learn about learning while they are learning. Through a process called demystification, they help students whose neurodevelopmental profiles do not currently mesh with expectations to learn about their own strengths and weaknesses and acquire the terms for the specific processes that they need to work on. With profile advisors as their consultants, regular classroom teachers take the lead in formulating management plans for these students.

Where We Need to Go

The core theme of K-12 education in this century should be straightforward: high standards with an unwavering commitment to individuality. In proposing that educators reexamine assessment, curriculum, and the role of teachers, I am advocating neurodevelopmental pluralism in our schools—the celebration of all kinds of minds. Such an ethos will be the most effective and humane way of realizing our commitment to leave no child behind.

Note

1. More information about the Schools Attuned program and All Kinds of Minds is available online at www.allkindsofminds.org.

References

Kavale, K. A., & Forness, S. R. (2000). What definitions of learning disability say and don't say: A critical analysis. *Journal of Learning Disabilities, 33*, 239-256.

Levine, M. (1994). *Educational care* (2nd ed.). Cambridge, MA: Educators Publishing Service.

Levine, M., & Reed, M. (1999). *Developmental variation and learning disorders* (2nd ed.). Cambridge, MA: Educators Publishing Service.

Author's note: Mary Dean Barringer, Stacy Parker-Fisher, Chris Osmond, and Tamara Nimkoff contributed to this article.

Mel Levine, M.D., is a professor of pediatrics at the University of North Carolina Medical School in Chapel Hill, North Carolina; Director of the University's Clinical Center for the Study of Development and Learning; and the founder of All Kinds of Minds. His most recent books are *A Mind at a Time* (Simon and Schuster, 2002) and *The Myth of Laziness* (Simon and Schuster, 2003).

No More Friday Spelling Tests?

An Alternative Spelling Assessment for Students With Learning Disabilities

Kelly A. Loeffler

"Is it true that you do not give spelling tests?" questioned a perplexed mother at back-to-school night. I was prepared for this question and knew that parents would have difficulty accepting that their children could learn how to spell without the weekly ritual of helping their children study for the traditional spelling test. I quickly explained to her why I changed my assessment to a spelling rubric rather than a traditional spelling test.

A traditional spelling test does not provide insight into the spelling cues that the students are using, (See box, "What Cues Do Writers Use to Spell Words Accurately?") However, a spelling rubric can measure the student's ability to find misspelled words, correct them, and use an appropriate spelling strategy. Students with learning disabilities often do well on weekly spelling tests by memorizing their lists of words, rather than by internalizing spelling strategies. They are quick to forget their weekly words when given a written assignment. Assessing my students' spelling ability was more important to me than evaluating their memorization skills. Heald-Taylor (1998, p. 405) elaborates, "Learning to spell is a complex, intricate cognitive and linguistic process rather than one of rote memorization." (See box, "What Does the Literature Say?")

What Does the Literature Say About the Need for Alternative Spelling Assessments?

Students with learning disabilities frequently misspell words. Darch, Kim, Johnson, and James (2000) explained that students with learning disabilities have difficulty spelling because they are less skilled at deducing and using spelling strategies and rules. The researchers concluded that students with learning disabilities do not use their knowledge of sound and symbol correspondences effectively. Students often substitute an incorrect vowel or leave out the vowel altogether. Jones (2001) stated that children with learning disabilities have difficulty detecting their own spelling errors. Teaching students to monitor their misspelled words is crucial to their lifelong growth as writers. A weekly test does not encourage students to monitor their spelling within the context of their writing.

In their study, Gill and Scharer (1996) developed a rubric to provide parents with ratings of their children's spelling performance without administering a spelling test. The researchers found that parents were more appreciative of this information than with obtaining the results of a weekly test.

What Cues Do Writers Use to Spell Words Accurately?

While writing, good spellers attend to one, two, or a combination of spelling cues to spell words accurately.

- One cue that a writer uses is phonics, or sounding-out the words.
- A writer also uses visual cues.
- A writer can use familiar spelling patterns and ask himself or herself whether the word looks right.
- A writer can use high-frequency words. These are words that the writer knows how to spell simply from exposure to the words through reading.

Developing an Alternative Spelling Assessment

For the first 2 years of my teaching career, I assigned spelling words on Monday, provided practice throughout the week, gave a pretest, and finally administered a spelling test on Friday. No undergraduate class taught me to teach spelling this way. I simply imitated the spelling methods from my own elementary school years. In grading spelling tests, I found that students with strong memorization ability were able to score 100% on their tests each week. Students with weaker memory skills became frustrated when they earned

Figure 1. Spelling Rubric

Name: _____   Date: _____

Spelling Rubric

Title of Writing Assignment: _____   Spelling Strategy Used: _____

Criteria	5	4	3	2	1
Circles all misspelled words	Student found and circled all misspelled words.	Student circled 75%-99% of misspelled words.	Student circled 50%-74% of misspelled words.	Student circled 25%-49% of misspelled words.	Student circled 1%-24% of misspelled words.
Accurately corrects all circled misspelled words	Student accurately corrected all circled misspelled words.	Student accurately corrected 75%-99% of circled misspelled words.	Student accurately corrected 50%-74% of circled misspelled words.	Student accurately corrected 25%-49% of circled misspelled words.	Student accurately corrected 1%-24% of circled misspelled words.
Always uses sounding out, spell-checker, dictionary, or similar words to spell words without help	Student always used one of the taught spelling strategies to spell words correctly on his or her own.	Student almost always used one of the taught spelling strategies to spell words correctly on his or her own.	Student sometimes used one of the taught spelling strategies to spell words correctly on his or her own.	Student always used one of the taught spelling strategies to spell words correctly with some help from an adult.	Student sometimes used one of the taught spelling strategies to spell words correctly with some help from an adult.
Spells all words correctly in writing	Student correctly spelled all the words in his or her writing.	Student correctly spelled 74%-75% of the words in his or her writing.	Student correctly spelled 50%-74% of the words in his or her writing.	Student correctly spelled 25%-74% of the words in his or her writing.	Student correctly spelled 1%-24% of the words in his or her writing.
Grade	/20 points	% =	Letter grade =		

Comments:

Parent Signature

a poor grade. However, most of my students did not generalize their weekly spelling words to their writing. Spelling lists and tests became a waste of instructional time for my upper-elementary students. I realized that this traditional method of spelling instruction did not work for my students with learning disabilities. So I decided to try a different method.

An alternative spelling assessment was in the works. I needed a tool that promoted my instructional objectives. I wanted students to be able to find their misspellings, choose a strategy to fix them, and write legibly. From these goals I devised an original rubric (Figure 1) that grades spelling within the context of student writing.

Implementing a Spelling Rubric

I use the rubric with fifth-grade students in a resource room setting. The children are excited and pleased when I announce that I do not give spelling tests. However, winning over their parents is a little more difficult. During the first week of school, I send home a copy of the spelling rubric, along with a letter describing the rationale for its use. I encourage parents to contact me with comments and questions. Parents respond well to the rubric when it is explained clearly to them.

Assessing their spelling ability was more important to me than evaluating their memorization skills.

Explaining to the students how the new spelling "test" works is much easier. During the first month of school, I use an overhead to model finding words that "don't look right." I show students how to circle these words but continue their writing. Continuing to write is the most difficult part for the students. Students with learning disabilities usually recognize that they are not the best spellers. They want to correct their errors as quickly as possible.

To help students detect their errors. I model a spelling self-check routine to the class. The students learn to verify that each syllable has a vowel and that each syllable starts and ends with the appropriate letters. After students circle all their misspelled words, they go back and attempt to correct their spelling. The rubric requires that students use one spelling strategy on their own. The strategies can involve any of the following:

• Asking a friend.
• Sounding out the word slowly by using sound boxes or finger tapping.
• Using a dictionary.

• Using similar words to help them spell the troublesome word.
• Using a spell-checker.

Most students choose to use an electronic spell-checker. MacArthur, Graham, Haynes, and DeLaPaz (1996) found that students with learning disabilities were able to correct 37% of their errors when they used a spell-checker. Without the support of a spell-checker, students could only correct 9% of their errors. Consequently, a spell-checker can be an invaluable tool for students with learning disabilities.

Teaching students to monitor their misspelled words is crucial to their lifelong growth as writers.

To maintain a focus on writing content and creativity. I do not assess students on each composition. I alert them when I will assess their written work for spelling. When students turn in both their rough drafts and their final drafts, I use the rubric to assess their spelling. I compare the rough draft with the final draft to see the improvements that they have made. The rough drafts include their circled misspelled words with their corrections written above the word. The final

Who Benefits From the Spelling Rubric?

- Upper elementary to secondary students.
- Students who have difficulty generalizing their spelling words to their writing.
- Students in general and special education settings

drafts show their use of spelling strategies. Students are thrilled when their written pieces show few or no spelling errors. When we review their compositions, I hold a one-on-one conference with the students and use their graded rubrics. We discuss the strategies that they used to correct their misspellings. The conference also allows me to introduce new spelling strategies that are based on the errors that the students did not find. The spelling rubric helps me individualize spelling instruction and assessment for my students with learning disabilities (see box, "Steps in Using a Spelling Rubric").

After seeing my students' improvement in spelling, general and special educators in my school became interested in the rubric. They, too, were frustrated because their students were not able to generalize their weekly spelling words, (See box, "Who Benefits From a Spelling Rubric?") Even students not identified as having a learning disability have benefited from using the spelling rubric rather than a spelling test. My principal is also supportive of the alternative assessment. Because her son has a learning disability, she recognizes that not everyone benefits from memorizing lists of spelling words. Her support has encouraged other teachers to undertake the challenge of alternative assessments.

Benefits of a Spelling Rubric

Using a spelling rubric has many benefits including the following:

- Students receive credit for identifying misspelled words.
- Students use an effective strategy to counteract their disability.

Steps in Using a Spelling Rubic

1. Send a letter home to parents describing the rubric. Be sure to attach a copy of the rubric to the letter.
2. Model finding words that "don't look right."
3. Model checking for a vowel in each syllable, as well as checking for appropriate beginning and ending sounds.
4. Explain strategies for correcting spelling errors.
5. Hold a conference with students about the graded spelling rubric.

- Teachers identify the spelling strategies that students are using effectively.
- Spelling becomes more meaningful when it is used in context.
- Spelling rubrics allow teachers to evaluate spelling in context and provide grades that replace traditional spelling scores.
- The students' self-esteem improves.

Spelling Assessment and Instruction

Although the spelling rubric is nontraditional, spelling instruction in my classroom continues to be direct and systematic. I instruct my upper-elementary students by using the Wilson Reading System (Wilson, 1996). Within the system, students learn to tap out words to help them segment the sounds. The spelling rubric is simply another form of assessment, not to be used solely for spelling instruction. Continuing formal spelling instruction in a manner that supports each student's needs is important.

Caution

Students with learning disabilities are often very smart and tend to find the quickest way out of a writing assignment. One problem with the spelling rubric was that students would write brief compositions with words they already knew how to spell. To encourage substantial compositions, I arrange the focused correction areas to include at least five words that the students have never used. I also stipulate

how many paragraphs they must write. Students are able to write substantial compositions when I give them a structural framework.

Final Thoughts

The greatest joy that came from the implementation of this spelling assessment came from Chrissy. As she was writing in her journal about her show dog, she asked me to help her spell a word. I told her to do the best she could and circle the word if it did not look right. Following this single prompt, she continued to write and diligently circled other misspelled words. She then used a spell-checker to correct those words.

This child had never received an A on a spelling test, but that day she received an A from me!

References

Darch, C., Kim, S., Johnson, S., & James, H. (2000). The strategic spelling skills of students with learning disabilities: The results of two studies [Electronic version]. *Journal of Instructional Psychology, 27*(1), 15–27.

Gill, C. H., & Scharer, P. L. (1996). "Why do they get it on Friday and misspell it on Monday?" Teachers inquiring about their students as spellers. *Language Arts, 73,* 89–96.

Heald-Taylor, B. G. (1998). Three paradigms of spelling instruction in grades 3 to 6. *The Reading Teacher, 51*(5), 404–413.

Jones, C. J. (2001). Teacher-friendly curriculum-based assessment in spelling. *TEACHING Exceptional Children, 34*(2), 32–38.

MacArthur, C. A., Graham, S., Haynes, J. B., & DeLaPaz, S. (1996). Spelling checkers and students with learning disabilities: Performance comparisons and impact on spelling. *The Journal of Special Education, 30*(1), 35–57.

Wilson, B. A. (1996). *Wilson reading system* (3rd ed.). Milbury: Barbara A. Wilson.

Kelly A. Loeffler, *Learning Support Teacher. Cumberland Valley School District, Mechanicsburg, Pennsylvania.*

Address correspondence to Kelly A. Loeffler, Cumberland Valley School District, 6746 Carlisle Pike, Mechanicsburg, PA 17050. (e-mail: kloeffler@cvschools.org).

Group Intervention
Improving Social Skills of Adolescents With Learning Disabilities

Deborah Court • Sarah Givon

The move to integrate students with learning disabilities into the general education system calls for assistance in helping them in adjusting socially. Children and adolescents with learning disabilities have social difficulties in comparison with their peers (Asher, Parker, & Walker, 1996; Elliot, 1988; Margalit & Levin-Alyagon, 1994). They report feelings of loneliness, isolation, and lack of fulfillment in social situations. This social isolation deepens over time, contributing to negative self-image and difficulty in social functioning at maturity (Elliot, 1988).

One Israeli middle school developed a social skills intervention program as part of the general support framework that was offered to students with learning disabilities. Twelve students, ages 13 and 14, participated in a case study of this program. This article describes the program, discusses the results and their implications for other educators, and provides practical suggestions for teachers.

Social Skills Deficits and Friendship Groups

Adolescence is a critical time in the social world in terms of self-evaluation and self-confidence. Healthy social interaction is important and helps to prepare youth for normal adult functioning, including independence and fitting in to a work environment. (Bauminger, 1990).

> **STUDENTS WHO HAVE CHALLENGES IN SOCIAL SKILLS OFTEN DEVELOP SOCIAL ISOLATION THAT DEEPENS OVER TIME, CONTRIBUTING TO NEGATIVE SELF-IMAGE.**

According to Smilansky (1988), during a child's process of maturing, friendship groups fulfill essential functions in terms of socialization: support, social comparison, models to imitate, conscience, the giving of status and authority, support in separating from parents, and a basis for future connections. The group offers

training in social connections and different kinds of social interactions.

For these reasons, social skills training in a group setting can be especially helpful to youngsters with social difficulties. Group treatment is built on three elements that have been shown to be effective: (a) creation of a social situation, (b) active participation in discussion, and (c) the use of group support (Shectman, 1993). Group counseling has been shown to be an important element of a treatment program for adolescents with learning disabilities (Margalit, 1991). In such a group, the adolescent is equal with the other members and can cope with social skills in an active way. This is an important factor in improving social skills.

The present case study involved two groups, one with six boys and one with six girls, all 13 or 14 years in age. Interviews with the students, observations in various settings, and a loneliness questionnaire (Margalit, 1995) determined students' feelings. Six of the students had nonverbal disabilities (four of these were extroverted and socially rejected, and two were introverted and socially rejected), and six had verbal learning disabilities (four were introverted and socially neglected, and two were more extroverted and somewhat more accepted by classmates).

The Nature of the Life Skills Program

Each group met once a week during a 5-month period. Meetings were built into students' regular class timetables so as not to be disruptive. This was a multifaceted, modular treatment program. The model includes practice in problemsolving strategies, as well as emotional development and self-awareness that are affectively based (expressing feelings and imagining the feelings of others; see Figure 1).

Students participated in 20 hour-long meetings during which they discussed a variety of topics concerning social skills. Topics included making friends, getting to know people, assertiveness, dealing with anger, small talk, and listening. Each lesson presented one particular skill.

Each lesson included visual, verbal, and written media so that each participant could grasp the material, no matter what his or her learning disability was. The students examined different methods of solving imagined problems, and the students related problems they had experienced or seen in real life. The tools and rationale presented by the group leader (the researcher) helped students to advance in social (and self) understanding. They learned

new skills, practiced during the week, and talked about what happened at the next meeting. They also tried to observe other people using these skills in social situations.

Results

Though these results were unanticipated, we did find marked differences in self-evaluation and self-image between boys and girls. Boys saw the treatment groups as a place to solve problems in a legitimate way, as they would in a lesson offering extra academic assistance, for example, and perhaps because of this they felt no stigma or social embarrassment about attending the sessions.

Despite their willingness to attend, however, they had more difficulty than girls in discussing and developing awareness of their problems. The extroverted boys, especially, expressed a need to "fix" the environment and their friends rather than confronting their own problems.

In contrast, it was difficult to convince the girls to come to the room where the sessions took place. They worried about the opinions of their peers, trying to arrive stealthily and unseen by others. Despite this behavior, all the girls were very aware of their own social difficulties. They were open and, even in the pretreatment interviews, spoke with pain about their social situations.

Identification and Expression of Social Feelings—The Emotional Realm

Almost all the participants showed great improvement in identifying and expressing their feelings and understanding their social situation. Only two boys did not, and their inconsistent results were likely caused by interruptions in the Ritalin they were taking. These boys passed through stages of denial, blaming the environment, demanding change in others, and lacking understanding of their social situations.

The other 10 students, those with verbal and those with nonverbal disabilities, reached the stage where they were able to check and evaluate their standing and their social situations, to discuss them clearly and with good communication, to express feelings, and to correctly identify their own feelings. Not everyone succeeded in identifying *others'* feelings. This was most prominent among those with nonverbal disabilities who found it difficult to "read" social situations and the feelings of others. They were absorbed in their own situation and had difficulty explaining others. One of these boys said during treatment, "I feel that I understand what I need to do, but I don't yet understand how to do it." One of the girls said, "I understand the words that you're saying, but with my friends it doesn't happen."

Figure 1. The Life Skills Program

Topics	Activities
• Self-development	• Role playing and simulations of real and hypothetical situations
• Friendship	
• Communication skills and behavior	• Group analysis of hypothetical events
• Problem-solving and decision making	
• Coping with situations of stress and change	• Discussions of problems seen on TV and read about in stories
• Assertiveness	
• Self- and program evaluation	• Discussions of personal problems and success in the social realm

Note: While the authors would be happy to supply the entire life skills program upon request, at present it exists only in Hebrew.

Social Skills—The Cognitive and Executive Realm

Most of the participants advanced in the area of social skills, though in some cases the advancement was slight, probably because of the relatively short duration (5 months) of the treatment. Two of the boys regressed. These were the two with attention deficit disorder who took Ritalin inconsistently.

The most significant changes in social skills were found among students with verbal learning disabilities. There was an especially dramatic change among four participants with verbal learning disorders who, before treatment, were neglected by their classmates; were introverted, shy, and taciturn; and did not take part in conversations or discussions in their home classes or peer groups. The greatest change among these four was in problem-solving.

It appears that the model of problem-solving presented during treatment strongly influenced all participants and was helpful to those with both verbal and nonverbal disabilities. Those with verbal disabilities improved in terms of communication and identification and expression of feelings.

One girl from this group said at the end of the treatment, "Using the things I learned here really helped me… Now I have more confidence to speak and to express my opinion because usually I'm quiet. But in the small group, I felt that I did speak enough, and I said what I had to say."

All students had difficulty in initiating social contacts, and no improvement was seen in this area. All agreed that the treatment time was too short and that more time was needed.

Interpersonal Relations and Social Interactions—The Social Realm

Most of the participants felt that there was a slight change in their social standing after the treatment. Four participants who were socially neglected, introverted, and had a verbal learning disability changed their social standing, not only according to their own assessment, but according to the before-and-after treatment sociometric questionnaires in their classrooms and their teachers' assessments. This was especially true if they had a particular friend in the home classroom (even if the classroom teacher assisted the friendship).

Improved social skills made it easier to find a friend, and having a friend seemed in itself to make classmates view participants more favorably. Improved social standing, however, did not affect participants' feelings of loneliness, and, in some cases, feelings of loneliness increased.

Four participants with nonverbal disabilities who were socially rejected, extroverted, and aggressive—especially the two boys who stopped taking their Ritalin—reported increased loneliness. Two participants with nonverbal disabilities who were introverted and had a tendency to blame themselves, experienced greater feelings of loneliness as their awareness and understanding of their social situations increased. They became depressed and experienced feelings of failure because, despite their improved personal skills and strong efforts to participate more socially, their peer group was not responsive, seeming unable to grasp that changes had taken place in these students.

One of the girls said, "I really want to change my standing in the classroom. It's hard for me to get into a popular group in the class. The kids still relate to my old image. … There are closed groups in the class. No one understands that I am starting to change, and they won't give me a chance to get into a group."

Feedback from parents indicated that in most cases, they saw significant improvement in their children's afterschool connections with friends. Many reported that their children started to go to afterschool activities at school and that the atmosphere at home surrounding interactions within the family (i.e., with siblings and parents) improved. Some participants started to attend youth groups, and some found new friends in their neighborhoods and had more confidence when playing outside. This was more pronounced among boys, except for the two boys who experienced interruptions in their Ritalin schedule. All the participants expressed the feeling that they had advanced in terms of social connections and interaction; but, again, they felt that others in the environment were not responsive.

One of the introverted boys said, "I feel that I have advanced. I am more assertive and don't always give in." One of the boys who was extroverted and aggressive said, "Now I am trying to 'think positively.'"

Some of the participants expressed their desire to use some of the techniques they had learned to improve the atmosphere at home. One of the girls said, "I have to help more at home, so Dad will understand us and not yell so much… He denies that he's a 'hothead.'"

Parents made similar comments: "She is trying to teach us… She tells us to 'think positively.'" The parents confirmed that their children's attempts to be a positive influence at home gave them a "push" and that the atmosphere was indeed improved.

Friendship Connections and Feelings of Loneliness—The Interpersonal Realm

One of the interesting findings was that most of the participants had increased feelings of loneliness after treatment. Before treatment, most had difficulty defining friendship. The need for an intimate friend increased with treatment. Two girls and two boys who felt they had undergone real change after treatment stated that others in the environment were not aware of their changes and that their classmates related to them as if they had not changed. Thus, it was still hard for them to find friends. Four of the participants, whose classroom teachers helped to match them with a friend, felt more confident and expressed less loneliness, even though the friendships were not of the same quality as those naturally formed.

As far as the kind of connections participants had with these teacher-orchestrated friends, it appeared that they were of lower quality, less concrete, and less intimate than naturally formed friendships. All participants expressed their desire for naturally formed, equal friendships, and most hoped a friend would help them, spend time with them, understand them, and do things together that they liked to do.

The girls showed more signs of intimacy and emotional connection in their descriptions of a good friend. At the end of treatment, girls said things like the following:

- "[A friend is] someone who won't forget me and will always help me."
- "We would have interesting and personal conversations."
- "We would play together outside and at home."
- "Always together."
  Boys said things like these:
- "[A friend is] someone who always does what I want, like my servant."
- "A friend [is someone] that likes what I like, like soccer and basketball."

Implications for Educators

There seem to be connections among several factors in the lives of the students in our study: (a) the kind of learning disability, (b) the nature of the adolescent's behavior, and (c) his or her social standing and social skills. In our study, students with verbal learning disabilities made greater social advancements than did those with nonverbal learning disabilities. This correlates with findings from other studies that children with nonverbal learning disabilities are at high risk for social difficulties and are the least socially adaptive (Gross-Tsur et al., 1995). We found that social skills prac-

tice did not greatly influence these participants or change their situation, in spite of their desire for change and their good verbal ability. Those with nonverbal disabilities may have a defective ability to acquire communication skills. Those with verbal disabilities can acquire these skills because of their better ability to understand gestures, read facial features, and speak with normal intonation.

THE TEACHER HAS A CRUCIAL ROLE IN DIRECTING STUDENTS, FINDING POTENTIAL FRIENDSHIP PAIRS, AND CREATING SITUATIONS THAT REQUIRE COOPERATION.

Given these factors, it may be that students with nonverbal disabilities would prosper under a different kind of treatment that teaches them in a specific way how to substitute socially positive behaviors for problem behaviors. To design such a program that includes this tailor-made dimension, educators would first need to identify problem behaviors through a functional behavior assessment of the kind suggested in the Individuals with Disabilities Education Act (IDEA; Fitzsimmons, 1998). Part of the rationale for such assessments is that problem behaviors fulfill social needs, such as the need for attention. If new social skills and positive behaviors can fulfill these same needs, there is a good chance that students with nonverbal disabilities can learn to replace old behaviors with new. In future development of the Life Skills program, we will introduce functional behavior assessments for students with nonverbal learning disabilities as part of the pretreatment assessment.

One of the surprises in our findings was that most of the participants' feelings of loneliness increased after treatment. With advancement in social skills and in the students' expectations

for change, understanding of their situations increased, as well as their feelings of loneliness. Students whose teachers matched them with a friend felt less lonely. We agree with Bergen (1993) and Margalit (1991) that the teacher has a crucial role in directing students, finding potential friendship pairs, and creating situations that require cooperation, as well as helping and encouraging parents to nurture these friendships outside of school.

The relatively slight improvement in social standing achieved by all participants may have been affected by the short, 5-month duration of the treatment. Their peer group did not have enough time to sense the changes. Social stigmas that are sometimes attached to those with learning disabilities can be hard to change, and it may be that some kind of directed intervention is needed in the home classrooms. If teachers and counselors worked consistently toward the goal of changing classroom culture, it might be possible to create an environment that is more flexible and more accepting of differences.

WITH ADVANCEMENT IN SOCIAL SKILLS AND IN THE STUDENTS' EXPECTATIONS FOR CHANGE, UNDERSTANDING OF THEIR SITUATIONS INCREASED AS WELL AS THEIR FEELINGS OF LONELINESS.

More research is needed on the relationship between verbal and nonverbal learning disabilities and adolescents' social skills. Research should also investigate the effects of different kinds of intervention, including group and individual treatment and the role of the teacher in encouraging friendships. Our study suggests the importance of detailed diagnosis of each student to design appropriate intervention. On the basis of our results, we propose several ideas for teachers and counselors in the areas of diagnosis, social skills intervention design, friendships, and classroom culture. The goal is to help adolescents with learning disabilities have fuller, happier social lives.

Suggestions for Teachers

Diagnosis

- Special education teachers and classroom teachers should utilize all diagnostic and anecdotal evidence available to determine whether a student's disability is verbal or nonverbal in nature.

- Students with nonverbal disabilities could also benefit from a functional behavior assessment.

- Evidence should be collected as to whether the student is socially neglected or rejected, introverted or extroverted, and whether he or she has friends at school and at home.

Intervention Design

- Analysis of these areas should be done to decide what kind of social skills treatment program is likely to be most beneficial and whether group or individual treatment is preferable. Possibly, those with nonverbal learning disabilities are more in need of learning how to replace specific problem behaviors with new behaviors, strengthening their sense of self, and one-on-one counseling and emotional support to improve their ability to cope with characteristics that they cannot change. Those with verbal learning disabilities may respond better to group counseling.

- The topics covered in our Life Skills program and the various discussion and simulation methods employed were helpful to students. We would add a section on initiating social contacts.

Friendships and Classroom Culture

- Assistance by the classroom teacher in helping students form friendships is important, even if these friendships are not of the same quality as naturally formed friendships. Students with any kind of friendship may feel less lonely and may experience increased self-esteem that will lead to greater overall social ease.

- The classroom teacher should engage in teaching *all* students in the home classroom in a structured, systematic way how to help support those with learning disabilities. This could increase the success of intervention programs and improve the integration of those with learning disabilities into general education classrooms. The goal is to help these adolescents become independent adults able to fully integrate into the activities of society.

References

Asher, S. R., Parker, J. G., & Walker D. L. (1996). Distinguishing friendship from acceptance: Implications for intervention and assessment. In W. M. Bukowski, A. F. Newcomb, & W. W. Hatup (Eds.), *The company they make: Friendships in childhood and adolescence.* Cambridge: Cambridge University Press.

Bauminger, N. (1990). *Main characteristics of social skills in adolescents with learning disabilities.* Unpublished master's thesis, The Hebrew University of Jerusalem, Israel (in Hebrew).

Bergen, D. (1993). Teaching strategies: Facilitating friendship development in inclusion classrooms. *Childhood Education, 69*(4), 234–236.

Dimitrovsky, L., Spector, H., Levy-Shiff, R., & Vakil, E. (1998) Interpretation of facial expressions of affect in children with learning disabilities with verbal or nonverbal deficits. *Journal of Learning Disabilities, 31*(3), 286–292.

Elliot, S. N. (1988, April). *Children's social skill deficits: A review of assessment methods and measurement issues.* Paper presented at the annual convention of the American Educational Research Association, New Orleans, LA.

Fitzsimmons, M. (1998). *Functional behavior assessment and behavior intervention plans.* Reston, VA: ERIC Clearinghouse on Disabilities and Gifted Education. ERIC/OSEP Digest E571.

Gross-Tsur, V., Shalev, R. S., Manor, O., & Amir, N. (1995). Developmental right-hemisphere syndrome: Clinical spectrum of the nonverbal learning disability. *Journal of Learning Disabilities, 28*(2), 80–86.

Levin, G. (1997). *Emotional style and emotional problems of learning disabled children.* Unpublished master's thesis, The Hebrew University of Jerusalem, Israel (in Hebrew).

Margalit, M., & Levin-Alyagon, M. (1994). Learning disability subtyping, loneliness, and classroom adjustment. *Learning Disability Quarterly, 17*(4), 297–310.

Margalit, M. (1991). Understanding loneliness among students with learning disabilities. *Behaviour Change, 8*(4), 167–173.

Margalit, M. (1995). Development trends in special education: Advancement in coping with loneliness, social connections and feelings of coherence. In *Education for the 21st century* (pp. 489–510). Tel-Aviv, Israel: Ramot Publishers (in Hebrew).

Rourke, B. P. (1988). Socioemotional disturbances of learning disabled children. *Journal of Consulting and Clinical Psychology, 56*(6), 801–810.

Rourke, B. P. (1989). *Nonverbal learning disabilities: The syndrome and the model.* New York: Guilford.

Shectman, Z. (1993). Group counseling in school in order to improve social skills among students with adaptation problems. *The Educational Counselor, 3*(1) (pp. 47–67) (in Hebrew).

Smilansky, S. (1988). *The challenge of adolescence.* Tel Aviv, Israel: Ramot Publishers (in Hebrew).

Deborah Court, *Lecturer, School of Education, Bar-Ilan University, Ramat-Gan, Israel.* **Sarah Givon,** *Doctoral Candidate, Bar-Ilan University, Ramat-Gan, Israel, and Lecturer, Jerusalem College, Israel. Address correspondence to Deborah Court, School of Education, Bar-Ilan University, Ramat-Gan, Israel 52900. (e-mail: d_court@inter.net.il).*

UNIT 4

Speech and Language Impairments

Unit Selections

12. **Language Differences or Learning Difficulties**, Spencer J. Salend and AltaGracia Salinas
13. **A Speech-Language Approach to Early Reading Success**, Adele Gerber and Evelyn R. Klein

Key Points to Consider

- How can a multidisciplinary team help prevent the over assignment of linguistically diverse children to communication disordered placements? How can assessment tools be selected and adapted for sensitivity to cross-cultural perspectives?

- What can speech-language clinicians teach us about the assessment and remediation of communication and the improvement of reading skills?

Student Website

www.mhcls.com/online

Internet References

Further information regarding these websites may be found in this book's preface or online.

Issues in Emergent Literacy for Children With Language Impairments
http://www.ciera.org/library/reports/inquiry-2/2-002/2-002.html

Speech Disorders WWW Sites
http://www.socialnet.lu/handitel/wwwlinks/dumb.html

Speech and language impairments, although grouped together as a category of disability by the IDEA (Individuals with Disabilities Education Act), are not synonymous. Language refers to multiple ways to communicate (for example by writing, signing, body, or voice), whereas speech refers to vocal articulation.

Many children have difficulty learning to read because of speech and/or language impairments. If they cannot receive language and/or express speech sounds correctly, the total lexicon makes less sense. Likewise, some children assessed as dyslexic (difficulty with the lexicon) are reading disabled primarily because of their disorders with speech and/or language. Telling these disorders apart can be challenging. Learning to communicate may also be difficult for children with hearing impairments, developmental disorders, some physical disorders (eg. Cerebral palsy) and some emotional disorders (eg. Elective mutism).

Speech is the vocal utterance of language. It is considered disordered in three underlying ways: voice, articulation, and fluency. Voice involves coordinated efforts by the lungs, larynx, vocal cords, and nasal passages to produce recognizable sounds. Voice can be considered disordered if it is incorrectly phonated (breathy, strained, husky, hoarse) or if it is incorrectly resonated through the nose (hyper-nasality, hypo-nasality). Articulation in-

volves the use of the tongue, lips, teeth, and mouth to produce recognizable sounds. Articulation can be considered disordered if sounds are mispronounced, or if sounds are added, omitted, or substituted for other sounds, such as using the z sound for the s sound or w for l.

Fluency involves appropriate pauses and hesitations to keep speech sounds recognizable. Fluency can be considered disordered if sounds are very rapid with extra sounds (cluttered) or if sounds are blocked or repeated, especially at the beginning of words. Stuttering is an example of a fluency disorder of speech.

Language is the rule-based use of voice sounds, symbols, gestures, or signs to communicate. Language problems refer to the use of such devices in combinations and patterns that fail to communicate, fail to follow the arbitrary rules for that language, or lead to a delay in the use of communication devices relative to normal development in other areas (physical, cognitive, social).

The prevalence rates of speech and language disorders are higher than the rates for any other condition of disability in primary school. The exact extent of the problem, however, has been questioned because assessment of communication takes a variety of forms. Shy children may be diagnosed with delayed language. Bilingual or multilingual children are often mislabeled as having a language disorder because they come from linguistically and culturally diverse backgrounds. Many bilingual children do not need the special services provided by speech-language clinicians but do benefit from instruction in English as a second language.

All children with language or speech disorders are entitled to assessment and remediation as early in life as the problem is realized. Because children's speech is not well developed between birth and age 3, most disorders are not assessed until preschool. Students with speech-language disorders are entitled to a free and appropriate education in the least restrictive environment possible and to transitional help into the world of work, if needed, after their education is completed.

Disordered language is usually more difficult to remedy than delayed language. Disordered language may be due to a receptive problem (difficulty understanding voice sounds), an expressive problem (difficulty producing the voice sounds that follow the arbitrary rules for that language), or both. Language disorders include aphasia (no language) and dysphasia (difficulty producing language). Many language disorders are the result of a difficulty in understanding the syntactical rules and structural principles of the language (form), or they are the result of a difficulty in perceiving the semantic meanings of the words of the language (content). Many language disorders are also due to a difficulty in using the language pragmatically, in a practical context (function).

Most speech and language impairments are remediated between elementary school and high school. An exception to this is speech problems that persist due to physical impairments such as damage or dysfunction of lungs, larynx, vocal cords, or nasal passages. Another exception is language problems that persist due to concurrent disabilities such as deafness, autism, compromised mentation, traumatic brain injuries, or some emotional and behavioral disorders.

Speech-language clinicians usually provide special services to children with speech and language impairments in pull-out sessions in resource rooms. Computer technology is also frequently used to assist these children in both their regular education classes and in pull-out therapy sessions.

The first article addresses the confusion that exists over whether a child has a cultural/linguistic difference in speech/language or whether the child is, in fact, disabled in the area of communication. Students with limited English proficiency should not be labeled communication disordered unless they are significantly disabled in their mother tongue as well.

The second article discusses a two-stage program for assessment and remediation of early speech or language impairments. Working with young children in the areas of phonetic awareness, discrimination of faulty production of sounds, listening to the sounds of language and correct articulation of sounds will not only correct communication disorders but improve reading skills.

Language Differences or Learning Difficulties

The Work of the Multidisciplinary Team

Spencer J. Salend and AltaGracia Salinas

Maria moved to the United States from Mexico and was placed in Ms. Shannon's fourth-grade class where she sat quietly at her desk and kept to herself. Whenever directions were given, she seemed lost and later had difficulty completing tasks and participating in class discussions. During teacher-directed activities, Maria often either looked around to see what her classmates were doing and then mimicked them, or played with materials at her desk.

Ms. Shannon was concerned about Maria's lack of progress in developing English proficiency and her inability to pay attention and complete her work. Ms. Shannon thought Maria might have a learning disability and referred her to the multidisciplinary team to determine if she needed special education. The team organized the assessment process for Maria by considering the following questions:

- Who can assist the team in making decisions about Maria's educational program?
- What factors should the team consider in determining Maria's educational strengths and needs?
- What strategies should the team employ to assess Maria's educational strengths and needs?
- Should the team recommend a special education placement for Maria?

Educators often refer students like Maria for placement in special education (Ortiz, 1997). As Ortiz indicated, students learning a second language and students with learning disabilities often exhibit similar difficulties with learning, attention, social skills, and behavioral and emotional balance. As a result, multidisciplinary teams are increasingly working with educators like Ms. Shannon to conduct meaningful assessments and determine appropriate educational programs for a growing number of students whose primary language is not English.

Recommendations for Multidisciplinary Teams

Using the experiences of Maria and her teachers, this article provides recommendations for helping multidisciplinary teams accurately and fairly assess second-language learners and differentiate language differences from learning difficulties. The article includes six recommendations, as follows:

- Diversify the composition of the multidisciplinary teams and offer training.
- Compare student performance in both the native and secondary languages.
- Consider the processes and factors associated with second-language acquisition.
- Employ alternatives to traditional standardized testing.
- Identify diverse life experiences that may affect learning.
- Analyze the data and develop an appropriate educational plan.

These recommendations also can assist multidisciplinary teams in developing educational programs for second-language learners and in complying with the Individuals with Disabilities Education Act (IDEA), which states that students should not be identified as having a disability if their eligibility and school related difficulties are based on their proficiency in English, or their lack of opportunity to receive instruction in reading or mathematics.

Diversify the Composition of the Multidisciplinary Teams and Offer Training

IDEA requires that a multidisciplinary team of professionals and family members, with the student when appropriate, make important decisions concerning the education of students referred for special education. Initially, the team determines if students are in need of and eligible for special education services. When teachers refer second-language learners to the multidisciplinary team, the team frequently faces many challenges, such as differentiating linguistic and cultural differences from learning difficulties, and developing an appropriate educational program that addresses students' linguistic, cultural, and experiential backgrounds.

The composition and training of the multidisciplinary team are critical factors in determining the educational needs of second-language learners (Ochoa, Robles-Pina, Garcia, & Breunig 1999). Therefore, the team should include family and community members, as well as professionals who are fluent in the student's native language, understand the student and the family's culture, and can help collect and interpret the data in culturally and linguistically appropriate ways. The inclusion of these people allows the team to learn about the family's and the student's cultural perspective and experiential and linguistic background, and to assist in the determination of the origins of the student's learning difficulties. Team members can help determine what students' learning difficulties can be explained by sociocultural perspectives, experiential factors, and sociolinguistic variables.

The composition of multidisciplinary teams for second-language learners should include educators who are trained in assessing second-language learners and designing educational programs to meet their varied needs. Such membership may include English as a Second Language (ESL) teachers, bilingual educators, and migrant educators. Whereas ESL teachers offer instruction in English to help students build on their existing English language skills, bilingual educators teach students in both their native language and in English. Because bilingual educators are fluent in the family's native language, they can be instrumental in involving family and community members in the team process and in assessing students' skills in their native language. In the case of migrant students like Maria, the team also can benefit from the input of migrant educators, who provide individualized instruction to migrant students and serve as a liaison between the family, the school and the community (Salend, 2001).

> For example, the multidisciplinary team assembled for Maria was expanded to include Ms. Garcia, a bilingual migrant educator who worked with Maria and her family in their home and had training and experience with the second language acquisition process, as well as in working with students from culturally and linguistically diverse backgrounds. Ms. Garcia worked with other members of the team to gather information about Maria's school, home-life and experiential background, to interact with and collect information from Maria, her mother, and other family members, to assess Maria's skills in Spanish, and to identify strategies to support Maria's learning.

The multidisciplinary team can foster the success of the process by working as a collaborative and interactive team (Chase Thomas, Correa, & Morsink, 2001; Salend, 2001). The collaborative and interactive nature of the team can be enhanced by agreeing upon goals, learning about each other's beliefs, experiences and expertise, understanding and coordinating each other's roles, being sensitive to cross-cultural perspectives and communication styles, establishing equal status relationships, and addressing differences directly and immediately. Successful teams adopt a problem solving approach and employ effective interpersonal and communication skills so that all team members feel comfortable identifying issues to be considered by the team, collecting and sharing information, seeking clarification from others, participating in discussions, and making decisions via consensus.

Multidisciplinary teams work with educators to conduct meaningful assessments and determine appropriate educational programs for a growing number of students whose primary language is not English.

Teams can enhance the effectiveness of the process for second-language learners by offering training to team members. Teams should provide this training to all school personnel, and it can help the team members be aware of the effect of sociocultural perspectives, experiential backgrounds, and linguistic variables on students' behavior and school performance. Team members also will benefit from training in employing culturally responsive instructional, behavior management and mental health interventions, understanding the second language acquisition process and the problems associated with the assessment of students from culturally and linguistically diverse backgrounds, and selecting and adapting assessment instruments (Salend, Dorney, & Mazo, 1997).

Teams often face mismatches between members of the team and second-language learners in terms of their different cultural, linguistic, and socioeconomic backgrounds (Gay, 2002).

- What is my definition of diversity?

- What are my perceptions of students from different racial and ethnic groups? With language or dialects different from mine?
- What are the sources of these perceptions?
- How do I respond to my students based on these perceptions?
- What kinds of information, skills, and resources do I need to acquire to effectively teach from a multicultural perspective?
- In what ways do I collaborate with other educators, family members and community groups to address the needs of all my students? (p. 4).

Thus, team members may find it helpful to engage in activities to examine their own cultural perspectives and consider how their cultural beliefs affect their expectations, beliefs, and behaviors and may differ from those held by students and their families (Cartledge, Kea, & Ida, 2000; Hyun & Fowler, 1995; Obiakor, 1999). Montgomery (2001) offered a self-assessment tool that team members can use to reflect upon their understanding of diversity. The tool includes the following questions:

Compare Student Performance in Both the Native and Secondary Languages

After multidisciplinary team members meet, they need to make a plan for assessment. The assessment plan for second-language learners should collect data to compare student performance in both the native and secondary languages. Team members can collect data relating to students' performance in both languages through the use of informal and standardized tests, language samples, observations, questionnaires, and interviews. These methods can be employed to examine students' language proficiency, language dominance, language preference, and code switching. Language proficiency relates to the degree of skill in speaking the language(s) and includes receptive and expressive language skills. Although proficiency in one language does not necessarily mean lack of proficiency in another language, language dominance refers to the language in which the student is most fluent and implies a comparison of the student's abilities in two or more languages. Language preference identifies the language in which the student prefers to communicate, which can vary depending on the setting. Code switching relates to using words, phrases, expressions and sentences from one language while speaking another language.

Collect data relating to students' performance in both languages through the use of informal and standardized tests, language samples, observations, questionnaires, and interviews.

Through observations, informal assessment, and interviews with Maria and her family members, the multidisciplinary team found out that Maria was proficient in Spanish but lacked proficiency in English. It was observed that when Maria spoke Spanish, she was expressive, used the correct tense and age-appropriate vocabulary, and understood all the communications directed to her. Whereas Maria used Spanish to initiate and maintain interactions with others in an organized and coherent manner, her English was characterized by the use of gestures and short, basic sentences to communicate. In addition, observations and interviews revealed that Maria preferred to speak Spanish in all settings, and that Spanish was the dominant language spoken at home, since Maria's mother did not speak English.

Consider the Processes and Factors Associated with Second Language Acquisition

The assessment process for second-language learners like Maria should recognize that learning a second language is a long-term, complex, and dynamic process that involves different types of language skills and various stages of development (Collier, 1995). Therefore, when assessing second-language learners, the multidisciplinary team needs to consider the factors that affect second-language acquisition and understand the stages students go through in learning a second language.

Because proficiency in a second language involves the acquisition of two distinct types of language skills, the team needs to assess students' basic interpersonal communication skills and cognitive/academic language proficiency. The former, the interpersonal skills are the social language skills that guide the development of social relationships (e.g., "Good morning. How are you?"). Even though they are relatively repetitive, occur within a specific and clearly defined context, and are not cognitively demanding, research indicates that they typically take up to 2 years to develop in a second language (Cummins, 1984).

Cognitive proficiency, on the other hand, refers to the language skills that relate to literacy, cognitive development, and academic development in the classroom. It includes understanding such complex academic terms as photosynthesis, onomatopoeia, and least common denominator. Because this proficiency does not have an easily understood context, and tends to be cognitively demanding, it often takes up to 7 years for children to develop and use these language skills. Since cognitive skills developed in one's first language foster the development of cognitive proficiency in one's second language, we must gather information on students' proficiency and educational training in their native language.

An analysis of Maria's English language skills indicated that she was starting to develop a mastery of interpersonal language skills and struggling in terms of her cognitive language proficiency. For example, Ms. Shannon reported that when Maria was given directions to perform a classroom activity in English, she had difficulty completing it. However, when the directions were explained in Spanish, she was able to complete the task.

In learning a second language, students go through developmental stages that team members should consider when evaluating students' learning.

In learning a second language, students also go through developmental stages (see Figure 1) that team members should consider when evaluating students' learning (Maldonado-Colon, 1995). Initially, second-language learners' understanding of the new language is usually greater than their production. Many second-language learners go through a silent period in which they process what they hear but refrain from verbalizing. This is often misinterpreted as indicating a lack of cognitive abilities, disinterest in school, or shyness. Once students are ready to speak their new language, their verbalizations gradually increase in terms of their semantic and syntactic complexity.

Observations of Maria in her class indicated that she was focusing on understanding via mimicking others and using visual and context clues, and that she communicated via pointing, physical gestures and the occasional use of one to three-word phrases. Therefore, the multidisciplinary team felt that she was functioning at the preproduction and early production stages of learning English.

The team should also be aware of other factors that may affect students and their developmental progress in maintaining their native language and learning their new language such as age, educational background, and language exposure. Students who have been educated in their native language often progress faster in learning a new language that those who have not had a formal education (Thomas & Collier, 1997). In addition, students may attempt to apply the rules of their first language to their second language, which can affect their pronunciation, syntax, and spelling (Tiedt & Tiedt, 2001). And as some students learn a second language, they may experience language loss in their native language. Similarly, children who simultaneously learn two languages from

birth may initially experience some temporary language delays in achieving developmental language milestones and some language mixing. These tend to disappear over time (Fierro-Cobas & Chan, 2001).

Figure 1. Stages of Second-Language Learning

1. **Preproduction or Silent period.** Students focus on processing and comprehending what they hear but avoid verbal responses. They often rely on modeling, visual stimuli, context clues, key words and use listening strategies to understand meaning, and often communicate through pointing and physical gestures. They may benefit from classroom activities that allow them to respond by imitating, drawing, pointing, and matching.
2. **Telegraphic or Early Production period.** Students begin to use two- or three-word sentences, and show limited comprehension. They have a receptive vocabulary level of approximately 1,000 words and an expressive level that typically includes approximately 100 words. They may benefit from classroom activities that employ language they can understand, require them to name and group objects, and call for responses to simple questions.
3. **Interlanguage and Intermediate Fluency period.** Students speak in longer phrases and start to use complete sentences. They often mix basic phrases and sentences in both languages. They may benefit from classroom activities that encourage them to experiment with language and develop and expand their vocabulary.
4. **Extension and Expansion period.** Students expand on their basic sentences and extend their language abilities to employ synonyms and synonymous expressions. They are developing good comprehension skills, employing more complex sentence structures, and making fewer errors when speaking. They may benefit from classroom literacy activities and instruction in vocabulary and grammar.
5. **Enrichment period.** Students are taught learning strategies to assist them in making the transition to the new language.
6. **Independent Learning period.** Students begin to work on activities at various levels of difficulty with heterogeneous groups.

SOURCE: *Creating Inclusive Classrooms: Effective and Reflective Practices* (4th ed., p. 91) by S. J. Salend, 2001, Columbus, OH: Merrill/Prentice Hall. Reprinted by permission of Pearson Education, Inc.

Employ Alternatives to Traditional Standardized Testing

As mandated by the latest reauthorization of IDEA, rather than relying solely on potentially biased, standardized tests, the multidisciplinary team should employ a variety of student-centered, alternative assessment procedures to assess the educational needs of students from culturally and linguistically diverse backgrounds accurately. Such assessment alternatives include performance-based and portfolio assessment, curriculum-based measurements, instructional rubrics, dynamic assessment, student journals and learning logs, and self-evaluation techniques (Salend, 2001). These assessment alternatives can provide the Multidisciplinary Team with more complete profiles of students like Maria including their academic strengths and needs, learning styles and the impact of the school environment on their learning.

In the case of Maria, the multidisciplinary team worked with Maria and Ms. Shannon to create a portfolio that showed that Maria's decoding and reading comprehension skills in Spanish were age appropriate. It also revealed that she reads phonetically, engages in self-correction, and uses context and semantic cues. These results were also confirmed by Maria's performance on a standardized Spanish reading test.

Identify Diverse Life Experiences That May Affect Learning

Many second-language learners have diverse life experiences that can have a significant effect on their learning. These experiences may include being separated from family members for extended periods of time (Abrams, Ferguson, & Laud, 2001). Identifying these experiences can help the team determine if students' learning difficulties are related to the existence of a disability or other experiential factors. Therefore, the team can use the guidelines in Figure 2 to collect information to determine if a student's difficulties in learning result from language, cultural, and experiential factors, acculturation, psychological and family traumas, economic hardships, racism, or lack of exposure to effective instruction.

Learning a second language is a long-term, complex, and dynamic process that involves different types of language skills and various stages of development.

Ms. Garcia was able to obtain information about Maria by speaking with Maria and her mother. Ms. Garcia reported that Maria had not had an easy life. She lived in a rural village in Mexico and sporadically attended a school that had limited resources. Maria traveled to the United States with her mother and her three siblings a year ago to join her father and two older brothers who had been working in the United States. Two other siblings remained in Mexico with the hope of joining the family when enough money could be saved to bring them to the United States. Two other siblings remained in Mexico with the hope of joining the family when enough money could be saved to bring them to the United States. However, within 6 months of living in the

United States, Maria's parents separated; and her father returned to Mexico. Maria reported that she misses her life in Mexico and her siblings who are still living there.

Upon arriving in the United States, Maria's mother found a job working as a migrant farmworker. Because she doesn't speak English, did not attend school, and works long hours to make ends meet, Maria's mother finds it difficult to help Maria with her schoolwork and relies on Maria to help take care of the younger children, and to cook and clean. Maria's mother also said that although her children watch cartoons in English, the interactions in the home are in Spanish. Interactions with the family also revealed that the family has few links to and interactions with the community, and that their lifestyle parallels the traditions of Mexico.

Code switching relates to using words, phrases, expressions and sentences from one language while speaking another language.

This information was helpful to the multidisciplinary team in providing information regarding Maria's learning abilities. First, it revealed that Maria's learning ability may be related to the fact that she has not regularly attended school and that the school she attended in Mexico is very different form her current school. Second, Maria's mother relies on her to help around the house; and Maria has quickly learned to perform these roles, which shows that she learns by active participation and is viewed by her mother as responsible and independent. Third, Maria has had limited exposure to English, which affects her progress in learning English and performing in school.

Analyze the Data and Develop an Appropriate Educational Plan

After the team has collected the data, team members meet to analyze the data and make decisions about students' educational programs. For second-language learners, the analysis should focus on examining the factors that affect learning and language development, determining if learning and language difficulties occur in both languages, and developing an educational plan to promote learning and language acquisition. Damico (1991) offered questions that can guide the team in examining the data to assess the extent to which students' diverse life experiences and cultural and linguistic backgrounds serve as

Figure 2. Life Experience Factors and Questions

Length of Residence in the United States

- How long and for what periods of time has the student resided in the United States?
- What were the conditions and events associated with the student's migration?
- If the student was born in the United States, what has been the student's exposure to English?

Students may have limited or interrupted exposure to English and the U.S. culture, resulting in poor vocabulary and slow naming speed, and affecting their cultural adjustment. Trauma experienced during migration or family separations as a result of migration can be psychological barriers that affect learning. Being born and raised in the United States does not guarantee that students have developed English skills and have had significant exposure to English and the U.S. culture.

School Attendance Patterns

- How long has the student been in school?
- What is the student's attendance pattern? Have there been any disruptions in school?

Students may fail to acquire language skills because of failure to attend school on a regular basis.

School Instructional History

- How many years of schooling did the student complete in the native country?
- What language(s) were used to guide instruction in the native country?
- What types of classrooms has the student attended (bilingual education, English as a second language, general education, speech/language therapy services, special education)?
- What has been the language of instruction in these classes?
- What is the student's level of proficiency in reading, writing, and speaking in the native language?
- What strategies and instructional materials have been successful?
- What were the outcomes of these educational placements?
- What language does the student prefer to use in informal situations with adults? In formal situations with adults?

Students may not have had access to appropriate instruction and curricula, resulting in problems in language acquisition, reading, and mathematics.

Cultural Background

- How does the student's cultural background affect second language acquisition?
- Has the student had sufficient time to adjust to the new culture?
- What is the student's acculturation level?
- What is the student's attitude toward school?

Since culture and language are inextricably linked, lack of progress in learning a second language can be due to cultural and communication differences and/or lack of exposure to the new culture. For example, some cultures rely on the use of body language in communication as a substitute for verbal communication. Various cultures also have different perspectives on color, time, gender, distance, and space that affect language.

Performance in Comparison to Peers

- Does the student's language skill, learning rate, and learning style differ from those of other students from similar experiential, cultural, and linguistic backgrounds?
- Does the student interact with peers in the primary language and/or English?
- Does the student experience difficulty following directions, understanding language, and expressing thoughts in the primary language? In the second language?

The student's performance can be compared to that of students who have similar traits rather than to that of students whose experiences in learning a second language are very different.

Home Life

- What language(s) or dialect(s) are spoken at home by each of the family members?
- When did the student start to speak?
- Is the student's performance at home different from that of siblings?
- What language(s) or dialect(s) are spoken in the family's community?
- Is a distinction made among the uses of the primary language or dialect and English? If so, how is that distinction made? (For example, the non-English language is used at home, but children speak English when playing with peers.)
- What are the attitudes of the family and the community toward English and bilingual education?
- In what language(s) does the family watch television, listen to the radio, and read newspapers, books, and magazines?
- What is the student's language preference in the home and community?
- To what extent does the family interact with the dominant culture and in what ways?

Important information concerning the student's language proficiency, dominance, and preference can be obtained by soliciting information from family members. Similarly, the student's acquisition of language can be enhanced by involving family members.

Health and Developmental History

- What health, medical, sensory, and developmental factors have affected the student's learning and language development?

A student's difficulty in learning and acquiring language may be related to various health and developmental variables.

Source: Creating Inclusive Classrooms: Effective and Reflective Practices (4th ed.; p. 94–95) by S. J. Salend, 2001, Columbus, OH: Merrill/Prentice Hall. Reprinted by permission of Pearson Education, Inc.

Figure 3. Differentiating Instruction for Second-Language Learners

- Establish a relaxed learning environment that encourages students to use both languages.
- Label objects in the classroom in several languages.
- Encourage and show students how to use bilingual dictionaries and Pictionaries.
- Use repetition to help students acquire the rhythm, pitch, volume, and tone of the new language.
- Use simple vocabulary and shorter sentences, and limit the use of idiomatic expressions, slang, and pronouns.
- Highlight key words through reiteration, increased volume and slight exaggeration, and writing them on the chalkboard.
- Use gestures, facial expressions, voice changes, pantomimes, demonstrations, rephrasing, visuals, props, manipulatives, and other cues to communicate and convey the meaning of new terms and concepts.

- Preview and teach new vocabulary, phrases, idioms, structures and concepts through use of modeling, and hands-on experiences.
- Supplement oral instruction and descriptions with visuals such as pictures, charts, maps, graphs, and graphic organizers.
- Offer regular summaries of important concepts and check students' understanding frequently.
- Emphasize communication rather than form.
- Correct students indirectly by restating their incorrect comments in correct form.

Sources: Choice of Languages in Instruction: One Language or Two?, by A. Brice and C. Roseberry-MeKibbin, 2001, *TEACHING Exceptional Children, 33*(4), pp. 10–16.
The Changing Face of Bilingual Education, by R. Gersten, 1999, *Educational Leadership, 56*(7), pp. 41–45.
Below the Tip of the Iceberg: Teaching Language Minority Students, by V. Fueyo, 1997, *TEACHING Exceptional Children, 30*(1), pp. 61–65.

explanations for the difficulties they may be experiencing in schools. These questions include the following:

- What factors and conditions may explain the student's learning and/or language difficulties (e.g., stressful life events, lack of opportunity to learn, racism, acculturation, and experiential background)?
- To what extent does the student demonstrate the same learning and/or language difficulties in community settings as in school and/or in the primary language?
- To what extent are the student's learning and/or language difficulties due to normal second language acquisition, dialectical differences, or cultural factors?
- Did bias occur prior to, during, and after assessment such as in the reliability, validity,and standardization of the test as well as with the skills and learning styles assessed?
- To what extent were the student's cultural, linguistic, dialectic and experiential backgrounds considered in collecting and analyzing the assessment data (e.g., selection, administration, and interpretation of the test's results, prereferral strategies, learning styles, family involvement)?

These questions also can guide the team in differentiating between two types of second-language learners (Rice & Ortiz, 1994), and planning appropriate educational programs for these students. One type of second-language learner demonstrates some proficiency in the native language but experiences difficulties in learning a new language that are consistent with the typical difficulties individuals encounter in learning a second language. Although these kinds of behavior are similar to those shown by students with learning difficulties, these students' educational needs can best be addressed through participation in a bilingual education or an English as a Second Language (ESL) program.

The other type of second-language learner exhibits language, academic, and social behavior in the first and second languages that are significantly below those of peers who have similar linguistic, cultural, and experiential backgrounds (Ortiz, 1997). These students may benefit from a special education program and individualized educational programs (IEPs) that address their own linguistic, cultural, and experiential needs (Garcia & Malkin, 1993; Ortiz, 1997). Both types of second-language learners would benefit from the use of strategies for differentiating instruction presented in Figure 3.

Team members will benefit from training in employing culturally responsive instructional, behavior management and mental health interventions.

In the case of Maria, the multidisciplinary team determined that she did not have a disability. The assessment data led the team to conclude that Maria had age-appropriate decoding, reading comprehension, and speaking skills in Spanish and that her difficulties in learning English appeared to be related to the normal process of second-language acquisition and cultural and experiential factors. They also decided that Maria didn't qualify for special education services under the IDEA because her school-related difficulties were based on her lack of proficiency in English and the limited opportunities she has had to receive instruction.

The multidisciplinary team determined that Maria would benefit from the services of a bilingual educator because she needed to strengthen her native language skills to learn academic content and to provide a better foundation for learning English. They also recommended strategies for establishing home-school partnerships and communications, and encouraged her teachers to use cooperative learning strategies and the strategies in Figure 3. The team also developed a plan to collect data to examine the effectiveness of these intervention strategies on Maria's learning, language development, socialization, and her success in school.

Final Thoughts

The ability to acquire and use language has a great effect on students' learning behavior and educational performance. As a result, many second-language learners like Maria exhibit types of behavior that resemble students with learning difficulties and are referred to the multidisciplinary team. Because the team process may vary across school districts, educators need to consider how the recommendations can be incorporated into their assessment process to differentiate between language differences from learning difficulties, and to provide second-language learners with appropriate educational programs.

References

Abrams, J., Ferguson, J., & Laud, L. (2001). Assessing ESOL students. *Educational Leadership, 59*(3), 62–65.

Brice, A., & Roseberry-MeKibbin, C. (2001). Choice of languages in instruction: One language or two? *TEACHING Exceptional Children, 33*(4), 10–16.

Cartledge, G., Kea, C. D., & Ida, D. J. (2000). Anticipating differences—Celebrating strengths: Providing culturally competent services for students with serious emotional disturbance. *TEACHING Exceptional Children, 32*(3), 30–37.

Chase Thomas, C., Correa, V., & Morsink, C. (2001). *Interactive teaming: Enhancing programs for students with special needs* (3rd ed.). Columbus, OH: Merrill/Prentice-Hall.*

Collier, V. (1995). Acquiring a second language for school. *Directions in Language and Education, 1*(4), 1–12.

Cummins, J. (1984). *Bilingualism and special education: Issues in assessment and pedagogy.* San Diego, CA: College-Hill.

Damico, J. S. (1991). Descriptive assessment of communicative ability in Limited English Proficient students. In E. Hamayan & J. S. Damico (Eds.), *Limiting bias in the assessment of bilingual students* (pp. 157–218). Austin, TX: PRO-ED.*

Fierro-Cobas, V., & Chan, E. (2001). Language development in bilingual children: A primer for pediatricians. *Contemporary Pediatrics, 18*(7), 79–98.

Fueyo, V. (1997). Below the tip of the iceberg: Teaching language minority students. *TEACHING Exceptional Children, 30*(1), 61–65.

Gay, G. (2002). Preparing for culturally responsive teaching. *Journal of Teacher Education, 53*(2), 106–116.

Gersten, R. (1999). The changing face of bilingual education. *Educational Leadership, 56*(7), 41–45.

Langdon, H. W. (1989). Language disorder or difference? Assessing the language skills of Hispanic students. *Exceptional Children, 56,* 160–167.

Maldonado-Colon, E. (1995, April). *Second language learners in special education: Language framework for inclusive classrooms.* Paper presented at the international meeting of the Council for Exceptional Children, Indianapolis.

Montgomery, W. (2001). Creating culturally responsive, inclusive classrooms. *TEACHING Exceptional Children, 33*(4), 4–9.

Obiakor, F. E. (1999). Teacher expectations of minority exceptional learners: Impact on accuracy of self-concepts. *Exceptional Children, 66,* 39–53.

Ochoa, S. H., Robles-Pina, R., Garcia, S. B., & Breunig, N. (1999). School psychologists' perspectives on referrals of language minority students. *Multiple Voices, 3*(1), 1–13.

Ortiz, A. A. (1997). Learning disabilities occurring concomitantly with linguistic differences. *Journal of Learning Disabilities, 30,* 321–332.

Rice, L. S., & Ortiz, A. A. (1994). Second language difference or learning disability? *LD Forum, 19*(2), 11–13.

Salend, S. J. (2001). *Creating inclusive classrooms: Effective and reflective practices* (4th ed.). Columbus, OH: Merrill/Prentice-Hall.*

Salend, S. J., Dorney, J. A., & Mazo, M. (1997). The roles of bilingual special educators in creating inclusive classrooms. *Remedial and Special Education, 18,* 54–64.

Thomas, W. P., & Collier, V. P. (1997). *School effectiveness for language minority students.* Washington, DC: National Clearinghouse for Bilingual Education.

Tiedt, P. L., & Tiedt, I. (2001). *Multicultural teaching: A handbook of activities, information, and resources* (6th ed.). Boston: Allyn & Bacon.*

Spencer J. Salend (CEC Chapter #615), Professor, Department of Educational Studies, State University of New York at New Paltz.
AltaGracia Salinas, Special Education Teacher, Alexandria City Public Schools, Virginia.

Address correspondence to Spencer J. Salend, Department of Educational Studies, OMB 112, SUNY New Paltz, 75 South Manheim Blvd., New Paltz, NY 12561 (e-mail: salends@ newpaltz.edu).

From *Teaching Exceptional Children,* March/April 2003, pp. 36–43. © 2003 by The Council for Exceptional Children. Reprinted by permission.

A Speech-Language Approach to Early Reading Success

Adele Gerber • Evelyn R. Klein

We are both speech-language pathologists who, in earlier periods of our careers, have served as specialists in school settings. A substantial part of our caseloads consisted of young children with articulation delays and disorders to whom we provided therapy. One of the procedures we frequently employed was intensive training in speech-sound perception that enabled the children to develop a heightened awareness of the difference between their error production and the corresponding standard sound.

On several occasions, first-grade teachers told us that children receiving articulation therapy excelled in phonics. On the basis of this information, in 1970, I (Adele Gerber) designed a program called Beginning Reading Through Speech in a format appropriate for use in kindergarten and first-grade classrooms. Recently we have revised the procedures to a format suitable for use by tutors or teachers providing individual or small-group training for children needing help mastering emergent literacy and early reading skills.

Over the past few decades, teachers have been informed about results of extensive research that has produced compelling evidence of a strong relationship between phonological awareness and the acquisition of reading awareness—that is, the perception of skills (Chaney, 1998). In particular, professional development programs have placed a heavy emphasis on phonemic awareness—that is, the perception of the speech sounds that form words—and its relevance to the mastery of letter-sound correspondences required for phonic decoding of the written word.

According to most theories of reading development today, phonological decoding is essential to reading.

Having served as a consultant in the Norristown, Pennsylvania Area School District, I received a request from the reading specialist to train teachers in the area of phonemic awareness, providing assistance in understanding the process and information about procedures for its development in children engaged in early reading acquisition. A corps of elementary school teachers participated in an inservice program that presented the rationale and procedures for a speech-language approach to early reading success.

This article describes this speech-language approach, which we designed to help young children learn to associate letters with consonant sounds and to assist children who are struggling with early reading skills. Here, we also provide rationale for this innovative approach and results showing its efficacy.

Rationale for the Speech-Language Approach

According to testimony from the International Reading Association before a congressional briefing regarding effectiveness of reading instruction, "If you want to make a difference, make it different." (National Institute of Child Health and Human Development, 2000). The speech-language approach does employ procedures that differ from traditional approaches to teach letter-sound associations, one of the essential building blocks of early reading success. This approach is unique because it stems from another discipline: speech-language-hearing science.

The necessity of phoneme awareness for reading success is supported by much evidence. Poor readers have deficits in this ability when compared to normal readers of the same age and younger (Badian, 2001; Goswami & Bryant, 1994; Wagner & Torgensen, 1987). According to most theories of reading development today, phonological decoding is essential to reading. The ability to learn the sound-letter associations for decoding printed words is directly related to awareness of the sounds of speech (Kamhi & Catts, 2002).

The Speech-Language Approach

This approach consists of two stages. Stage 1 contains six steps; Stage 2 consists of four steps.

Stage 1: Training Phonemic Awareness for Consonant-Sound Perception

A phoneme is the smallest discrete speech sound in a word that has the capability to distinguish one word from another. For example, the difference between *boy* and *toy* is determined by the initial phonemes /b/ and /t/. Because the sound is embedded in the meaningful context of a word, it is difficult for some children (and some adults) to perceive it as a discrete entity.

Failure in response to conventional phonics instruction is frequently due to attempts to match the abstract form of a letter to a sound that is not perceived.

Phonemic awareness development is critical to the speech-language pathologist's methods of treating articulation disorders. To heighten discrimination between a defective and a standard production of a speech sound, the phoneme is removed from the surrounding sounds in a word and presented in isolation (as a *phone*). Under this condition, the distinctive features of a speech sound are most apparent.

We designed the procedures in this approach to ensure success in a step-by-step progression from identification of each targeted consonant in isolation to recognition of the sound-letter correspondences in words.

According to a report from the National Reading Panel to the National Institute of Child Health and Human Development (2000), phonemic awareness training has caused reading and spelling improvement. The benefits have lasted beyond the end of training.

Step 1: Introduce the sound with a picture-sound symbol. Introduce each consonant sound with its associated picture-sound symbol. The sound picture and associated label capitalize on onomatopoeia (sounds that imitate what they denote).

Cut out each of the 16 picture-sound symbols from Figure 1, and present them individually with a corresponding story that includes multiple productions of the sound in isolation. For example, a student is presented with a story (see Figure 2) about the sound of the letter. The *bubble sound*, /b/, is repre-

Figure 1. The 16 Picture-Sound Symbols

Bubble Sound b   Angry Cat Sound f   Humming Sound m   Clock Sound t

Baby Sound g   Motorboat Sound p   Drumming Sound d   Rooster Sound k-c

Happy Sound h   Motorcycle Sound v   Nasty Sound n   Puppy Sound w

Singing Sound l   Hissing Sound s   Growl Sound r   Jump-rope Sound

Figure 2. The Bubble Story for the /b/ Sound

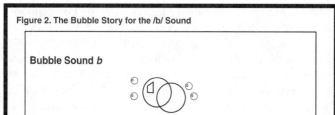

Bubble Sound *b*

(It is recommended to have a large glass ½ full of milk or another preferred drink, a straw, and a bubble blower with soapy water or bubble solution available, if possible). The sound of 'b' is produced as an isolated sound without the vowel sound as in 'buh'.

I'm going to tell you a story about Betty. Betty was a good little girl. She helped her mother make the beds. She never talked back. But there was one thing that she did that her mother did not like. Betty loved to blow bubbles in her glass of milk. Whenever she drank milk she would blow through her straw, like this. (demonstrate) She loved to hear the bubbly sound. The bubbles seemed to say, "b b b b b," etc.

Her mother said, "Betty, why do you like to blow bubbles in your glass?"

Betty said, "Because I love to hear the bubbles say, b b b b b."

Betty's mother said, "I'll buy you a bubble blower and you can blow all the bubbles you want." So Mother bought a little bottle of liquid bubbles and a bubble blower.

Betty blew lots of pretty bubbles. But one day she said to her mother, "Mommy, these bubbles are pretty, but they don't talk."

"What do you mean, the bubbles don't talk?" asked her Mother.

"They don't say, b b b b b," said Betty, "like my milky bubbles do."

"Well," said Mother, "I want you to drink your milk, not blow bubbles in it. But I want you to have fun, too. I have a good idea. I'll put the liquid bubbles in a glass and you can blow talking bubbles with your straw." So Mother put the liquid bubbles in a glass and Betty blew into it with a straw. She heard the bubbles say b b b b b any time she wanted to. But she drank her milk without blowing bubbles. So Mother was pleased, and Betty was happy with her talking bubble sound.

Can you make the bubble sound with me?

Figure 3. Picture-Sound Symbol and Letter Cards

Step 4: Touch the picture of the sound symbol when hearing the sound in easy words. Following the child's approximately 90% correct identification, tell her, "I'm going to say some words. When you hear the bubble sound at the beginning of a word, touch the picture of the bubble. If it is the first word, touch this circle." Point to the circle on the left side, then continue, "And if it is the last word, touch this circle." Point to the circle on the right side. Produce a series of minimally contrastive CVC words that rhyme and include some that start with the /b/ sound. Use two drawn circles (one on the left side of page and one on the right side) to complete this step. Say, "Bat-hat; rake-bake, bin-fin; fill-bill," and so on.

Step 5: Touch the picture of the sound symbol when hearing sound in words. Following the child's approximately 90% correct identification, say, "I'm going to say words one at a time. Touch the picture of the bubble sound when you hear a word that begins with the bubble sound." Produce a randomized list of single words, starting with one-syllable words. If the child masters the task, increase the length of the words. Say, "Bark, house, boy, paint, sing, face, book, lady, tiger, big, party, Bobby, Carlos, Kim, Felix, Billy, Keisha, Luis, Tanya," and so on.

Step 6: Match the correct sound-symbol picture with one of four sounds. After completing Steps 1 through 5 with 4 of the 16 consonants sounds from Figure 1, display those four picture-sound symbols on the workspace. Tell the child, "I'm going to say words that start with different sounds. You point to the picture of the sound you hear at the beginning of each word." The first four picture-sound symbols recommended are: /b/, /f/, /m/, and /t/. Say, "boy, fun, basket, money, tie, fork, talk, big, milk," and so on.

sented by a picture of a bubble displayed to the child (see Figure 3). We encourage teachers to develop their own stories similar in content and style to this example.

Step 2: Touch the picture of the sound symbol when hearing isolated sound. (This procedure applies to each new picture and sound.) Display a picture of the bubbles (picture-sound symbol) on a workspace. Tell the child, "I will say some sounds. Some will be the bubble sound and some will be other sounds. When you hear the bubble sound, touch the bubbles." Produce a series of isolated consonant sounds; for example, "/b/, /l/, /b/, /b/, /f/, /k/, /b/," and so on.

Step 3: Touch the picture of the sound symbol when hearing the sound in syllables. After he achieves approximately 90% correct identification, tell the child: "I'm going to talk baby talk. That means I will talk like a baby. When you hear me say the bubble sound, touch the bubble." Produce a random series of consonant-vowel (CV) nonsense syllables, some starting with the bubble sound. Say, "Ba-ba, fo-fo, bi-bi, sa-sa, ta-ta, ba-ba," and so on.

Stage 2: Matching Letter to Sound—Introductory Systematic Phonics

Step 1: Introduce letters with corresponding picture sound symbols. Display a picture-sound symbol card and a letter card beside it. Tell the child, "This is the letter that goes with the bubble sound. Its name is 'B.' This is the letter that goes with the angry cat sound. Its name is 'F.'" We recommend continuing with the four letters previously taught.

Step 2: Match the picture-sound symbols with letters. Display a group of letter cards and a group of picture-sound symbol cards on the workspace in random order. (The number of cards displayed depends on the level of mastery demonstrated in Step 1.) Tell the child, "We are going to play a matching game. Here are some sound pictures and some letter cards. See how many letters and sound pictures you can match."

Step 3: Identify sound-symbol pictures with various words. If the child achieves approximately 90% accuracy at Step 2, display a group of single-syllable word cards beginning with the targeted consonants; for example: bat, fan, man, tail. Tell the child, "I will say the word. You find the picture of the sound you hear at the beginning of the word. For example, if I say 'bat,' you point to the bubble sound picture."

Step 4: Match the beginning letters with the corresponding words. If the child achieves approximately 90% accuracy at Step 3, display a group of corresponding consonant-letter cards. Tell the child, "I will say some words that begin with these sounds. You pick up the letter that matches the first sound you hear when I say the word." Produce a list of words in random order, matching the picture-sound symbols to the letters. Say one word at a time. We recommend that initially the words consist of single-syllable rhyming groups such as pat, fat, bat, mat, and so on. When the child achieves 90% accuracy at this level, introduce more varied word patterns.

Evidence of Effectiveness

The speech-language approach to early reading success was used in the Norristown, Pennsylvania, School District to reduce the incidence of students with reading delay. In an extended-day tutorial program staffed by classroom teachers, children in first and second grades who scored at the below basic level of reading on the Houghton Mifflin Emergent Literacy Test were scheduled in groups of five per instructor for one-half hour sessions three times per week. A midyear test of progress was administered after a period extending from October, 2001 to February, 2002. Table 1 reflects the pre-and posttest results secured at the beginning of March, 2002.

Table 1. Progress of Students on Tested Emergent Literacy Skills After 5 Months of Training

Emergent Literacy Subtest	Number Students/Grade	Percentage of Students	October 2001 Skill Level	March 2002 Skill Level
Rhyme	31/1st	100%	Below Basic	Proficient
Beginning Sounds	31/1st	100%	Below Basic	Proficient
Blending Onsets/Rimes	31/1st	100%	Below Basic	Proficient
Concepts of Print	31/1st	100%	Below Basic	Proficient
Letter Naming	31/1st	100%	Below Basic	Proficient
Segmenting Onsets/Rimes	31/1st	100%	Below Basic	Basic
Phoneme Blending	31/1st	100%	Below Basic	Basic
Phoneme Segmentation	31/1st	100%	Below Basic	Basic
Word Recognition	31/1st	100%	Below Basic	Basic
Fluency	31/1st	100%	Below Basic	Basic
Word Writing	31/1st	100%	Below Basic	Basic
Sentence Dictation	31/1st	100%	Below Basic	Basic
Rhyme	7/2nd	100%	Below Basic	Proficient
Concepts of Print	7/2nd	100%	Below Basic	Proficient
Letter Naming	7/2nd	100%	Below Basic	Proficient
Fluency	7/2nd	100%	Below Basic	Proficient
Beginning Sounds	7/2nd	100%	Below Basic	Proficient
Blending Onsets/Rimes	7/2nd	100%	Below Basic	Basic
Segmenting Onsets/Rimes	7/2nd	100%	Below Basic	Basic
Phoneme Blending	7/2nd	100%	Below Basic	Basic
Phoneme Segmentation	7/2nd	100%	Below Basic	Basic
Word Recognition	7/2nd	100%	Below Basic	Basic

Of the students tested, seven second-grade students had I.Q. scores in the 60-70 range. Although prior instruction throughout the first grade had not succeeded in the development of emergent literacy skills in these students at the basic or proficient levels, 5 months of instruction in this program achieved progress—to the basic or proficient level skills for all seven students, considered to be developmentally delayed.

The data in Table 1 indicate noteworthy gains that impressed the teachers who implemented the methods. In first grade, 5 of 12 tested areas (42%) showed improvement from below basic to proficient levels and 7 of 12 of the areas (58%) improved from below basic to basic levels for all 31 first graders. In the second grade, half the tested areas showed improvement from below basic to proficient, and the other half of the tested skills areas showed improvement from below basic to basic for all 7 second graders.

The effectiveness of this step-by-step approach to reading success evidenced by the reported gains was further reflected by the reactions of teachers. The reading specialist who was the administrator of the remedial reading program stated, "The teachers loved it." She further expressed her intent to introduce the program into kindergarten classrooms at the beginning of the next school year.

> ## The effectiveness of this step-by-step approach to reading success evidenced by the reported gains was further reflected by the reactions of teachers.

Final Thoughts

The methods used in this program emphasized the importance of connecting the auditory signal of the letter sound to the visual letter. Onomatopoeias relating common items such as the roaring sound of a lion for the sound of /r/ or the sound of a hissing snake for /s/ are used to help make an imprint to associate the concrete sound with the abstract symbol. Tying in a high-interest story that captivates the young listener by using auditory bombardment with repetitive sounds embedded in a story line keeps the children engaged and ready to learn how to associate consonant sounds with letters.

Studies have demonstrated that in early intervention, including phonological awareness, phonetic decoding, letter naming, sound knowledge, whole-word identification, and writing skills, along with reading connected text can be very effective (Vellutino, Scanlon, & Sipay, 1996). From an extensive review of research and practice in the area of emergent literacy, Whitehurst & Lonigan (1998) determined that well-developed language skills, letter knowledge, and some form of phonological sensitivity are necessary for reading and

Students need to have a strong understanding of spoken language before they can understand written language. Our goal is to reduce the incidence of students with reading delay. As reading specialists in an urban-school setting where our less-skilled readers tend to have difficulty identifying, separating, and blending sound segments, we incorporated the speech/language approach in our extended day tutorial reading program. The gains have been noteworthy.
—Reported from teachers in the Norristown School District, 2002

writing and that the origins of these components of emergent literacy are found during the preschool years (Treiman, Tincoff, Rodruquez, Mouzaki, & Frances, 1998).

The early intervention methods used in the speech-language approach incorporate these skills and combine memory-enhancing strategies with phoneme awareness to help prevent problems during emergent literacy and the early reading period. This program approach has been found effective with beginning readers in first and second grades who were functioning at below basic level of early reading prior to instruction and at basic and proficient levels after training.

References

Badian, N. A. (2001). Phonological and orthographic processing: Their roles in reading prediction. *Annals of Dyslexia, 51*, 179-199.

Chaney, C. (1998). Preschool language and metalinguistic skills are links to reading success. *Applied Psycholinguistics, 19*, 433-446.

Goswami, U., & Bryant, P. (1994). *Phonological skills and learning to read.* Hove, UK: Lawrence Erlbaum.

Kamhi, A. G., & Catts, H. W. (2002). The language basis of reading: Implications for classification and treatment of children with reading disabilities. In K. G. Butler & E. R. Silliman (Eds.), *Speaking, reading, and writing in children with language learning disabilities* (pp. 45–72). Mahwah, NJ: Lawrence Erlbaum.

National Reading Panel. (2000). Teaching children to read: An evidence-based assessment of the scientific research literature on reading and its implications for reading instruction (NIH Publication No. 00-4769.) Report of the National Reading Panel. National Institute of Child Health and Human Development. Washington, DC.

Treiman, R., Tincoff, R., Rodriguez, K., Mouzaki, A., & Frances, D. J. (1998). The foundations of literacy: Learning the sounds of letters. *Child Development, 69*(6), 1524-1540.

Vellutino, F. R., Scanlon, D. M., & Sipay, E. R. (1996). Toward distinguishing between cognitive and experiential deficits as primary sources of difficulty in learning to read: The importance of intervention in diagnosing specific reading disability. In B. Blachman (Ed.), *Foundations of reading acquisition and dyslexia: Implications for early intervention* (pp. 347-379). Mahwah, NJ: Lawrence Erlbaum.

Wagner, R. K., & Torgensen, J. K. (1987). The nature of phonological processing and its causal role in the acquisition of reading skills. *Psychological Bulletin, 101*, 192-212.

Whitehurst, G. J., & Lonigan, C. J. (1998). Child development and emergent literacy, *Child Development, 69*, 848-872.

Adele Gerber, Professor Emeritus, Temple University, Department of Communication Sciences, Philadelphia, Pennsylvania. **Evelyn R. Klein** (CEC Chapter #388), Assistant Professor, Department of Speech, Language, Hearing Science, La Salle University, Philadelphia, Pennsylvania.

Address correspondence to Adele Gerber, 600 East Cathedral Road, H316, Philadelphia, PA 19128 (e-mail: adeleg410@aol.com).

From *Teaching Exceptional Children,* Vol. 36, No. 6, July/August 2004, pp. 8-14. Copyright © 2004 by Council for Exceptional Children. Reprinted by permission.

UNIT 5

Developmental Disabilities/ Autistic Spectrum Disorders

Unit Selections

14. **When Does Autism Start?**, Claudia Kalb
15. **Service-Learning Opportunities That Include Students With Moderate and Severe Disabilities**, Harold Kleinert, et al.
16. **Inscrutable or Meaningful? Understanding and Supporting Your Inarticulate Students**, Robin M. Smith

Key Points to Consider

- When does autism start? Can the autistic spectrum disorders be diagnosed earlier?

- Can service-learning be used for assessment as well as education of students with developmental disabilities?

- Students with developmental disabilities may have atypical facial expressions and speech. Are these inscrutable or meaningful? How can teachers and others interpret and use these messages?

Student Website

www.mhcls.com/online

Internet References

Further information regarding these websites may be found in this book's preface or online.

Arc of the United States
   http://www.thearc.org
Disability-Related Sources on the Web
   http://www.arcarizona.org/dislnkin.html
Gentle Teaching
   http://www.gentleteaching.nl

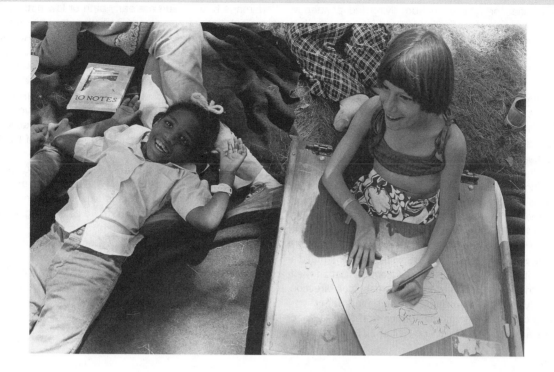

In our efforts to be more "politically correct" and to not inflict pain, we now avoid labels such as "mentally retarded." We always put the individual first and add the condition of disability second (when and if it is necessary). Students and adults who have cognitive skills falling two standard deviations below the norm for their age are now considered cognitively developmentally disabled. Children who have sustained brain damage through traumatic brain injury, even if they score two standard deviations below the intellectual norm for age, are traumatically brain injured, not developmentally disabled or intellectually impaired. Children and adults with autism or autistic spectrum disorder (such as Asperger's syndrome) are subsumed under a separate disability category by the U.S. Individuals with Disabilities Education Act (IDEA). Three out of four individuals with classic autism score two standard deviations below the IQ mean. Nevertheless, cognitive developmental disorders, traumatic brain injuries, and autistic spectrum disorders are each recognized as separate disability categories by IDEA.

Children with significantly subnormal intelligence were once classified as "educable," "trainable," or "custodial" for purposes of placement. These terms are strongly discouraged today. Even severely developmentally disabled children are educable and can benefit from some schooling. They must leave where they are, to be where we hope they can be. The current preferred categorical terms for children who are developmentally challenged are "intermittent," "limited," "extensive," and "pervasive." These terms refer to how much support the individuals need to function and to succeed as much as possible.

IDEA mandates free and appropriate public school education for every child, regardless of mentation. While the legal windows on education are from ages 6 to 16 in the United States, individuals with developmental disabilities are entitled to a free and ap-propriate education from age of assessment (birth, early childhood) to age 21. This encompasses parent-child education programs and preschool programs early in life and transitional services into the community and world of work after the public school education is completed.

The inclusion of children with disabilities in regular education classes has been controversial throughout the time span since 1975. Some school systems have succeeded brilliantly in integrating students with cognitive developmental disabilities into their regular classes. Other schools have fought the law every step of the way. Their dark histories are full of lawsuits brought by parents to try to obtain the services to which the law entitles them. The less-than-stellar school systems, and some U.S. states that have been notorious laggards, complain that the law is too cumbersome. There have been few negative consequences for school systems or whole state education departments who have resisted placing cognitively disabled students in regular classrooms. Therefore some parents still invoke formal complaint procedures against schools to get their children out of full-time special classes or special schools.

A child with a cognitive developmental disability (intellectual impairment) who is in the mildest "intermittent" classification needs support at school at times when special needs arise and at times of life transitions. This terminology is generally used for children whose disabilities do not create an obvious and continual problem. These children have slower mentation but also have many abilities.

The next level of support, classified as "limited," is usually used for children whose disabilities create daily limitations on their abilities but who can achieve a degree of self-sufficiency after an appropriate education in the least restrictive environment. Limited refers to the period of time from diagnosis until adulthood (age 21). The "extensive" support classification extends the support throughout the lifespan for individuals whose developmental disabilities prohibit them from living independently. The "pervasive" support classification is used infrequently. It is only for those individuals whose disabilities prevent them from most activities of self-help. Pervasive support is intensive and life-sustaining in nature.

The majority of children with developmental disabilities (intellectual impairments) can be placed in the intermittent support classification. To casual observers, they often do not appear to have any disabilities. However, their ability to process, store, and retrieve information is limited. In the past, this group of children was given IQ measurements between two and three standard deviations below the mean (usually an IQ below 70 but above 55). Intelligence testing is an inexact science with problems of both validity and reliability. The current definition of developmental disability endorsed by the American Association on Mental Deficiency (AAMD) does not include any IQ scoring results other than to use the phrase "subaverage intellectual functioning." It emphasizes the problems that individuals with developmental disabilities have with adaptive skills such as communication, self-care, home living, social skills, community use, self-direction, health and safety, functional academics, leisure, and work.

The causes of developmental disabilities and autistic spectrum disorders are unclear. About one-half of all individuals are suspected of having sustained some brain damage prenatally, neonatally, or in childhood. Among the better-known factors that damage brain tissue are early birth or low birth weight, anoxia, malnutrition, drugs, viruses, radiation, trauma, and tumors.

The first article in this unit, "When Does Autism Start," describes the autistic spectrum disorders. Claudia Kalb discusses the surge in these diagnoses in recent years, and the incomplete understanding we have of causation. Advanced technology may make it possible to assess the autistic spectrum disorders at earlier ages. New treatments, and more family involvement, will allow better remediation of social and cognitive abilities.

The second article discusses the impact of PL 107-110 (No Child Left Behind) on the education of students with developmental disabilities/cognitive impairments. The use of service-learning projects as a means of demonstrating proficiency in certain core academic subjects is explained. Service-learning has many benefits beyond assessment as well (eg. education, peer interaction, parental involvement).

The third article, "Inscrutable or Meaningful?" discusses the importance of deciphering the emotions, behaviors, and atypical speech and language processes of students with developmental disabilities. Understanding and supporting inarticulate students is critical to their education.

When Does Autism Start?

Scientists are now looking for the earliest signs of the mysterious disorder as desperate parents hunt for treatments that may improve their children's lives.

By Claudia Kalb

It's a winter night in Northbrook, Ill., and brothers David and Jason Craven are on the move. They're watching a "Baby Beethoven" video. They're bouncing on a mattress in their basement playroom. They're climbing up their dad's legs. David, 7, and Jason, 5, with their mops of brown hair, look physically healthy. But both boys are suffering from a devastating developmental disorder: autism. David speaks only about 10 words, still wears diapers at night and sucks on a pacifier. Jason drinks from a baby bottle. Neither one can vocalize his glee as he plays. Neither one can communicate pain or joy in words. Neither one can say "I love you."

Since their sons were diagnosed, both at the age of 2, Barry and Dana Craven have tried a dizzying array of therapies: neurofeedback, music therapy, swimming with dolphins, social-skills therapy, gluten-free diets, vitamins, anti-anxiety pills and steroids. To reduce the boys' exposure to environmental chemicals, which the Cravens believe might aggravate their conditions, the couple replaced their carpeting with toxin-free wood floors and bought a special water-purifying system. They even installed a $3,500 in-home sauna, which they think will help remove metals like mercury and arsenic from the boys' bodies. Warm and loving parents, the Cravens spent $75,000 on treatments last year alone. "I'm willing to try just about anything if it makes sense," says Dana.

In the six decades since autism was identified, modern medicine has exploded: antibiotics cure infections, statins ward off heart disease, artificial joints combat osteoarthritis. And yet autism, a vexing brain disorder, remains largely a mystery. Researchers still don't know what causes it, nor do they know how best to treat a condition that prompts one child to stop speaking and another to memorize movie scripts. With a tenfold spike in numbers over the past 20 years—one in every 166 children is now diagnosed with an Autism Spectrum Disorder (ASD)—researchers, advocacy groups and the government are racing to improve the lives of children and their families, many of them emotionally and financially drained. This year the National Institutes of Health will spend $99 million on autism research, up from $22 million in 1997.

"I haven't been this excited about research in a very long time."
—Wendy Stone, Vanderbilt University

Some of the most exciting new work involves efforts to spot clues of the disorder in infants as young as 6 months. In the complicated world of autism, where controversies reign and frustration festers, a two-word rallying cry is growing louder by the day: early diagnosis. This week the Centers for Disease Control and Prevention launches a $2.5 million autism-awareness campaign, "Learn the Signs. Act Early." The goal: to educate healthcare providers and parents about red flags, to intervene as quickly as possible—and to give kids with autism a shot at productive, satisfying and emotionally connected lives. "This is an urgent public-health concern," says the CDC's Catherine Rice.

Today, most children aren't even seen by specialists until they've passed their 2nd birthdays, and many aren't diagnosed until at least the age of 3. Kids with Asperger's, on the higher-functioning end of ASD, may be overlooked until well into elementary school. "If we had a way of screening for autism at birth and then could begin very early to retrain the brain, that would really be the ticket," says Dr. Thomas Insel, head of the National Institute of Mental Health. Scientists are now attempting to do just that. In a joint effort by the National Alliance for Autism Research and the National Institute of Child Health and Human Development, researchers at 14 sites, from Harvard to the University of Washington, are studying the baby siblings of children with autism, who have a genetic liability for the disorder. By measuring the infants' visual and verbal skills and their social interactions, scientists hope to identify early markers of autism before children turn 1. "I haven't been this excited about research in a very long time," says consortium member Wendy Stone of Vanderbilt University. "Not only are we getting clues about the earliest features of autism, but we're helping these families along the way."

Canadian researchers Dr. Lonnie Zwaigenbaum and Susan Bryson have enrolled 200 siblings, half of whom have been observed to the age of 2. Roughly 10 percent have been diagnosed with autism. Zwaigenbaum, of McMaster University in Ontario, says that signs of the disorder, though at first subtle, are often there from the very beginning. Preliminary data show that 6-month-olds who are later diagnosed with autism generally have good eye contact, but they're often quieter and more passive than their peers. And they may lag behind in motor developments, like sitting up or reaching for objects.

The signs often become more obvious as children reach their 1st birthdays. By then, some show patterns of extreme reactivity, either getting very upset when a new toy or activity is presented or barely noticing at all. Others already exhibit repetitive behaviors characteristic of autism—rocking back and forth or becoming fixated on an object, like a piece of string dangling in front of their eyes. And they're less responsive to playful interactions with others. When a typically developing child plays peekaboo, her face lights up, she looks at the person she's playing with, she makes sounds, she reaches for the peekaboo blanket. Children with autism, by contrast, show little facial expression. They may not look at their playmate, and it can take enormous energy to elicit a reaction. "What's been striking," says Zwaigenbaum, "is the lack of response or the distress that these activities can elicit."

The Baby Sibs consortium is also looking for early physical markers of the disorder, starting with the size of children's heads. A landmark study published in 2003 found that kids with autism experienced unusually rapid head growth between 6 and 14 months. Consortium members want to see if their young siblings do, too. Scientists aren't sure what accounts for the increase, but one theory is that it has to do with an overgrowth of neuronal connections. Normally, the brain clears out biological debris as it forms new circuits. "Little twigs fall off to leave the really strong branches," says University of Michigan researcher Catherine Lord. In kids with autism, however, that pruning process may go awry.

In their hunt for neurological clues, scientists are unveiling the inner workings of the autistic mind. Using eye-tracking technology, Ami Klin, of the Yale Child Study Center, is uncovering fascinating differences in the early socialization skills of children with autism. Klin has found that when affected toddlers view videos of caregivers or babies in a nursery, they focus more on people's mouths—or on objects behind them—than on their eyes. Klin's toddler study echoes findings in adults and adolescents with autism when they watched clips of "Who's Afraid of Virginia Woolf?" "Richard Burton and Elizabeth Taylor were engaged in a passionate kiss, and they're focusing on the light switch," says Klin. "Our goal is to identify these vulnerabilities as early as possible."

Might it be that the autistic brain's operating platform is different, as if it's a Mac in a world of PCs? Functional MRI scans show that the brain's "fusiform face area," the control tower for face recognition, is underactive in people with autism. The more severe the disorder, the more disabled the fusiform. But is it actually dysfunctional? Or is it just not interested in people? In an intriguing early study, Yale's Robert Schultz took brain scans of a child with autism who had trouble distinguishing human faces but loved the cartoon character Digimon. "Lo and behold," says Schultz, "his fusiform showed strong activity." Schultz and James Tanaka at the University of Victoria in Canada are hoping computer games can help kids with autism learn how to engage with human faces and identify emotions. The children follow directions to shoot at smiley faces or click on the guy who looks sad. In "Emotion Maker," they choose features—angry eyes, a scowling mouth—to create their own faces. And in "Who's Looking at Me?" they scan an array of faces to sensitize them to eye contact. So far, says Schultz, the kids appear to be improving. But will it help change the course of their lives? "That's the million-dollar question," he says.

An intellectual thief, autism infiltrates children's brains, stalling or stealing cognitive and social development. In classic autism, babies fail to coo or babble by their 1st birthdays. Or words that do develop ("dada," "up," "toy") inexplicably disappear. One-year-olds don't respond to their names. A child once bursting with potential finds spinning tops more captivating than her mother's smile. Kids with Asperger's may not be as closed off, but they suffer severe social deficits. Many are verbal fanatics, immersing themselves in long-winded monologues about obscure topics, like fat fryers or snakes. Klin recalls a child who bowed and spoke in Shakespearean English, "almost as if I had plucked him from 14th-century Verona." Such oddities can make these children social pariahs. Baffled by human interactions and frustrated by their inability to make friends, some kids spiral into debilitating fits of anxiety and depression. Many children on the autism spectrum will never live independent lives. "We're talking about children who need lifelong care," says NIMH's Insel. "This is an astonishingly devastating disease."

And its current treatment is all over the map. Every day, it seems, there's a new "cure." With no known cause and no clear guidance, parents must navigate a maze of costly therapies, most of which have little hard-core science to prove their effectiveness. Many children now take medications, ranging from anticonvulsants (about one third suffer from seizures) to stimulants like Ritalin to calm hyperactivity. Low doses of antidepressants such as Prozac may help reduce the severity of repetitive behaviors. And risperidone, an anti-psychotic drug, can quell aggression and tantrums, says Dr. Christopher McDougle, of the Indiana University School of Medicine. The drug, whose side effects include weight gain and sedation, is now before the FDA and could become the first medication approved specifically for autism.

"I am willing to try just about anything if it makes sense."

—**Dana Craven,** mother of two boys with autism

Drugs, however, won't help a child learn to speak. One of the few treatments that just about everyone agrees is critical is behavioral intervention, which uses word repetition, game-playing and specialized exercises to develop a child's language and social skills. At the Lovaas Institute in Los Angeles, senior instructor Sona Gulyan engages Adam Ellis, who turns 4 next month, in language drills known as discrete trials. "Say 'hi'," says Gulyan. Adam, a chubby-cheeked little boy in jeans and a white T shirt, responds with a "k" sound. "No, 'hi'," says Gulyan. After several failed attempts, Gulyan switches the focus. "Do this," she says, pointing to her nose. Adam imitates the gesture and is congratulated. And then it's back to the original task: "Say 'hi'." Finally, success—and an orange balloon as a reward. In 1987, founder Ivar Lovaas reported that children who received an average of 40 hours a week of his intensive one-on-one therapy called Applied Behavior Analysis increased their IQs by 30 points, compared with a control group. Other studies, however, have been mixed, and critics believe the program is too militaristic. But for Adam's mother, Megan, it's progress that matters. "He has mastered so many skills," she says. "It's just amazing."

Things are more relaxed at Cleveland's Achievement Centers for Children, where Lisa and Tim Brogan play with their son, Alex. Alex is learning to communicate through an intervention called Floortime, which focuses on a child's individual strengths and his relationships with others. Kids learn to engage with their parents through "circles of communication." If Alex wants to line up toy cars in a row, his dad will join him, then nudge one out of place. The move prompts Alex to interact with his father—a circle of communication—rather than isolate himself with the toys. "We have come such a very long way," says Lisa.

Children with autism have as many styles and personalities as any group of toddlers. A behavioral intervention that suits one child (or his parent) won't necessarily work for another. Many treatment centers now mix techniques from different approaches, including one of the newest on the block: Relationship Development Intervention, or RDI. Here, parents learn how to use everyday events as teachable moments. A trip to the grocery store, for example, becomes an opportunity for kids to learn to adapt to sensory overload—the chatter of shoppers, 100 different kinds of cereal. In the past, Pam Carroll's son, Morgan, now 9, was fixated on instant oatmeal with blueberries, and he melted down if it wasn't available. Now he roams the aisles in Gainesville, Fla., and helps his mom shop. Linda Andron-Ostrow, a clinical social worker in Los Angeles, likes the way RDI empowers parents and allows for creative thinking. "Life isn't structured," she says.

With autism's medley of symptoms—which can include a heightened sensitivity to sound and picky eating habits—many families search for alternative treatments. Kacy Dolce and her husband, Christopher, recently took their son, Hank, 4, to see Mary Ann Block, an osteopath in Hurst, Texas, for a $2,500 assessment. Block prescribes vitamins and minerals, diets free of wheat and dairy, and a controversial treatment, chelation, which strips the body of metals like mercury. Block believes these toxins could come from vaccines and are at the core of autism. Mainstream doctors, pointing to scientific studies showing no connection, worry that chelation puts children at serious risk. Despite the possibility of dangerous side effects, like liver and kidney problems, the Dolces say they'd consider it. "We don't know enough yet to say no," says Kacy. "I'll do anything to help our child."

What parents really need is a road map. Earlier this month six U.S. medical centers joined forces to launch the Autism Treatment Network, which will evaluate therapies, pool data and, ultimately, create guidelines. "We can't have parents chasing down the latest treatment," says Peter Bell of Cure Autism Now, a research and advocacy group allied with the effort. "We need to understand what works." At the forefront of ATN is Massachusetts General's Ladders program, where Dr. Margaret Bauman is using a multidisciplinary approach. In addition to offering standard regimens like physical therapy and behavioral intervention, Bauman assesses overall health. When she saw a teenager crying and twisting her body, symptoms other doctors attributed to autism, Bauman sent her to a gastroenterologist, who found ulcers in her esophagus. The writhing was caused by pain. A boy's head-banging went away after he was treated for colitis. "We really have to start thinking out of the box," says Bauman.

And thinking early. Today many kids aren't getting treatment until well after their 3rd birthdays. Diagnosing an infant with autism at 6 months or a year—maybe even one day in the delivery room—could mean the difference between baby steps and giant leaps. At the Kennedy Krieger Institute in Baltimore, a handful of 2-year-olds toddle at the next frontier in autism treatment. The children are part of an NIH-funded study run by Rebecca Landa to see if early intervention, before the age of 3, can improve the trajectory of cognitive and social development. As Landa looks on, David Townsend fusses and stamps his feet. Then, he notices his twin sister, Isabel, turning the pages of "Ten Little Ladybugs." David looks at Isabel, watches her hands, then flips a page himself, accomplishing what autism experts call "joint engagement." "That was beautiful," says Landa. A fleeting moment, a developmental milestone—and, if all goes well, a new world of possibilities for a sweet little boy with dimples.

With Karen Springen, Ellise Pierce, Joan Raymond and Jenny Hontz

---

Service-Learning Opportunities That Include Students With Moderate and Severe Disabilities

Harold Kleinert   Virginia McGregor   Michelle Durbin   Tina Blandford
Karen Jones   Josh Owens   Beth Harrison   Sally Miracle

Picture this scenario:

For Young at Heart, a monthly social and recreational event targeted specifically for senior citizens, students with moderate and severe disabilities worked with Key Club members to plan and cook a dinner for seniors, as well as plan the entertainment for the evening. During the event, students helped prepare the meal, served it, and participated in the social activities. After a successful evening, the students wrote letters to local businesses to solicit funding for the next event. Students and their peer partners composed reflections and planned a celebration. Teachers included videotaped reflections and activities into students' alternate portfolios to document their learning.

The article describes the experiences of four high schools in Kentucky that have worked to develop inclusive service-learning activities for students with moderate and severe disabilities and their peers (see box, "What Does the Literature Say?"). The students worked through the Kentucky Peer Service-Learning Project. One of the projects was the Young at Heart program, which we describe in more detail later.

Implementing a Service-Learning Project

In implementing our service-learning projects, we have used the steps developed by *Students in Service to America* (2003), with special consideration to the needs and learning characteristics of students with moderate and severe disabilities. *Students in Service to America* described a 10-step process, to which we have added an 11th step, which is to link inclusive service-learning activities to the evidence of learning required for your state's alternate educational assessment under the Individuals with Disabilities Education Act (Amendments of 1997, IDEA '97). We illustrate each step with details of the Young at Heart program, which one of the schools conducted. We also briefly discuss other service-learning projects undertaken by various school districts.

Step 1: Assess the Resources and Needs of Your Community and School

It is essential that we include all students in locating resources and needs. Students with moderate and severe disabilities rarely have the opportunity to plan their learning activities and how they would like to contribute to their community. Students with disabilities and their peers can jointly talk with civic groups and school organizations.

Another strategy is to consider assisting in an existing service-learning activity in your school or community.

For example, in one of our schools, students with disabilities and peer tutors jointly talked with the school principal, counselors, other students in the school, and school service clubs. The students with disabilities and peer tutors found out that the school's Key Club was looking for another group to help out with Young at Heart, A monthly social and recreational event targeted specifically for senior citizens. At this monthly event, students planned and cooked a dinner for seniors, as well as planned the entertainment for the evening.

Step 2: Develop Community Partnerships

Seek out the assistance of community organizations (e.g., churches and nonprofit organizations) in identifying the needs of your community. These organizations can provide direction and consultation to your project. Students with moderate and severe disabilities, in partnership with their typical peers, can meet with these organizations. Such experiences provide valued opportunities to practice communication, social, and problem-solving skills and allows those in the community to perceive students with disabilities in a new light.

- -

Community organizations, like churches and nonprofit agencies, can provide direction and consultation to your project.

- -

In the Young at Heart example, the students not only met with the Key Club members, but also contacted the Center for Senior Citizens each month to let them know the time, date, and theme for each event.

Step 3: Set Clear Educational Goals and Curriculum

Make sure that targeted service-learning skills are an extension of educational goals and individualized education program (IEP) objectives. Teachers can plan to measure achievement of goals through a variety of strategies, including instructional data on IEP objectives, student journals, peer reflections (written by collaborating peers), and letters by local civic groups or community organizations documenting the students' achievements.

In the Young at Heart example, student IEP objectives included

- Initiating and sustaining social interactions,
- Cooking and meal planning skills.
- Functional math skills (planning a budget, purchasing items, measuring, and counting items for each participant).
- Recreational skills (playing card and other table games).

Step 4: Choose Project and Begin Planning

During this step, the students and teacher should complete their evaluation of needs, as well as the extent of their own resources. In selecting the service-learning project, teams should consider community and school partnerships (what part will each play?). In addition, the planning teams should think about how the goals of the service-learning activity will be continued after the project is completed.

In the Young at Heart example, students with moderate and severe disabilities were actively involved in each stage of the planning (e.g., identifying the theme for each evening, the menu, and the recreational activities). The teacher and students have already begun planning how this service-learning project can continue beyond the current year.

In subsequent years, the teacher plans to have her students write letters to businesses to see if they can donate money, supplies, or time to Young at Heart.

Step 5: Plan Project in Detail

During this step, students should develop a specific action plan and a timeline for completing their project, determine a project budget, and assign tasks for themselves, as well as work with any community partners to identify the steps or activities the partners will undertake (*Students in Service to America*, 2003). This step provides students with disabilities and their peers with excellent opportunities to practice time, budgeting, and money management skills and to learn to divide goals into a series of smaller steps or sub-goals.

What does the Literature Say About Service Learning?

Definition. Service learning is a well-recognized strategy for enabling students to integrate and apply the knowledge and skills they learn in school to address significant needs in their schools or communities (Yoder, Retish, & Wade, 1996). Students choose to do activities to benefit their community; within those activities, teachers infuse the academic curriculum and individualized student goals.

What separates service learning from simple volunteer or community service activities is the links to *both* the curriculum *and* to the students' reflections on what they have learned as a result of that activity. Service learning is thus directly tied to the academic curriculum, and for students with disabilities, into their individualized education program (IEP) objectives.

Benefits and Results. Educators are increasingly recognizing service learning as an important learning tool for *all* students.

- In a survey of 13 special educators involved in service-learning projects with their students, Brill (1994) found increases in attendance, academic skills, and social relationships with peers for the students with disabilities.
- Yoder et al. (1996) described an inclusive service-learning program between seventh- and eighth-grade students with learning disabilities, students with limited English proficiency (LEP), and general education students. These authors noted several benefits for this heterogeneous group of students, including increased self-esteem, self-knowledge, communication, problem-solving skills, and social skills.

- The Web site for *Students in Service to America* (2003) has identified other benefits, including enhanced student engagement in school, the opportunity to learn about new careers, and a stronger sense of being part of one's community.
- Little research exists on the use of service learning for students with moderate and severe cognitive disabilities, especially in the context of *inclusive* learning opportunities with their peers. In one such study, Burns, Storey, and Certo (1999) described an inclusive-learning project that included high school students with severe disabilities and students without disabilities. The peers who participated demonstrated significantly more positive attitudes toward people with severe disabilities than they had before their participation. In contrast, these authors found that high school students who engaged in service activities directed solely to *helping* students with severe disabilities (e.g., Special Olympics) did not evidence significant changes in attitude.
- Gent and Gurecko (1998) have also discussed the appropriateness of service learning for students with severe disabilities, and the potential benefits of creating more natural peer supports, responsible citizenship, and integrated learning and assessment strategies. These authors have noted that even students with severe disabilities can learn to reflect on the impact of what they have learned.
- A recent study described service learning as a vehicle for authentic community-referenced instruction for all students (Kluth, 2000). The study showed that the project enabled students with disabilities to practice important life skills, while providing students without disabilities opportunities to connect what they learn in class to the real world.

In the Young at Heart project, students were actively involved in all steps (including the budget) and the teacher carefully considered how each student with a disability could work with a peer.

- -

Students with moderate and severe disabilities were activity involved in each stage of the planning (e.g., identifying the theme for each evening, the menu, and the recreational activities).

- -

Step 6: Seek Necessary Funding and Resources

Some service-learning projects may require additional resources. Other school clubs, faculty, students, parents, faith-based organizations, and local businesses may be willing to help, if asked. In our Young at Heart example, the teacher was able to secure a grant from a nonprofit agency for the activity.

Step 7: Implement and Manage the Project

As students begin their project, teachers should assist them in continuously monitoring their progress. Students with disabilities might even track their own performance on key learning objectives during this step (e.g., a money management skill for a student who has that skill on his or her IEP).

In the Young at Heart program, the students were in charge of decorations, food, and entertainment for each monthly event. For the Thanksgiving event, the students decided to have formal seating for the dinner, with a peer and a student with a disability seated at each table with several senior citizens in order to get to know the seniors better.

One student with a moderate disability, whose IEP objectives included initiating and sustaining interactions, evaluated her own performance on how well she did each time in practicing those skills. She learned not only to initiate interactions, but to even request her favorite tasks each month for Young at Heart.

Step 8: Devise Reflection Activities

Involve students, on an ongoing basis, in reflecting on what they have achieved and learned. Peers can assist students with moderate and severe disabilities in composing their reflections. Students can also document their learning by taking photographs and videotapes, or through a pictorial or photographic story. They can also integrate digital photographs into a peer service-learning project Web site. Reflections and other documentation of student learning can be excellent additions to student portfolios and can help to promote students' sense of ownership and control over their own learning (Ezell and Klein, 2003).

In the Young at Heart example, both students with disabilities and peer tutors have written reflections about their participation in Young at Heart (see boxes).

Peer Tutor Reflection

"Watching the students with disabilities open up and communicate with other people made me realize how much of a regular life they can live if given the opportunity to do so. I saw students in totally a new light outside of the classroom and outside of the daily math and reading work. They carried on conversations and worked at assisting everyone else just like the peer tutors did.

"Young at Heart not only helped the students with disabilities to interact with their peers and community, but it helped me to realize how incredible these students actually are. I honestly feel that I learned so much more from this experience than they did. I learned exactly how much they have to offer this world and how capable they are of doing things.

"Hopefully this event also helped to impact the community's opinions on students with disabilities. I hope the senior citizens that took part in this experience gained a better understanding for people with disabilities and realized they're people, too."
— *Kali Arison, Peer, Hopkins County Central High School*

Step 9: Assess and Evaluate Your Service-Learning Program

Teachers can assist students in collecting data on their own performance. Teachers and students can also conduct interviews with others (community organization, service recipients, and other teachers) to evaluate the effect of their service-learning activity.

For example, one strategy' for evaluating the success of Young at Heart would be to survey the senior citizens about their participation at the end of the year. Such a survey would give students further opportunities for practice on IEP skills (e.g., initiating and sustaining interactions, calculating and charting the number of participants who reported that they had enjoyed the monthly activities).

Step 10: Celebrate Students' Achievements

Celebration is crucial to any service-learning project. For all students involved in the activity, it is a chance to celebrate the results of their work. For students with moderate and severe disabilities, a celebration provides the opportunity to give back to the community and to be recognized for that achievement. Participation in a service-learning project can be a great source of pride and of a sense of one's own competence.

A celebration is also a time for recognizing the contributions of one's partners. In the Young at Heart program, the teacher, students with disabilities, and peer tutors have planned a cookout the last week of school to recognize student achievements and to celebrate their achievements. They will also recognize individual students for their participation in the program with a certificate. As they plan for next year, they are hoping to include even more students in the service-learning project.

Step 11: Include the Service-Learning Project Into Alternate Portfolio Entries, If Applicable

As we have noted, service-learning activities provide a wonderful source of evidence for student portfolios. In several states, that evidence can be used to document

- The achievement of targeted IEP objectives.
- Generalized performance across school and community settings.
- The student's ability to work toward a group goal with peers.
- Opportunities to explore a potential career option.

Portfolio evidence can include journal entries and other self-reflections, photographs, student instructional performance data, peer reflections about the student's work, and letters from participating community agencies on the success of the project (Kleinert & Kearns, 2001).

In the Young at Heart example, students with moderate and severe disabilities have had their reflections included in their alternate assessment portfolios, along with evidence of achieving their targeted skills. Peers have included their own reflections as one of the required writing pieces in Kentucky's writing portfolio required for graduation.

Young at Heart has been so successful that the students with moderate and severe disabilities and peers have decided to start their own service-learning club. *Together as Peers,* and have designed a shirt for their club with *Together as Peers* on the front and the signatures of all the club members on the back of each shirt. The club motto is "Attitudes Are the Real Disabilities." The club now has 67 members, with students with disabilities and peers paired for each office (e.g., President, Vice-President). Each student member has to have 6 service-learning hours, and officers must complete 9 hours.

Other Examples of Service-Learning Projects

The following are other examples of service-learning projects across our participating schools.

Care Packages

Students collected nonperishable supplies for care packages for soldiers stationed overseas, and especially in war-torn areas. Students had to identify recently graduated, former students from their school who were serving overseas, determine an overall budget for their project (including the approximate cost of care packages and postage), what they could send that the soldiers would need, collect or purchase the supplies, make the care packages and take them to the post office. Students also learned a part of the history of the region in which the men and women were serving (e.g., Iraq), learned about the origins of the conflict, and followed the progress of other soldiers' efforts.

One school raised money for this project by conducting a bake sale that was promoted by the local Wal-Mart; students had to bake and sell the Items, while learning targeted IEP objectives in measuring, following directions, counting money, working in a group and on interpersonal skills.

In purchasing the items for the care packages, the students had to select the best buys for their money, learning valuable lessons in consumerism. One school also included teddy bears in care packages, so soldiers could give the bears to Iraqi children.

Reflections From Students With Disabilities

"We decorated the cafeteria and had a meal for them (Senior Citizens) and I sung for the Young at Heart. There was about 40 senior citizens there." "We wanted to help people in need." "We learned about service." "It was a lot of fun to help others."

Community Health

Students helped to plan a Community Health Fair. One of our schools has a Sports Medicine and Health Department that collaborates with a local hospital. Several of the students with disabilities take Sports Medicine classes. Together with their peers, they are planning a spring Community Health Fair open to the public.

The fair will include free blood pressure and cholesterol checks, information about preventative health care and common diseases that are especially prevalent in Kentucky (e.g., diabetes, heart disease), as well as women's and children's health issues. Students are responsible for working together to obtain the health care workers for each booth, and in the process, are learning important elements of living healthy lives themselves.

Students participating in the state alternate assessment will be able to include this activity as an important part of their Health entry for their required portfolios. These entries will document the state learner standards of "Students demonstrate the skills that they need to remain physically healthy and to accept responsibility for their own physical well-being" and "Students demonstrate the skills to evaluate and use services and resources available in their community."

Service-learning projects provide opportunities for students to practice time, budgeting, and money management skills and to learn to divide goals into a series of smaller steps.

Reading Program

Students created children's books and read those books to preschool and primary-age students. Together, students with moderate and severe disabilities and peers at three of our schools have created story books and story boards (illustrations) of children's books to read to preschool and primary-age children. Not only does this activity increase valued literacy skills for students with disabilities, but it also provides these students an added opportunity to practice those skills with students just beginning reading instruction.

Targeted skills incorporated into this service-learning activity included increased oral communication skills, sight word vocabulary, reading comprehension, and writing in complete sentences.

Toy Drive

Students conducted a drive to collect used toys in good condition to package and distribute to local facilities for Christmas. The students and peers decided where the toys would go. This activity was done as a whole school project (i.e., all students were invited to participate), to increase the number of toys brought in.

Teacher and Parent Reflections on Service Learning

Teacher Reflection

"The only thing I would do different is start sooner. I have been depriving my students by not giving them a way to give back to their community and feeling they have value. This project has built confidence and self-esteem for students with and without disabilities. Service learning has helped me to remember why I am a teacher!"—*Virginia McGregor, Teacher, Hopkins County Central High School*

Parent Reflection

"Service learning helps students with disabilities learn about helping others. Students with disabilities often receive a great deal of help. It is so wonderful for them to help someone else. It has given Karli a great sense of awareness about how she can help others in need. This project also provided opportunities where Karli could feel that she was doing something important. I can see how gratifying it is for Karli to help someone else and make someone smile."—*Lori Edds, Parent*

The students also held a Christmas craft sale to raise the funds needed to package and wrap the gifts, purchase batteries, and buy other accessories. During the craft sale, the students worked on IEP objectives for measuring, completion of task, following directions, handling money and making change, salesmanship, and detail to the craftsmanship of the items they were making.

Recycling

Students held a school wide recycling project in collaboration with the School Ecology Club and with a unit on recycling that was part of Earth Science class. Students learned to weigh and calculate the amount of usable recyclables collected each week, as well as the difference between hazardous and safe materials.

Students had to do research in the library on what could be recycled, and they had to take home a survey and interview neighbors and relatives on whether they recycled, and why they did or did not do so.

Meals on Wheels

A student with a moderate to severe disability and a peer were paired for this activity. Together, they counted out what was needed for each meal (meals, utensils, drinks, desserts, etc.), and delivered the meals with staff supervision on their prescribed route. The student with a disability worked on critical communication skills (greeting each person and engaging in social conversations) and on targeted IEP math skills related to counting and addition. After graduating, the student with a disability found paid employment in a similar job delivering ink cartridges to businesses.

Clothing Drive

Students conducted a clothing drive for a garage sale to benefit Habitat for Humanity. Students were responsible for collecting, sorting, cleaning, and packing the clothes, in preparation for the Habitat for Humanity Garage Sale.

As a follow-up activity for Habitat for Humanity, students are working to construct a storage shed to house the tools used in building a Habitat house. When the house is completed, the tool shed will remain as a storage shed for the new home owners. Student learning objectives included independent living skills, math skills (measurement), and working in a group to accomplish an overall goal.

Children's Hospital

Students collected toys, books, and money for children served by the local Hospice program. Money collected was used to purchase books; students used their own knowledge of favorite children's books to make their choices. Students worked on money management (counting money, purchasing within a budget), as well as reading skills in selecting appropriate books.

Pledges for a Benefit

Students raised pledge money and volunteered at the local Down Syndrome Buddy Walk, to benefit children and adults with Down syndrome (two schools participated in this project).

Benefits of Service Learning for Students With Moderate and Severe Disabilities

Service learning provides students with moderate and severe disabilities the opportunity to give back to their communities. Too often, educators and other service providers view these students only as the recipients of services (Brill, 1994), be it through such formal services as special education, vocational rehabilitation, related services or through more informal supports, such as peer tutoring.

In addition to the benefits reported in the literature for students with and without mild disabilities (e.g., increased self-esteem, problem-solving skills, social skills), we have found that service-learning opportunities for students with moderate and severe disabilities have led to improved attitudes of peers about these students' true capabilities.

We have also found that inclusive service-learning activities allow students with disabilities who are participating in their state's alternate assessment to document increased evidence of generalization of targeted skills across multiple settings, increased use of natural supports, and document higher levels of self-direction and self-determination. Direct evidence of targeted skills, the generalization of those targeted skills, natural supports, and measures of self-determination are currently included within the scoring rubric of several states' alternate educational assessments under IDEA '97 (Browder et al., in press; Kleinert, Green, Hurte, Clayton & Oetinger, 2002). Thus service learning can provide students with an important vehicle for demonstrating what they know and are able to do.

Incorporating Student Projects Into Alternate Assessments

Students have included their service-learning projects into our state's alternate assessment in a variety of ways, as follows:

- Service-learning projects provide excellent vehicles for students to demonstrate their learning in targeted skills in such general curriculum areas as Science (the ecology service project noted previously) and Health (the Community Health Fair project noted previously). Math skills have included purchasing, choosing the best buys (comparative shopping), managing a budget, and measurement skills. Language arts skills have been incorporated through the students' own reflections on service learning, and through writing and adapting stories for young children. Targeted skills in these and related areas are included in most states' alternate assessments (Browder et al., in press), and content from the areas of Reading, Math, and Science are now a requirement for alternate assessments under No Child Left Behind.

- Through service learning, students are able to show that they can apply what they have learned in the classroom to other settings throughout their school and community. A number of states have included measures of generalization and multiple settings as part of their scoring rubrics for alternate assessments (Browder et al, in press).

- Service learning allows students to document sustained social interaction and cooperative group skills, also measured in several states' alternate assessments. Kentucky, as well as several other states, includes a measure of a student's network of social relationships as a part of its alternate assessment. Service-learning projects such as Young at Heart, in which students with and without disabilities are actively engaged with senior citizens and others in the community, provides vivid examples of such social networks.

- Service learning provides excellent ways for students to demonstrate such skills as planning a project and monitoring and evaluating its success. Choosing, planning, monitoring, and evaluating one's performance are all essential components of self-determination (Agran, King-Sears, Wehmeyer, & Copeland, 2003), an educational outcome that researchers have shown to be directly related to postschool success (Wehmeyer & Palmer, 2003).

Service learning provides students with moderate and severe disabilities the opportunity to give back to their communities.

Peer, Student, Teacher, and Parent Reflections

We collected reflections by a peer and reflections by students with disabilities about their service-learning projects, respectively (see boxes). We also noted perspectives from a teacher and a parent. In our interviews at participating schools, we found that administrators, general and special educators, students with and without disabilities, and parents of students with and without disabilities saw positive effects from these students' involvement with service learning.

For example, one administrator noted that, as a result of his school's peer tutoring and service-learning program, "students seem more enthusiastic about their school work and responsibilities and accomplishing the tasks and also the goals that they have during their high school years."

A parent of a participating peer at another of our schools echoed that theme:

> He's found a purpose in life and a goal to reach. It seemed like he was just running and didn't know what he wanted to do.... But it seems like he has finally found something that he has found satisfaction and enjoyment out of at the same time.

Clearly the benefits of these programs go both ways—for students with and without disabilities!

References

Agran, M., King-Sears, M., Wehmeyer, M., & Copeland, S. (2003). *Teachers' guides to inclusive practices: Student-directed learning.* Baltimore: Paul H. Brookes.

Brill, C. (1994). The effects of participation in service-learning on adolescents with disabilities. *Journal of Adolescence, 17,* 369-380.

Browder, D., Ahlgrim-Delzell, L., Flowers, C., Karvonen, M., Spooner, F., Algozzine, R. (in press). How states implement alternate assessments for students with disabilities and recommendations for national policy. *Journal of Disability Policy Studies.*

Burns, M., Storey, K., & Certo, N. (1999). Effect of service learning on attitudes towards students with severe disabilities. *Education and Training in Mental Retardation and Developmental Disabilities, 34,* 58-65.

Ezell, D., & Klein, C. (2003). Impact of portfolio assessment on locus of control of students with and without disabilities. *Education and Training in Developmental Disabilities, 38,* 220-228.

Gent, P., & Gurecka, L. (1998). Service learning; A creative strategy for inclusive classrooms. *Journal of the Association of Persons with Severe Handicaps, 23,* 261-271.

Kleinert, H., Green, P., Hurte, M., Clayton, J., & Oetinger, C. (2002). Creating and using meaningful alternate assessments. *TEACHING Exceptional Children. 34*(5), 40-47.

Kleinert, H., & Kearns, J. (2001). *Alternate assessment: Measuring outcomes and supports for students with disabilities.* Baltimore: Paul H, Brookes.

Kluth, P. (2000). Community referenced learning and the inclusive classroom. *Remedial and Special Education, 21,* 19-26.

No Child Left Behind Act of 2001, Pub. L. No. 107-110, 115 Stat. 1425 (2002).

Students in Service to America. (2003). Retrieved December 10. 2003, from http://www.studentsinservicetoamerica.org/

Wehmeyer, M., & Palmer, S. (2003). Adult outcomes for students with cognitive disabilities three-years after high school: The impact of self-determination. *Education and Training in Developmental Disabilities, 38*, 131-144

Yoder, D., Relish, E., & Wade, R. (1996). Service learning: Meeting student and community needs. *TEACHING Exceptional Children. 28*(4), 14-18.

Harold Kleinert (CEC Chapter #180), Executive Director, Interdisciplinary Human Development Institute, University of Kentucky, Lexington. **Virginia McGregor** (CEC Chapter #278), Teacher, Hopkins County Schools, Madisonville, Kentucky. **Michelle Durbin,** Teacher, Jefferson County Public Schools, Louisville, Kentucky. **Tina Blandford,** Teacher, Daviess County Public Schools, Owensboro, Kentucky. **Karen Jones** (CEC Chapter #5), Teacher, Woodford County Public Schools, Versailles, Kentucky. **Josh Owens** (CEC Chapter #960), Teacher, Scott County Public Schools, Georgetown, Kentucky. **Beth Harrison,** Project Director, Interdisciplinary Human Development Institute, University of Kentucky, Lexington. **Sally Miracle** (CEC Chapter #180), Consultant, Central Kentucky Special Education Cooperative, University of Kentucky, Lexington.

Address correspondence to Harold Kleinert, Interdisciplinary Human Development Institute, University of Kentucky, 126 Mineral Industries Blds., Lexington, KY 40506-0051 (e-mail: hklein@uky.edu)

This article was supported, in part, by the U.S. Administration on Developmental Disabilities (Grant No. 90DN0107/01). However, the opinions expressed do not necessarily reflect the position or policy of the U.S. Administration on Developmental Disabilities, and no official endorsement should be inferred.

Inscrutable or Meaningful?

Understanding and Supporting Your Inarticulate Students

Robin M. Smith

**Interpreting movement.
Time.
Assistive technology.
Choice.
Audiotapes.
Sticky notes.**

What do these dissimilar items or concepts have in common? Teachers can use them all in adapting lessons for students who have difficulties in communicating with others.

This article explores ways teachers can build competence in such students, rather than focus on their deficits. Along the way, you can learn how to observe your students to discover their strengths and weaknesses, translate body language, unravel the ways they process language, appreciate indications of humor, and interpret different kinds of behavior and its intent. Tips include ways to encourage group membership and participation, ways to influence student behavior, and ways to encourage communication and independent decision making by students.

Understanding Teaching Approaches

All three students described in this article (see box, "What Does It Mean to be Nonverbal?") studied with two kinds of teachers—which we will refer to as deficit-oriented and competence-oriented (Smith, 2000). How these teachers perceive their students affected how they taught and evaluated them. Their students often responded according to how they were treated and perceived in class (Smith, Ryan, & Salend, 2001). How teachers perceive their students will influence how they instruct, evaluate, and affect their students (Biklen & Duchan, 1994; Rosenthal, 1997; Smith, 1999).

Focusing on Deficits

Deficit-oriented teachers often perceive their students with developmental disabilities as inscrutable—that is, because the students are difficult to understand, they think the students must therefore be lacking basic understanding of the things going on around them. Those students who also have cognitive disabilities may not have typical speech or facial expression; and the students may also experience language-processing disabilities, such as problems with word retrieval, delayed understanding of complex speech, or need for a longer response time in conversation.

Deficit-oriented teachers tend to teach to a medial model of repairing the (often) irreparable individual. Their descriptions of students foster ranking, sorting, and diagnosing. Such medical-model descriptions obscure the individual abilities of students who may have unusual approaches to communicating their understanding, wants, and needs. For example, teachers may consider a nonverbal student who is labeled with severe mental retardation to be unable to participate in class discussions, and therefore may have the student doing something different elsewhere in the classroom or even in another room.

Deficit-oriented teachers who think their students are inscrutable and uncomprehending may miss student communications and key skills and strengths or fail to see their relevance. In the example of Tyrone (see box), his deficit-oriented teacher had no idea Tyrone understood the class discussion and therefore made few requests that he respond. Tyrone's teacher accepted his homework assignments but did not ask about missing assignments.

Focusing on Competence

Competence-oriented teachers, on the other hand, perceive students as whole persons and teach with the students' strengths in mind. Instead of questioning if students can participate in a class activity, these teachers think about *how* students can be involved in the activity. Such teachers acquire the skill of "reading" students who communicate in ways that greatly differ from their peers. They learn how students show engagement, boredom, contentment, and dissatisfaction. They are aware of their students' strengths and how these strengths might be used to support learning and achievement.

Competence-oriented teachers' descriptions of students tend to foster understanding and communication with students. For example, in Teresa's case (see box), whereas her competence-oriented teacher assisted her with exams, essays, and had meaningful typed conversations with her, her deficit-oriented teacher frequently encountered passive and active resistance from Teresa and experienced little or no meaningful communication with her.

Understanding Student Communication

You might compare students like Teresa, Tyrone, or Gerard—who differ from peers in the way they move, process information, and communicate—to a foreign visitor who does not speak your language very well but is likely to understand it. As the "native speaker," you as teacher can take on the role of interpreter as you learn the student's own language.

The following guidelines, summarized in Table 1, are designed to help you

What Does It Mean to be Nonverbal? Three Students

Many of us tend to focus on the student's disability, not the person, and thus see students who are nonverbal or inarticulate as simply "difficult to understand." Students who are labeled mentally retarded or who have impaired communication, especially, are the victims of such first impressions (Goode, 1989).

The three students described here have studied with two kinds of teachers, which will become evident as you read. The first type of teachers regarded their students as inscrutable or incompetent, rather than as sources of meaningful activity and communication. They had difficulty seeing intelligence and using the strengths of their students. The second category of teachers not only saw the students' intelligence and competencies, but also helped them engage academically.

Gerard was a high school student labeled mentally retarded who spoke in short phrases. When asked a direct question, he often responded, "I don't know." Several of his teachers, both general and special education, said that he understood little of what was going on in class. A paraprofessional who did feel Gerard understood his schoolwork was working with him on some questions in a textbook about managing money. She asked him what he should do with his paycheck. Gerard shook his head and said, "I don't know." She said,

"Let me put this another way. When you work at [your job], what do you do with your check? Does your mom put it in the bank or do you spend it?" He said, "Bank."

Tyrone, a student with autism, spoke in short phrases and often repeated favorite expressions and topics in his conversation. Two teachers described him as "a mystery" and had no idea if he understood what was happening in class. One day, one of these teachers was questioning the students about a history worksheet they had done on the early 1900s, asking them about historic people and events. "John Jacob Astor?" A student replied, "American Fur Company." The teacher mentioned the Broadway musical about the Astor family, asking for the title. Tyrone called out, "Scrooge." The teacher laughed, "Good guess."

Teresa was nonverbal and communicated inconsistently by pointing and making sounds. Teachers supported her pointing to answer choices written on Post-It notes. With gentle physical support, she could sustain pointing to letters in a large keyboard for a short time. She took quizzes and typed short conversations with a teacher assigned to help her with communication skills. Her other teacher assigned for the same purpose, however, was unable to engage Teresa in typed conversations and said, in her presence, "I don't think she knows her letters."

learn about your students and become an effective interpreter.

Get to Know Your Students' Communication Strengths and Needs

Your ability to engage students depends on your knowledge of their communication strengths and needs. If you spend some time getting to know your students, you can identify these strengths and needs by doing the following:

- Sharing with the students that you are trying to get to know them, their communication styles and patterns, and their interests, and thus explaining why you are asking some questions that might seem obvious to them. Let them know you want to learn about what they have invented as strategies to communicate.

- Drawing on the knowledge of others who know the student—for example, paraprofessionals, family members, and friends.

- Observing students and asking yourself questions like these:
  —How does this student typically show interest?
  —How does this student show understanding?

  —Are there atypical or meaningful body movements that are special to this student?

  —Is this student following the conversation even when looking around or pacing? How do I know?

Understand Movement Differences

Some students have movement differences associated with their disability. We must not misinterpret movement differences as discipline problems, resistance, boredom, or incomprehension. For example, although Tyrone often walks around the room during a discussion, he is a full participant, understanding others' communication and making relevant contributions on request.

When Tyrone is seated in class, however, he has a different way of being in motion. Although he often writes a list of five names over and over, apparently engrossed in his notebook, he will answer a question when asked. Though some teachers may consider him disengaged, his repetitive writing helps him concentrate by blocking out other distractions. You can learn about and examine your students' movement differences by observing them and asking yourself:

- Does this student have trouble starting, executing, stopping, combining, continuing, or switching activities? These are some common movement differences identified by Donnellan and Leary (1995, p. 80) in people with autism and mental retardation. These behaviors reflect neither intention nor intelligence. They reflect the need for understanding and accommodation.

- Do the movements have particular meaning? Sometimes the movements have no meaning. Students with Tourette's syndrome, for example, cannot control certain words, shouts, or twitches.

Understand Language-Processing Differences

Some students can speak, but are inarticulate. Whereas students may be capable of one- or two-word sentences or short phrases, their teachers may think they are intellectually limited or lazy.

Some common indications that students have difficulty with processing language are as follows:

- Difficulty with word retrieval when answering a direct question. Gerard (see box) was inarticulate and also had difficulty finding the words he

Table 1. Understanding Students' Communication

Get to know communication strengths/needs	Let them know you want to learn about their communication strategies.
	Draw on the knowledge of others: family, friends, paraprofessionals.
	Observe how students show interest and understanding.
	Learn how unique body movements can be interpreted as meaningful.
Understand movement differences	Identify problems with starting, executing, stopping, combining, continuing, or switching activities.
	Identify meanings of recurring movements or intensity of movements.
Understand processing differences such as:	Difficulty with word retrieval
	Limited response repertoire
	Longer wait time to respond
	Difficulty responding to someone else's initiated conversation
Look for signs of sophisticated thinking	Humor
	Insight
Understand refusal or resistance relating to:	Personal considerations or preferences
	Academic considerations such as needs for modifications; appropriateness of the task; need for coaching; ability to physically carry out the task.
Understand unintentional behaviors	Abrupt behaviors may not be related to noncompliance, nonunderstanding, or lack of interest.
	Student may be "stuck" in a repetitive thought or feeling.
	Less participation may be fatigue rather than disinterest.

needed to communicate with others. Sometimes, when he replied, "I don't know," his conversation partner repeated the question in a different way that also gave him extra time to come up with an answer. Sometimes Gerard could immediately answer a question if his attention were already on the topic, such as during a class discussion. In the previous example, Gerard selected the correct answer from choices presented to him.

- Some students may have a limited response repertoire. As a result, they rely on consistent alternative responses. When asked a direct question, Gerard responded "Yes," "No," or "I don't know." In health class, he responded appropriately to every question the teacher asked, including rhetorical ones. ("Would you get on a plane if the pilot were high?" "No.")
- Some students need a longer wait time to prepare and articulate their responses. Therefore, teachers need to provide students with a sufficient amount of time in which to respond.
- Some students have difficulty responding in conversations that someone else has initiated. Regarding Gerard's social conversation skills, his special education teacher said he was lazy because he answered, "I don't know" so often.

Yet, he initiated a conversation with a teacher about plans for the weekend; and when asked what he was going to do, said that his parents were taking him to a concert.

You can change the way you communicate with students once you realize they process language differently. You can speak slower or with longer wait time in between thoughts. You also can ask more "yes/no" questions or phrase questions to include the words students need to respond appropriately. When students appear to be restless, you can ask them if they are bored or need a break.

Look for Signs of Sophisticated Thinking, Such as Humor or Insight

Students who are nonverbal or inarticulate may show sophistication with a few choice words, a joke, a comeback, or the timing of a behavior.

For example, Tyrone's naming the Astor play, "Scrooge," was an obvious sign of sophistication. Tyrone's jokes and his correct one-word answers in other classes were also a sign of sophisticated thinking. One time his paraprofessional yawned when helping with a worksheet and said, "Excuse me." Tyrone responded, "You need a blanket."

Understand Refusal and Resistance

Although teachers generally consider refusal and resistance unproductive and inappropriate, for some students these strategies may be their most effective method of communication. This is particularly true of students who lack the motor coordination to write or type and who do not speak.

For example, one day a teacher was absent; and the students had a period of reading, resting, and chatting. Gerard's paraprofessional tried in vain to get him to work on yesterday's assignment. Gerard looked around and leafed through a magazine.

After a few minutes, the paraprofessional asked, "Are you being this way because all the other kids don't have to work today and you don't want to, either?"

He responded, "Yes."

Like Gerard's paraprofessional, you can attempt to understand your students' refusal and resistance by examining the following:

- Are there personal considerations and preferences? Ask students questions to find out if they are tired, sick, thirsty, bored, dislike this topic, or want to do the same thing as other students.
- Are there academic considerations? Does the task need to be modified in any way? Does the expected task

Table 2. Competence-Oriented Supports	
Plan ahead for student participation	Pre-arrange a time to call on students Call on students for yes/no or choice answers Assign a task the student can do to contribute to the whole class Prepare choices students can point to during group discussions Prepare prerecorded choices and answers the student can activate with a switching device
Maximize student decision making	Support decisions at each step of a project Use sticky notes to write exam choices Use augmentative communication systems: communication, picture/symbol/word books; pointing, recording devices, keyboard devices, etc. Use alternative forms of written communication (e.g., arranging sentence cards for essays) Ask student to confirm answers or meaning of their communication.
Minimize effect of unintentional behaviors	Study consistency of certain behaviors Discover appropriate prompts to help students through problematic movements

make sense to the student? Does the student need coaching to stay focused and on task? Can the student physically carry out the task?

Understand When Students' Behaviors Are Unintentional

Sometimes students have unusual verbal responses and utterances, as well as nonverbal actions they cannot control. Understanding such behavior will help you to carefully interpret unusual and unexpected verbal responses and nonverbal behavior.

Because students' processing delays and unintentional verbal and physical types of behavior may be misinterpreted, based on the responses of typical students, you can inquire into such differences by considering the following:

- Is unintentional behavior misinterpreted as noncompliance, nonunderstanding, or lack of interest? Some students with developmental disabilities have unintentional types of behavior, appearing as abrupt behavior changes. Students may have tics, use inappropriate language, call out irrelevant phrases, pace, strike or challenge others, or walk out of the room or building. An event, a feeling, or a physical response to the environment, such as the sound of fluorescent lights or computer hard drives, may trigger some of this behavior.
- Are repetitive words or phrases signs that student is "stuck" in an emotion? A student may be involuntarily involved in a repetitive thought or feeling, particularly when nervous. Some coaching or prompting may help a student move

on. It may help to ask the student if he or she is "stuck."

- Is less-than-usual participation or speech misinterpreted as lack of interest? For some students, this lack of participation may be a sign of the effort it takes to suppress an involuntary behavior, such as a movement, sound, or tic.

Competence-Oriented Supports to Involve Inarticulate or Nonspeaking Students

As you get to know your students, you do not have to wait until you are expert in "their language." The use of competence-oriented strategies, summarized in Table 2, can cause you to see how your students demonstrate engagement and understanding.

In addition, you will be providing more opportunity for participation. Eugene Marcus (personal communication, 1994), a man with autism who communicates by typing said, "Treat every individual who you meet as a dignitary from another country who does not speak your language very well." The following are some suggestions for implementing Marcus's mandate in your classes.

Plan Ahead for Participation During Group Discussions

Pre-arrange a time to call on students. For example, Teresa's special education teacher met with the health teacher and arranged with him to call on Teresa for a particular question from the homework assignment. Then, she prerecorded the answer into Teresa's speaking device. Teresa pushed a button on her speaking

device when called on in class to answer the question.

Call on students for yes/no or choice answers. For example, a student named Nick could not speak but nodded his head when the teacher asked him if he agreed with what another student said.

Assign a task students can do to contribute to a small group or the whole class. For example, Gerard's social studies teacher asked him to find a picture of the Great Wall in the school library. With the help of his paraprofessional, he found the picture while the class was doing a written assignment; and then he showed the photo to his social studies class during a discussion about China.

Arrange choices for students to point to when answering questions during whole-group and small-group lessons and during exams. Teachers, paraeducators, or peers can prepare these choices in advance or spontaneously use Post-it notes or an erasable white board.

Use recording devices with switches students can operate. For example, with the help of teachers and peers, students can answer questions with prerecorded responses, give reports, turn on background sounds for others' reports, and even prepare small-talk conversations in advance using a cassette recorder.

Maximize Students' Decision Making

Support students to decide during each step of a project they cannot physically do alone. For example, Tyrone did not have the fine-motor coordination to cut and paste pictures for a collage in his health class. His paraeducator asked him to decide on a topic for a collage. Tyrone chose the materials, the color scheme, which pictures to cut out, and where to glue them.

Use Post-it notes to record possible choices during exams or spontaneous conversations and ask students to select their responses. For example, during an exam, the teacher wrote the choices for fill-in-the-blank questions on Post-it notes; and Teresa then pointed to her choice. Because Teresa was not always consistent in her movements, the teacher then confirmed the choice by changing the order of the three choices—and Teresa would point to the same one.

Use communication books (pictures with words, phrases, or sentences on laminated cards) for the common conversations. Communication books work well in role-plays, pairs, and small groups, as peers or teachers support students to participate and contribute.

Use alternative forms of written communication. Teachers can help students write drafts using Post-it notes or cards, and then make sure the students approve of the order. For an essay on health careers, Teresa chose sentences from texts that her paraprofessional wrote on cards. She later put them in order, along with transitional sentences suggested by her paraeducator.

Use augmentative communication systems, such as typing, pointing to letters or pictures, or facilitated communication to facilitate independent choice making. Nick, who did not speak and lacked fine-motor coordination, was looking at menu choices that were in small type and close together. When the paraeducator wrote the prices larger and farther part, Nick was able to point to the correct choice through a type of facilitated communication: Paraeducator provided only slight resistance by pulling back on his sleeve (Biklen & Cardinal, 1997).

Seek confirmation when students are too concise, inconsistent, or are engaging in automatic and repetitive phrases. You can encourage detail by saying, "I don't understand what you meant; please type/say it again," or "Please say more." If a

student is inconsistent when pointing and is taking an exam, you might ask after each choice, "Is that your answer?"

Minimize the Effect of Unintentional Behavior

Learn if there is consistency for particular unintentional behaviors. For example, teachers can learn if behaviors such as pacing or walking out of the room are related to anxiety and try to discover ways to ease students' anxiety.

Discover appropriate prompts and indirect means to overcome unintentional and problematic differences in movement. Some students have trouble initiating and need pre-arranged cues to begin a task, whereas others have problems completing several steps of a task and need a series of cues to complete the task. Still others will have difficulty stopping. Necessary accommodations will be different for each student, and these supports will help with such problems as difficulty in starting, continuing, and stopping an activity (see Donnellan & Leary, 1995).

For example, touching Teresa's elbow enabled her to begin pointing to her answers on a test. A picture schedule helped another student, Sally, go through the steps of a classroom activity that included getting out her supplies, using them correctly, and putting them away without prompting.

Both teachers and peers can incorporate all these suggestions. Peers can learn to draw out responses from each other and may even provide the educators with creative, fresh approaches.

Final Thoughts

We need to think of our roles not only as developers of social, academic, and functional skills in students, but also as interpreters and communication allies of inarticulate students. These are the same sensitivities we automatically use with students without disabilities in general education settings, with our peers, and often with young children—when we re-

member how much they really do understand.

References

Biklen, D., & Cardinal, D. (1997). *Contested words, contested science: Unraveling the FC controversy.* New York: Teachers College Press.

Biklen, D., & Duchan, J. (1994). I am intelligent: The social construction of mental retardation. *Journal of the Association for Persons with Severe Handicaps, 19*(3), 173–184.

Donnellan, A. M., & Leary, M. R. (1995). *Movement differences and diversity in autism/mental retardation: Appreciating and accommodating people with communication and behavior challenges* (4th ed.). Madison, WI: DRI Press.

Goode, D. A. (1989). Who's Bobby? Ideology and method in the discovery of a Down syndrome person's competence. In P. M. Ferguson, D. L. Ferguson, & S. J. Taylor (Eds.), *Interpreting disability: A qualitative reader* (pp. 197–212). New York: Teachers College Press.

Rosenthal, R. (1997). *Interpersonal expectancy effects: A forty-year perspective.* Paper presented at the American Psychological Association Convention, Chicago. (ERIC Document Reproduction Service No. ED 415 460)

Smith, R., Ryan, S., & Salend, S. (2001). Watch your language: Closing or opening the special education curtain. *TEACHING Exceptional Children, 33*(4), 18–23.

Smith, R. M. (1999). Academic engagement of students with significant disabilities and educators' perceptions of competence. *The Professional Educator, 22*(1), 17–31.

Smith, R. M. (2000). View from the ivory tower: How academics construct disability. In B. B. Swadner & L. Rogers (Eds.), *Semiotics and disability: Interrogating the categories of difference* (pp. 55–733). New York: State University of New York (SUNY) Press.

Robin M. Smith *(CEC Chapter #615), Assistant Professor of Special Education, Educational Studies, State University of New York at New Paltz, New York.*

Address correspondence to the author at Educational Studies Department, State University of New York–New Paltz, 75 S. Manheim Blvd., New Paltz, NY 12561 (e-mail: smithrm@newpaltz.edu)

From *Teaching Exceptional Children*, March/April 2002, pp. 28-33. © 2002 by The Council for Exceptional Children. Reprinted by permission.

UNIT 6

Emotional and Behavioral Disorders

Unit Selections

17. **Psychiatric Disorders and Treatments: A Primer for Teachers**, Steven R. Forness, Hill M. Walker, and Kenneth A. Kavale
18. **I Want to Go Back to Jail**, Lynn Olcott
19. **The Importance of Teacher Self-Awareness in Working With Students With Emotional and Behavioral Disorders**, Brent G. Richardson and Margery J. Shupe
20. **Classroom Problems That Don't Go Away**, Laverne Warner and Sharon Lynch

Key Points to Consider

- Which emotional and behavioral disorders should be referred for psychiatric treatment? How can teachers detect them?

- Would you want to teach emotionally and behaviorally disordered young women in jail? Find out why one teacher found it a choice assignment.

- After reading the article by Brent Richardson and Margery Shupe, suggest why teachers need to be in touch with their own feelings and how they can increase self-awareness.

- How can chronic and intense behavioral difficulties be ameliorated in the classroom to allow learning to take place?

Student Website

www.mhcls.com/online

Internet References

Further information regarding these websites may be found in this book's preface or online.

Educating Students With Emotional/Behavioral Disorders
http://www.nichcy.org/pubs/bibliog/bib10txt.htm
Pacer Center: Emotional Behavioral Disorders
http://www.pacer.org/ebd/

T he definition of a student with emotional behavioral disorder (EBD) usually conjures up visions of the violence perpetrated by a few students who have vented their frustrations by taking guns to school. One of the hot topics in special education today is whether or not students with emotional and behavioral disorders are too dangerous to be included in regular education classes. The statistics show that students with EBDs are as likely to be the victims of violence or bullying by nondisabled classmates as to be the troublemakers. The definition of EBDs broadly includes all emotionally disordered students with subjective feelings such as sadness, fear, anger, guilt, or anxiety that give rise to altered behaviors that are outside the range of normal.

Should children with chronic and severe anger, already convicted of problem behaviors such as violent acts or threats of violence, be re-enrolled in inclusive regular education classes with Individualized Education Plans (IEPs)? Although teachers, other pupils, and school staff may be greatly inconvenienced by the presence of one or more behaviorally disordered students in every classroom, the law is clear. The school must "show cause" if a child with EBD is to be permanently moved from the regular classroom to a more restrictive environment.

The 1994 Gun-Free Schools Act in the United States requires a one-year expulsion of a student who brings a firearm to school. The Individuals with Disabilities Education Act (IDEA) in its 1997 reauthorization made a compromise for students with EBDs or other conditions of disability. If bringing a gun to school is related to their disability (for example, as the result of being teased or bullied), they are exempt from the Gun-Free Schools Act legislation. They can be expelled, but only for 10 days while the school determines their degree of danger to others. If they are judged to really be dangerous, they can temporarily be given an alternate educational placement for 45 days, subject to reassessment. Their IEPs should not be rewritten to place them in a permanent restrictive setting unless their acts were clearly unrelated to their disabilities (hard to prove). This double standard is very controversial. Students without disabilities are expelled with no educational provisions for one full year.

For educational purposes, children with behavior disorders are usually divided into two main behavioral classifications: (1) withdrawn, shy, or anxious behaviors and (2) aggressive, acting-out behaviors. The debate about what constitutes a behavior disorder, or an emotional disorder, is not fully resolved. The Diagnostic and Statistical Manual of Mental Disorders (4th edition) (DSM-IV) sees serious behavioral disorders as a category first diagnosed in infancy, childhood, or adolescence. Among the DSM-IV disorders of childhood are, eating disorders, tic disorders, elimination disorders, separation anxiety disorders, reactive attachment disorders, oppositional defiant disorder, and conduct disorder .

An alliance of educators and psychologists proposed that IDEA remove the term "serious emotional disturbances" and instead focus on behaviors that adversely affect educational performance. Conduct usually considered a sign of emotional disorder, such as anxiety, depression, or failure of attachment, can be seen as behaviorally disordered if it interferes with academic, social, vocational, and personal accomplishment. So, also, can eating, elimination, or tic disorders and any other responses outside the range of "acceptable" for school or other settings. Such a focus on behavior can link the individualized educational plan curriculum activities to children's behavioral response styles.

Inclusive education does not translate into acceptance of disordered behaviors in the regular education classroom. Two rules of thumb for the behavior of all children, however capable or incapable, are that they conform to minimum standards of acceptable conduct and that disruptive behaviors be subject to fair and consistent disciplinary action. In order to ensure more orderly, well-regulated classroom environments, many schools are instituting conflict management courses.

What causes students to act out with hostile, aggressive behaviors directed against school personnel or other students? An easy, often-cited reason is that they are barraged with images of violence on the news, in music, on videos, on television programs, and in movies. It is too facile: Media barrage is aimed at everyone, yet only a few decide that they want to become violent and harm others. Aggressive, bullying children commonly come from homes where they see real violence, anger, and insults.

They often feel disconnected, rejected, and afraid. They do not know how to communicate their distress. They may appear to be narcissistic, even as they seek attention in negative, hurtful ways. They usually have fairly easy access to weapons, alcohol, and other substances of abuse. They usually do not know any techniques of conflict management other than acting out.

The first article describes the more common psychiatric disorders which contribute to students' symptoms of EBDs. Forness, Walker, and Kavale, discuss the problems with both assessment and treatment of these disorders. Both behavioral therapy and drug therapy may be needed as well as good communication and collaboration between parents, students, and teachers.

Lynn Olcott, in the second article writes "I Want to Go Back to Jail," and she did, as a teacher. She describes the rewards of helping emotionally and behaviorally disordered young women earn their general education diplomas.

Brent Richardson and Margery Shupe, in the third selection, point out how self-awareness in educators can reduce conflicts with students with EBD. They identify strategies to increase teachers' self-awareness.

The fourth article, "Classroom Problems That Don't Go Away" gives suggestions for ameliorating and/or preventing conflicts, and antisocial acts, within the regularized education curriculum by teaching alternative behaviors.

Psychiatric Disorders and Treatments

A Primer for Teachers

Steven R. Forness • Hill M. Walker • Kenneth A. Kavale

Children who have social or emotional problems require understanding and support from teachers and family members and may occasionally require counseling to help the child deal with his or her feelings and explore ways of coping. Psychiatric disorders, on the other hand, are generally much more disabling, more difficult to diagnose correctly, and sometimes require very specific therapeutic or medical treatments, meaning treatment with psychopharmacology (medications used to help the child control his or her emotional or behavioral symptoms).

Child psychopharmacology is a controversial field that is often sensationalized in the popular media. Coverage in the media often suggests that large numbers of children are being prescribed medication for only minor problems. Studies suggest that only a small fraction of children with serious psychiatric disorders are actually receiving such medication (Jensen et al., 1999; Zito et al., 1998). In the hands of a competent pediatrician or child psychiatrist, moreover, these medications are not only effective but an essential component of an overall treatment program for many, if not most, children with psychiatric disorders.

> Psychiatric disorders are likely to be prevalent in children or adolescents receiving special education.

Careful treatment with these medications has been shown not only to effect dramatic improvement in behavioral or emotional responses of these children, but also to improve their social and academic functioning. Specific behavioral and related therapies are also critical. These may be used alone, prior to, or concurrent with psychopharmacologic treatment; and combined behavioral and psychopharmacologic treatments are often better than either used alone (Forness & Kavale, 2001; Forness, Kavale, & Davanzo, 2002).

Psychiatric disorders are classified in the fourth edition of the American Psychiatric Association's *Diagnostic and Statistical Manual (DSM IV;* 1994). *DSM IV* is used primarily by psychiatrists and psychologists to diagnose mental health problems in both children and adolescents. The diagnostic information contained here is taken directly from *DSM IV,* and treatment issues are referenced separately. All of these disorders were diagnosed only after a thorough evaluation that included

1. Screening for health, vision, or hearing problems.
2. Review of the child's developmental history.
3. Interviews with the parents and the child.
4. Review of information from teachers or school records.
5. Careful consideration of context and occurrence of symptoms.

Psychiatric disorders are likely to be prevalent in children or adolescents receiving special education (Garland et al., 2001). Educators working with these children should be familiar enough with such disorders so they can readily detect and refer children to mental health professionals and collaborate with these professionals in ongoing treatment. These disorders are discussed in the following paragraphs in terms of definition or diagnosis and therapeutic and psychopharmacologic treatment.

Oppositional Defiant and Conduct Disorders

Diagnosis

Both oppositional defiant and conduct disorders involve disruptive behavior. Oppositional defiant disorder often seems developmentally to precede a later diagnosis of conduct disorder. Both disorders probably occur in at least 4% of children or adolescents (Forness, Kavale, & Walker, 1999). Children with oppositional defiant disorder are those who have persistent patterns of negativistic, hostile, or defiant behavior directed primarily toward adults. Children with conduct disorder show consistent patterns of behavior in which they violate the rights of others or transgress age-appropriate social norms.

In oppositional defiant disorder, symptoms may include
- Persistent temper tantrums.
- Arguing with adults.
- Refusing to comply with reasonable adult requests.
- Annoying others.
- Vindictiveness.

The symptoms of an oppositional defiant disorder bother adults but are not considered as troublesome as conduct disorder, in which symptoms usually cluster into more serious patterns of
- Overt aggression toward people or animals.
- Destruction of property.
- Deceitfulness or theft.
- Serious violations of rules such as staying out all night and truancy from school.

As is the case with all psychiatric disorders, oppositional defiant disorder and conduct disorder are diagnosed in *DSM IV* when the child meets a set number of symptoms

from among a list of several symptoms typical of the disorder. Children must have 4 from a list of 8 symptoms to be diagnosed with oppositional defiant disorder and at least 3 from a list of 15 symptoms to be diagnosed with conduct disorder. These symptoms must also meet the criteria of causing significant impairment in social, academic, or related functioning. In conduct disorder, presence of only 3 symptoms is termed *mild conduct disorder*, whereas moderate and severe conduct disorder are characterized by increasing numbers of symptoms and increasingly greater harm to others.

> The symptoms of an oppositional defiant disorder bother adults but are not considered as troublesome as conduct disorder.

Treatment

The primary treatment for both oppositional defiant disorder and conduct disorder is behavioral therapy (Kavale, Forness, & Walker, 1999). Usually this takes the form of a reward or a reinforcement system in which the child earns points for appropriate behavior and is ignored or even given time-outs for inappropriate behavior. Points are usually exchanged for privileges or tangible awards at home or school. A major part of such behavioral therapy is parent or teacher consultation, so that adults can learn how to praise or reward good behavior and ignore inappropriate behavior. Social skills training is also helpful for children who do not seem to know how to behave or interact appropriately.

Unlike most psychiatric disorders, medication is not usually used to control symptoms of oppositional defiant disorder or conduct disorder directly. Both disorders, however, are very likely to co-occur or be comorbid (more than one condition existing at the same time) with a wide range of other psychiatric disorders

(Forness, Kavale, & Walker, 1999). Psychopharmacology for these disorders (such as attention deficit hyperactivity disorder, depression, or anxiety disorders) may often improve symptoms of oppositional defiant disorder or conduct disorder, as well.

Attention Deficit/Hyperactivity Disorder

Diagnosis

This disorder is found in 3%-5% of children or adolescents (Forness & Kavale, 2002). It is diagnosed when a child has persistent problems in inattentive or in hyperactive-impulsive behavior. At least some of these symptoms must have appeared prior to 7 years of age. The symptoms must also persist to a degree that markedly impairs the child's functioning in two or more settings, such as home and school.

Symptoms of inattention include
- Failing to give close attention to details in school work or related activities.
- Difficulty in sustaining attention.
- Seeming not to listen.
- Difficulty in organization.
- Distractibility.

Symptoms of hyperactivity or impulsivity include
- Excessive fidgeting.
- Inability to sit still in the classroom or other situations when this is expected.
- Running about or even climbing things excessively.
- Extreme restlessness or talkativeness.
- Difficulty waiting for turn.
- Interrupting conversations.

The child must usually meet criteria in *DSM IV* for six of nine symptoms in inattention or six of nine symptoms of hyperactivity-impulsivity. Children can thus be diagnosed with three subtypes of attention deficit/hyperactivity disorder (ADHD): predominantly inattentive, predominantly hyperactive-impulsive, or combined. It is usually important to rule out other psychiat-

Titration

The process of determining the right dose of medication, called titration, requires close collaboration between child, parents, and teachers (Wilens, 2001). The goal of titration is to use the lowest effective dose of medication while avoiding unwanted side effects.

Side effects occur because these medications, while very helpful, are still imperfect. Although stimulants target certain areas of the brain, they sometimes also spill over into other areas for which they were not intended, thus causing side effects such as loss of appetite, insomnia, dizziness, or irritability. These side effects may occur only at higher doses for some children or may occur with some children for some stimulants and not for others. At other times, these side effects may diminish as time goes by or as the child gets used to the drug. For some children, they may persist to the point where another medication or treatment must be tried instead.

In recent medication studies, researchers present side effects that occur on the drug as well as side effects that occur on placebo pills that contain no active medication. Interestingly, many children with ADHD seemed to show problems with irritability, insomnia, and poor appetite even when not on medication. Medication side effects are usually only slightly more frequent than problems that, upon careful observation, existed previously in these children before they were placed on medication.

Titration is somewhat easier with stimulants because these medications usually act within an hour or so and generally wash out of the body within a few hours or by the end of the day. The process of finding the right dose or switching to another medication may be accomplished within a few days or weeks.

Antidepressant medications, on the other hand, may take at least 3 or more weeks to obtain a full therapeutic effect. Other medications such as antipsychotics or neuroleptics for schizophrenia or other treatment-resistant disorders may take weeks to establish the most effective regimen. Thus, effective titration for these medications may commonly take weeks or even months. The side effects of these medications are also likely to be more debilitating and may also include

- Sedation.
- Dizziness.
- Problems in heart rhythms, especially in children with a family history of heart disease.
- Tremors.
- Significant weight gain.

Prescribing physicians should warn patients and their families about what to look for in terms of both therapeutic effects and adverse side effects. Physicians should also schedule regular follow-up visits to assess and monitor both the effects and the side effects of each medication. Competent physicians do careful patient and family education to prepare the child and his or her family for the titration process. During titration, they will usually provide the family and the child's teachers with checklists of symptoms and side effects so that significant adults in the child's environment can also monitor and provide regular feedback to the physician on how the medication is working.

Certain medications require more careful screening and monitoring of health status or drug effects through blood work, electrocardiograms, and the like. Physicians should give families careful instructions for regular administration of these medications, as well as numbers to call in case of unexpected emergencies.

ric disorders (such as depression, anxiety disorder, schizophrenia, or autism) before diagnosing ADHD, since these diagnoses may be more serious and usually take precedence. In many cases, a child may have both ADHD and one or more of these other disorders.

Treatment

The most effective treatment for ADHD generally combines both psychopharmacologic and behavioral interventions (MTA Cooperative Group, 1999a,1999b). Stimulant medications such as Ritalin, Adderall, or Dexedrine are usually the first medications considered. While it often seems paradoxical to treat an overactive child with stimulants, these drugs stimulate brain chemicals, called neurotransmitters, to work more effectively, thus allowing the child to slow down and concentrate. Children not responding to stimulant medications have sometimes been treated with other psychopharmacologic medications, such as antidepressants like Tofranil or Wellbutrin. There are other medications that can be used if the child does not respond to these drugs or when ADHD co-occurs or is comorbid with certain other psychiatric disorders.

Selecting the appropriate medication involves a process called titration (see box). Table 1 depicts some of the primary stimulants and the approximate length of time each drug lasts or has noticeable effects in the child being treated. Some of the primary side effects (see Table 1)

may occur only during the titration phase of treatment and may disappear in all but a few children.

Children with ADHD may also respond to psychosocial or behavioral treatments (Forness & Kavale, 2002). Behavioral interventions include establishing predictable routines and expectations for children, both at home and at school, and reinforcing the child for meeting these expectations. By increasing goals gradually, the child does not have to be "perfect" at the outset but can accomplish small steps over a period of days or weeks. Parent education and teacher consultation can help adults in the child's life to set reasonable expectations, reinforce effective behavior, ignore hyperactive or distractible behavior, use time-out effectively, and collaborate by developing consis-

Table 1. Stimulants	
Generic (and Trade) Name	**Duration**
Methylphenidate or MPH (Ritalin)	3-4 hours
Dextroamphetamine (Dexedrine)	6-8 hours
Amphetamine (Adderall)	7-10 hours
Sustained MPH (Concerta)	10-12 hours

Side effects: appetite loss, stomachache, headache, insomnia

tent expectations and reinforcers between home and school.

Research evidence on treatment of ADHDs comes both from a re-analysis of 115 recent medication studies (Forness, Kavale, Sweeney, & Crenshaw, 1999) and from a long-term nationwide study of nearly 600 children funded by the National Institute of Mental Health (NIMH; MTA Cooperative Group, 1999a, 1999b). This evidence suggests that psychopharmacologic treatment seems to be a critical factor in effective intervention for ADHD. The message from this research is also clear that best practice is a combination of medication and behavioral therapies (Swanson et al., 2001). In the NIMH study, combined treatment also tended to improve scores on reading tests and on ratings of social skills on long-term follow-up, if children remained on medication (Arnold et al., 2000).

Evidence suggests that the presence of co-occurring or comorbid psychiatric disorders in children with ADHD may influence treatment outcome (Jensen et al., 2001). Children with ADHD and no other disorders tend to respond best, sometimes with only medication. Children with ADHD and comorbid anxiety disorders seem to respond almost as well, either to medication or to behavioral therapy. Children with ADHD and comorbid oppositional defiant disorder or conduct disorder also respond relatively well

but only if combined psychopharmacologic and behavioral treatments are used.

Depression or Other Mood Disorders

Diagnosis

Although childhood onset of depressive or other mood disorders does not occur as frequently as ADHD, it is not uncommon and may affect more than 2% of children and at least twice that number of adolescents (Birmaher & Brent, 1998). There are essentially three major types of mood disorders: depression, dysthymia, and bipolar or manic depressive disorder. Depression is diagnosed in *DSM IV* when the child has a depressed or irritable mood or loss of interest or pleasure in most activities. Other symptoms may include

- Unexplained fluctuations in weight.
- Insomnia.
- Loss of energy.
- Diminished ability to think or concentrate.
- Feelings of excessive guilt or worthlessness.

Of nine different symptoms, at least five must occur nearly every day during a 2-week period for depression to be diagnosed.

Dysthymia is diagnosed by a depressed or irritable mood on most days for at least a year and must also be accompanied by at least two of six other symptoms. Including

- Insomnia.
- Low energy or fatigue.
- Low self-esteem.
- Poor concentration.
- Feelings of hopelessness.

The diagnosis of bipolar or manic depressive disorder depends on fluctuations in mood, from depressed episodes, as noted previously, to manic episodes. Manic episodes are characterized by distinct periods in which the child or adolescent has an abnormal and persistently elevated or expansive mood and in which three of seven other symptoms are present, such as

- Decreased need for sleep.
- Excessive talkativeness.
- Distractibility.
- Psychomotor agitation.

> The most effective treatment for attention deficit hyperactivity disorder generally combines both psychopharmacologic and behavioral interventions.

All of these disorders must cause significant distress or functional impairment and require that certain other disorders, such as schizophrenia or substance abuse, be ruled out before making the diagnosis. Bipolar disorders in children are relatively rare and may be difficult to diagnose because of less distinct patterns of cycling than occur in adults; however, they become more common during adolescence and early adulthood.

Treatment

Treatment for depression usually involves cognitive behavioral therapies and psychopharmacologic treatment. Psychopharmacology for dysthymia is less predictable because symptoms may not always be consistently present, but it may be used depending on the child's or adolescent's age and presentation of symptoms (Wagner & Ambrosini, 2001).

In medicating for depression, physicians usually begin with one of the drugs known as selective serotonin reuptake inhibitors (SSRIs), such as Zoloft, Prozac, or Paxil. If the child or adolescent fails to respond to two or more of these medications, tricyclic antidepressants such as Tofranil or atypical antidepressants, such as Wellbutrin, may be tried.

In bipolar or manic depressive disorder, physicians may begin with lithium and, in some cases, attempt a trial of other mood stabilizers such

Table 2. Antidepressants/Mood Stabilizers

Class (Examples)	Full Effects
SSRI (Zoloft, Paxil, Luvox, Prozac)	2 to 4 weeks
Tricyclics (Tofranil, Elavil)	2 to 4 weeks
Atypicals (Wellbutrin, Effexor, Serzone)	2 to 4 weeks
Stabilizers (Lithium, Depakote)	7 to 10 days

Side effects: stomachache, agitation, headache, dry mouth, dizziness.

as Depakote. Examples of these medications in each classification are provided in Table 2, along with the approximate time it may take to obtain a full therapeutic effect. Table 2 also lists some of the most frequently occurring side effects.

Psychopharmacologic treatment in each of these disorders, however, can be quite complex because large numbers of children or adolescents may not respond favorably enough to continue treatment or may suffer from side effects that tend to lead to discontinuation of the drug. In a significant number of cases, more than one medication may be required for effective treatment. Pediatricians usually do not have sufficient training to manage such treatment effectively, so most children with these disorders should be referred to board certified child or adolescent psychiatrists for the best outcome.

Cognitive behavioral therapies may also be effective for treatment of depressive disorders (Asarnow, Jaycox, & Tompson, 2001). Such treatment focuses on the child or adolescent monitoring his or her mood, involvement in activities, stress, or other symptomatic behaviors and is then taught to coach himself or herself through "self talk," which is designed to give a sense of control over the symptoms and negate feelings of despair, low self-esteem, helplessness, and the like. Supportive therapy and education about the nature of the child's partic-

ular disorder can help and may assist in better outcomes for psychopharmacologic treatment, if warranted.

Monitoring suicidal symptoms is especially critical in children or adolescents with these disorders. These disorders also sometimes tend to have a diagnostic progression, with dysthymia putting a child at higher risk for depression and depression putting a child at higher risk for bipolar or manic depressive disorder. Early detection and treatment is therefore very critical.

Anxiety Disorders

Diagnosis

Anxiety disorders occur in approximately 4% of children and in a slightly larger percentage of adolescents (Bernstein & Shaw, 1997). *DSM IV* lists several types of anxiety disorders, including obsessive-compulsive disorder, generalized anxiety disorder, separation anxiety disorder, and posttraumatic stress disorder. Obsessive-compulsive disorder is marked by obsessions or compulsions that cause marked distress, are excessively time consuming, or significantly interfere with the child's or adolescent's functioning or social relationships. Obsessions are recurrent and persistent thoughts or impulses that seem to have no relationship to real-life problems or that the child or adolescent seems unable to ignore or suppress, despite the fact that he or she recognizes these as merely a product of his or her own mind.

Compulsions are repetitive behaviors (such as hand washing, ordering of objects, checking on things) or mental acts (such as counting objects or repeating words silently) that, according to rigid rules, the child or adolescent feels driven to perform and are aimed at preventing or reducing some imagined distress. These behaviors or mental acts do not seem to be connected in a realistic way to this distress or are clearly excessive.

Children or adolescents may be diagnosed with generalized anxiety disorder when they demonstrate excessive worry about events or activities (such as social functioning or school performance) and find it difficult to control these responses. Worrying must cause clinically significant impairment in social or academic functioning and also be associated with at least three of six anxiety symptoms:

- Restlessness.
- Fatigue.
- Concentration problems.
- Irritability.
- Muscle tension.
- Sleep disturbance.

Separation anxiety disorder is diagnosed when a child has developmentally inappropriate and excessive anxiety concerning separation from home or family. This must cause clinically significant distress or impairment and be accompanied by at least three of eight symptoms, such as

- Excessive worrying about injury or loss of a major family member.
- Anxiety about separation from family through being kidnapped or getting lost.
- Persistent refusal or reluctance to attend school because of fear of separation.
- Sleep disturbance.
- Complaints of physical symptoms whenever separation from a major family member occurs or is anticipated.

The diagnosis of posttraumatic stress disorder is made when a child or adolescent has experienced or witnessed a traumatic event that involved intense fear, helplessness, or horror. Subsequently, following that actual event, other symptoms have to occur. The traumatic event has to be persistently re-experienced in terms of at least one of the following:

- Intrusive recollections.
- Recurrent dreams.
- Feeling that the event is actually recurring.

- Intense distress upon exposure to cues that remind the child of the event or a physiologic reaction to such cues, like shaking or sweating.

There must also be persistent avoidance of at least three things that remind the child or adolescent of the traumatic event, such as

- Avoiding thoughts or situations.

- Inability to recall important details of the trauma.

- Feeling detached from others.

- Restriction of emotional range.

Finally, the child must demonstrate at least two of five symptoms of increased arousal, such as

- Sleep disturbance.

- Irritability.

- Difficulty concentrating.

- Hypervigilance.

- Exaggerated startle response.

> Community agencies and regional centers often provide education for parents in using behavioral approaches to further develop social and functional skills at home.

Treatment

Treatment for each of these anxiety disorders varies, depending on the specific diagnosis, but generally involves cognitive or behavioral therapies and possible psychopharmacologic treatment (Ollendick & King, 1998). The cognitive therapies generally focus on providing the child both with ways to monitor his or her own internal anxieties and with a sense of control through "self talk." For example, a young child with an obsessive-compulsive disorder may be taught to pretend that his or her ob-

sessions or compulsions are like a "little monster" trying to trick him or her into performing these rituals. The child is then shown ways to make the monster less threatening or powerful.

Other cognitive or behavioral approaches focus, in similar ways, on the unreality of the anxiety and how to anticipate responding in a more adaptive way. Reinforcement schemes may also be employed to assist or motivate the child in establishing a sense of control and participating more gradually over a period of time in anxiety-provoking events.

Psychopharmacologic treatment may involve anxiolytic or antidepressant medications (Green, 2001). The anxiolytic or anxiety-breaking medications are drugs such as Klonopin, Ativan, or Buspar. These medications are relatively fast-acting and must often be taken two or three times per day. Their major side effects include sedation or drowsiness and, in a few children, may cause a sudden onset of agitation, silliness, talkativeness, or even increased anxiety, a response that usually wears off within a couple of hours.

Stopping these drugs abruptly may also lead to increased agitation or anxiety, so their use should be withdrawn gradually, as is the case with most other psychopharmacologic medications discussed. Usually anxiolytics are used in children on a short-term basis only. The antidepressants that have been found most helpful for anxiety disorders are SSRI medications (such as Paxil or Luvox) or atypical antidepressants (such as Effexor). For children and younger adolescents, SSRIs and atypical antidepressants have become the first choice for treatment of most anxiety disorders.

Schizophrenic or Other Psychotic Disorders

Diagnosis

These disorders are exceedingly rare, especially in children—the rate

is probably less than a tenth of a percent (McClellan & Werry, 2000). *DSM IV* diagnoses children or adolescents with schizophrenia when at least two of the following symptoms are present:

- Delusions (such as thinking one has special powers or feeling that people are out to do one harm).

- Hallucinations (such as hearing voices or seeing things that no one else experiences).

- Disorganized speech.

- Grossly disorganized behavior.

- Certain symptoms of social withdrawal.

These symptoms must generally be present over a period of at least 6 months and must markedly affect one or more areas of functioning, like school or interpersonal relationships. Separate diagnoses exist for brief or atypical psychotic disorders, which last less than a month or do not meet full criteria.

Treatment

Treatment is usually a combination of behavioral training (including social skills training) and psychopharmacology (Vitiello, Bhatara, & Jensen, 1999). Medications for schizophrenia are currently the new or atypical neuroleptic or antipsychotic drugs such as Risperdal, Zyprexa, and Seroquel. These medications may diminish agitation almost immediately but take days to diminish hallucinations. After several weeks, these medications will improve disorganized thinking and social withdrawal. Side effects, however, can be severe, including sedation or even abnormal facial or motor movements.

These side effects tend to limit their use especially in children but, in rare cases, are seen as unavoidable or preferable in the face of full-blown psychosis, which can be devastatingly frightening to children or adolescents with the disorder and to those around them. In some instances, these newer neuroleptic drugs are also being used for treatment resistant depression and anxiety disorders.

Autistic Spectrum Disorders

Diagnosis

These disorders also occur quite infrequently but may not be as rare as childhood- onset schizophrenia (Volkmar, Cook, Pomeroy, Realmuto, & Tanguay, 1999). Autistic spectrum disorder is diagnosed by at least six symptoms across three areas:

1. Social impairment, such as
- Lack of eye contact.
- Failure to develop peer relationships.
- Lack of sharing enjoyment or interests with others.
- Lack of social or emotional give and take.

2. Communicative impairment, such as
- Delays in spoken language.
- Inability to initiate or sustain conversations.
- Repetitive or odd use of phrases.
- Lack of make-believe or social-imitative play.

3. Restrictive or repetitive behavior, such as
- Intense preoccupations with restricted patterns of interest.
- Inflexible routines or rituals.
- Repetitive motor mannerisms such as hand-or finger-flapping.
- Preoccupation only with parts of objects.

At least some of these symptoms must have occurred prior to 3 years of age. About three of every four children with autism may also have severe cognitive delays as well.

Asperger's disorder is diagnosed if at least three symptoms are present from the social impairment and restricted or repetitive behavior lists above but there are no significant delays in language or cognitive development. Pervasive developmental disorder may be diagnosed if it is not clear that symptoms were present prior to 3 years of age or if sufficient symptoms are not clearly present.

Treatment for children with autistic spectrum disorders relies primarily on developing basic language and social skills using behavioral strategies and reinforcement systems. Academic skills are taught according to the child's cognitive or intellectual levels. Community agencies and regional centers often provide education for parents in using behavioral approaches to further develop social and functional skills at home. There are as yet no recognized psychopharmacologic medications to treat autism directly. Some children with autism may also be at risk for other psychiatric disorders or symptoms, however, and they might be responsive to psychopharmacologic medications for such disorders (Sweeney, Forness, & Levitt, 1998).

Other Diagnoses in *DSM IV*

DSM-IV includes learning disorders, mental retardation, and communication disorders. Although they are not strictly considered mental health disorders, they are sometimes closely associated with certain psychiatric disorders. Children with these disorders are also at significantly higher risk for comorbid or co-occurring psychiatric disorders (Beichtman, Cantwell, Forness, Kavale, & Kauffman, 1998; King, DeAntonio, McCracken, Forness, & Ackerman, 1994). Eating disorders such as anorexia nervosa are listed as psychiatric disorders in *DSM IV* and involve refusal to maintain normal weight for height and age (usually defined as less than 85% of expected weight), coupled with an intense fear of gaining weight and a disturbance of body image related to weight. This disorder affects primarily adolescent girls who are often apt to focus obsessively on academic achievement, in addition to their obsession with weight or diet (Lewis, 2002).

Tourettes disorder is also listed in *DSM IV* and involves chronic motor and sometimes vocal tics occurring many times a day, usually in bouts. This disorder is often treated by SSRI

or antihypertensive medications such as Clonidine (Sweeney et al., 1998).

Substance-related disorders, such as alcohol or drug abuse are listed in *DSM IV* as psychiatric disorders and involve recurrent substance use that results in poor work or school performance, hazardous behavior such as impaired driving, or recurrent social or personal problems.

Final Thoughts

This is neither an exhaustive list nor a comprehensive description of childhood psychiatric disorders but, rather, an introduction for teachers and other school professionals to some of the major diagnoses that can impair school learning or classroom behavior. Detection and treatment of these disorders may sometimes greatly improve academic progress and social adjustment of children with more serious school learning or behavior problems. A behavioral checklist for teachers and parents has therefore been developed that is based on *DSM IV* and provides both primary and possible comorbid psychiatric diagnoses (Gadow & Sprafkin, 1994). Introductory materials to further educate teachers and parents about psychopharmacology have also been developed for those interested in particular medications (Konopasek, 2002; Wilens, 2001).

References

American Psychiatric Association. (1994). *Diagnostic and statistical manual of mental disorders* (4th ed.). Washington, DC: Author.

Arnold, L. E., Jensen, P. S., Hechtman, L., Hoagwood, K., Greenhill, L., & MTA Cooperative Group. (2000, October). *Do MTA treatment effects persist? New followup at 2 years.* Paper presented at the annual meeting of the American Academy of Child and Adolescent Psychiatry, New York.

Asarnow, J. R., Jaycox, L. H., & Tompson, M. C. (2001). Depression in youth: Psychosocial interventions. *Journal of Clinical Child Psychology, 30,* 33–47.

Beichtman, J. H., Cantwell, D. P., Forness, S. R., Kavale, K. A., & Kauffman,

J. M. (1998). Practice parameters for the diagnostic assessment and treatment of children and adolescents with language and learning disorders. *Journal of the American Academy of Child and Adolescent Psychiatry, 37*(10 Supplement), 42S–62S.

Bernstein, G. A., & Shaw, K. (1997). Practice parameters for the assessment and treatment of children and adolescents with anxiety disorders. *Journal of the American Academy of Child and Adolescent Psychiatry, 36*(10 Supplement), 69–84.

Birmaher, B., & Brent, D. (1998). Practice parameters for the assessment and treatment of children and adolescents with depressive disorders. *Journal of the American Academy of Child and Adolescent Psychiatry, 37*(10 Supplement), 63–83.

Forness, S. R., & Kavale, K. A. (2001). Ignoring the odds: Hazards of not adding the medical model to special education decisions. *Behavioral Disorders, 26,* 269– 281.

Forness, S. R., & Kavale, K. A. (2002). Impact of ADHD on school systems. In P. S. Jensen & J. R. Cooper (Eds.), *Attention deficit hyperactivity disorder: State of the science best practices. (pp. 1–20, 24).* Kingston, NJ: Civic Research Institute.

Forness, S. R., & Kavale, K. A., & Davanzo, P. A. (2002). Interdisciplinary treatment and the limits of behaviorism. *Behavioral Disorders, 27,* 168–178.

Forness, S. R., Kavale, K. A., Sweeney, D. P., & Crenshaw, T. M. (1999). The future of research and practice in behavioral disorders: Psychopharmacology and its school treatment implications. *Behavioral Disorders, 24,* 305–318.

Forness, S. R., Kavale, K. A., & Walker, H. M. (1999). Identifying children at risk for antisocial behavior: The case for comorbidity. In R. G. Gallimore, C. Bernheimer, D. L. MacMillan, & D. Speece (Eds.), *Developmental perspectives on children with high incidence disabilities* (pp. 135– 155). Mahwah, NJ: Lawrence Erlbaum.

Gadow, K., & Sprafkin, J. (1994). Child Symptom Inventory manual. Stony Brook, NY: Checkmate Plus.

Garland, A. F., Hough, R. L., McCabe, K. M., Yeh, M., Wood, P. A., & Aarons, G. A. (2001). Prevalence of psychiatric disorders in youths across five sectors of care. *Journal of the American Academy of Child and Adolescent Psychiatry, 40,* 409–418.

Green, W. H. (2001). *Child and adolescent clinical psychopharmacology* (3rd ed.). New York: Guilford Press.

Jensen, P. S., Hinshaw, S. P., Kraemer, H. C., Lenora, N., Newcorn, J. H., Abikoff, H. B., March, J. S., Arnold, L. E., Cantwell, D. P., Conner, C. K., Elliott, G. R., Greenhill, L. L., Hechtman, L., Hoaz, B., Pelham, W. E., Severe, J. B., Swanson, J. M., Wells, K. C., Wigal, T., & Vitiello, B. (2001). ADHD comorbidity findings from the MTA study: Comparing comorbid subgroups. *Journal of the American Academy of Child and Adolescent Psychiatry, 40,* 147–158.

Jensen, P. S., Kettle, L., Roper, M. T., Sloan, M. T., Dulcan, M. K., Hoven, C., Bird, H. R., Bauermeister, J. J., & Payne, J. D. (1999). Are stimulants overprescribed? Treatment of ADHD in four U.S. communities. *Journal of the American Academy of Child and Adolescent Psychiatry, 38,* 797–804.

Kavale, K. A., Forness, S. R., & Walker, H. M. (1999). Interventions for ODD and CD in the schools. In H. Quay & A. Hogan (Eds.), *Handbook of disruptive behavior disorders* (pp. 441–454). New York: Plenum.

King, B. H., DeAntonio, C., McCracken, J. T., Forness, S. R., & Ackerman, V. (1994). Psychiatric consultation to persons with severe and profound mental retardation. *American Journal of Psychiatry, 151,* 1802– 1808.

Konopasek, D. E. (2002). *Medication "Fact Sheets": A medication reference guide for the non-medical professional.* Anchorage, AK: Arctic Tern.

Lewis, M. (Ed.). (2002). *Child and adolescent psychiatry: A comprehensive textbook* (3rd ed.). New York: Guilford Press.

McClellan, J., & Werry, J. (2000). Summary of the practice parameters for the assessment and treatment of children and adolescents with schizophrenia. *Journal of the American Academy of Child and Adolescent Psychiatry, 39,* 1580–1582.

MTA Cooperative Group, (1999a). A 14–month randomized clinical trial of treatment strategies for attention deficit/hyperactivity disorder. *Archives of General Psychiatry, 56,* 1073–1086.

MTA Cooperative Group. (1999b). Moderators and mediators of treatment response for children with attention deficit/hyperactivity disorder. *Archives of General Psychiatry, 56,* 1088–1095.

Ollendick, T., & King, N. (1998). Empirically supported treatments for children with phobic and anxiety disorders: Current status. *Journal of Clinical Child Psychology, 27,* 156–167.

Swanson, J. M., Kraemer, H. C., Hinshaw, S. P., Arnold, L. E., Conners, C. K., Abikoff, H. B., Clevenger, W., Davies, M., Elliot, G. R., Greenhill, L. L., Hechtman, L., Hoza, B., Jensen, P. S., March, J. S., Newcorn, J. H., Owns, E. B., Pelham, W., Schiller, E., Severe, J. B., Simpson, S., Vitiello, B., Wells, K., Wigal, T., & Wu, M. (2001). Clinical relevance of the primary findings of the MTA: Success rates based on severity of ADHD and ODD symptoms at the end of treatment. *Journal of the American Academy of Child and Adolescent Psychiatry, 40,* 168–179.

Sweeney, D. P., Forness, S. R., & Levitt, J. G. (1998). An overview of medications commonly used to treat behavioral disorders associated with autism, Tourette's disorder, and pervasive developmental disorders. *Focus on Autism and Other Developmental Disabilities, 13,* 144–150.

Vitiello, B., Bhatara, V. S., & Jensen, P. S. (1999). Special section: Current knowledge and unmet needs in pediatric psychopharmacology. *Journal of the American Academy of Child and Adolescent Psychiatry, 38,* 501–565.

Volkmar, F., Cook, E. H., Pomeroy, J., Realmuto, G., & Tanguay, P. (1999). Practice parameters for the assessment and treatment of children, adolescents, and adults with autism and other pervasive developmental disorders. *Journal of the American Academy of Child and Adolescent Psychiatry, 38*(12 Supplement), 32–54.

Wagner, K. D., & Ambrosini, P. J. (2001). Childhood depression: Pharmacological therapy/treatment (Pharmacotherapy of childhood depression). *Journal of Clinical Child Psychology, 30,* 88–97.

Wilens, T. E. (2001). *Straight talk about psychiatric medication for kids.* New York: Guilford Press.

Zito, J. M., Safer, D. J., Riddle, M. A., Johnson, R. E., Speedie, S. M., & Fox, M. (1998). Prevalence variations in psychotropic treatment of children. *Journal of Child and Adolescent Psychopharmacology, 8,* 99–105.

Steven R. Forness, (CEC Chapter #520), Professor and Chief Educational Psychologist, UCLA Neuropsychiatric Hospital, Los Angeles, California. **Hill M. Walker** (CEC OR Federation), Professor and Director, Institute on Violence and Destructive Behavior, University of Oregon, Eugene. **Kenneth A. Kavale,** Professor, Division of Curriculum and Instruction, University of Iowa, Iowa City.

Address correspondence to Steven R. Forness, UCLA Neuropsychiatric Hospital, 760 Westwood Plaza, Los Angeles, CA 90049.9.

I Want to Go Back to Jail

At the Onondaga County Justice Center, Ms. Olcott entered the lives of the students who had disappeared from the radar screen of American education.

LYNN OLCOTT

I WANT to go back to jail. I'm serious. I was a more honest, more effective teacher there. I trusted my students, and they trusted me. We worked together toward the next scheduled GED (General Education Development) test and filled ourselves with as much literature as I could put in their willing hands. Every day I went deep into a maximum-security facility to the women's pod, where my students lived and ate and studied. Every day I encountered students who were eager to learn and glad for the simple materials I brought. I rediscovered pure, joyous teaching. In that stark environment, I rediscovered the educational power of kindness and respect.

Like so many of us now, I was a card-carrying member of the "sandwich generation," caregiver for my father while I still had a teenager at home. When my father died, I was exhausted, sad, and thoroughly disillusioned with long-term care, Medicare, and every other kind of care. I was eager to return to teaching, my late father's profession as well as mine. I responded to an ad in the paper looking for a teacher for an incarcerated education program, with no real idea of what that meant. My father's funeral was on a stormy Friday in January. The next week, I was thrilled to be hired as a GED teacher at the Onondaga County Justice Center. My new life had begun.

From the very beginning, I was struck by the contrast between the bleak correctional environment and the rich educational experiences offered there. The offerings were not limited to GED courses but included training in office technology, anger management, food service, and many other subjects. The Syracuse City School District, in conjunction with the Onondaga County Sheriff's Office, has operated the Incarcerated Education Program for several years. It is a "showcase program" in that it is well respected in corrections services circles. But it is practically unknown to the general public, even in the county where it exists. The Justice Center houses about 600 prisoners at any one time, and perhaps 60 or 70 of them are women. It is a non-sentenced facility, so students might be in the program for a few days or a few months before being bailed out, sentenced upstate, or transferred to other facilities. The GED test is given in-house about every two months. Pass rates, about 50%, equal and sometimes exceed those on the "outside."

In New York State, inmates aged 16 through 21 who lack a GED or high school diploma are required to attend classes. Many students over 21 attend voluntarily. Most of the girls and women I met were African American and had left school around 10th grade, usually due to pregnancy or childbirth. Most were incarcerated for economic crimes—prostitution, shoplifting, passing bad checks, selling drugs, and occasionally burglary and assault. Most scored between the fourth- and sixth-grade levels on the TABE (Test of Adult Basic Education), the test we used as a baseline. Most were involved with men who never came to see them. Most had children, whom they missed very much, being cared for by relatives.

The first student I met was Sally. She was about 40 years old, and her children were being raised by her father and stepmother. Several acts of violence had brought her here and to prison in the past. Sally instantly became my self-appointed assistant and made it her priority to have the heavy tables dragged together and the shaky whiteboard erected and ready for us every morning. She worked hard and encouraged the other students with persuasive personal lectures on the importance of education. When she left to serve time in a state prison, I missed her.

Sally's close friend Sheryl took over the role of encourager, but she left the moving of the heavy tables to the kids. I usually had eight or 10 students at a time, of different ages and working at different levels. I invented a simple, individualized system that students could enter easily and could use to track their own achievements. I taught math, science, and social studies as well as language arts. I liked the diversity of subject matter and was grateful for my own liberal arts education. Though technically I taught this medley of subjects, I was primarily a teacher of remedial reading and writing, a teacher of reading comprehension, a teacher of guerrilla English.

Teaching writing was fascinating. My students had a great deal to write about. Sheryl wrote about living in the South and about how her family had made a living picking cotton before coming north with her brave mother and cruel stepfather. Tina wrote a moving essay about wanting to gather her scattered family and cook Sunday dinner for them. A tough high school girl named Ilene wrote an amazing piece of irony about stolen watches and doing time. I was not really teaching writing at all; I was merely opening the drawstrings on bags of experiential treasure. What I was teaching—to students who had not written 250 words together in decades, if ever—was the format expected in a successful GED essay.

At the request of one of the high school girls, we read Sophocles' play *Antigone*. The students argued fiercely and eloquently over the judgment of King Creon against Antigone, who insisted on honoring her dead brother. Later we read parts of *Romeo and Juliet*. The students' soft ghetto voices gave the Elizabethan speech a powerful new music. Their favorite play was *A Raisin in the Sun*, by Lorraine Hansberry. We all knew people like Lena, the matriarch, and her weak, handsome son, from our own lives. We read excerpts from *Inside the Brain*, by Ronald Kotulak. One student traced her own learning difficulties to her mother's drug use during pregnancy. Another took heart at the awesome resilience of the adult brain, feeling that it was possible for her to master math and pass the GED, though the work was very hard for her. She had not stayed in school long enough to learn algebra, and this was a real disadvantage for GED students.

In quiet moments, I would look out on the tables of students and admit undeniably that these were the kids (whatever their ages) that we had failed to reach. These are kids we all had in our classes, kids who were often behavior problems, kids who had a hard time with learning, either because of circumstances or brain wiring or both. We passed or failed them, or we placed them elsewhere and forgot about them. They quit school, but they did not go away. I felt like Alice, stepping through the looking glass of American education and meeting firsthand these tales of almost incomprehensible woe.

Some days at the GED table were heartbreaking. There was Lily, who sometimes had to excuse herself from class, eyes brimming with tears, because the image of her teenage son, lying dead of a gunshot wound, was still too raw. Her own drug use could only intermittently obscure the pain. There was Ellie, just 18, who braided her own hair into shining French braids and who had been incarcerated one way or another since she was 10. There were girls and women with scars and burn marks and injured eyes. There were girls and women who had had their front teeth knocked out. Some were safer in jail than at home. Every day when I left the jail, I took a deep breath of fresh air, but my students were locked away, and their stories and their anguish and their unique female rage were locked away with them.

I have great respect for the deputies in the residence pods. I just came in every morning with my case of GED materials and enjoyed a few hours of pure and joyful teaching. It was the deputies who handled the round-the-clock despair of incarcerated lives.

Winter ripened into spring. My students left for prison, or for rehab, or for home, and there were new students almost every day. I could no longer support my family on the part-time salary, and we needed health insurance. Dutifully I applied for every full-time English teaching job within commuting distance from home. I am sure that I bombed more than one interview just by being too enthusiastic about jail! On the last day of summer before school started, I was hired for a long-term English substitute position in a suburban high school an hour from home. I would be able to make ends meet again, with the family insured. My father would approve. Or would he? I could not shake the feeling that, in terms of my calling as a teacher, I was selling out. I was abandoning students who needed me for students who probably didn't.

My new students are well dressed and college-bound. They have jet skis and cellphones, and if they ever get into trouble, it is unlikely that they will have to rely on a court-appointed attorney—or even need to know what one is. I do not have a classroom. But what am I complaining about? I have a cart that I take from room to room. In the jail, I lugged around a plastic case. Maybe it is the role of substitute that makes me feel tentative. Maybe it is the constant interruptions, the reminders about "crazy sock" day, the announcements about senior baby pictures, and the grade-level fund-raisers. Maybe I just want to go back to jail.

Recently I got a letter from Sally. She is doing one to three years at "Miss Betty's House," the insider's term for the Bedford Hills Correctional Facility. She tells me she is attending GED classes again, determined to pass this time. She says she will never give up, and I believe her. She thanks me for encouraging her to write. She reminds me that I always told the students that the world will be a better place when more women tell their stories. She says she plans to put her life down in a book someday, and I believe she will.

I miss the dull roar of electric doors closing behind me. I miss the courage of the students who came to the GED table ready to learn, despite broken lives, despite deep worries and uncertain futures. I miss the sense that I am somehow making it up to them for our educational failures of the past. Sure, I know it is a drop in the bucket. But I also know that each day, as I went deeper into the experiences of these women, I came closer to students who honored me with their willing minds. Each day in the jail, I was true to my calling. In jail I was a teacher.

LYNN OLCOTT *is a high school teacher and freelance writer living in Homer, N.Y. She is an adjunct professor in the Foundations and Social Advocacy Department at the State University of New York, Cortland. Since writing this article, she has returned to jail.*

The Importance of Teacher Self-Awareness in Working With Students With Emotional and Behavioral Disorders

Brent G. Richardson & Margery J. Shupe

What are your primary concerns in the classroom? Are you constantly involved in power struggles with some students? Do you yearn for good relationships with all your students? Are you stressed out? This article may help.

The frequency and intensity of students' emotional and behavioral disorders have increased in the past several decades (Bartollas & Miller, 1998; Knitzer, 1993; Lerner, 1995; Long, Morse, & Newman, 1996). In surveys, teachers consistently reveal that disruptive student behavior and classroom discipline are their primary educational concerns (Long, 1996a). Teachers who work with students with emotional and behavioral disorders can enhance their effectiveness and job satisfaction, minimize power struggles, and build more positive relationships with children with disabilities by taking proactive steps to increase their own self-awareness. Gold and Roth (1993) identified teacher self-awareness as a key component for managing stress.

> Teachers revealed that disruptive student behavior and classroom discipline are their primary educational concerns.

Gold and Roth (1993) defined self-awareness as "a process of getting in touch with your feelings and behaviors" (p. 141). Increased self-awareness involves a more accurate understanding of how students affect our own emotional processes and behaviors and how we affect students, as well. Self-awareness is particularly important for teachers who work with students with emotional and behavioral disorders. Seldom are we unaffected by their behavior. Often, these students reflect the best and worst in ourselves (Richardson, 2001). Our development as teachers depends on our willingness to take risks and regularly ask ourselves which of our own behaviors are helping or hindering our personal and professional growth. "If we could allow ourselves to become students of our own extraordinary self-education, we would be very well placed to facilitate the self-education of others" (Underhill, 1991, p. 79).

> Our development as teachers depends on our willingness to take stock of our own behavior.

This article identifies questions and strategies to help teachers become more self-aware regarding their interactions with students with behavioral and emotional disorders.

Five Key Questions to Increase Teacher Self-Awareness

1. Am I taking proactive steps to identify and defuse my own "emotional triggers"?

Cheney and Barringer (1995) asserted: "More than any other group, students with emotional and behavioral disorders appear to present problems that affect staff members on a very personal level" (p. 181). Unfortunately, teacher education does not always highlight the connection between a teacher's self-awareness and his or her ability to build and maintain meaningful relationships with youth with emotional and behavioral disabilities. Although teachers need to learn how to recognize signs of emotional distress in their students, it is equally important to acknowledge that teachers' own personalities, learned prejudices, and individual psychological histories have helped shape their attitudes and responses to certain behaviors (Long et al., 1996). Fritz Redl, a pioneer in working with students with emotional disturbances, emphasized that self-awareness is a key ingredient for succeeding with this population:

> As teachers we have a room, a group, equipment, materials, a curriculum, instructional methods, and grades, but most of all, we have ourselves. What happens to us emotionally in the process of teaching emotionally disturbed kids is the critical factor in determining our effectiveness. (cited in Long, 1996a, p. 44)

Helping youth with emotional and behavioral disabilities begins with understanding ourselves, particularly our own emotional processes that occur in the midst of conflict. Although psychological soundness and effective interpersonal skills are essential characteristics for teachers who work with this population (Kaufman, 1997; Webber, Anderson, & Otey, 1991), certain students can provoke even the most concerned, reasonable, and dedicated teachers to act in impulsive, acrimonious, and rejecting ways (Long, 1996a). Students experiencing stress have the capacity to locate and activate unresolved issues in our own personal lives. Few of us possess the inner peace to respond in a calm and professional manner without conscious effort. Awareness of our primary emotional triggers improves our chances of making rational decisions based on conscious choice, rather than unconscious emotional conditioning.

Helping youth with emotional and behavioral disabilities begins with understanding ourselves, particularly our own emotional processes that occur in the midst of conflict.

Further, the psychological fit between a teacher's need to stay in control and a youth's inability to maintain control can lead to counterproductive power struggles (Long, 1996a). Long asserted that by taking ownership of "negative" feelings such as anger, frustration, and disdain, we are more likely to recognize the difference between having feelings and being had by our feelings. Teachers who are aware of their own emotional processes are more likely to minimize the frequency and intensity of these counterproductive power struggles (see box, "Strategy for Identifying and Defusing Emotional Triggers").

2. Am I paying attention to what I need to pay attention to?

Most teachers recognize the power and necessity of using positive reinforcement (Johns & Carr, 1995). By consciously noticing and reinforcing positive behavior, the classroom becomes a more positive environment—one in which the recognition of both academic and behav-

---

Strategy for identifying and Defusing Emotional Triggers

Take periodic "timeouts" before, during, or after both "negative" interactions with students. Ask yourself:
- "What led me to respond this way?"
- "Is this way of responding helping or hurting this relationship?"
- "Is it helping me grow as an educator?"
- "Is it helping the youth make better choices?"

It is important to remember that we are often unaware of our primary emotional triggers. Actively seek consultation from colleagues and supervisors regarding behaviors and/or attitudes which are helping or hurting your effectiveness in the classroom.

Ask a colleague or supervisor:
- "What do you see as my biggesst strength in working with students with behavioral and emotional disorders?"
- "What types of problems or student behaviors do I find the most difficult?"

---

ioral accomplishments leads to increased student self-esteem (Fagan, 1996). In an extensive study of effective teaching behaviors for students with disabilities, Larrivee (1982) found that "giving positive feedback" to be a behavior positively correlated with student performance measures. Johns and Carr recommended that at least 70% of comments teachers give students should be positive. Although researchers have found teacher praise to be linked to improved behavioral and academic outcomes of students with emotional and behavioral disorders, the use of praise in these classrooms is often low (Sutherland & Wehby, 2001).

Teachers often inadvertently neglect to recognize and build on students' positive behaviors and strengths.

Good and Brophy (1984) found that teachers' perceptions of students can affect teaching outcomes. Teachers who work with students with emotional and behavioral disabilities can become so attuned to problem behaviors and perceived weaknesses, they inadvertently neglect to recognize and build on positive behaviors and strengths. A Minnesota youth poll by Hedin, Hannes, & Saito (as cited in Braaten, 1999) revealed that two thirds of respondents believed that they were perceived negatively by the significant adults in their lives. Only 25% believed that adults held positive images of them. Furthermore, a large proportion did not believe the adults' perceptions of them to be accurate. The researchers concluded that the youths believe that adults do not value or trust them and do not treat them with respect, and this belief increases as

Strategy for Shifting Your Focus (The Penny Transfer Technique)

Take five pennies and place them in your left pocket. Identify a student in your classroom who regularly needs to be redirected. Ideally, this should be a student whom you find difficult to engage. Every time you are able to verbally encourage that student for something he or she does well, transfer a penny to your right pocket. It is important to avoid phony or superficial affirmations (e.g., "I like your new jeans"). Your goal is to move all five pennies to the right pocket by the end of the day. Repeat this exercise each day for 2 weeks. (Note: You may need to use less pennies or extend the timeframe several days if you are only with the student one period.)

the youths grow older. In their study of teacher behaviors, Sutherland and Wehby (2001) found that ongoing teacher self-assessment had a positive impact on teacher praise.

People often expect teachers to assume not only academic roles, but also those of instructional model, disciplinarian, surrogate parent, social worker, and counselor.

The Penny Transfer Technique is one strategy teachers can use to help them shift their focus to more positive student behaviors and attributes (see box, "Strategy for Shifting Your Focus"). Richardson (2001) noted that professionals who have used the Penny Transfer Technique have found that (a) they began to automatically notice positive behaviors of problem students and (b) they were able to change their perceptions and thus improve their relationships with these youth.

3. Am I using effective strategies to reduce burnout and nurture my own mental health?

Teaching students with emotional and behavioral disorders is one of the most perplexing and challenging roles in education (Cheney & Barringer, 1995). These teachers are faced with enormous pressures and simultaneous challenges (Cheney & Barringer; Pullis, 1992) and report high levels of emotional exhaustion (Male & May, 1997). They are evaluated primarily on their ability to help students make tangible, academic improvements (Long, 1996b); yet they are also expected to assume multiple roles, such as model, disciplinarian, surrogate parent, social worker, and counselor.

Many teachers find it difficult to perform all these roles in the midst of decreasing budgets and increasing class sizes. Teachers find themselves struggling to find time to adequately cover each of the learning objectives while also attending to the emotional needs of their students. Teacher stress can adversely affect the teachers, their students, and the classroom climate. Cheney and Barringer (1995) found that stress "can be manifested as (a) a reluctance to consider factors beyond the immediately observable behavior of the student, and (b) a rigid focus on school rules as a way of coping with problematic social interactions" (p. 181).

We must develop effective strategies for regularly monitoring and managing our own stress.

To survive and thrive in the classroom, teachers who work with students with emotional and behavioral disabilities must develop effective strategies for regularly monitoring and managing their own stress.

Teachers need safe places to express their feelings and frustrations and recharge their emotional batteries. In a survey of special education teachers, Pullis (1992) found that talking with supportive colleagues is one of the most effective coping strategies. In fact, 96% of teachers rated collaborating and talking with special education colleagues as one of their most effective strategies for coping with stress (see box, "Strategy for Reducing Burnout and Nurturing Teacher Mental Health").

We need to recognize the difference, however, between the need to vent and a pattern of negativity and complaining. Assessing our results will help us make this distinction. Venting is only helping us if we are actually *venting* pent-up feelings. If this process only adds to our

Strategy for Reducing Burnout and Nurturing Teacher Mental Health

Recognize the difference between productive venting and an unproductive pattern of negativity and complaining. Take time to assess your conversations with friends and colleagues about your classroom and students. Ask yourself whether these conversations are helping to reduce or amplify your stress level. Periodically gauge your feelings and coping skills and seek out positive models.

Stop and ask yourself, "What is your vision for the children and youth that you teach?" If necessary, explore new strategies (e.g., exercising, seeking professional help, reframing student behavior, finding humor in potentially humorous situations, commending yourself for ways you are making a difference) for managing your stress and increasing your own morale.

stress level and frustration, we might want to employ a different strategy. A pattern of "unproductive venting" in the teacher's lounge, in the copy room, at lunch breaks, and at home is often the most foreboding precursor to burnout. We must regularly assess our coping skills and seek out positive colleagues and role models who will engage in supportive, constructive dialogue.

4. Am I using an appropriate sense of humor to build relationships, diffuse conflict, engage learners, and manage my own stress?

A number of educators have stressed that an appropriate sense of humor is absolutely essential for long-term success in working with youth with emotional and behavioral disorders (Richardson, 2001; Tobin, 1991, Webber et al., 1991). These students often are trying to make sense out of a variety of highly charged emotional stressors (e.g., poor reading skills, changing family structure, parental abuse and neglect) and will likely direct their hurt and frustration at teachers and peers. Students need to be held accountable for their behavior. If we take their actions personally or too seriously, however, we place ourselves at risk for both overreacting and burnout. Teachers want to approach their jobs diligently and sincerely; however, we need to recognize when we are taking ourselves, our students, or our jobs too seriously.

An appropriate sense of humor is an effective strategy for engaging students who seem to be disengaged.

While working as a high school counselor, one of the authors was informed that 80% of the disciplinary referrals to the assistant principal came from only 10% of the teachers. When asked if there were commonalities among those teachers, the assistant principal remarked,

> They all seem to take themselves and their jobs too seriously. They seem unhappy when they teach. Ironically, while they have very little tolerance for "acting-out" behaviors, students tend to act out more in their classrooms.

On the other hand, "teachers with a sense of humor are usually happy, relaxed, fun-loving, and reinforcing to others" (Webber et al., 1991, p. 291). A recent study supported these observations. Talbot and Lumden (2000) found that teachers who were more likely to use humor in their classroom reported lower emotional exhaustion and a higher sense of personal accomplishment.

Also, many writers have pointed out that an appropriate sense of humor is an effective strategy for engaging students who seem to be disengaged (Johns & Carr, 1995; Sommers-Flanagan & Sommers-Flanagan, 1997; Webb er et al., 1991). These authors also noted that humor is also one of the most effective means of de-escalating potential

crisis situations. Webber et al. observed that it is difficult for a student to continue to act aggressively or destructively while he or she is laughing. Crowley (1993) interviewed students with severe behavioral disorders regarding helpful teacher attitudes and behaviors and found that these students repeatedly talked about the relevance of humor in the classroom.

Victor Borge, the comedian, could have been talking about educators and students when he said, "Laughter is the shortest distance between two people." Sultanoff (1999) asserted, "One of the greatest potential gifts we can provide for children is to present ourselves as "humor beings." By living with a humorous perspective, we teach children to effectively manage life's challenges with far less stress" (p. 2).

Humor that heals is sensitive, is good natured, defuses difficult situations, and brings people closer together.

Having a sense of humor in the classroom is less about telling jokes and more about maintaining a relaxed and upbeat attitude and outlook about our jobs and life's bizarre twists. Teachers who have an appropriate sense of humor convey to their students that they

---

Strategy for Assessing Our Ability to Use an Appropriate Sense of Humor

To assess whether you might be incorporating an appropriate sense of humor into your classroom, periodically ask yourself the following questions:

- "How often do I laugh as I teach?"
- "Do students seem to enjoy learning in my classroom?"
- "For the most part, do I enjoy working with students with behavioral and emotional disorders?"
- "Do I use humor as a technique to defuse difficult situations or avoid potential power struggles?"
- "Does humor used in my classroom (by me or my students) tend to bring people closer together or push them further away?"

Based on your responses to these questions, it may be helpful to seek consultation or additional resources to more effectively incorporate humor into the classroom. Also, remember that qualifying language was used in these questions ("for the most part," "tend to"). You do not need to inject humor into every lesson plan or difficult situation. An honest self-assessment, however, will likely provide you with direction regarding areas where a change in attitude or behavior may be helpful.

enjoy their jobs, like their students, relish playful exchanges, and do not take themselves too seriously. Most importantly, they recognize the difference between humor that hurts and humor that heals. Richardson (2001) noted that humor that hurts is sarcastic, caustic, and pushes people away from one another, whereas humor that heals is sensitive, good natured, defuses difficult situations, and brings people closer together. As educators, we need to periodically assess our use of humor in the classroom and make adjustments when warranted (see box, "Strategies for Assessing Our Ability to Use an Appropriate Sense of Humor").

5. Do I regularly acknowledge significant ways I (and others) are making a difference in the lives of students?

In conducting workshops for professionals who work with youth with emotional and behavioral disabilities, one of the authors shared the following story of a young boy rescuing starfish on the beach:

> A young boy was walking along the beach in the middle of a sweltering, summer day. As the tide was retreating, he noticed thousands of starfish washed up on the dry sand. As the boy began throwing starfish back into the ocean, a man was passing by and said, "Son, look how many there are—you will never make a difference." Smiling, the boy looked at the starfish in his hand, threw it into the ocean, and declared, "I'll make a difference to that one."

The plight of students with disabilities is analogous to starfish washed up on the dry sand. It is easy to become paralyzed by the magnitude of the task and fail to recognize ways teachers are making a difference. It is easy to allow negative television newscasts, periodic setbacks, and seemingly unappreciative students and adults to discolor our perceptions and rob us of the idealism that propelled us to be a teacher. It is also easy to become so busy attending meetings and attending to students, we fail to attend to ourselves and our colleagues. Because of professional role demands, teachers of students with behavioral and emotional disabilities are frequently isolated from interaction with colleagues and particularly susceptible to this symptom of burnout (Zabel, Boomer, & King, 1984).

Kaufman and Wong (1991) found that teachers who perceive themselves as having the ability to bring about desired student results are more likely to perceive their students as teachable and worthy of their attention and effort. One study defined teacher efficacy as "the extent to which the teacher believes he or she has the capacity to affect student performance" (Bergman, McLaughlin, Bass, Pauly, & Zellman, 1977, p. 137). These teachers with a high sense of self-efficacy were also less likely to personalize the misbehaviors of students and more likely to maintain an attitude of tolerance for difficult students. Recognizing ways that they and others are making a dif-

---

Strategy for Recognizing Difference Makers: The Starfish Calendar

This technique is similar to the "Penny Transfer Technique"; however, the objective is to recognize the positive behavior of teachers. First, find a calendar. Draw and cut out pictures of yellow and orange starfish. When you recognize another educator making a difference (e.g., taking extra time after class, encouraging a student to talk to their counselor, using a creative intervention), communicate in some way that you appreciate their efforts.

Then, write a brief description of the behavior on a yellow starfish and paste it on the date in your Starfish Calendar. At the end of the day, identify a specific way you made a difference, and paste an orange starfish each day. This should only take a few minutes. If you happen to miss a day, try to find two the following day.

---

ference can affect the teachers' perceived self-efficacy (see box, "Strategy for Recognizing Difference Makers").

Although many teachers make a habit of overextending themselves, burnout is just as likely to result from a persistent feeling that they are not truly making a difference. The Starfish Calendar (see box) is one simple way to encourage ourselves and others to be proactive in acknowledging the contributions of teachers.

Final Thoughts

Many teachers have not received adequate training to recognize how their own psychological histories and personalities affect their interactions with youth with emotional and behavioral disabilities. Although the success of educators to reach and teach these young people depends on many factors (e.g., frequency and intensity of student behaviors, organizational structure, administrative support), this article focused on an important area in which teachers have more direct control— increasing their own self-awareness.

Many goals outlined here are challenging and may not be fully attainable. As vulnerable human beings, teachers will never discover all their emotional triggers, build positive relationships with every student, or completely avoid counterproductive power struggles. If teachers make conscious, ongoing efforts to increase their own self-awareness, they will likely enhance their effectiveness and their job satisfaction. Teachers who are willing to take prudent risks and try new strategies will inevitably make some mistakes. We need to view past conflict and unsuccessful interventions as helpful feedback, rather than personal failure. We must remember that the overall attitude of the teacher and the classroom climate affect students much more than most other techniques or interactions.

References

Bartollas, C., & Miller, S. J. (1998). *Juvenile justice in America* (2nd. ed.). Upper Saddle River, NJ: Prentice-Hall.

Bergman, P., McLaughlin, M., Bass, M., Pauly, E., & Zellman, G. (1977). *Federal programs supporting educational change: Vol. VII. Factors affecting implementation and continuation.* Santa Monica, CA: RAND. (ERIC Document Reproduction Service No. 335 341)

Braaten, J. L. (1999). Self-concept and behavior disorders. *Journal of Youth and Adolescence, 39*(1), 218-225.

Cheney, D., & Barringer, C. (1995). Teacher competence, student diversity, and staff training for the inclusion of middle school students with emotional and behavioral disorders. *Journal of Emotional and Behavioral Disorders, 3*(3), 174-182.

Crowley, E. P. (1993). Reflections on "A qualitative analysis of mainstreamed behaviorally disordered aggressive adolescents' perceptions of helpful and unhelpful teacher attitudes and behaviors." *Exceptionality, 4*(3), 187-191.

Fagan, S. A. (1996). Fifteen teacher intervention skills for managing classroom behavior problems. In N. Long, W. C. Morse, & R. G. Newman (Eds.), *Conflict in the classroom: The education of at-risk and troubled students* (5th ed., pp. 273-287). Austin, TX: Pro-Ed.

Gold, Y., & Roth, R. A. (1993). *Teachers managing stress and preventing burnout: The professional health solution.* Washington, DC: The Falmer Press.

Good, T. L., & Brophy, J. E. (1984). *Looking in classrooms* (3rd. ed.). New York: Harper & Row.

Johns, B. H., & Carr, V. G. (1995). *Techniques for managing verbally and aggressive students.* Denver: Love.

Kaufman, J. M. (1997). *Characteristics of behavior disorders of children and youth* (6th ed.). Columbus, OH: Merrill.

Kaufman, J. M., & Wong, K. L. (1991). Effective teachers of students with behavioral disorders: Are generic teaching skills enough? *Behavioral Disorders, 16*(3), 225- 237.

Knitzer, J. (1993). Children's mental health policy: Challenging the future. *Journal of Emotional and Behavioral Disorders, 1*(1), 8-16.

Larrivee, B. (1982). Identifying effective teaching behaviors for mainstreaming. *Teacher Education and Special Education, 5,* 2-6.

Lerner, R. M. (1995). *America's youth in crisis: Challenges and options for programs and policies.* Thousand Oaks, CA: Sage.

Long, N. (1996a). The conflict cycle paradigm on how troubled students get teachers out of control. In N. Long, W. C. Morse, & R. G. Newman (Eds.), *Conflict in the classroom: The education of at-risk and troubled students* (5th ed., pp. 244-265). Austin, TX: Pro-Ed.

Long, N. (1996b). Inclusion of emotionally disturbed students: Formula for failure or opportunity for new acceptance. In N. Long, W. C. Morse, & R. G. Newman (Eds.), *Conflict in the classroom: The education of at-risk and troubled students* (5th ed., pp. 116-126). Austin, TX: Pro-Ed.

Long, N., Morse, W. C., & Newman, R. G. (Eds.). (1996). *Conflict in the classroom: The education of at-risk and troubled students* (5th ed.). Austin, TX: Pro-Ed.

Male, D. B., & May, D. (1997). Stress, burnout and workload in teachers of children with special education needs. *British Journal of Special Education, 24*(3), 133-140.

Pullis, M. (1992). An analysis of the occupational stress of teachers of the behaviorally disordered: Sources, effects, and strategies for coping. *Behavioral Disorders, 17*(3), 191-201.

Richardson, B. G. (2001). *Working with challenging youth: Lessons learned along the way.* Philadelphia, PA: Brunner-Routledge.

Sommers-Flanagan, J., & Sommers-Flanagan, R. (1997). *Tough kids, cool counseling.* Alexandria, VA: American Counseling Association.

Sultanoff, S. M. (1999). President's column. *Therapeutic Humor, 13*(4), 2.

Sutherland, K. S., & Wehby, J. H. (2001). The effect of self-evaluation on teaching behavior in classrooms for students with emotional and behavioral disorders. *The Journal of Special Education, 35*(3), 161-171.

Talbot, L. A., & Lumden, D. B. (2000). On the association between humor and burnout. *Humor: International Journal of Humor Research, 13,* 419-428.

Tobin, L. (1991). *What to do with a child like this? Inside the lives of troubled children.* Deluth, MN: Whole Person Associates.

Underhill, A. (1991). The role of groups in developing teacher self-awareness. *English Language Teaching Journal, 46*(1), 71-80.

Webber, J., Anderson, T., & Otey, L. (1991). Teacher mindsets for surviving in BD classrooms. *Intervention in School and Clinic, 26,* 288-292.

Zabel, R. H., Boomer, L. W., & King, T. R. (1984). A model of stress and burnout among teachers of behaviorally disordered students. *Behavioral Disorders, 9*(3), 215- 221.

Brent G. Richardson, *Associate Professor; and* **Margery J. Shupe,** *Assistant Professor, Education Department, Xavier University, Cincinnati, Ohio.*

Address correspondence to Brent G. Richardson, Education Department, Xavier University, Cincinnati, OH 45207-6612 (e-mail: Richardb@xu.edu).

Classroom Problems That Don't Go Away

Laverne Warner and Sharon Lynch

W*ade runs "combat-style" beneath the windows of his school as he makes his getaway from his 1st-grade classroom. It is still early in the school year, but this is the third time Wade has tried to escape. Previously, his teacher has managed to catch him before he left the building. Today, however, his escape is easier, because Mrs. Archie is participating with the children in a game of "Squirrel and Trees" and Wade is behind her when he leaves the playground area. She sees him round the corner of the school, and speedily gives chase. When she reaches the front parking lot of their building, however, she cannot find him. Wade is gone!*

Experienced and inexperienced teachers alike, in all grade levels, express concern about difficult classroom problems—those problems that don't ever seem to go away, no matter what management techniques are used. Wade's story and similar ones are echoed time and again in classrooms around the world as adults struggle to find a balance between correcting children's behavior and instructing them about self-management strategies.

Educators emphasize an understanding of appropriate guidance strategies, and teachers learn about acceptable center and school district policies. An abundance of books, videotapes, and other teacher resources are available to classroom practitioners to enhance their understanding of appropriate guidance strategies. Professional organizations such as the Association for Childhood Education International define standards of good practice. Textbooks for childhood educators define well-managed classrooms and appropriate management techniques (e.g., Marion, 2003; Morrison, 2001; Reynolds, 2003; Seefeldt & Barbour, 1998; Wolfgang, 2001).

Despite this preparation, educators daily face problems with guiding or disciplining children in their classrooms. Understanding the developmental needs of children and meeting their physical needs are two ingredients to happy classroom management. It is also important to look at the larger problems involved when children's misbehaviors are chronic to the point that youngsters are labeled as "difficult." Are these children receiving enough attention from the teacher? Are they developing social skills that will help them through interactions and negotiations with other children in the classroom?

Mrs. Archie's guidance philosophy is founded on principles that she believes are effective for young children. Taking time at the end of the day to reflect on Wade's disappearance, Mrs. Archie concluded that she had done what she could, as always, to develop a healthy classroom climate.

She strives to build a classroom community of learners and act with understanding in response to antisocial behavior in the classroom, and she knows that the vast majority of children will respond positively. Mrs. Archie's classroom layout promotes orderly activity throughout the day and is well-stocked with enough materials and supplies to keep children interested and actively engaged in their learning activities. Although the activities she provides are challenging, many simple experiences also are available to prevent children from being overwhelmed by classroom choices.

Furthermore, Mrs. Archie's attitude is positive about children, like Wade, who come from families that use punitive discipline techniques at home. Her discussions with Wade's mother prior to his escape had been instructive, and she thought that progress was being made with the family. Indeed, when Wade arrived at home the day he ran off, his mother returned him to school immediately.

So what is the teacher to do about children, like Wade, with chronic and intense behavioral difficulties? If serious behavior problems are not addressed before age 8, the child is likely to have long-lasting conduct problems throughout school, often leading to suspension, or dropping out (Katz & McClellan, 1997; Walker et al., 1996). Since the window of opportunity to intervene with behavior problems is narrow, childhood educators must understand the nature of the behavior problem and design an educative plan to teach the child alternative approaches.

The ABC's of the Problem

The first step in analyzing the behavior problem is to determine the "pay-off" for the child. Challenging behaviors usually fall into one of the following categories: 1) behavior that gets the child attention, either positive or negative; 2) behavior that removes the child from something unpleasant, like work or a task; 3) behavior that results in the child getting something she or he wants, like candy or a toy; and 4) behavior that provides some type of sensory stimulation, such as spinning around until the child feels dizzy and euphoric.

To understand the pay-off for the child, it is important to examine the ABC's of the behavior: the antecedents, behaviors, and consequences associated with the problem. The *antecedent* requires a record, which describes what was happening just prior to the incident. The actual *behavior* then can be described in observable, measurable terms: instead of saying that the misbehaving child had a tantrum, detail that he threw himself to the floor, screamed, and pounded his fists on the floor for four minutes. Finally, we examine the pay-off (*consequences*) for the behavior.

Did the behavior result in close physical contact as the child was carried into the adjoining room and the caregiver attempted to soothe him? Did the behavior result in his being given juice so that he could calm down? Did the behavior result in scolding by the teacher, providing the kind of intense individual attention that some youngsters crave because it is the only demonstration of love and caring they have experienced? When teachers and caregivers examine the ABC's of the behavior, they are better able to understand the child's motivation, establish preventive strategies, and teach alternative social skills the child can use to meet his or her needs.

Prevention Strategies

Mrs. Archie knows that she needs to learn specific strategies that will help her work with "difficult" behaviors, like those of Wade, because these problems certainly don't seem to go away on their own. The following intervention methods are designed to preempt anti-social behaviors and often are referred to as prevention strategies. It is always better to prevent the behavior as much as possible.

Accentuate the Positive For the child who demonstrates inappropriate behavior to gain attention, the teacher should find every opportunity to give the child positive attention when he or she is behaving appropriately. Often, these opportunities to "catch the child being good" occur relatively early in the day. When children receive plenty of positive attention early in the day and the teacher continues to find opportunities for praise and attention as the day goes on, the child is not as likely to misbehave for attention as his need is already being met (Hanley, Piazza, & Fisher, 1997). This intervention is based on the principle of deprivation states. If the child is deprived of attention and is "hungry" for adult interaction, he will do anything to gain the attention of others, even negative attention.

Player's Choice When educators see a negative pattern of behavior, they can anticipate that the child is likely to refuse adult requests. This is often referred to as "oppositional behavior." A teacher may remark, "It doesn't matter what I ask her to do, she is going to refuse to do it." One successful strategy for dealing with this type of oppositional behavior is to provide the child with choices (Knowlton, 1995). This approach not only gives the child power and control, but also affords the child valuable opportunities for decision making. Example of choices include, "Do you want to carry out the trash basket or erase the chalkboard?," "Do you want to sit in the red chair or the blue chair?," or "Do you want to pick up the yellow blocks or the green blocks?"

The teacher must be cautious about the number of choices provided, however. Many children have difficulty making up their minds if too many choices are presented—often, two choices are plenty. Also, adults need to monitor their own attitude as they present choices. If choices are presented using a drill sergeant tone of voice, the oppositional child is going to resist the suggestions.

On a Roll When adults anticipate that a child is going to refuse a request, teachers can embed this request within a series of other simple requests. This intervention is based on the research-based principles of high-probability request sequences (Ardoin, Martens, & Wolfe, 1999). The first step in this procedure is to observe the child to determine which requests she consistently performs. Before asking the child to perform the non-preferred request, ask her to do several other things that she does consistently. For example, 8-year-old Morgan consistently resists cleaning up the dollhouse area. While she is playing with the dollhouse, her teacher could ask her to "Give the dolls a kiss," "Show me the doll's furniture," and "Put the dolls in their bedrooms." After she has complied with these three requests, she is much more likely to comply with the request to "Put the dolls away now" or "Give them to me."

Grandma's Rule This strategy often is referred to as the Premack Principle (Premack, 1959). When asking a child to perform an action, specifying what he or she will receive after completing it more often ensures its completion. Examples here include: "When you have finished your math problems, then we will go outside," "When you have eaten your peas, you can have some pudding," and "After you have rested awhile, we will go to the library."

A Spoonful of Sugar Helps the Medicine Go Down This principle involves pairing preferred and non-preferred activities. One particular task that is difficult for preschoolers, and many adults, is waiting. Most of us do not wait well. When asking a child to complete a non-preferred activity such as waiting in line, pairing a preferred activity with the waiting will make it more tolerable.

Businesses and amusement parks use the principle of pairing when they provide music or exhibits for customers as they wait in line. Similarly, with young children, teachers can provide enjoyable activities as children wait. Suggested activities that can be used during waiting periods include singing, looking at books, reading a story, or holding something special such as a banner, sign, or toy.

Another difficult activity for many young children is remaining seated. If the child is given a small object to hold during the time she must remain seated, she may be willing to continue sitting for a longer period. The principle of pairing preferred and non-preferred activities also gives the child increasing responsibility for her own behavior, instead of relying on teacher discipline.

Just One More This particular intervention is most effective when a child behaves inappropriately in order to escape a low-preference task. The purpose of the intervention is to improve work habits and increase time on task. The first step is to identify how long a particular child will work at a specific task before exhibiting inappropriate behavior. Once the teacher has determined how long a child will work on a task, the teacher can give the child a delay cue to head off misbehavior. Examples of delay cues are "Just one more and then you're finished," "Just two minutes and then you're finished," or "Do this and then you're finished."

In this intervention, a teacher sets aside preconceived ideas about how long children *should* work on a task and instead focuses on improving the child's ability to complete tasks in reference to his current abilities. As the children's challenging behaviors decrease, the adult gradually can increase the time on task, and the amount of work completed, before giving them the delay cue and releasing them from the task.

The More We Get Together Another way to improve task completion is by making the job a collaborative effort. If a child finds it difficult to complete non-preferred activities, then the instructor can complete part of the task with the student. For example, when organizing the bookshelf, the adult completes a portion of the task, such as picking up the big books as the student picks up the little books. She prefaces that activity by stating, "I'll pick up the big books, and you pick up the little books." As the child becomes more willing to complete her part of the task, the caregiver gradually increases the work expectations for the child while decreasing the amount of assistance.

Communication Development

In addition to preventing inappropriate behavior, another tactic is replacing the problem behavior by teaching the child alternative behaviors. The key to this process is "functional equivalence." Teachers must determine the *function* or pay-off for the inappropriate behavior and then teach an alternative *equivalent* action that will service the same purpose as the negative behavior. This often is referred to as the "fair pair" rule (White & Haring, 1976). Rather than punishing the behavior, teaching children a better way to behave assists in meeting their needs.

Bids for Attention The first step in addressing attention-seeking negative behaviors is to reduce their occurrence by providing plenty of attention for the child's appropriate behaviors. The next step is to teach the child appropriate ways to gain attention from others. Most children learn appropriate social skills incidentally from their family and teachers; some children, however, have learned negative ways to gain social attention. Some of the social skills that may need to be taught include calling others by name, tapping friends on the shoulder for attention, knowing how to join others in play, and raising one's

hand to gain the teacher's attention. Numerous other social skills may require direct instruction. Any time a behavior is considered inappropriate, adults need to teach the child a better way to have his needs met.

When teaching social skills to chldren, break the skill into a maximum of three steps. Then model the steps and have the child demonstrate the skill. Provide positive and negative examples of the step and have the children label the demonstration as correct or incorrect. Use class discussion time to role-play and talk about when this particular social skill is appropriate. Throughout the day, set up situations that allow practice of the social skill and encourage the child to use the new skill. Finally, promote carry-over of the skill by communicating with the family about the social skills instruction in order for the child to practice the social skills outside of the classroom—on the playground, in the lunch room, and at home.

Ask for Something Else If we know that the child has disruptive behaviors when presented with tasks that are disliked, then the teacher can present the child with an alternative task or materials, something she likes, *before* the problem behavior occurs. Then the child can be taught to ask for the alternative activity or object. When the child requests the alternative, provide it and preempt the negative behavior. In this way, children can learn to communicate their needs and prevent the challenging behavior from occurring.

Ask for Help Many children behave disruptively because they are frustrated with a task. Teachers usually can determine when the child is becoming frustrated by observing and reading non-verbal communication signals. Possible signs of frustration might be sighing, fidgeting, reddening of the face, or negative facial expressions. Noticing these signs helps the teacher know that it is time to intervene. Rather than offering help when the child needs it, the teacher says, "It looks like you need some help. When you need help, you need to tell me. Now you say, 'I need help.'" After the child has responded by saying, "I need help," the teacher provides assistance. This strategy is much more effective if the group already has role-played "asking for help."

Ask for a Break This strategy is similar to the two listed above; in this case, educators teach the child to ask for a break during a difficult and frustrating task. Prior to presenting the task, the teacher can explain that she knows that the activity can be difficult, but that the child can have a break after spending some time working hard at it. Then, the child can be taught to request a break while other students are engaged in various tasks.

Although teachers would like to think that instruction and activities are always fun for children and that learning should be child-directed, certain important activities must be mastered if children are to become successful in school. Especially as children progress into the primary grades, teachers expect them to work independently on pencil-and-paper tasks. Teaching youngsters communication skills that will help them handle frustration and low-preference activities will improve their outcomes as learners in school and in life.

Reviewing Options

Mrs. Archie, in reviewing her options for working with Wade, is gaining confidence in her ability to work more carefully with the family and with Wade to ensure his successful re-entry to her classroom. Her resolve is to continue developing a "community of learners" (Bredekamp & Copple, 1997) by helping Wade become a functioning member of her group. She intends to teach him how to enter a play setting, negotiate for what he wants in the classroom, and learn how to make compromises, while nurturing him as she would any child. These are goals that she believes will help turn around Wade's negative behavior.

Mrs. Archie also knows that her administrator is a caring woman, and, if necessary, Wade could be placed in another classroom so that he could have a "fresh start" with his entry into school. Her hope is that this will be a last-resort strategy, because she understands how much Wade needs a caring adult who understands him and his needs. Her phone call to Wade's mother at the end of the day will be friendly and supportive, with many recommendations for how the school can assist the family.

A Long-Term Plan

Most children with chronic difficult behaviors did not learn them overnight. Many of these children experience serious ongoing problems in their families. As teachers, we cannot change home dynamics or family problems. Sometimes a parent conference or parent education groups can be helpful, as the family learns to support a difficult child at home. With others, we do well to teach the child socially appropriate behavior in the classroom. As a child learns socially appropriate behavior in school, she learns that the behavior is useful in other settings. Often, the school is the only place where the child has the opportunity to learn prosocial behaviors. Children's negative behaviors may have, in a sense, "worked" for them in numerous situations for a substantial period of time. When we work to teach the child a better way to get his or her needs met, we must recognize that this process takes time and effort. When we as educators invest this time and effort with children during childhood, we are pro-

viding them with the tools that can make the difference in their school careers and in their lives.

References

Ardoin, S. P., Martens, B. K., & Wolfe, L. A. (1999). Using high-probability instruction sequences with fading to increase student compliance during transitions. *Journal of Applied Behavior Analysis, 32*(3), 339–351.

Bredekamp, S., & Copple, C. (Eds.). (1997). *Developmentally appropriate practice in early childhood programs* (Rev. ed.). Washington, DC: National Association for the Education of Young Children.

Hanley, G. P., Piazza, C. C., & Fisher, W. W. (1997). Noncontingent presentation of attention and alternative stimuli in the treatment of attention-maintained destructive behavior. *Journal of Applied Behavior Analysis, 30*(2), 229–237.

Katz, L., & McClellan, D. (1997). *Fostering children's social competence: The teacher's role.* Washington, DC: National Association for the Education of Young Children.

Knowlton, D. (1995). Managing children with oppositional defiant behavior. *Beyond Behavior, 6*(3), 5–10.

Marion, M. (2003). *Guidance of young children* (3rd ed.). Englewood Cliffs, NJ: Prentice Hall.

Morrison, G. (2001). *Early childhood education today* (8th ed.). Englewood Cliffs, NJ: Prentice Hall.

Premack, D. (1959). Toward empirical behavior laws: I. Positive reinforcement. *Psychological Review, 66*, 219–233.

Reynolds, E. (2003). *Guiding young children* (2nd ed.). Mountain View, CA: Mayfield.

Seefeldt, C., & Barbour, N. (1998). *Early childhood education: An introduction* (4th ed.). Columbus, OH: Merrill.

Walker, H. M., Horner, R. H., Sugai, G., Bullis, M., Sprague, J. R., Bricker, D., & Kaufman, M. J. (1996). Integrated approaches to preventing anti-social behavior among school-age children and youth. *Journal of Emotional and Behavioral Disorders, 4*(4), 194–209.

White, O. R., & Haring, N. G. (1976). *Exceptional teaching.* Upper Saddle River, NJ: Merrill/Prentice Hall.

Wolfgang, C. H. (2001). *Solving discipline and classroom management problems* (5th ed.). New York: John Wiley and Sons.

Laverne Warner is Professor, Early Childhood Education, and Sharon Lynch is Associate Professor of Special Education, Department of Language, Literacy, and Special Populations, Sam Houston State University, Huntsville, Texas.

UNIT 7

Vision and Hearing Impairments

Unit Selections

21. **A Half-Century of Progress for Deaf Individuals**, McCay Vernon
22. **Using Tactile Strategies With Students Who Are Blind and Have Severe Disabilities**, June E. Downing and Deborah Chen

Key Points to Consider

- Looking back, what are the major accomplishments of a half-century of educating children with hearing impairments? Looking forward, what can we hope to accomplish in the next half-century?

- How can tactile strategies support learning for students with visual impairments and other severe disabilities?

Student Website

www.mhcls.com/online

Internet References

Further information regarding these websites may be found in this book's preface or online.

Info to Go: Laurent Clerc National Deaf Education Center
http://clerccenter.gallaudet.edu/InfoToGo/index.html

The New York Institute for Special Education
http://www.nyise.org/index.html

Earlier, more adequate prenatal care, preventive medicine, health maintenance, and medical technology have reduced the number of children born either blind or deaf. In the future, with knowledge of the human genome and with the possibility of genetic manipulation, all genetic causes of blindness and deafness may be eliminated. Now and in the future, however, environmental factors will probably still leave many children with vision and hearing impairments.

Children with visual disabilities that cannot be corrected are the smallest group of children who qualify for special educational services through the Individuals with Disabilities Education Act (IDEA). Legally, a child is considered to have low vision if acuity in the best eye, after correction, is between 20/70 and 20/180 and if the visual field extends from 20 to 180 degrees. Legally, a child is considered blind if visual acuity in the best eye, after correction, is 20/200 or less or if the field of vision is restricted to an area of less than 20 degrees (tunnel vision). These terms do not accurately reflect a child's ability to see or read print.

The educational definition of visual impairment focuses on what experiences a child needs in order to be able to learn. One must consider the amount of visual acuity in the worst eye, the perception of light and movement, the field of vision (a person blinded by tunnel vision may have good visual acuity in only a very small field of vision), and the efficiency with which a person uses any residual vision.

Public Law 99-457, fully enacted by 1991, mandated early education for children with disabilities between ages 3 and 5 in the least restrictive environment. This has been reauthorized as PL102-119. It requires individualized family service plans outlining what services will be provided for parents and children, by whom, and where. These family service plans (IFSPs) are updated every 6 months. This early childhood extension of IDEA

has been especially important for babies born with low vision or blindness.

In infancy and early childhood, many children with low vision or blindness are given instruction in using the long cane as soon as they become mobile. Although controversial for many years, the long cane is increasingly being accepted. A long cane improves orientation and mobility and alerts persons with visual acuity that the user has a visual disability. This warning is very important for the protection of persons with blindness/low vision.

Children with visual impairments that prevent them from reading print are usually taught to read braille. Braille is a form of writing using raised dots that are read with the fingers. In addition to braille, children who are blind are usually taught with Optacon scanners, talking books, talking handheld calculators, closed-circuit televisions, typewriters, and special computer software.

Hearing impairments are rare, and the extreme form, legal deafness, is rarer still. A child is assessed as hard-of-hearing for purposes of receiving special educational services if he or she needs some form of sound amplification to comprehend oral language. A child is assessed as deaf if he or she cannot benefit from amplification. Children who are deaf are dependent on vision for language and communication.

When children are born with impaired auditory sensations, they are put into a classification of children with congenital (at or dating from birth) hearing impairments. When children acquire problems with their hearing after birth, they are put into a classification of children with adventitious hearing impairments. If the loss of hearing occurs before the child has learned speech and language, it is called a prelinguistic hearing impairment. If the loss occurs after the child has learned language, it is called a postlinguistic hearing impairment.

Children whose hearing losses involve the outer or middle ear structures are said to have conductive hearing losses. Conductive losses involve defects or impairments of the external auditory canal, the tympanic membrane, or the ossicles. Children whose hearing losses involve the inner ear are said to have sensorineural hearing impairments.

In 1999 The Newborn and Infant Hearing Screening and Intervention Act in the United States provided incentives for states to test the hearing of newborns before hospital discharge. Thirty-four states now offer this test for a small fee. When an infant is diagnosed with deafness or hearing loss, an appropriate early education can begin immediately under the auspices of IDEA.

Students with vision or hearing impairments whose disabilities can be ameliorated with assistive devices can usually have their individualized needs met appropriately in inclusive classrooms. Students with visual or hearing disorders whose problems cannot be resolved with technological aids, however, need the procedural protections afforded by law. They should receive special services from age of diagnosis through age 21, in the least restrictive environment, free of charge, with semiannually updated individualized family service plans (IFSPs) until age 3 and annually updated individualized education plans (IEPs) and eventually individualized transition plans (ITPs) through age 21.

The numbers of children and youth who qualify for these intensive specialized educational programs are small.

Many professionals working with individuals who are deaf feel that a community of others who are deaf and who use sign language is less restrictive than a community of people who hear and who use oral speech. The debate about what has come to be known as the deaf culture has not been resolved.

The first article in this unit deals with the progress that has been made in the last fifty years in the education of children with hearing impairments or deafness. Six areas are reviewed: use of American Sign Language (ASL), audiology, medicine, mental health, vocation and career preparation, and legislation which has facilitated the first five areas. Despite the improved quality of life for individuals with hearing impairments, the author argues that there is still a long way to go.

The second article discusses the importance of the sense of touch for students with visual impairments. They not only need instructional materials that provide tactile information, they also need the teacher to convey expectations, mood, and other social messages through physical contact. June Downing and Deborah Chen consider many issues for educating using the sense of touch.

A Half-Century of *Progress* for Deaf Individuals

By McCay Vernon

Merv Garretson, a highly respected leader in the deaf community (who is deaf himself) recently commented, "The past 50 years saw an amazing increase in the quality of life for people who are deaf."

This article will look at those 50 years of progress from the viewpoint of a person who is deaf. Six major areas will be considered: vocational rehabilitation and careers, American Sign Language, education, audiology, medicine, mental health and legislation.

Vocational Rehabilitation and Careers

What follows is a personal example of what vocational rehabilitation was like in the 1950s.

My late wife, Edith, was deaf. Early in the 1950s, she went to vocational rehabilitation in order to get help for a job or for education. The counselor she was sent to could not sign, declined to write to her and provided no interpreter. Instead, he chased her around his office and tried to seduce her. When she broke down crying, he gave her 25 cents and told her to leave.

This is an extreme example, but until the 1960s, there were no specialized counselors who could sign in the Division of Vocational Rehabilitation nor were vocational rehabilitation counselors trained to serve deaf clients. This was critical, because most deaf people had to depend upon vocational rehabilitation if they wanted to go to college or get vocational training after leaving

school. Subsequent legislation has greatly improved this situation. Most states now have specially trained counselors who sign and can serve deaf clients. If not, there are funds for interpreters. Today, many rehab counselors are deaf themselves.

In terms of careers, a half-century ago, residential schools for the deaf had strong vocational departments. They taught trades such as printing, barbering, shoe repair, cabinet making, upholstering, body and fender work, etc. Many graduates of these schools learned one of these trades while in school and applied what they had learned to earn decent livelihoods for the rest of their working days.

For example, the printing trade used to be one of the highest paid of all crafts. It was unionized, and there was a constant demand for printers—especially linotype operators. Once a deaf person became a printer and got a union card, he could go anywhere in the United States or Canada and find work. Assured of a job, many drifted all over, seeing the country. Because schools for the deaf—and industry in general—were resistant to hiring deaf college graduates into decent professional jobs, many of the deaf men graduating from Gallaudet worked as linotype operators as late as the 1950s.

Technology has changed all of this. Today for a bright, educated deaf person there are many career options available with good pay and excellent working conditions. For the lower 60 to 70 percent of deaf people who lack good edu-

cation, jobs that pay much more than minimum wage are hard to come by. Many of these individuals have turned to SSI and SSDI, which is unfortunate.

American Sign Language

By far, the major contribution made by linguists was that of the late William Stokoe. Until his book proving American Sign Language (ASL) was a bona fide language, it was thought to be only a gross, primitive set of unattractive gestures, mime, and ugly facial expressions. Educators, audiologists and other professionals in deafness, as well as some deaf professionals, perceived it in this way. Stokoe was reviled for his book on ASL by his colleagues at Gallaudet, where he was a professor. Initially, his work was rejected by his peers in deafness. However, other linguists—scholars such as Norm Chomsky—and a nucleus of Stokoe's deaf and hearing students recognized the tremendous significance of his contribution. Gradually and begrudgingly, as Stokoe continued his work and disciples—such as Ursula Bellugi and others—followed in his path, sign language gained in stature.

Today, ASL plays a major role in deaf education and deaf theater. Books on sign language are by far the best selling publications in the field of deafness. Thousands of hearing people study American Sign Language in colleges, universities and through non-credit courses. In theater, it has become almost a form of choreography. An entire profession—that of sign language interpreters—has grown, in part as a result of the pioneering work of Stokoe and his students.

Deaf people have been given access to hundreds more educational opportunities than ever before because of Stokoe's contributions and their implications relative to interpreting services. Today, sign language has a status that makes deaf people proud instead of ashamed, as was the case 50 years ago.

The use of sign language in education… has improved educational achievement, but not to the levels that are needed for success in today's world.

Two examples illustrate the situation: In the 1950s, Gallaudet was the only college in the U.S. teaching signs. Even there, the only course offered related to sign language was called "dactology," in order to conceal the fact that Gallaudet was teaching sign language. At that time, such a stigma was attached to ASL that no academic institution wished to be associated with it. In the dactology class, fingerspelling was taught, as were signs, but not sign language (ASL). Students were taught to fingerspell and to sign a vocabulary of 150 to 200 words. No instruction was offered in the syntax of ASL—which, at that time, was still not thought to be a language.

Education

Unfortunately, when one looks at the bottom line, education has not made the progress that has been achieved in other areas. Today, 30 percent of deaf adults are still functionally illiterate. Average reading levels remain around fourth to fifth grade for most deaf school students.

However, there are pluses. Fifty years ago, the overwhelming majority of deaf youth attended classes in which sign language was forbidden. Few teachers even knew how to sign. Many schools forbid the use of sign language in classes, on playgrounds and in dormitories. However, starting in the late 50's and early 60's, research on the dismal educational results of oralism was being made

public. Coupled with the findings of linguists regarding sign language, educational methodology started to change. First, it went to simultaneous communication, known as "Total Communication." More recently, the bilingual-bicultural method is becoming widespread.

The use of sign language in the education of deaf students has improved educational achievement, but not to the levels that are needed for success in today's world.

At Gallaudet University in the 50's, deaf people wanting to teach were not permitted in the graduate program for teachers. Only hearing applicants were accepted. Whereas hearing students could practice teach at the Kendall Demonstration School on Gallaudet's campus, deaf would-be teachers were not allowed to practice teach at all, but could only do individual tutoring.

From the 1950's almost until the "Deaf President Now" movement at Gallaudet in 1988, deaf teachers were a relatively small minority in residential schools and only beginning to be accepted in mainstream programs. Those deaf teachers who were hired were usually given classes of very slow, difficult students and assigned additional time consuming activities, such as Boy Scout leader, coach, dormitory counselor, etc. There were no deaf school superintendents and only a few deaf lower level administrators. For many years, Tom Dillon in the New Mexico School was the only deaf educator to reach the level of principal.

This treatment of deaf educators, coupled with the stigma placed on sign language, bears considerable responsibility for the limited gains made in education over the last 50 years.

Currently, two trends in education are of concern: First is the lack of any national standards for mainstream programs. These programs are expanding rapidly, but in ways that are not always in the best interest of deaf youth. For example, most small mainstream programs are administered by school principals with no preparation or experience in deafness and often lacking interest in the field. This means that key decisions—such as those involving money, class size, psychological services, teacher

qualifications, educational curricula, interpreter standards, etc.—are often made by people who know little or nothing about deaf children. In large day schools, the situation is much better, but there are still no national standards, and key decisions are made by people who lack training and experience in deafness.

The other trend of concern is decreasing enrollments in residential schools. In the past, these schools educated the majority of deaf youth and have always hired the most deaf teachers and administrators. They are now in a fight for survival. There is a great need for national leadership on the part of the administrators of these schools if their schools are to survive as schools and not merely custodial facilities for severely multiply handicapped deaf youth.

On the positive side, educational opportunities are far better than ever before for bright, motivated deaf people. They can attend any college or university in the U.S. for which they are qualified and be provided an interpreter or CART service. Gallaudet continues to offer a fine liberal parts program. The National Technical Institute for the Deaf (NTID) provides excellent opportunities in technology and science. California State University at Northridge offers the same wide range of courses available in most large state universities, plus excellent support services for deaf students. There are also junior college programs in most states. These programs have both vocational and academic courses. Many also offer strong deaf support services.

This broad range of educational options was unheard of 50 years ago. At that time, it was essentially Gallaudet or nothing for a deaf person wanting to attend college.

Today, deaf individuals desiring to go into education have the opportunity to become teachers, principals, superintendents and state-level officials.

Audiology

For the last half century, audiology has been a bastion of oralism, and to some extent, still is. Through its influence in the powerful American Speech and Hearing Association (ASHA), it controlled many teacher preparation programs, all of which were oral and none of which hired deaf faculty or accepted deaf students.

In recent years, ASHA's position has modified some, but audiologists and speech therapists still have an influence on how deaf children are taught that far exceeds their knowledge of what deafness is all about.

On the plus side, audiologists have improved hearing aids dramatically. Fifty years ago, they were cumbersome instruments requiring the user to wear a box-like container in front with a wire attached to the ear mold. These devices were crude and tended to amplify as much noise as they did speech.

Today, hearing aids are so sophisticated that about 30 percent of the people who functioned as deaf 50 years ago are now "hard of hearing," meaning that with amplification they can converse orally, both expressively and receptively. For this, hearing impaired people owe audiologists a lot.

Medicine

The major contributions of medicine have been twofold; by discovering and perfecting antibiotics and vaccines, many major etiologies of deafness—such as scarlet fever, rubella, meningitis, whooping cough, mumps, etc.—have either been eliminated or greatly reduced as a cause of hearing loss.

Until the mid to late 1960s, complications of Rh factor caused a significant amount of childhood deafness. Half of these children were both deaf and had cerebral palsy. Through transfusion techniques and a vaccine, Rh factor is no longer a significant cause of deafness.

Currently, the major medical contributions have come from the invention and perfection of the cochlear implant and advances in genetics. Implants have proved a blessing to many individuals who were deafened adventitiously. Some have gone from being deaf to being able to understand speech. However, the procedure has also produced many failures. These tend to be covered up.

The use of cochlear implants with prelingually deaf children is far more controversial and has a lower rate of success. However, there is no question some

children born deaf have been helped by implants. Whether implants are significantly more effective than hearing aids for those born deaf remains a debatable issue.

Unfortunately, most of the published research on cochlear implants is being done by the surgeons, audiologists and speech therapists who are doing the surgery and rehabilitation—and making a fortune in the process. As a consequence, it is almost impossible to get any research published in audiological or medical journals that addresses the failures of cochlear implants. Many infants born with significant residual hearing are being implanted, despite laws to the contrary.

As indicated above, another new area of medical progress is genetics. About half of deafness is due to genetics. The locations of many of the genes causing different forms of deafness are being discovered; this offers the possibility for the future eradication of these particular causes of hearing loss.

Mental Health

Fifty years ago, there were about five psychologists in the United States and one psychiatrist who devoted as much as 20 percent of their time to the field of deafness. If a deaf person had a mental health problem, there were no outpatient clinical services that provided signing therapists or sign language interpreters. This meant there were no outpatient facilities that could offer meaningful help to patients who were deaf. Those who needed hospitalization were placed in mental hospitals where there were no staff who could sign, no interpreters, nor any other deaf patients. This was, in essence, anti-therapeutic custodial isolation, designed more for the convenience of society than for treatment of patients who were deaf. Consequently, deaf patients stayed in the hospital much longer than hearing patients.

Often they were misdiagnosed as mentally retarded by psychologists who used the wrong tests or by psychiatrists who confused their jumbled written syntax as being indicative of schizophrenia.

In the 1960s, a few pioneering psychiatrists—such as Rainer, Grinker, Alt-

shuler, Kallmann, and Robinson—took an interest in mentally ill deaf patients. They set up units for them in hospitals in New York, Chicago and Washington, D.C. Their research and publications led to other states establishing inpatient units for deaf patients and eventually to outpatient clinics. Gallaudet started programs to prepare school psychologists, school counselors and clinical psychologists. Both NTID and Gallaudet also established departments to train social workers. Many of the graduates of these programs are deaf.

As a consequence, today most deaf people have reasonable access to mental health services, except in rural areas. Most residential schools now have school psychologists and social workers, and some have school counselors and consulting psychiatrists. However, in the majority of mainstream programs, many of the psychologists responsible for working with deaf students have little or no experience with or preparation for evaluating youth who are deaf. This has led to a situation where misdiagnoses are common and the recommendations of these psychologists are often inappropriate and do damage to the deaf student.

Despite the "amazing increase in quality of life… there is still a long way to go."

In recent years, through the efforts of psychologists, such as Pollard and Marschark, and psychiatrists, such as Steinberg, work in mental health with deaf people has moved more into the mainstream of psychology and psychiatry. This is a very positive change from previous times, when deafness was of little interest to either the American Psychological Association or the American Psychiatric Association.

Legislation and Advocacy

Federal legislation—some facilitated by the Center for Law and Deafness—has been the basis for much of the progress made by deaf people over the last half century.

For several reasons, laws passed during the last 30 years have made possible what Merv Garretson referred to as "the amazing increase in the quality of life for people who are deaf." First, they guaranteed every deaf child an education up until 21 years of age. Second, they mandated affirmative action policies be implemented in all business, government and private agencies which receive any government funding. The Telecommunications Act is responsible for captioned TV and TDDs in essential places such as police stations, airports, fire stations, hospitals, etc.

The most sweeping law, the Americans with Disabilities Act of 1990, is intended to prevent discrimination in every aspect of society, including employment.

For example, it requires all state and local agencies, hotels, theaters, restaurants, etc. be accessible to those who are deaf.

The greatest progress made by people who are deaf has come from the political activism that has resulted in these revolutionary laws affecting deaf and hard of hearing people. Once this legislation started to be passed, the National Association of the Deaf—with the help of Gallaudet—set up the Law Center for the Deaf, and other advocacy law agencies came into being. These agencies brought test cases that established exactly what rights these laws provided for deaf people. More importantly, these test cases

facilitated the enforcement of these critically important laws.

Despite the "amazing increase in the quality of life for people who are deaf" referred to by Merv Garretson, there is still a long way to go, especially in the area of education. We also need to do much more for the 30–50 percent of deaf adults with educational levels at fourth to fifth grade or below.

McCay Vernon's career in deafness spans the 50 years he has written about in this article. He has worked as a psychologist, teacher, coach, professor and is an author of six books.

Using Tactile Strategies With Students Who Are Blind and Have Severe Disabilities

June E. Downing • Deborah Chen

Vision is a primary sense for learning. Teachers use pictures, photographs, and a variety of color-coded materials in their instruction. They also use demonstrations and considerable modeling, which requires the students' visual attention. Many students with severe and multiple disabilities have considerable difficulty understanding verbal information and so rely heavily on visual information (Alberto & Frederick, 2000; Hodgdon, 1995; Hughes, Pitkin, & Lorden, 1998).

But what about students who cannot perceive visual cues—or access verbal information? When students have severe and multiple disabilities, teachers must resort to alternative teaching strategies to provide effective and accessible instruction.

If these students are also blind or have limited vision, however, they need instructional materials that provide relevant tactile information. This article describes specific tactile strategies to support instruction of students who have severe and multiple disabilities and who do not learn visually.

> **When students have severe and multiple disabilities, teachers must resort to alternative teaching strategies to provide effective and accessible instruction.**

Getting in Touch

A teacher's instructional style certainly influences what a student learns. Teachers engage their students by providing visual and auditory information. They convey their mood through facial expressions, body language, and tone of voice. They give directions by gestures, pointing, and spoken words. If students cannot receive or understand these modes of communication, the teacher must use alternative strategies. The primary alternatives are tactile. The teacher must convey his or her instructional expectations, mood, and information through physical and direct contact with the student. Teaching through the sense of touch may be unfamiliar and uncomfortable for most teachers, including those with training in special education. Teachers should become aware of how they interact with the student through touch. To be most effective with tactile teaching, teachers must consider many issues:

- What impressions are conveyed to a student when he or she is touched?
- Do the teacher's hands convey different information depending on their temperature, tenseness of tone, speed of movement, and degree of pressure?
- Are teachers aware of the range of emotions that they can communicate through touch?
- Where do they touch the student (e.g., palms, back of hands, arms, legs, chest)?
- Do they touch the student's bare skin or clothing over the skin?
- How do students respond to different types of tactile input?

To be maximally effective, teachers must become aware of, interpret, monitor, and modify their tactile interactions from the student's perspective.

Tactile Modeling

Sighted students learn from demonstrations and through imitation. Students who are blind or have minimal vision need opportunities to feel the demonstrator's actions by touching the parts of the body or objects involved in the actions (Smith, 1998). For example, in a cooking class, a classmate demonstrates how to make meringue by whipping egg whites. The student who is blind can feel the peer's hand holding the bowl, the other hand grasping the electric mixer. This way, the student who is blind can "see" what his or her classmate is demonstrating. Like other tactile adaptations, the use of tactile modeling requires careful planning on the part of the teacher and extra time for the student to benefit from this instructional strategy.

Tactile Mutual Attention

Sighted students visually examine and make observations about something they are looking at together. The student with minimal or no vision should have opportunities for shared exploration with classmates through tactile mutual attention (Miles, 1999). For example, during a unit of study on masks, the student and a classmate may tactilely examine an African mask, placing their hands together as they explore the relatively smooth parts of the mask and find the leather strips, beads, and decorative feathers that border the mask. This way the student has a joint focus and shares observations with a classmate. Sighted classmates will have many creative ideas of ways to use tactile modeling and tactile mutual attention with peers who are blind and have additional disabilities (see Figure 1).

Tactile Learning and Teaching

When students with severe disabilities are unable to use their vision effectively for obtaining information, they require tactile information that is accessible to their hands or other parts of their body. Tactile information, however, has different characteristics from visual.

Unlike vision, touch provides a fragment of the whole; the student must put together a series of tactile impressions to understand what other students are looking at. For example, fourth-grade students are studying different aspects of life in the desert. One student, who is deaf and blind and does not know American Sign Language, is feeling a large desert tortoise. One hand is near the tail, and the other hand is feeling one edge of the shell near the tortoise's head. It will take this student considerable time and effort to tactilely examine and discover the physical characteristics of a tortoise, while his classmates can see that it is a tortoise in one glance.

> **Unlike vision, touch provides a fragment of the whole; the student must put together a series of tactile impressions to understand what other students are looking at.**

Certain concepts are easier to convey tactilely than others. Abstract concepts are much more difficult to adapt tactilely than more concrete facts. For instance, it is much easier to teach about helium using balloons than it is to teach historical events. The teacher must ensure that the tactile representation is truly representative of the concept and is relevant and meaningful to the student. For example, to teach that the solid state of water is ice, the use of raised (tactile) lines in waves to represent water and raised (tactile) straight lines to represent ice is not meaningful or understandable to most students with severe and multiple disabilities. In contrast, the use of water (wet, liquid) and ice (cold, solid) would clearly represent the critical aspects of the topic of study.

Figure 1. Considerations for Interacting Through Touch

1. Select the message that you want to communicate to the student (e.g., greeting, reassurance, encouragement, praise, redirection, demonstration).
2. Decide how best to communicate that message through the type of touch (i.e., duration, pressure, movement) and where to touch the student (e.g., back of hand, shoulder, or knee).
3. Identify how you will let the student know that you are close (e.g., by saying his name) before touching him or her (e.g., on the elbow).
4. Discuss whether and how to examine an item with the student (e.g., by having two students examine an African mask).
5. Decide whether and how to use tactile modeling (e.g., by asking a classmate to show the student how to blow up a balloon).
6. Observe the student's reactions to your tactile interactions and modify the interaction accordingly.
7. Identify how you will end the interaction (e.g., let the student know that you are leaving by giving him a double pat on the shoulder).

The educational team must decide what aspects of a lesson can be represented tactilely to make instruction most easily understood. At times, the best tactile representation may be tangential to the specific subject. For example, for a lesson on Lewis and Clark and their exploration of the West, artifacts of the Old West (e.g., pieces of clothing, fur, leather pieces, a whip, and tools) can be used to provide a tactile experience for the student with no usable vision. Such items would also benefit the entire class. Acting out the event using objects as props also adds clarity and interest to a seemingly abstract topic.

Obviously, students with different skills and abilities will develop different concepts of the topic of study. For example, whereas fifth-grade students without disabilities in geometry class learn how to find the area of a square, a student who has severe and multiple impairments, including blindness, may just be learning to sort square shapes from round ones. General and special educators need to understand such differences and still challenge students to learn what they can.

Presenting Tactile Information

You can provide visual (e.g., pictures or sign language) and auditory (e.g., speech) information to several students at once. These so called *distance senses* are quick and efficient. In contrast, tactile information requires individual physical contact and takes more time to understand. You must allow extra time for presentation of tactile information so the student has an opportunity to touch, handle, examine, and eventually synthesize and understand information (Downing & Demchak, 2002). Here are some reminders:

- Decide how to introduce an item to the student.

- The item should be accessible so the student can detect its presence and then manipulate it to determine its identity or relationship to familiar experiences.
- Touching the item to some part of the student's body (e.g., arm or side or back of hand) is less intrusive than manipulating the student's hand to take the item and therefore, such an approach is recommended (Dote-Kwan & Chen, 1999; Miles, 1999; Smith, 1998). Some students are timid about tactile exploration because they are wary and careful about handling unfamiliar or disliked materials.

> **Allow extra time for presentation of tactile information so the student has an opportunity to touch, handle, examine, and eventually synthesize and understand information.**

A teacher or peer may introduce a new object to the student, by holding the object, and placing the back of his or her hand under the student's hand. The student is more likely to accept the touch of a familiar hand than that of an unfamiliar object. Slowly the teacher or peer can rotate his or her hand until the student is touching the object. This way the student has physical support while deciding whether to touch and examine the object (Dote-Kwan & Chen, 1999). After the student detects the presence of the item, he or she is more likely to take the item and explore it (if physically possible).

Ideally, students will use their hands to explore; however, some students have such severe physical disabilities that they may use touch receptors in their tongue, on their cheeks, or inside of their arms. In all cases, you need to encourage the student's active participation (even if only partial) in accessing information.

Providing Effective Tactile Representation

To determine whether tactile information is truly representative of a specific concept, the representation must be tactilely salient and meaningful. Because it is natural for sighted teachers to have a visual perspective, it is difficult to make tactile adaptations that make sense tactilely. For example, tactile outlines of items (e.g., string glued to a drawing of a house) may be used to represent different concepts but may not be recognized tactilely or understood by the student. Although miniatures are convenient because of their size and are easy to handle, they are based on visual characteristics of the objects they represent. For example, a small plastic dog has no tactile characteristics in common with a real dog. Similarly, a miniature of a house, while visually recognizable, does not resemble a house when examined tactilely. A key that the student has used to open the front door of his house will form a more accurate concept of "house."

Experiment with what can be perceived tactilely by blindfolding yourself and examining the adaptation using only your sense of touch. In addition, avoid misconceptions as much as possible. For example, in a kindergarten classroom, a student brought a glass paperweight with a rose in it for show and tell. He talked about the rose as he passed it around the class. When a classmate who has no vision and limited language was allowed to hold the paperweight, he was confused when told "it's a rose." More appropriate language should be used to describe what this student is experiencing (e.g., "round," "smooth," "heavy," and "glass"). If this student is to understand the meaning of "rose," then you need to provide a real rose, so the student can perceive its shape, texture, size, and scent (see Figure 2 for other considerations).

Hyperresponsivity to Touch

Some students demonstrate strong reactions to tactile information, even though this may be the best way for them to receive information. These reactions are often referred to as *tactile defensiveness* and treated as a negative characteristic of the student. Some people have a low sensory threshold and are hyperreactive or hyperresponsive to certain sensory stimulation (Williamson & Anzalone, 2001). Tactile responsivity is simply the degree to which an individual responds to tactile stimulation. Some individuals can tolerate considerable and varied amounts of tactile input without much reaction (e.g., tactile hyporesponsivity), while others are very sensitive to certain types of tactile input (tactile hyperresponsivity). These responses vary from person to person. Some people can wear certain fabrics next to their skin while others cannot.

Teachers must be aware of and respect these individual differences. Teachers should not take students' hands and physically make them touch materials if they are not willing to do so (Smith, 1998). If students are forced to have aversive tactile experiences, they are less likely to explore tactilely. The term tactile defensiveness has a nega-

---

Figure 2. Considerations for Developing Tactile Adaptions

1. Identify the objective of the lesson or the instructional concept.
2. Select the materials to convey this concept.
3. Close your eyes and examine the material with your hands.
4. Take a tactile perspective, not visual, when deciding how and what to present.
5. If the entire concept (e.g., house) is too complicated to represent through a tactile adaptation, then select one aspect of the concept (e.g., key) for the tactile representation.
6. Consider the student's previous tactile experiences. What items has he or she examined?
7. How does the student examine materials through the sense of touch?
8. Decide how the item will be introduced to the student.
9. Identify what supports the student needs to tactilely examine the item.
10. Decide what language input (descriptive words) will be used to convey the student's experience of the material.

tive connotation that may interfere with effective intervention. If the student has a sensory modulation problem that results in hyperresponsiveness, then the educational team should include an occupational therapist. Creative ways to bypass this problem and assist the student to handle tactile information are needed.

A Team Effort

Making appropriate tactile accommodations (instructional strategies or materials) cannot be left to one member of the team (i.e., the teacher certified in the area of visual impairment). A team effort is required, with different team members contributing their skills, knowledge, experiences, and ideas (Downing, 2002; Silberman, Sacks, & Wolfe, 1998). A special educator specifically trained in the area of visual impairments and blindness can be helpful with teaching ideas and tactile resources. Depending on this teacher's professional training and experiences, however, he or she may be unfamiliar with the types of accommodations a particular student may need. The student who is blind, has spoken language, and reads braille has very different learning needs from those of a student who does not speak, does not read braille, and has limited receptive language.

Relying on one specialist to meet the tactile needs of a student who is blind with additional severe disabilities should be avoided. The ideas of all members of the team are needed, including family members and classmates who do not have disabilities (Downing, 2002). This way tactile adaptations and strategies are more likely to be used at home and school and with peers.

Team members should consider how the student perceives information through touch, the student's best physical position, the student's ability to move different parts of his body, and past experiences with tactile information. Family members can provide insight on the student's tactile experiences and preferences. Occupational therapists can provide valuable information on the student's use of his hands, responsivity to tactile items, and strategies to decrease hyperresponsivity. Physical therapists can help with positioning considerations and adaptive equipment that support tactile exploration. In collaboration with the general educator, the teacher certified in visual impairments can provide ideas for making tactile adaptations to instructional materials. Classmates can be asked for their ideas on how to use tactile modeling or to gather objects and tactile materials that can make a lesson more meaningful.

The ideas of all members of the team are needed, including family members and classmates who do not have disabilities.

Final Thoughts

Meeting the learning needs of students who have severe disabilities and who do not have clear access to visual information is a significant instructional challenge. Teaching through touch is unfamiliar and perhaps awkward for most sighted people, but learning though touch is essential for students who are blind or have minimal vision. Effective use of tactile strategies must consider the individual student's needs and abilities, learning environment, and task. These strategies can best support students' learning when there is a concerted effort on the part of the educational team, additional time for the presentation of tactile information, and systematic evaluation of adaptations.

References

Alberto, P. A., & Frederick, L. D. (2000). Teaching picture reading as an enabling skill. *TEACHING Exceptional Children, 33*(1), 60-64.

Dote-Kwan, J., & Chen, D. (1999). Developing meaningful interventions. In D. Chen (Ed.), *Essential elements in early communication visual impairments and multiple disabilities* (pp. 287-336). New York: American Foundation for the Blind Press.

Downing, J. E. (2002). Working cooperatively: The role of team members. In J. E. Downing (Ed.), *Including students with severe and multiple disabilities in typical classrooms: Practical strategies for teachers* (2nd ed., pp. 189-210). Baltimore: Paul H. Brookes.

Downing, J. E., & Demchak, M. A. (2002). First steps: Determining individual abilities and how best to support students. In J. E. Downing (Ed.), *Including students with severe and multiple disabilities in typical classrooms: Practical strategies for teachers* (2nd ed., pp. 37-70). Baltimore: Paul H. Brookes.

Hodgdon, L. A. (1995). *Visual strategies for improving communication. Vol. 1: Practical supports for school and home.* Troy, MI: QuirkRoberts.

Hughes, C., Pitkin, S. E., & Lorden, S. W. (1998). Assessing preferences and choices of persons with severe and profound mental retardation. *Education and Training in Mental Retardation and Developmental Disabilities, 33*, 299-316.

Miles, B. (1999). *Talking the language of the hands to the hands.* Monmouth, OR: DBLINK, The National Information Clearinghouse on Children Who Are Deaf-Blind. (ERIC Document Reproduction Service No. ED 419 331)

Silberman, R. K., Sacks, S. Z., & Wolfe, J. (1998). Instructional strategies for educating students who have visual impairments with severe disabilities. In S. Z. Sacks & R. K. Silberman (Eds.), *Educating students who have visual impairments with other disabilities* (pp. 101-137). Baltimore: Paul H. Brookes.

Smith, M. (1998). Feelin' groovy: Functional tactual skills. Retrieved January 24, 2000, from http://www.tsbvi.edu/Outreach/seehear/summer98/groovy.htm

Williamson, G. G., & Anzalone, M. (2001). *Sensory integration and self regulation in infants and toddlers: Helping very young children interact with their environment.* Washington, DC: Zero to Three. (ERIC Document Reproduction Service No. ED 466 317)

June E. Downing *(CEC Chapter #29), Professor; and* **Deborah Chen** *(CEC Chapter #918) Professor, Department of Special Education, California State University, Northridge.*

Address correspondence to June E. Downing, Department of Special Education, California State University, Northridge, 18111 Nordhoff St., Northridge, CA 91330-8265 (e-mail: june.downing@csun.edu).

The development of this article was supported by the U.S. Department of Education, Office of Special Education and Rehabilitative Services Grant # H3224T990025. The content, however, does not necessarily reflect the views of the U.S. Department of Education, and no official endorsement should be inferred.

UNIT 8
Multiple Disabilities

Unit Selections

23. **Making Inclusion a Reality for Students With Severe Disabilities**, Pamela S. Wolfe and Tracey E. Hall
24. **Choice Making: A Strategy for Students With Severe Disabilities**, Alison M. Stafford
25. **Empowering Students With Severe Disabilities to Actualize Communication Skills**, Paul W. Cascella and Kevin M. McNamara

Key Points to Consider

- What types of preplanning and planning are required to develop IEPs for students with multiple disabilities being integrated into general education settings? Why is collaboration essential?

- Do students with multiple disabilities have the ability to make choices for themselves? Should they be encouraged to do so? Why or why not?

- What types of augmentative technology can help students with multiple disabilities communicate? What other ways do they have to make their thoughts known?

Student Website

www.mhcls.com/online

Internet References

Further information regarding these websites may be found in this book's preface or online.

Activity Ideas for Students With Severe, Profound, or Multiple Disabilities
http://www.palaestra.com/featurestory.html

Severe and/or Multiple Disabilities
http://www.nichcy.org/pubs/factshe/fs10txt.htm

For most of the twentieth century, children with multiple disabilities (MD) were kept hidden in their parents' homes or put into institutions. Any father or mother presenting such a child at a public school for admission was ridiculed and turned away. In 1975 the Individuals with Disabilities Education Act (IDEA) in the United States turned this around. Such children may now be enrolled in general education classes if that is appropriate. They are entitled to a free education in the least restrictive environment that serves their needs. IDEA, in its years of existence, has allowed millions of students, who once would have been written off as "uneducable" to be given some form of schooling.

A child placed in the category of multiple disabilities (MD) has two or more co-occurring areas of exceptionality. Each child with MD is very special and very needy. Consider the physicist, Steven Hawking, who has a brilliant mind but cannot communicate or move without augmentative technology. While many MD students have some cognitive disabilities, many have normal or above normal intellect. Their impairments may be developmental disabilities, speech and language impairments, autism, traumatic brain injuries, emotional and behavioral disorders, visual impairments, hearing impairments, orthopedic impairments, health impairments, or any combination of these.

The practice of deinstitutionalization (removing individuals from hospitals and large residential institutions and keeping them in their own homes) and the legal initiatives requiring free and appropriate public education in the least restrictive environment have closed some of the cracks through which these children once fell.

Schools are attempting to provide students with MD with the best education possible. Often, when schools fail, it is some condition(s) outside of the school's control which share the onus of responsibility. Schools, when they fail to be effective, usually provide inadequate services due to lack of professional development. Without adequate teacher preparation, and sufficient teaching support, education of all children in inclusive classrooms becomes infeasible. Professional development must be both improved and expanded to give regularized education a leg to stand on.

Another problem that looms large in the appropriate education for children with MD is lack of acceptance and preparation by the lay public and the macrosystem to accept their inclusion in public schools. Advocates for the rights of disabled individuals have used the term handicapism to describe this prejudice and discrimination directed at disabled students. The greater the disability, the greater the prejudice. A disability (not able) is not the same as a handicap (hindrance, not at an advantage). The words should not be used interchangeably. A person who is not able to do something (walk, see, hear) has a disability but does not have to be handicapped. Schools and communities may impose handicaps (hindrances) by preventing the student with the disability from functioning in an alternative way. Thus, if a student who cannot walk can instead locomote in a wheelchair, he or she is not handicapped. If a building or classroom has no ramps, however, and is inaccessible to a wheelchair user, then the school has imposed a handicap by preventing access to that

particular property of the environment. If a student cannot use vocal cords to communicate, and is provided with an augmentative and alternate communication (AAC) system, he or she is not handicapped. If a building or classroom has no power supply or other provisions for use of the AAC system, then the environment again has imposed a handicap. There are millions of ways in which properties of our environments and characteristics of our behavior prevent children with multiple disabilities from functioning up to their potentialities.

Some public schools have resisted the regular education initiative (REI) that calls for general education classes rather than special education classes to be primarily responsible for the education of students with more severe and multiple disabilities. The inclusive school movement, which supports the REI, would have special education teachers become consultants, resource specialists, collaborative teachers, or itinerant teachers rather than full-time special education teachers. While arguments for and against the REI have not been resolved, most educators agree that an appropriate education for each child with a disability may require a continuum of services. Some children, especially those with multiple disabilities, may require an environment more restrictive than a general education classroom for at least part of the day in order to get the type of assistance they need to function up to their potentialities. Teacher education typically does not offer comprehensive preparation for working with children with MD who require extensive special educational services. In addition, children with MD often require related therapy, transportation) to enable them to learn in a classroom environment. Hopefully, teacher preparation, in-service education, and professional development sessions will address some of these concerns of service delivery in the near future.

Many children and youth with MD suffer from a lack of understanding, a lack of empathy, and handicapist attitudes that are directed at them. They present very special problems for teachers to solve. Often the message they hear is, "just go away." The challenge of writing an appropriate Individualized Education Plan (IEP) is enormous. Updating the IEP each year and preparing an Individualized Transition Plan (ITP), which will allow the student with MD to function as independently as possible after age 21, is mandated by law. These students must be served. Teachers must be given the time and support needed to do so. Excuses such as no time, no money, and no personnel to provide appropriate services are unacceptable. Teachers can expect progress and good results, even with the most multiply disabled.

The first article in this unit, "Making Inclusion a Reality for Students With Severe Disabilities" emphasizes the how, when, and where of inclusion. The time for debating whether to include students with MD is past. Collaborative planning is essential for appropriate integration and education of students with MD. A cascade of integration options makes it possible for students with MD to be included even during content area instruction. The authors give suggestions for designing IEPs with workable instructional objectives.

The second article in this unit suggests that students with multiple disabilities should have the opportunity to participate in choice-making about education and activities of daily living. Alison Stafford tells how persons in responsible positions could encourage them in this regard. Their preferences can be more readily determined by understanding their typical modes of response.

The unit's final article, "Empowering Students With Severe Disabilities to Actualize Communication Skills," discusses functional communication. Students can use gestures, sign language, and/or augmentative technological aids to express their needs and desires. Service providers can learn to translate their vocalizations, gestures, signs, and augmentative aids in order to provide more appropriate education and care.

Making Inclusion a Reality for Students With Severe Disabilities

Pamela S. Wolfe and Tracey E. Hall

Let's end the debate about *whether* to include students with severe disabilities in the general education classroom (see box, "What Does the Literature Say?"). Let's focus on *how* and *when* and *where*. This article provides helpful perspectives and suggestions for teachers, students, and parents in the struggle to provide an appropriate education for all students.

Here, we provide a cascade of integration options for inclusion. These integration options are based on the work of many researchers (Bradley, King-Sears, & Tessier-Switlick, 1997; Giangreco, Cloninger, & Iverson, 1998; Janney & Snell, 2000; Stainback & Stainback, 2000).

The social integration focus of inclusion negates the opportunity for the student with disabilities to receive instruction in content areas.

In these options, we have applied content area instruction to inclusive settings, using a case example. We have also outlined a system designed to facilitate collaborative planning between general and special education teachers, using a student's individualized education program (IEP) as a foundation for decision making. Use of the IEP ensures that educational programming is both individualized and integrated with the general classroom curriculum.

The Cascade of Integration Options

The Individuals with Disabilities Education Act (IDEA) promotes the concept of placement of students with disabilities into the least restrictive environment (LRE). The concept of LRE is based on the belief that educators must provide a range of placement options (Mastropieri &

Scruggs, 2000; Thomas & Rapport, 1998). A cascade of placement options can range from the home-school and general education class setting to institutional placements. This cascade of services highlights the need to individualize and base decisions for placement on the student's unique needs.

As noted, schools and districts are placing more students with severe disabilities in general education settings. But placement alone is insufficient to guarantee that the student with disabilities will benefit educationally. The optimal integration option is based on two factors:

- The type of activity undertaken in the general education setting.

- The objectives stated on the student's IEP.

Decisions about including a student with severe disabilities are frequently oriented toward fitting the student into the existing general education classroom activities and focus primarily on social integration (Scruggs & Mastropieri, 1996). The social integration focus negates the opportunity for the "included" student to receive instruction in content areas. Although we acknowledge the value of social integration, we advocate that programming should emanate from the student's IEP objectives. Teachers should consider content area coursework as a means by which the student may meet his or her IEP objectives. For example, teachers can address many objectives from the IEP in the general education setting by considering a range of adaptations and accommodations.

The Cascade of Integration Options illustrates a range of accommodations for students with severe disabilities who are included in general education settings (see box, "Cascade of Integration Options"). This cascade includes the following poles:

- The least restrictive inclusion option in which no changes are made (unadapted participation in the general education curriculum).

What Does the Literature Say About Inclusion for Students With Severe Disabilities?

The inclusion of students with severe disabilities into general education classrooms has become increasingly prevalent (Katsiyannis, Conderman, & Franks, 1995; Sailor, Gee, & Karasoff, 2000; U.S. Department of Education, 2000). Although IDEA '97 does not mandate the inclusion of students with disabilities, the legislation strongly encourages consideration of appropriate placement in general education settings.

Definition. The term *inclusion* has many interpretations. We have adopted the definition of inclusion noted by Mastropieri and Scruggs (2000) in which *students with disabilities are served in the general education classroom under the instruction of the general education teacher.* Specifically it involves providing support services to the student in the general education setting versus excluding the student from the setting and their peers. Inclusion requires the provision of adaptations and accommodations to classroom curriculum to ensure that the student will benefit from the placement. The definition, however, does not require that the student with special needs perform at a level comparable to peers without disabilities.

Benefits of Inclusion. Many research studies have shown that the inclusion of students with severe disabilities into general education settings is beneficial for all students (those with and without disabilities) particularly in relation to social acceptance, self-esteem, and social skills (Kennedy, Shukla, & Fryxell, 1997; Mu, Siegel, & Allinder, 2000). Although some research has indicated

academic gains, teachers are more challenged to appropriately include students with severe disabilities in the content areas (Heller, 2001). Content domain areas include social studies, sciences, health, and related academic subjects.

Role of IEP. Given that the goal of inclusion is to assure that *all* students benefit from instruction, educators must provide programming that meets the needs of *all* students including those with disabilities. For students with disabilities, the IEP serves as the document to guide program planning and instruction. Educators should use the IEP to determine *what* should be taught, *how* the content should be taught, and *who* can most appropriately provide instruction.

Roles of Professionals. There are many professions involved in providing services for students with severe disabilities in included settings. Two frequent members to this team of professionals are the general education and special education teachers. The collaboration of these teachers is essential to assure that the student with disabilities is successful in the placement both socially and academically (Jackson, Ryndak, & Billingsley, 2000; Salend, 2001; Salisbury, Evans, & Palombaro, 1997; Snell & Janney, 2000). Both teachers need to be aware of the student's IEP objectives and use this document to guide program planning decisions and data collection procedures. To meet the needs of students with disabilities in the general education classroom, changes in the curriculum may be necessary.

- A more restrictive option in which students with severe disabilities are temporarily removed from the setting (functional curriculum outside the general education classroom).

The cascade also includes a series of questions designed to help educators make decisions concerning the most appropriate integration options during content area instruction.

Collaborative Planning for Inclusion

As noted previously, the collaboration of educators involved with the student having severe disabilities is essential to ensure appropriate integration and educational programming. Special and general education teachers must share knowledge about teaching strategies when planning effective instruction. Through collaborative teaming, teachers set the stage for student achievement of goals.

We have identified two stages of planning for special and general education teachers when considering options for content area integration. Table 1 lists these stages as *preplanning* and collaborative *planning* activities.

- *In the preplanning stages,* the general education teacher reflects on the content area unit activities and conducts a task analysis to identify key components of the lessons. Once the general education teacher has identified components of the unit, the special education teacher is asked to reflect upon the individual student's IEP objectives and how those objectives can be addressed in the general education content area unit. This stage is a *thinking* or *reflection activity* before a meeting; or the teachers could hold a face-to-face meeting to think together.

- *In the collaborative planning stage,* the two teachers meet to determine the most appropriate integration options in relation to the IEP, what adaptations or accommodations will be re-

Cascade of Integration Options

Unadapted participation in the general curriculum
Same activities, same objectives, same setting
- Can student complete the activities as written for the general education classroom?
- Do one or more lesson objectives match the student's IEP?

Adaptations to the general curriculum
Same activities, different (related) objectives, same setting
- Can the student meet the lesson objectives with minor modifications (time, response mode)?

Embedded skills within the general curriculum
Similar activity, different (related) objectives, same setting
- Are there components of the activity that can be met by the students, even if not the central objective of the lesson but match an IEP objective?

Functional curriculum in the general education classroom
Different activities, different (related) objectives, same setting
- Are the class activities greatly unrelated to the student's IEP? Are there IEP? Are there IEP objectives that could be met in the same setting?

Functional curriculum outside general education classroom
Different activities, different (unrelated) objectives, different setting
- Are the class activities greatly unrelated to the student's IEP? Are IEP objectives better met in a different setting (require equipment, repetition, etc.)?

quired, what additional supports are needed, and how student progress will be monitored (see Table 1).

Case Study of Collaborative Planning

Table 2 shows a case example of the Cascade of Integration Options in operation, as educators implement accommodations for a student included in content area instruction. The example reflects the plan for a student named Billy, who is included in a sixth-grade classroom.

Billy's IEP contains instructional objectives in a variety of domain areas, including communication, functional academics, socialization, fine and gross motor skills, hygiene, and leisure and recreation. The teachers formed their instructional plan based on Billy's IEP objectives.

The teachers collaboratively determined how they could meet many of Billy's IEP objectives within the content area of social studies.

Critical to the successful application of the Cascade is a well-designed IEP with clearly stated instructional objectives

---

As Table 2 illustrates, the integration option varies across the activities and days of the instructional unit. Further, note that the teachers considered the need for additional support to implement instruction (adaptive equipment, additional personnel, technical support). In this case Billy was able to work on nearly all of his IEP objectives in the content area unit. The one exception is Billy's IEP objective related to hygiene; for programming related to showering and shaving, Billy is temporarily removed from the general education setting (functional curriculum outside the general classroom conducted during an adapted physical education class).

As Table 2 shows, teachers used a variety of integration options. Through the use of integration options, Billy was able to obtain instruction on important IEP objectives even though he did not always work on the general education social studies outcomes. Further, by employing the Cascade of Integration Options, Billy's teachers were able to provide Billy with the following:

- Social skills practice.
- Instruction on social studies information.
- Instruction on IEP objectives that focused on Billy's needs.

Although this article focused on the case of Billy, educators can apply the Cascade of Integration Options with most students and areas of instruction, throughout the school year. Critical to the successful application of the Cascade is a well-designed IEP with clearly stated instructional objectives.

Final Thoughts

Inclusion of students with disabilities requires the provision of curriculum and classroom adaptations. But inclusion does not require that the student with special needs perform at a level comparable to peers without disabilities. Students with disabilities may be included during content area instruction if teachers consider the Cascade of Integration Options.

If teachers collaborate to employ such options through carefully planned instruction, they can include students with severe disabilities in general education settings in meaningful ways—for *all* students.

Table 1. Stages of Planning for Curriculum Adaptations for Student With Disabilities in General Education Settings

Preplanning		Planning
General Education Teacher Unit Plan Analysis	*Special Education Teacher*	*General and Special Education Teacher Planning Meeting*
What are the objectives of my lessons? • What is the purpose of the unit? • What skills do I want students to obtain? What are the steps students must undertake to complete the unit? • What are the component activities within the series of lessons? (list in order) • Do the activities directly relate to the overall objective of the unit? • Are the steps logically sequenced? Will the completion of the unit include individual and/or group activities? • Cooperative Learning Groups • Individual • Group activities • Individual and Group What learner products are expected? • Written report • Oral Report • Tests • Computer Question • Concept maps/graphic displays What is the time frame to complete the activities for this unit? • Single day • Monthly • Weekly • Bimonthly • Longer term What are the required materials for the activities and/or unit? • Resource materials • Class text • Computer internet • Misc. materials (school, home) How will student progress be assessed throughout the unit? • End-of-unit test • Rubric • Performance or subjective evaluation	What are the IEP objectives for the included student(s)? What domain areas from the IEP can be addressed in the instructional unit? Does this student have characteristics that will require adaptations? Have I considered: • Cognitive skills • Motor skills • Communication skills • Social skills What levels of adaptations from the continuum are appropriate for this student for different activities within the unit? What required unit adaptations could be made for this student in terms of the following: • Materials • Time requirements • Product expectations	Based on the unit analysis, what IEP objectives can be worked on during content area instruction? What adaptations or accommodations will be required to work on these objectives? What other supports will the general education teacher need to successfully complete the activity? • Teaching assistant present • Adaptive equipment • Technical support • Materials adaptations • Co-teach with special education teacher Are the student's IEP objectives being addressed in this unit in a meaningful way? How will teachers communicate about student progress throughout the unit? • Informal discussion • Weekly meetings • Report from assistant • Communication journal How will progress toward attainment of IEP goal(s) be assessed?

Table 2. Case Example of Collaborative Planning in Content Area Instruction (Social Studies)

	Day 1	**Day 2**	**Day 3**	**Day 4**	**Day 5**
Preplanning					
Activity	Assign to one of three map groups. • Political map • Geographic map • Natural resources map Start research for map information. Textbook, Encyclopedia. Newspaper, Library books, CD-ROM, Internet. 30-minute library time.	Continue research. Draw the map on 3' x 5' poster board, include scale, legend, major cities, and landmarks. Each student must draw and color a minimum of 10 features for specific map in appropriate location. 1-hour map making.	Continue map making: Draw the map on 3' x 5' poster board, include scale, legend, major cities, and landmarks. Draw or color features for specific map in appropriate location. 1-hour map making.	Final map construction. Preparation for oral presentation. Division of speaking roles. 30-minutes map work. 30-minutes presentation work.	Three groups orally present maps to class. 30-minute presentations for each group.
IEP Objective	**Communication:** Initiate conversation about map with group members using communication device. **Functional Academics Reading:** Identify parts of newspaper for peers to find map information. **Social Skills:** Take turns interacting with peers during research; maintain appropriate personal space. **Gross Motor:** Manipulate wheelchair to and within library.	**Fine Motor:** Cut out three pictures that represent resources on the map with adaptive scissors. **Functional Academics Math:** Count the number of resource features group members made (10 each). **Communication:** Initiative with peers if ready for them to count if number of items is correct using communication device.	**Fine Motor:** Paste the three objects on the map. **Functional Academics Math:** Alert the group when time is up map making. **Communication:** Initiate communication with peers using device.	**Functional Academics Reading:** While students are completing research information for presentation, student uses newspaper to identify leisure activities (movie section, TV guide). **Leisure:** Select preferred leisure activity for the weekend. **Functional Academics Math:** Practice time-telling in preparation for group presentation, day 5.	**Communication:** Introduce members of the working group to the class using communication device. **Functional Academics Math:** Keep time for the group. Notify members when half-hour period is over.
Planning					
Level of Adaptation	Embedded skills within the general curriculum. Similar activities, different objectives, same setting.	Adaptations to the general curriculum. Same activities, different objectives, same setting.	Adaptations to the general curriculum. Same activities, different objectives, same setting.	Functional curriculum in the general education classroom. Different activities, different objectives, same setting.	Unadapted participation in the general curriculum. Same activities, same objective, same setting.
Support from Special Education Teacher	Co-teach presentation of the map assignment to class. Needed technical support.	Provide adapted scissors to general education room. Provide enlarged pictures for student to cut. Needed technical support.	Needed technical support.	Needed technical support.	None.

References

Bradley, D. F., King-Sears, M. E., & Tessier-Switlick, D. M. (1997). *Teaching students in inclusive settings.* Boston: Allyn & Bacon.

Heller, K. W. (2001). Adaptations and instruction in science and social studies. In J. L. Bigge, S. J. Best, & K. W. Heller (Eds.), *Teaching individuals with physical, health, or multiple disabilities* (4th ed., pp). Upper Saddle River, NJ: Merrill.

Giangreco, M. F., Cloninger, C. J., & Iverson, V. S. (1998). *Choosing outcomes and accommodations for children* (2nd ed.). Baltimore: Paul H. Brookes.

Jackson, L., Ryndak, D. L., & Billingsley, F. (2000). Useful practices in inclusive education: A preliminary view of what experts in moderate to severe disabilities are saying. *Journal of The Association for Persons with Severe Handicaps, 25*(3), 129–141.

Janney, R., & Snell, M. E. (2000). *Teachers' guide to inclusive practices: Modifying schoolwork.* Baltimore: Paul H. Brookes.

Katsiyannis, A., Conderman, G., & Franks, D. J. (1995). State practices on inclusion: A national review. *Remedial and Special Education, 16,* 279–287.

Kennedy, C. H., Shukla, S., & Fryxell, D. (1997). Comparing the effects of educational placement on the social relationships of intermediate school students with severe disabilities. *Exceptional Children, 64,* 31–47.

Mastropieri, M. A., & Scruggs, T. E. (2000). *The inclusive classroom. Strategies for effective instruction.* Upper Saddle River, NJ: Merrill.

Mu, K., Siegel, E. B., & Allinder, R. M. (2000). Peer interactions and sociometric status of high school students with moderate or severe disabilities in general education classrooms. *Journal of The Association for Persons with Severe Handicaps, 25*(3), 142–152.

Sailor, W., Gee, K., & Karasoff, P. (2000). Inclusion and school restructuring. In M. E. Snell & F. Brown (Eds.), *Instruction of students with severe disabilities* (5th ed.), *31–66.* Upper Saddle River, NJ: Merrill.

Salend, S. J. (2001). *Creating inclusive classrooms. Effective and reflective practices* (4th ed.). Upper Saddle River, NJ: Merrill.

Salisbury, C. L., Evans, I. M., & Palombaro, M. M. (1997). Collaborative problem-solving to promote the inclusion of young children with significant disabilities in primary grades. *Exceptional Children, 63,* 195–209.

Scruggs, T. E., & Mastropieri, M. A. (1996). Teacher perceptions of mainstreaming/inclusion 1958–1995: A research synthesis. *Exceptional Children, 63,* 59–74.

Snell, M. E., & Janney, R. (2000). *Teachers' guides to inclusive practices: Collaborative teaming.* Baltimore: Paul H. Brookes.

Stainback, S., & Stainback, W. (Eds.). (2000). *Inclusion: A guide for educators.* Baltimore: Paul H. Brookes.

Thomas, S. B., & Rapport, M. J. K. (1998). The least restrictive environment: Understanding the directions of the courts. *The Journal of Special Education, 32*(2), 66–78.

U.S. Department of Education. (2000). *Twenty-second annual report to Congress on the implementation of the Individuals with Disabilities Education Act.* Washington, DC: Author. (ERIC Document Reproduction Service No. ED 444 333)

Pamela S. Wolfe, *Associate Professor, Department of Educational and School Psychology and Special Education, The Pennsylvania State University, University Park.* **Tracey E. Hall** *(CEC Chapter #18), Senior Research Scientist/ Instructional Designer, Center for Applied Special Technology (CAST), Peabody, Massachusetts.*

Address correspondence to Pamela S. Wolfe, 212A CEDAR Building, The Pennsylvania State University, University Park, PA 16802 (e-mail; psw7@psu.edu).

From *Teaching Exceptional Children,* March/April 2003, pp. 56-61. © 2003 by The Council for Exceptional Children. Reprinted by permission.

Choice Making: A Strategy for Students With Severe Disabilities

Alison M. Stafford

Joni is a 6-year-old student with severe intellectual disabilities. She has limited communication skills, and many adults do not take the time to decipher her idiosyncratic communication. When given a snack, for example, Joni frequently tosses it on the floor. On many mornings, Joni struggles and cries while her mother dresses her; however, she cooperatively assists her mother with dressing at other times. Her mother is very confused about the causes of Joni's aberrant behavior. Joni's teachers also are frustrated, because some days Joni seems unmotivated to participate in daily activities, but on other days she is eager to participate and interact with her teachers and her classmates. Joni is typical of many children with severe disabilities who have difficulty communicating their needs and desires to caregivers, teachers, and peers. And the frustrations that Joni's teachers and parents experience also are typical.

Most of us take for granted our abilities and opportunities to make choices. Being able to make choices, as well as faking advantage of opportunities to make choices, is an integral part of what makes humans able to function independently within the community. Although no one would argue against the benefits of choice making for all persons or against allowing opportunities for choice making during an individual's daily activities, minimal documentation addresses methods of teaching choice making to individuals with severe disabilities (see box, "What Does the Literature Say About Choice Making?").

Choice is the action of an individual moving toward an item (Sigafoos & Dempsey, 1992); picking up an item (Parsons & Reid, 1990); or actively selecting an item (Guess et al., 1985). These definitions all imply that individuals must actively seek items in their environments to make a choice. In addition, merely looking at, touching, or interacting with an item, activity, or person can represent a choice.

But how many times can you recall a student, particularly one with severe disabilities, making such a choice only to discard or reject the selection and seek another item? If the opportunity for making a choice is new to a student, he or she may not understand what is being offered. Another possibility is that the student may not have experience with a person accepting his or her "choice" because well-meaning caregivers have "corrected" choices or provided the individual with an object or item that represented the caregiver's choice. Perhaps a student with severe disabilities who tosses an object aside is indicating that he or she first thought that he or she wanted the object, only to realize that he or she actually wanted something else. Individuals without severe disabilities often make a choice and then change their mind and make another selection. However, when a person with severe disabilities rejects a previously selected item, others may view this behavior as inappropriate rather than as an example of a choice.

What Does the Literature Say About Choice Making?

Individuals who lack the ability and the opportunity to make choices become dependent on others to make choices and decisions for them (Guess, Benson, & Siegel-Causey, 1985). Making choices is a fundamental right that most people take for granted (Brown, Belz, Corsi, & Wenig, 1993). In addition, opportunities for choice making can have beneficial behavioral effects. These benefits include an increased engagement level (Datilio & Rusch, 1985; Parsons, Reid, Reynolds, & Bumgarner, 1990) and improved behavior (Jolivette, Wehby, Canale, & Massey, 2001; Kern, Mantegna, Vorndran, Bailin, & Hilt, 2001; see also Romaniuk & Miltenberger, 2001, for a review).

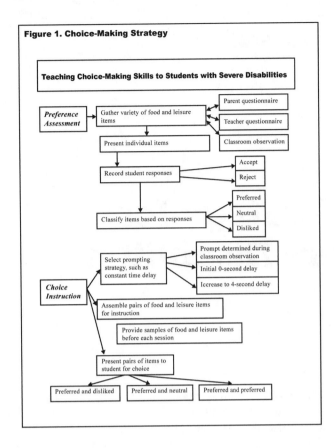

Figure 1. Choice-Making Strategy

Teaching Choice-Making Skills to Students with Severe Disabilities

students prompts that enable them to learn new skills more efficiently by limiting the number of errors. (For a description of time delay procedure, see box "Constant Time Delay.")

Preference Assessment

Before implementing this strategy for teaching choice making, the educator must identify items that the individual likes or prefers. Several reasons exist for identifying these preferences. First, educators must distinguish between individuals who accept a wide variety of items only to quickly discard them and individuals who do not attempt to obtain items even when given cues or prompts. In addition, a person who does not have recent knowledge of the items that students like cannot be sure whether they are choosing items on the basis of their preference or for an arbitrary reason, such as the item's proximity, color, or novelty.

If students do not actively attempt to obtain items that are within their reach, how can educators justify the assumption that they are not reaching for the items because they are choosing not to do so? For example, Joni is what most adults would consider a well-behaved child. She does not grab for items in her environment but waits until someone gives them to her, whether the item is a toy, an instructional item, or food. Many who work with Joni comment on how "easy" she is to have in class because when she is around, they do not have to guard certain items. Because Joni is accustomed to receiving items from adults, she does not attempt to obtain items that are within her reach. To some people, this behavior is evidence that Joni does not have preferences, because she does not actively attempt to obtain items that are not presented to her. Is it evidence that she does not have preferences, or has Joni been taught too well to wait? Assessing Joni's preference for specific items is therefore essential.

Is It evidence that she does not have preferences, or has Joni been taught to wait?

A number of strategies for teaching choice making to students with severe disabilities have appeared in the professional literature (Bambara & Roger, 1996; Beukelman & Mirenda, 1998; Lancioni, O'Reilly, & Emerson, 1996; Shevin & Klein, 1984), but little data support the effectiveness of any of these procedures. The strategy that this article describes has been effective in teaching choice-making skills to children who are 5- to 10-years old and who have severe intellectual disabilities (Stafford, Alberto, Fredrick, Heflin, & Heller, 2002). The key components of this strategy (see Figure 1) include the following:

- Preference assessments.
- A sequence of choice levels.
- Constant time delay.

The first two components of this strategy give individuals with severe disabilities multiple opportunities to develop their choice-making abilities by offering them immediate reinforcement in the form of a preferred item. After the choice-making skill has been established, the strategy allows the individual additional opportunities to practice the skill. During these opportunities, the individual can choose between a pair of preferred items.

This strategy includes the final component, constant time delay, because of its effectiveness as a teaching strategy for students with severe disabilities (Westling & Fox, 2004). Constant time delay provides a systematic method of teaching skills by routinely giving

Because an individual's preferences can change over time (Bambara & Koger, 1996; Stafford et al., 2002; Umbreit & Blair, 1996), not only must educators ascertain current preferences, but they should also repeat the preference assessments on a regular basis. For example, Stafford et al. found that the preferences of young children with severe intellectual disabilities changed at least weekly. How many times have you observed a student suddenly rejecting favorite activity, toy, or person? Sometimes people, including children with severe disabilities, just want something different.

Gathering an Array of Items and Sorting Them

Before you begin to assess your students' preferences, you must gather an array of items. Several ways of selecting these items are possible.

- You can initially spend time observing students to note items that consistently engage their interest or items that they consistently reject or ignore.
- You can interview teachers and other professionals in the school setting to ascertain their observations regarding the student's preferences.
- You can gain information from parents, either through informal conversations or by requesting that parents complete a choice questionnaire.

An additional consideration when assessing preferences is whether the choice items are age-appropriate for a specific student. To obtain this information, teachers can observe students of the same chronological age who do not have disabilities or ask them about their preferences.

After you have assembled a number of items that you believe are possible items of preference for your students with severe disabilities, include in your array other items that you either know or suspect that the students dislike. Doing so will furnish you with a group of items that includes both preferred and disliked items from which the students can develop their choice-making skills (Lohrmann-O'Rourke, Browder, & Brown, 2000).

Next, sort the items according to individual students' likes and dislikes, and be certain that you have included enough items. You want to have a sufficient number of items to enable you to determine preferred, neutral, and disliked items for each student. After you have identified such items for specific students, you can begin to carry out the choice-making instructional strategy.

Assessing Students' Responses

Many individuals with severe disabilities use atypical responses to indicate preferences (see box, "What Does the Literature Say About the Ways That Students With Severe Disabilities Express Their Preferences?"). Joni, for example, does not talk. This inability is very frustrating for her family and teachers because they are often unable to interpret her attempts at communication. However, Joni is able to make a wide range of facial expressions and sounds. Although her family and teachers try to respond in ways that they believe are appropriate, Joni frequently does not appear satisfied with their responses.

When conducting preference assessments, the teacher should look for two basic responses: accept and reject. Stafford et al. (2002) defined *accept* as follows:

- For food items, the consumption of the item within 5 seconds.
- For leisure items, the student showing interest in or manipulating the item within 5 seconds of presentation, as well as

---

Constant Time Delay

Constant time delay (CTD) is an instructional strategy that has been found to be both effective and efficient when teaching individuals with severe disabilities (Doyle, Wolery, Gast, Ault, & Wiley, 1990; Gast, Ault, Wolery, Doyle, & Belanger, 1988; McDonnell, 1987; McDonnell & Ferguson, 1989). CTD works by initially pairing the instructional cue with a prompt that increases the probability of a correct response. Prior to the start of instruction, the teacher selects the prompt (verbal, gesture, model, or physical) that he or she feels will elicit the desired response. Following the presentation of the instructional cue, the teacher provides the prompt. "Time delay" refers to the delay between the presentation of the instructional cue and the presentation of the prompt. Initially a 0 second delay is used, resulting in the cue and the prompt being presented simultaneously or, in the case of a verbal prompt, the prompt immediately following the cue. Providing the prompt this quickly virtually ensures a correct response from the learner. After a predetermined number of opportunities, usually five, the delay following the instructional cue is increased. While the teacher may determine the delay, the recommended length is 4 seconds. There are five possible responses: anticipation, wait, non-waiting error, waiting error, and a no response. An anticipation indicates that the learner provided the correct response before the prompt was given, while a wait indicates that he or she provided the correct response following the prompt. While both of these responses are technically correct, only anticipations count toward criterion. The remaining three possible responses are considered errors. A non-waiting error occurs when the learner provides an incorrect response prior to the presentation of the prompt, while a waiting error indicates that an incorrect response was provided following the prompt. The final type of response, no response, indicates that the learner did not provide a response at any time during the opportunity. For a full description of the time delay procedure, readers are encouraged to see Snell and Gast (1981).

---

maintaining his or her interest or manipulation for an additional 5 seconds.

This definition of accept presents another challenge; namely, how can the teacher decide whether the student is interested? Possible indications of interest include positive facial affect, such as smiling or looking at the item, or positive vocalizations. A student rejects an item by throwing it aside, spitting it out of his or her mouth, exhibiting negative facial affect or vocalizations, or showing no interest. Until you have a good idea of the responses that your students will use to indicate acceptance or rejection of an item, you should provide enough trials that you can rule out any misinterpretation of your students' responses. At the beginning of the preference assessment, each student should have 10 opportunities to sample each of the items. However, after you are comfortable with your assessment of the idiosyncratic responses of your students, you may find that you can complete the preference assessment for a particular item following the acceptance or rejection of an item after only four or five presentations. For a description of a way of abbreviating these time-consuming preference assessments, see box, "How to Shorten the Preference Assessment Process."

If you are using food items to determine preference, preparing single portions ahead of time will enable you to have one portion of food available. Using portion cups, such as those used in restaurants and cafeterias, allows you to put aside a tablespoon or so of yogurt or to have bite-sized pieces of cookies readily available. When selecting an array of leisure items, check the appropriateness of specific items both for the environment in which you will use them and for the age of the student. Likewise, use the actual item, not a picture or some other representation. Using the item is critical, since you are teaching choice making and not symbolic representation.

Presenting the Items

For each trial of the preference assessment, present an item to the student and then state the student's name and the name of the item. If the student is able or seems to be willing to take the item independently, then permit him or her to do so. Otherwise, you may need to provide physical assistance so that the student can sample the item. After the student samples the item, you should observe the student's reaction to the item and record her

or his response on a data sheet. Repeat this procedure for all items in the array; your goal is to allow 10 trials per item. The literature documents this method of individual presentation as

an effective way to assess the preferences of individuals with significant disabilities (Goode & Gaddy, 1976; Green et al., 1988; Pace, Ivancic, Edwards, Iwata, & Page, 1985), because presenting items in pairs or groups permits educators to assess preferences in individuals who have not demonstrated their ability to choose (Lohrmann-O'Rourke et al., 2000).

Classifying the Items

After you complete the preference assessment, classify the items as preferred, neutral, or disliked. To classify the items, calculate the percentage of acceptance for each item. Categorize items that the student accepts at 80% or more of the presentations as preferred, categorize items that the student accepts at 40% to 60% of the presentations as neutral, and categorize items that the student accepts at 20% or less of presentations as disliked. Identifying neutral items is critical to the choice-making strategy. Including items that the student likes "some of the time" shapes the choice-making ability of the student by gradually moving him or her toward the type of choice that is most common in real situations: two or more preferred options. The box entitled "Assessing Responses and Categorizing Items" summarizes the definitions of the terms accept, reject, preferred, neutral, and disliked.

Some of the items that you present will not fit into a category. Joni, for example, accepted a book about horses 3 out of 10

Assessing Responses and Categorizing Items

Since students with severe disabilities may use atypical responses to indicate preferences, use the following guidelines to define *accept* or *reject*:

- *Accept*: consumes food item within 5 seconds; shows interest in or manipulates item within 5 seconds and maintains interest (showing positive facial affect such as smiling or looking at the item, using positive vocalizations, or manipulating the item for an additional 5 seconds; manipulation need not be appropriate, since student's preference, not the ability to appropriately use the item, is important).

- *Reject*: throws item aside, spits out (for food items), exhibits negative facial affect, emits negative vocalizations, or otherwise shows no interest.

After conducting the preference assessment, calculate the percentage of acceptance for each item. Use the following criteria for categorizing the items as preferred, neutral, or disliked:

- *Preferred*: Items accepted for at least 80% of presentations.
- *Neutral*: Items accepted for 40% to 60% of presentations.
- *Disliked*: Items accepted for 0% to 20% (rejected at least 80%) of presentations.

---

times. That 30% acceptance ratio was too high for the book to fall in the disliked category but too low for it to fall in the neutral category. This strategy only considers items that clearly fall into the preferred, neutral, or disliked categories; omitting items that do not clearly meet the criteria for those categories allows the teacher to have greater confidence in pairing items during the choice-making instruction phase. Joni, for example, accepted a Barbie doll 6 out of 10 times (60%, neutral), a brightly colored necklace 9 out of 10 times (90%, preferred), and a book about baseball only 1 out of 10 times (10%, disliked) during a preference assessment.

Choice Instruction Strategy

The next component in the choice-making strategy is presenting students with a pair of items. The sequence of pairings is as follows:

- Preferred–disliked.
- Preferred–neutral.
- Preferred–preferred.

Begin choice instruction with pairs consisting of one preferred item (accepted at 80% or more of presentations) and one disliked item (accepted at 20% or less of presentations). For example, the results of Joni's preference assessment indicate that her teacher might pair the brightly colored necklace (a preferred item) with the book about baseball (a disliked item). The rationale for the initial pairing is that presenting a preferred item

with a disliked item results in an obvious response and allows for immediate reinforcement of a student's action, thereby allowing the student to experience natural consequences (Beukelman & Mirenda, 1998). A teacher who began instruction with two preferred items would not know whether the student selected an item because of a preference or whether he or she selected it for some other reason. The subsequent pairings of preferred items with neutral items and preferred items with preferred items help students practice and improve their choice-making abilities, with the final pairings more similar to those found in naturally occurring choice opportunities.

For the first pairings in the sequence, use 10 pairs of items, with each pair consisting of a preferred item and a disliked item. Be sure to include a variety of items, and be certain to vary the order in which you present them. In other words, balance the preferred and disliked items so that you do not always present the preferred item first. At this point, as well as before all instructional sessions, each student should have an opportunity to sample the items so that he or she can make an informed choice.

For each trial, you should present the pair of items to the student along with the verbal cue "(Student), I have (first item) and (second item). Do you want (first item) or (second item)?" For example, when giving Joni a choice between the necklace and the book about baseball, the teacher would say, "Joni, I have a book about baseball and a necklace. Do you want the book or the necklace?" Record the item that the student chooses, and repeat this procedure until the student has reached the criterion that you have set. Stafford et al. (2002) established a criteria of 80% for three consecutive sessions before moving to the next phase. This criteria enabled the students to demonstrate their ability to make a choice at each level before the choice options became more complex. If a student is not making progress and/or appears to be making random selections, the teacher should return to a 0 second delay for at least one full session before again implementing a 4 second delay.

After the student has reached the criterion with the initial pairings, present pairings consisting of a preferred item and a neutral item. At this level, one of the pairs for Joni might be the necklace (preferred) with the Barbie doll (neutral). Present each pair in the same manner as the previous pairings. When the student has reached the criterion with the pairs of preferred and neutral items, assemble pairs of preferred items and follow the same procedure that you used with the preferred–disliked pairs and the preferred-neutral pairs. This final type of pairing parallels many of the choices that people encounter every day: a choice between items that they prefer relatively equally. Although that type of pairing is a more realistic choice format, the strategy includes the preferred–disliked and preferred–neutral pairings to offer students opportunities to make choices that will be more reinforcing to them. Students need to learn about natural consequences; although people sometimes make poor choices, they must accept the choices that they make.

At this stage, if the student "chooses" items that the preference assessment classified as disliked (during the first group of pairings) or neutral (during the second group of pairings), conduct another preference assessment. As previously indicated, preferences can and do change over time, and the preferences of students with severe disabilities are no exception. Regularly scheduled preference assessments will enhance the effectiveness of this strategy.

Final Thoughts

Choice making is an integral part of the daily lives of all people. The strategy that this article presents for teaching choice-making skills provides practitioners and family members with a method of ensuring that those with severe disabilities can take advantage of choice-making opportunities. This instruction will benefit not only the individual with a severe disability but also his or her family and other caregivers because it results in improved participation in daily life, improved behavior, and less dependence on others.

References

Bambara, L. M., & Koger, F. (1996). *Innovations: Opportunities for daily choice making*. Washington, DC: American Association on Mental Retardation.

Beukelman, D. R., & Mirenda, P. (1998). *Augmentative and alternative communication: Management of severe communication disorders in children and adults*. Baltimore: Paul H. Brookes.

Brown, F., Belz, P., Corsi, L., & Wenig, B. (1993). Choice diversity for people with severe disabilities. *Education and Training in Mental Retardation. 28*, 318–326.

Brown, F., Gothelf, C. R., Guess, D., & Lehr, D. (1998). Self-determination for individuals with the most severe disabilities: Moving beyond chimera. *Journal of the Association for Persons with Severe Handicaps, 23*, 17–26.

Butterfield, N., & Arthur, M. (1995). Shifting the focus: Emerging priorities in communication programming for students with a severe intellectual disability. *Education and Training in Mental Retardation and Developmental Disabilities, 30*, 41–50.

Datillo, J., & Rusch, F. R. (1985). Effects of choice on leisure participation for persons with severe handicaps. *Journal of the Association for Persons with Severe Handicaps, 10*, 194–199.

Doyle, P. M., Wolery, M., Gast, D. L., Ault, M. J., & Wiley, K. (1990). Comparison of constant time delay and the system of least prompts in teaching preschoolers with developmental delays. *Research in Developmental Disabilities, 11*, 1–33.

Gast, D. L., Ault, M. J., Wolery, M., Doyle, P. M., & Belanger, S. (1988). Comparison of constant time delay and the system of least prompts in teaching sight word reading to students with moderate retardation. *Education and Training in Mental Retardation, 23*, 117–128.

Goode, D. A., & Gaddy, M. R. (1976). Ascertaining choice with alingual, deaf-blind and retarded clients. *Mental Retardation, 14*(6). 10–12.

Green, C. W., Reid, D. H., White, L. K., Halford, R. C, Brittain, D. P., & Gardner, S. M. (1988). Identifying reinforcers for persons with profound multiple handicaps. *Journal of Applied Behavior Analysis, 21*, 31–43.

Guess, D., Benson, H. A., & Siegel-Causey, E. (1985). Concepts and issues related to choice-making and autonomy among persons with severe disabilities. *Journal of the Association for Persons with Severe Handicaps, 10*, 79–86.

Jolivette, K., Wehby, J. H., Canale, J., & Massey, N. G. (2001). Effects of choice-making on the behavior of students with emotional and behavioral disorders. *Behavioral Disorders, 26*, 131–145.

Kern, L., Mantegna, M, E., Vorndran, C. M., Bailin, D., & Hilt, A. (2001). Choice of task sequence to reduce problem behaviors. *Journal of Positive Behavioral Interventions, 3*, 3–10. .

Lancioni, G. E., O'Reilly, M. F., & Emerson, E. (1996). A review of choice research with people with severe and profound developmental disabilities. *Research in Developmental Disabilities, 17*, 391–411.

Lohrmann-O'Rourke, S., Browder, D. M., & Brown, F. (2000). Guidelines for conducting socially valid systematic preference assessments. *Journal of the Association for Persons with Severe Handicaps, 25*, 42–53.

McDonnell, J. (1987). The effects of time delay and increasing prompt hierarchy strategies on the acquisition of purchasing skills by students with severe handicaps. *Journal of the Association of Persons with Severe Handicaps, 12*, 227–236.

McDonnell, J., & Ferguson, B. (1989). A comparison of time delay and decreasing prompt hierarchy strategies in teaching banking skills to students with moderate handicaps. *Journal of Applied Behavior Analysis, 22*, 85–91.

Pace, G. M., Ivancic, M. T, Edwards, G. L., Iwata, B. A., & Page, T. J. (1985). Assessment of stimulus preference and reinforcer value with profoundly retarded individuals. *Journal of Applied Behavior Analysis, 18*, 249–255.

Parsons, M. B., Reid, D., Reynolds, J., & Bumgarner, M. (1990). Effects of chosen versus assigned jobs on the work performance of persons with severe handicaps. *Journal of Applied Behavior Analysis, 23*, 253–258.

Parsons, M. B., & Reid, D. H. (1990). Assessing food preferences among persons with profound mental retardation: Providing opportunities to make choices. *Journal of Applied Behavioral Analysis, 23*, 183–195.

Romaniuk, C., & Miltenberger, R. G. (2001). The influence of preference and choice of activity on problem behavior. *Journal of Positive Behavior Interventions, 3*, 152–159.

Shevin, M., & Klein, N. K. (1984). The importance of choice-making skills for students with severe disabilities. *Journal of the Association for Persons with Severe Handicaps, 9*, 159–166.

Siegel, E., & Wetherby, A. (2000). Nonsymbolic communication. In M. E. Snell & R Brown (Eds.), *Instruction of students with severe disabilities* (5th ed., pp. 409–452). Upper Saddle River, NJ: Merrill/ Prentice Hall.

Sigafoos, J., & Dempsey, R. (1992). Assessing choice making among children with multiple disabilities. *Journal of Applied Behavior Analysis, 25*, 747–755.

Snell, M. E., & Gast, D. L. (1981). Applying time delay procedure to the instruction of the severely handicapped. *Journal of the Association for the Severely Handicapped, 6*(3), 3–14.

Stafford, A. M., Alberto, P. A., Fredrick, L. D., Heflin, L. J., & Heller, K. W. (2002). Preference variability and the instruction of choice making with students with severe intellectual disabilities. *Educa-

tion and Training in Mental Retardation and Development Disabilities. 37, 70–88.

Umbreit, J., & Blair, K. (1996). The effects of preference, choice, and attention on problem behavior at school. *Education and Training in Mental Retardation and Developmental Disabilities. 31*, 151–161.

Westling, D. L., & Fox, L. (2004). *Teaching students with severe disabilities* (2nd ed.). Upper Saddle River, NJ: Merrill/Prentice Hall.

Alison M. Stafford (CEC Chapter #112). Assistant Professor, Department of Special Education and Speech Language Pathology, University of West Georgia, Carrollton.

Address correspondence to Alison M. Stafford. University of West Georgia, 1601 Maple Street, Carrollton, GA 30118. (e-mail: astaffor@westga.edu)

Empowering Students With Severe Disabilities to Actualize Communication Skills

Paul W. Cascella • Kevin M. McNamara

Jessica is an 11-year-old child who attends the sixth grade at a local middle school. Jessica has a history of severe mental retardation, secondary to childhood meningitis and seizures. Jessica is essentially nonverbal and nonambulatory, and she relies on her parents and caregivers for eating, dressing, toileting, and participation in typical home and school events. Jessica has normal hearing, and she wears eyeglasses.

Jessica participates in both an academic and functional life skills program at her school. During most mornings, Jessica participates in middle school academic subjects within the general education context. Her middle school has a rotating daily class schedule; and Jessica attends sixth-grade classes in math, science, social studies, language arts, and Spanish. She eats lunch with students from her academic classes.

After lunch, Jessica participates in her school's functional life skills program. This program is a multi-aged group of 8 to 10 students; and the curriculum is threefold: prevocational job exploration, community experience, and recreation. Prevocational job exploration includes opportunities to participate in basic maintenance tasks (e.g., cleaning the school's library), gardening (e.g., working in the school's greenhouse), delivering snacks (e.g., as a volunteer at a local nursing home), and kitchen work (e.g., using an industrial-size kitchen at a local restaurant on Mondays when the restaurant is closed).

Activities of daily living include opportunities to set a table for meals, do laundry, go grocery shopping, and practice hygiene skills in the school's locker room. Community experience opportunities occur when Jessica participates in visits to the local public library and browses at local shop window displays.

When a speech-language pathologist or a special education teacher meets a child like Jessica, he or she might wonder about what to do for speech-language therapy and communication goals. Jessica presents an interesting challenge, not only because of her significant developmental disability, but also because she is enrolled in a general education curriculum.

Many questions come to mind: Is Jessica a candidate for speech-language therapy? What is her prognosis for communication improvement? What are some realistic communication outcomes for her? What specific skills should the educator target? Gestures? Speech? Augmentative communication? What instructional format should the educator use? Should therapy be direct or indirect? How can specialists and teachers implement goals within both general and special education activities? This article addresses these questions and provides some concrete steps for promoting effective communication.

Students With Severe Mental Retardation

Students with severe to profound mental retardation need an extensive and pervasive array of supports to fully participate in everyday learning situations, community events, adaptive skills, self-determination, and social relationships (American Association on Mental Retardation, 2002). Reports suggest that these students have rich and diverse communication abilities, including contact and distal gestures (i.e., actions that convey interest in something out of direct reach), vocalizations, verbalizations, sign language, aberrant behavior, concrete object use, and picture symbol use. These students communicate for many reasons; for example, to direct someone else's behavior, to repair a misunderstood message, to request desired activities and objects, and to protest disliked events (Mar & Sail, 1999; McLean, Brady, McLean, & Behrens, 1999; Romski, Sevcik, & Adamson, 1999).

Skill Actualization and Functional Communication

To address the questions raised previously, the speech-language pathologist and the special education teacher should consider realistic and functional outcomes. For students with severe mental retardation, educators need to establish functional communication goals that target social and learning interactions within daily school routines (Calculator, 1995; McCarthy et al., 1998). This model relies on communication partners who encourage and respect communication skills, even when the skills are nonverbal and require interpretation (Ferguson, 1994; Payne & Ogletree, 1995).

For people with severe mental retardation, a functional communication model includes modifications to the physical environment and the structure of the curriculum so as to embed communication goals into naturally occurring daily school and life routines (Cascella, 1999; National Joint Committee, 2002). A functional model depends on treatment decisions made by a transdisciplinary team and the development of a cumulative set of objectives to foster skills across multiple settings and partners (Ervin, 2003; Farrell & Pimentel, 1996). This approach is consistent with milieu teaching strategies often employed in early childhood education settings that inte-grate language skills into naturally occurring class activities (Horn, Lieber, Li, Sandall, & Schwartz, 2000).

A critical aspect of functional communication is that it emphasizes *skill actualization*, where teachers give students the opportunity to use their already developed (i.e., extant) communication skills across multiple everyday situations (McLean & McLean, 1993). Skill actualization goals are represented on the individualized education program (IEP), as statements such as, "The child will use (an already developed communication action) to (their reason for communicating) during (a particular class or social routine)."

Student with severe to profound mental retardation need many supports to participate in learning situations, community events, and social relationships.

This model matches the child's extant skill set to the classroom curriculum and the supports that are needed to enable the child's full participation in the general education classroom. This requires a careful analysis of the child's abilities and the communication expectations of teachers and peers, as well as class activities, materials, and natural opportunities for communication (Rowland & Schweigert, 1993).

For Jessica, these objectives shift from acquisition goals (i.e., developmental skills) to practical outcomes that enable her to actively participate in the school day (see Figure 1).

Figure 1. Examples of Developmental Versus Functional IEP Communication Goals	
Receptive Vocabulary	
Developmental	Jessica will identify 5 common objects during speech therapy with 80% accuracy.
Functional	Jessica will get 5 objects that are needed to participate in art activities after a request by the teacher.
Articulation	
Developmental	Jessica will produce the consonants /f/, /t/, and /s/ with 80% accuracy in word-initial position (e.g., fun, ton, sun).
Functional	Jessica will repeat herself when teacher asks for clarification of misunderstood messages during free play activities outside.
Speech	
Developmental	Jessica will imitate consonant-vowel (CV) and vowel-consonant (VC) combinations in 8/10 trials.
Functional	Jessica will vocalize to indicate her presence during morning roll call.

Steps in Creating Communication Actualization Outcomes

Step 1: Create a Communication Profile

The first step toward developing skill actualization goals for students with severe mental retardation is to create a communication profile. A communication profile is a comprehensive list of the child's communication forms and functions. Communication forms are the methods the child uses to communicate, and communication functions are the identified reasons why the child communicates (see Figures 2 and 3).

The child's communication profile includes not only obvious communication actions (e.g., pointing, head nods) and functions (e.g., requests, protests) but also communication behaviors unique to the child. For example, at a recent meeting, one teacher commented, "Sometimes when Jessica has had enough work, she pushes the work away with her hands, but other times I know when she's had enough because her head tilts like this" (teacher demonstrates the head tilt).

The members of the child's educational team create the communication profile during a team meeting that lasts for about 1 hour. At this meeting, one team member is assigned the role of facilitator while another team member acts as a recorder. The facilitator directs the discussion by asking the team to think about all of the child's possible communication skills, ones that the child deliberately uses, and ones that team members interpret from the child's behavior. The facilitator can assist the team by asking form-specific questions, such as "How does she tell you she is upset?" and "Describe how she conveys interest in an activity."

The facilitator can also guide a discussion with function-specific questions like "What is she trying to tell us when she takes someone's hand to lead them?" and "Why does she vocalize first thing in the morning?" The facilitator can also ask situation-specific questions, such as "What and how does she communicate at lunch?" "During physical therapy?" or "At the end of the day?"

After the meeting, the recorder summarizes the discussion into a succinct chart of the child's communication forms and functions. When the list is completed, team members share it with all of the people who might interact with the child during the school day. These people include the core members of the child's educational team who developed the profile and many other people—the bus driver, the librarian, the school secretaries, the lunchroom workers, the school janitors, and a select peer group. The team shares the communication profile with all of these people to encourage incidental communicative support across daily routines. Two useful phrases that school staff and peers can use are "It looks like you're telling me_____" and "Am I right that you're telling me _____?"

If the educational team has too many conflicting schedules and cannot meet together, another option is for the speech-language pathologist to take a lead role in creating the communication profile. In this strategy, the speech-language pathologist actively seeks the input of all the

---

Figure 2. Examples of Communication Forms

Vocalizations and sounds
Real words and phrases
Sign language or modified signs
Leading gestures (e.g., pulling someone)
Pushing objects (toward and away)
Pointing gestures
Reaching gestures
Showing gestures
Eye gaze
Head nod or shake
Body orientation (standing near or away)
Pointing to or exchanging pictures
Holding or pointing to real objects
Facial expressions

Figure 3. Examples of Communication Functions

Name objects, people, activities
Tell people what to do
Secure help
Convey social pleasantries ("Hi," "Bye")
Convey interest in an activity
Protest
Convey emotional or physical state
Ask for objects, people, activities
Make a choice
Request and/or report information

---

vested parties and develops a profile that accurately reflects their input. The speech-language pathologist completes observations of the child across all school events and discusses the child's communication with each of the teachers who routinely have contact with the child. Such tasks may seem like yet another hard-to-manage expansion of the already burdensome role of the school speech-language pathologist. It is consistent, however, with shifting practice patterns away from exclusively providing direct service to engaging in collaborative consultation.

Step 2: Identify the Communication Patterns of Class Routines

The second step toward communication skill actualization is to integrate the child's communication skills into classroom events and curricula activities. To do this, members of the educational team must first know about the typical dialogues, communication expectations, and communication opportunities that occur within every class situation and school activity.

In Jessica's case, her academic and life skill curricula activities are observed, and her teachers are interviewed. The speech-language pathologist and/or the special education teacher note the communication expectations that teachers and peers make in her classes. For example, the math teacher might greet the students at the beginning of class and expect them to reply a particular way. Or, perhaps the science teacher uses cooperative learning groups, and students are expected to engage in group verbal problem-solving activities.

The observer identifies the communication agendas of the people in the room and the expectations made within any classroom situation. The observer also interviews the teachers and a select group of peers to confirm whether the observations were relatively typical to that class or school activity. These interviews require the observer to understand the child from the perspective of each classroom teacher and acknowledge the strategies each teacher might already use to support the child.

Afterward, the observer creates a record of the typical communication events of the child's class activities, a summary of the expected content of those communicative acts, and the natural supports already in place. This record requires at least 1 day of class observations and teacher interviews.

Step 3: Integrate the Communication Profile Into School Routines and the Curriculum

The third step to facilitate communication actualization occurs when the educational team has a second hour-long meeting in which they brainstorm and build a communication support plan focused on enabling the child to use communication across daily routines. This integration occurs by specifically matching the child's communication abilities to the communication expectations of each of the classes and activities.

This process results in a communication plan that specifically identifies what the child can do (the communication form), the reason for the action (the communication function), and the specific setting or event in which communication takes place. For example, Jessica's IEP can include statements such as "Jessica will look up (form) to convey she wants to go home (function) during the afternoon dismissal time (setting)."

Step 4: Expand the Communication Profile

Another strategy that supports actualization is to create communication opportunities so that the child can expand and diversify his or her skill base by generalizing an already established skill.

Many people in school—the bus driver, the librarian, the school secretaries, the lunchroom workers, the school janitors, and a select peer group—can become involved in students' functional communication plans.

For example, if Jessica already uses pushing away gestures to protest during free time after lunch, her teachers can encourage her to expand her skills by using other communication forms, such as body orientation, modified signs, and a vocalization. The teacher can say something like "Oh, you're telling me you don't like that. Let's use a sign, too." The premise underlying the examples in Figure 4 is that Jessica is encouraged to expand her existing communicative repertoire, based on the skills she already possesses.

Step 5: Evaluate the Effectiveness of the Communication Support Plan

All members of Jessica's educational team must periodically review the effectiveness of her communication and the progress she is making toward functional communication outcomes. Using a dynamic assessment model, the team should periodically observe and measure the degree to which Jessica maintains her extant communication abilities over time and across different communication settings and partners. The educational team should continuously review their own ability to provide meaningful opportunities for Jessica to use her communication skills to affect her surroundings.

Two published options are available to educational teams that want to self-evaluate their communication supports for students with severe mental retardation. One protocol is the *Communication Supports Checklist* (McCarthy et al., 1998). This instrument was specifically designed to enable school and human service personnel to evaluate their ability to serve the communication needs of people with severe disabilities. This 97-item checklist encourages self-evaluation of program supports for communication, assessment practices, goal setting practices, program implementation, and team competencies.

A second protocol. *Analyzing the Communication Environment (ACE)*, contains 52 items to assess opportunities for communication, adult interaction, specific activities, group dynamics, the materials being used, and the child's communication system (Rowland & Schweigert, 1993).

The educational team should *continuously* provide meaningful opportunities for Jessica to use her communication skills.

Final Thoughts

Although children who have severe mental retardation may present unusual challenges to school personnel, the use of a communication profile integrated into daily class events helps to establish functional communication goals and realistic outcomes. A communication profile carefully documents the child's existing communication forms and functions, and it allows the educational team to create opportunities that encourage the use of existing as well as new skills across daily school routines and the child's curriculum.

Figure 4. Individualized Education Program (IEP) Goal Content to Support Communication Actualization

1. Actualization by Communication Form

Jessica's Action	Function	The Setting
Modified sign	To protest	During free time after lunch
Body orientation		
Pushing away gesture		
Vocalization		

2. Actualization by Communication Function

Jessica's Action	Function	The Setting
Vocalization	To protest	Geography group projects
	To request help	
	To gain attention	
	To state a feeling	

3. Actualization Across Communication Setting

Jessica's Action	Function	The Setting
Vocalization	To gain attention	During math roll call
		During lunch group
		Passing a teacher in hallway

References

American Association on Mental Retardation (AAMR). (2002). *Mental retardation: Definition, classification, and systems of supports* (10th ed.). Annapolis Junction, MD: AAMR Publications.

Calculator, S. N. (1995). Communication sciences. In O. C. Karan & S. Greenspan (Eds.), *Community rehabilitation services for people with disabilities*, (pp. 277–293). Stoneham, MA: Butterworth-Heineman.

Cascella, P. W. (1999). Communication disorders and children with mental retardation. *Child and Adolescent Psychiatric Clinics of North America, 8*(1), 61–75.

Ervin, M. (2003). Autism spectrum disorders: Interdisciplinary teaming in schools. *The ASHA Leader, 8*(7), 4–5, 14.

Farrell, S. E., & Pimentel, A. E. (1996). Interdisciplinary team process in developmental disabilities. In A. J. Capute & P. J. Accardo (Eds.), *Developmental disabilities in infancy and childhood: Vol. 2. The spectrum of developmental disabilities* (2nd ed., pp. 431–441). Baltimore: Paul H. Brookes.

Ferguson, D. L. (1994). Is communication really the point? Some thoughts on interventions and membership. *Mental Retardation, 32*(1), 7–18.

Horn, E., Lieber, J., Li, S., Sandall, S., & Schwartz, I. (2000). Supporting young children's IEP Goals in inclusive settings through embedded learning opportunities. *Topics in Early Childhood Special Education, 20*(4), 208–224.

Mar, H. H., & Sali, N. (1999). Profiles of the expressive communication skills of children and adolescents with severe cognitive disabilities. *Education and Training in Mental Retardation and Developmental Disabilities, 54*(1), 77–89.

McCarthy, C. F., McLean, L. K., Miller., J. F., Paul-Brown, D., Romski, M. A., Rourk, J. D., et al. (1998). *Communication supports checklist*. Baltimore: Paul H. Brookes.

McLean, L. K., Brady, N. C., McLean, J. E., & Behrens, G. A. (1999). Communication forms and functions of children and adults with severe mental retardation in community and institutional settings. *Journal of Speech, Language, and Hearing Research, 42*, 231–240.

McLean, L. K., & McLean. J. E. (1993). Communication intervention for adults with severe mental retardation. *Topics in Language Disorders, 13*(3), 47–60.

National Joint Committee on Persons with Severe Disabilities. (2002). Adults with learning disabilities: Concerns about the application of restrictive "eligibility policies." *Communication Disorders Quarterly, 23*(3), 145–153.

Payne, H. W., & Ogletree, B. T. (1995). Training team members to respond to the communicative behaviors of children with profound handicaps. *Focus on Autistic Behavior 10*(5), 1–15.

Romski, M. A., Sevcik, R. A., & Adamson, L. B. (1999). Communication patterns of youth with mental retardation with and without their speech-output communication devices. *American Journal on Mental Retardation. 104*(3), 249–259.

Rowland, C., & Schweigert, P. (1993). *Analyzing the communication environment.* Tucson, AZ: Communication Skill Builders.

Paul W. Cascella *(CEC Chapter #58), Associate Professor, and* **Kevin M. McNamara,** *Clinic Director, Department of Communication Disorders, Southern Connecticut State University, New Haven. Address correspondence to Paul W. Cascella, Department of Communication Disorders, Southern Connecticut State University, 501 Crescent Street, New Haven CT 06515 (e-mail: cascellapl@southemct.edu)*

From *Teaching Exceptional Children,* Vol. 37, No. 3, January/February 2005, pp. 38-43. Copyright © 2005 by Council for Exceptional Children. Reprinted by permission.

UNIT 9

Orthopedic and Health Impairments

Unit Selections

26. **Savior Parents**, Elizabeth Weill
27. **Accommodations for Students With Disabilities: Removing Barriers to Learning**, MaryAnn Byrnes
28. **Trick Question**, Michael Fumento
29. **Finding What Works**, Peg Tyre

Key Points to Consider

- What hope have biotechnology and the mapping of the human genome given to parents of children with orthopedic and/or health impairments?

- What kinds of accommodations are appropriate for students with health impairments (e.g. cancer, asthma, epilepsy)?

- Why should parents and teachers be consulted before medications are prescribed for children with health impairments (e.g. ADHD)?

Student Website

www.mhcls.com/online

Internet References

Further information regarding these websites may be found in this book's preface or online.

Association to Benefit Children (ABC)
   http://www.a-b-c.org

An Idea Whose Time Has Come
   http://www.boggscenter.org/mich3899.htm

Resources for VE Teachers
   http://www.cpt.fsu.edu/tree//ve/tofc.html

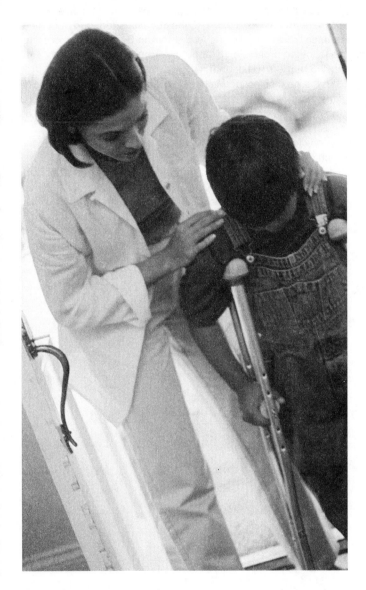

Orthopedic impairments are usually defined as those that hinder physical mobility or the ability to use one or more parts of the skeletomuscular system of the body. Orthopedic problems may be neurological (brain or spinal cord) or skeletomuscular (muscles or skeletal bones). Regardless of etiology, the child with an orthopedic impairment usually has a problem with mobility. He or she may need crutches or other aids in order to walk or may be in a wheelchair.

Health impairments are usually defined as those that affect stamina and predominantly one or more systems of the body: the cardiovascular, respiratory, gastrointestinal, endocrine, lymphatic, urinary, reproductive, sensory, or nervous systems. Children with health impairments usually have to take medicine or follow a medical regimen in order to attend school. The degree of impairment (mild, moderate, profound) is usually based on limitations to activity, duration of problem, and extent of other problems.

Attention-deficit hyperactive disorder (ADHD) is formally recognized as a health impairment, as well as a learning disability. Often children with ADHD are also assessed as gifted or as emotionally-behaviorally disordered. It is possible for a child with ADHD to have characteristics of all of these categories. ADHD will be covered in this unit.

Orthopedic and health impairments are not always mutually exclusive. Many times a child with an orthopedic impairment also has a concurrent or contributing health impairment, and vice versa. In addition, children with orthopedic and health impairments may also have concurrent conditions of educational exceptionality.

Some children with orthopedic and health impairments have only transitory impairments; some have permanent but nonworsening impairments; and some have progressive impairments that make their education more complicated as the years pass and may even result in death before the end of the developmental/educational period.

Each of the dimensions defined in the preceding paragraphs makes educational planning for children with orthopedic and health impairments very complicated.

The reauthorization of IDEA mandated that schools must pay for all medical services required to allow orthopedically or health impaired students to attend regular education classes. The only exceptions are the actual fees for physician-provided health services. Thus, if children need ambulances to transport them to and from school, the schools must pay the tab. Federal appropriations for special educational services only pay about 10 percent of the bills. Thus high-cost special needs students can quickly drain the funds of state and local education departments.

Teachers may resent the need to spend teacher time giving medications or providing quasi-medical services (suctioning, changing diapers) for students with health impairments in the many U.S. schools that no longer have school nurses.

Resentment is common in parents of nondisabled students who feel that the education of high-cost disabled students robs their children of teacher time, curriculum, and supplies to which they should be entitled. More than 95 percent of special needs students attend regular schools today. About 3 percent attend separate schools and about 2 percent are served at home, in hospitals, or in residential facilities.

Two civil rights laws, the Americans With Disabilities Act (ADA) and section 504 of the Rehabilitation Act, prohibit discrimination against students with disabilities. They also mandate reasonable accommodations for them in education. Together with the Individuals With Disabilities Education Act (IDEA) and the No Child Left Behind Act (NCLB), the United States has clearly articulated its desire that students with orthopedic and health impairments be given equal access to free and appropriate public education.

Children and youth with orthopedic and health impairments can be divided into classifications of mild, moderate, and profound. Within most impairments, the same diagnosis may not produce the same degree of disability. For example, children with cerebral palsy may be mildly, moderately, or profoundly impaired.

When orthopedic or health impairments are diagnosed in infancy or early childhood, an interdisciplinary team usually helps plan an Individualized Family Service Plan (IFSP) that includes working with parents, medical and/or surgical personnel, and preschool special education providers.

When the orthopedic or health impairment is diagnosed in the school years, the school teachers collaborate with outside agencies, but more of the Individualized Educational Planning (IEP) is in their hands. Children who have orthopedic or health impairments need psychological as well as academic support. Teachers need to help them in their peer interactions. Teachers should also work closely with parents to ensure a smooth transition toward a lifestyle that fosters independence and self-reliance. By middle school, Individualized Transition Plans (ITPs) should be developed. They should be implemented throughout high school and until age 21 when the students move to adult living, and they must be updated every year. Schools are held accountable for their success in helping students with orthopedic and health impairments to make smooth transitions to maturity.

The first article, "Savior Parents" emphasizes the importance of parental advocacy to insure that children with orthopedic and health impairments get the most up-to-date diagnoses and therapeutic assistance. New technologies are making remediation and/or cures possible, that in the past were unthinkable. Educators must stay current of the on-going progress and join parents in the role of saviors to students with such impairments.

The second selection for this unit suggests some of the accommodations that school systems must make to ensure that students with orthopedic and health impairments receive an appropriate education. It explains the 504 plans required under the Americans with Disabilities Act. MaryAnn Byrnes points out that the teaching profession is about allowing students to learn. Removing barriers will do that.

In the next selection Michael Fumento questions the veracity of the diagnosis of attention deficit hyperactive disorder (ADHD). Many persons have declared the label a hoax, and the use of medication to treat it a conspiracy to make boys more like girls. The article presents evidence that it is a neurological disorder which can usually be successfully treated with medicine.

In the last selection Peg Tyre questions "what works?" There have been years of controversy about medications for children with attention deficit disorder, and other health impairments. What and how much to prescribe should be determined in collaboration with educators and parents who see results. Other therapies, such as applied behavioral analysis (ABA), can also reduce the dosage required of many medications.

Savior Parents

Rescuing an ailing child can become a crusade and a career

ELIZABETH WEILL

Jannine and John Cody were packing to move from Sheppard Air Force Base in Wichita Falls, Texas, to Brooks Air Force Base in San Antonio in 1985 when a military doctor gave them some devastating news. Their 6-week-old daughter Elizabeth was missing part of her 18th chromosome. To explain what that meant, the doctor showed Jannine a textbook with a horrifying picture and caption that she still keeps in her files. It read, "They are probably the most seriously afflicted among carriers of chromosome abnormalities. They maintain the froglike position observed in infants and are reduced to an entirely bedridden and vegetative life." The young mother was incredulous. "That just didn't jibe with what I was seeing," Cody vividly recalls. "It had been raining for a week, everything was wet, the packers were angry. I had a 3-year-old, a 6-week-old and a mother-in-law to deal with. I was on total overload, so I said to myself, O.K., this doesn't quite fit; she doesn't seem like a vegetable. I'll deal with that later."

Elizabeth's first year included three surgeries to fix a cleft palate and a cleft lip. By age 2, she had slipped far behind on the growth charts. Her pediatrician seemed to think that was inevitable, but her mother demanded that Elizabeth's symptoms be treated, a radical notion at the time. She took her daughter to an endocrinologist, who put Elizabeth on daily injections of human growth hormone, a therapy that caused her to grow like a weed and blossom developmentally as well. When Elizabeth had difficulty learning to speak, Cody pushed for her to see a neurologist, who determined that the problem had more to do with the impairment of her hearing than with her intelligence. The 3-year-old was fitted with a hearing aid and began learning sign language.

The journey to save Elizabeth took both mother and daughter to unexpected places. Cody went back to college and earned a Ph.D. in human genetics at age 42. Her dissertation topic: syndromes of the 18th chromosome. Today this former homemaker and president of her local embroiderers' guild conducts genetic research at the University of Texas Health Science Center. Her work has helped raise Elizabeth's IQ into the normal range and has provided a model for helping the approximately 500 other kids in the U.S. with the same defect. Cody also set up the Chromosome 18 Registry and Research Society—a foundation that connects affected families with one another and funds research.

This month Cody will reap a huge personal reward for her efforts: Elizabeth will graduate from high school. A few years ago, Cody sat watching Elizabeth's pep squad perform at a football game, wearing red, white and blue, the school colors. "Suddenly I'm watching, and I realize I can't pick her out of the crowd. She wasn't so bad!" says Cody. "I just burst into tears. I never ever thought I would see the day when she'd just be one of the girls in high school, out there on the field with all the other kids. It was amazing."

Being a parent brings out the most extreme traits in all of us—capacities for love, fear, persistence you never knew you had—and those traits are only magnified when a kid is in danger. You stay up all night when your daughter spikes a 101° fever. You drive across town in five minutes flat when your son falls out of a tree. But parenting a child who has a serious genetic disease transcends that entirely, as movies like *Lorenzo's Oil* have shown. It turns Clark Kents into Supermen and former science-phobes into experts in molecular biology. "For a long time in the pediatric community, [the attitude was] if you have a major chromosomal abnormality, you're going to not grow well, you're going to be developmentally delayed, you're going to be mentally retarded, and there's not a darn thing we can do about it," says Dr. Daniel Hale, a pediatric endocrinologist who works closely with Cody. These days the situation is different. At the molecular level, genetic diseases are better understood, and new avenues are opening for dealing with them, thanks in part to the advocacy of parents like Cody who embrace the notion that kids with chromosomal abnormalities have a right to reach their fullest potential.

"I'm a person, **NOT A DISEASE!**" insists Sam Berns, age 7

Particular Clark Kents, of course, turn into particular superheroes because of varying talents and inclinations. Leslie Gordon and Scott Berns, for example, were both multidegree doctors—she has an M.D. and a Ph.D., he has an M.D. and a master's in public health—when a doctor friend diagnosed progeria in their 21-month-old son Sam, now 7 (the rare disease causes accelerated aging and often leads to death by early adolescence). The next day, Gordon took a leave from her training in pediatric ophthalmology. Within nine months, she created the Progeria Research Foundation to bring attention to and research funds for the disease, which affects just 1 in 4 million babies. "There was nothing out there. Zero," says Gordon from her home in Foxboro, Mass., her voice brimming with fierce enthusiasm. "I was surprised because as a doctor, you train, you train, you train, and when you get out there you realize there are holes."

Gordon and Berns are committed to the idea that Sam, who inhabits the body of a 70-year-old, should just be a kid. Currently he's obsessed with baseball, school and drums, and when a new friend informs him he has no hair, he says, "Tell me something I don't know. Let's go play." Gordon, in just over five years, has started a tissue bank, raised serious money and lured top scientists into studying her son's disease. In October 2002, she, along with an international team, succeeded in isolating the progeria gene. Progeria, it turns out, is caused by a tiny point mutation in a child's DNA, a one-letter typo in the chromosomal book. But even after that research triumph—the culmination of an 11-month, white-hot burn of constant phone and e-mail conversations—Gordon did not take a break. Sam, she reasons, has no time to waste. A stroke could hit at any time, and the same is true for the more than 50 other kids with progeria whom Gordon has come to know and love. "Somebody called me a barracuda once, and I said thank you," Gordon says. "You can't hand a child a paper saying we found the gene, and here, you're cured. Isolating the gene was the end of Chapter One. We now have a gene that leads to a protein defect that researchers can sink their teeth into. Fantastic labs can ask fantastic questions. We can pull in a lot more terrific researchers, ask better questions and start moving toward treatment."

Taking on the responsibility of finding a cure for your child's rare genetic disease can be both comforting and painful, like all parental obligations, except in this case the stakes aren't seeing a child's soccer game vs. working out, but seeing your child's future birthdays vs. (perhaps) not blaming yourself if you don't.

"You don't want to ever have to tell your kids someday that you didn't try your best," says Brad Margus, a Harvard M.B.A. and the former owner of a Florida shrimp-processing company who switched careers after discovering that two of his four boys had a rare, degenerative disease. "Being a dad, you're expected by your kids to be able to fix anything, right? So they're counting on you to do something about it," says Margus, who is now CEO of Perlegen Sciences, a Silicon Valley biotech firm.

Margus' nightmare started when he and his wife Vicki still had three boys in diapers, and his second eldest, Jarrett, then 18 months, developed difficulty walking and his speech slurred. At first doctors thought the cause was mild cerebral palsy. Then around his 18-month mark, Margus' next eldest boy, Quinn, started developing the same symptoms as Jarrett's, which suggested that the problem was genetic. The boys endured blood tests, spinal taps, muscle biopsies. After spending $60,000 and turning up nothing, the Marguses took their sons to see Dr. Jean Aicardi, a world-famous French neurologist who happened to be visiting Miami Children's Hospital. "In the first five minutes, he saw our kids and said, 'It looks an awful lot like ataxia-telangiectasia,' which we couldn't even pronounce. 'I assume you've tested for this?' All it takes is a $20 blood test. The local doctors just looked at their feet." The Marguses recognized the name (it's pronounced ay-*tack*-see-uh teh-*lan*-jick-*tay*-sha), but all they knew was that A-T was really bad. At home that night they read that about 40% of kids with A-T get cancer by age 12; 100% deteriorate neurologically, so they're in wheelchairs as early as age 8; most die of lung problems or cancer by their late teens or early 20s. "You kind of go through a grief process," Margus says. "Your kids aren't dead, but the kids you thought you had are gone."

"You don't want to ever have to tell your kids that YOU DIDN'T TRY your best."

Like progeria, A-T is what might be called a superorphaned disease. It affects so few kids—just 400 in the U.S.—that scientists and drug companies don't bother with it. So Margus began applying his business brain to the problem of how to find a cure. He broke it down into smaller problems, assembling a list of things he needed to learn about: molecular biology, how the government funds research, how you capture the interest of top-notch scientists, what lobbying is all about. He decided his approach would be to pollinate as many excellent labs as possible, funding postdocs to work under superstars and hoping that whenever researchers discovered something relevant, they might at least ask themselves, Could this help Brad's kids? "Early on, you're naive enough that you don't know how challenging the problem really is, so you give it a shot." The result? Margus has raised more than $15 million to date, and he funded the research that isolated the A-T-mutated gene nine years ago.

Still, Margus sounds distinctly sad. Sure, he has raised a lot of money and even made a savvy career switch that puts him in regular contact with executives from five of the top 10 pharmaceutical companies. Yet, in his mind, "so far we haven't done squat." His kids, now 13 and 15, are deteriorating daily. This summer he hopes to move his family from Florida to California, where he spends most of his time, but first he will need to retrofit a house "for two teenagers in power wheelchairs who can't control their motor skills very well, so they take out huge chunks of drywall." When his boys ask their father about his work, Margus is honest. "Quinn is quite tough on me," Margus says. "He asks what those researchers are doing. And candidly, I have to say that we've failed. We've set up a center at Johns Hopkins, so at least there's one place in the world that's accumulating a lot of data on the kids. But as far as a treatment or cure or even slowing the progression of the disease, we still haven't done it."

The struggles of parents like Brad Margus and Leslie Gordon are less lonely than they were in the pre-Internet era. Numerous websites help such parents reach out and learn from one another; among them are sites created by the Genetic and Rare Diseases Information Center at the National Institutes of Health and the Genetic Alliance, an advocacy group. This June in San Antonio, Jannine

Cody is convening the first World Congress on Chromosome Abnormalities. More than 1,000 parents, doctors and researchers are expected to attend. Sessions will range from "Neurological and Anatomical Imaging" to "Potty/Sleep Solutions." The event is the culmination of 15 years of work, with twin goals of building stronger advocacy groups for children with chromosomal abnormalities and establishing a nucleus of scientists dedicated to addressing their problems. "Somebody ought to give that lady a MacArthur," says Dr. Hale.

On a recent afternoon, Elizabeth Cody comes bounding down the stairs to greet her mother, who has just returned from work. There is nothing froglike or vegetative about the bright-eyed 19-year-old, who flops onto the sofa and expresses relief that her mother has remembered to bring home a chart showing exactly which part of her 18th chromosome is missing. "A boy at my school used to make fun of me, so I wanted to show him this," Elizabeth explains. After graduation in May, Elizabeth plans to attend a local community college, and then become a teacher's assistant in a hearing-impaired classroom and perhaps move out to California. One thing she can count on: her mother will be cheering all the way.

Accommodations for Students with Disabilities: Removing Barriers to Learning

Secondary school principals frequently encounter questions about educating students with disabilities. Sometimes the questions revolve around seeking a deeper understanding of the disability and the best way to meet student needs. Other times, the questions focus on all the changes that must be made to ensure students receive an appropriate education. What questions do teachers ask about accommodations for students with a disability?

By MaryAnn Byrnes

Think about taking a driver's test without wearing glasses (if you do, that is). Not fair, you say; you need the glasses to see. You have just identified an accommodation that you need. Wearing glasses does not make a bad driver better or make driving easier; rather, wearing glasses makes driving possible. Glasses are so much a part of our lives that we do not even consider that they remove a barrier caused by a disability.

Secondary school teachers encounter students every day on an Individualized Education Plan (IEP) or 504 Plan, both of which address programs for students with disabilities. Most likely, the person charged with monitoring this plan has indicated that particular students need changes in teaching style, assignments, or testing strategies.

It is usually easy to understand the need for glasses or wheelchairs or hearing aids. These sound like changes the student must make. Other adjustments, modifications, or accommodations on these plans, such as extended time, may not be as clear.

What is an accommodation?

An accommodation is an adjustment, to an activity or setting, that removes a barrier presented by a disability so a person can have access equal to that of a person without a disability. An accommodation does not guarantee success or a specific level of performance. It should, however, provide the opportunity for a person with a disability to participate in a situation or activity.

Think of that pair of glasses, or the time you broke your leg and could not drive. Think of how your life was

affected by these conditions. Your competence did not change. Your ability to think and work did not change. Your ability to interact with (have access to) the reading material may be very limited without your glasses. Your ability to get to (have access to) work or the grocery store may be very limited without someone to transport you. The support provided by the glasses—or the driver—made it possible for you to use your abilities without the barrier presented by less than perfect vision or limited mobility.

An accommodation is an adjustment, to an activity or setting, that removes a barrier presented by a disability so a person can have access equal to that of a person without a disability.

The accommodations in IEPs or 504 Plans serve the same purpose. They identify ways to remove the barrier presented by a person's disability.

Why do we need to provide accommodations?

Accommodations are required under Section 504 of the Federal Rehabilitation Act of 1974 as well as the Americans with Disabilities Act. Both these federal laws prohibit discrimination against individuals who have a disability. Situations that limit access have been determined to be discriminatory.

Accommodations must be provided not just by teachers to students, but by employees for workers and governments for citizens. Curbs have been cut to provide access. Doors have been widened and door handles altered to provide access to people for whom the old designs posed a barrier. Employers provide computer adaptations or other adjustments in work schedules and circumstances.

For employers and schools, individuals with disabilities may have a document called a 504 Plan, which details the types of accommodations that are required. Students who have a 504 Plan will not require special education services, just changes to the environment or instructional situation.

Students who have a disability and require special education services in addition to accommodations will have this information contained in an IEP, which also details the types of direct services that need to be provided and the goals of these services. Accommodations will be listed within this IEP.

With the recent changes in IDEA '97, the federal law governing special education, you will be addressing accommodations that must be made so a student with a disability can participate in large-scale districtwide or statewide assessment systems as well as classwork and school life.

Who needs accommodations?

According to Section 504, an individual with a disability is any person who has "a physical or mental impairment that limits one or more major life activities." IDEA '97, the federal special education law, lists the following disabilities: autism, deaf-blindness, deafness, hearing impairment, mental retardation, multiple disabilities, orthopedic impairment, other health impairment, serious emotional disturbance, specific learning disability, speech or language impairment, traumatic brain injury, and visual impairment.

Students who have a 504 Plan will not require special education services, just changes to the environment or instructional situation.

Some conditions are covered by Section 504, but not special education. These can include attention deficit disorder—ADD, (also attention deficit hyperactivity disorder—ADHD); chronic medical conditions (such as cancer, Tourette Syndrome, asthma, or epilepsy); communicable diseases; some temporary medical conditions; physical impairments; and disorders of emotion or behavior. To qualify, there must be a demonstrated and substantial limitation of a major life activity.

Students (or adults) who have disabilities may require accommodations to have equal access to education. Not every student with a disability will require accommodations, and not every student with a disability requires the same accommodation all the time.

Think of Jim, a student who has limited mobility in his hands, affecting his ability to write. This disability will present a barrier in a class that requires the student to take notes quickly or write long essays in class. In a class that does not require either of these activities, no barrier may be present. Equal access is possible without accommodation. The student can learn and demonstrate what he knows and can do unaffected by his disability.

What kind of accommodations are there?

Just as there is no limit to the range of disabilities, there is no limit to the range of accommodations. The point is to understand disability and determine if it presents a barrier to equal access. If so, decide whether an accommodation can be identified to remove the barrier—and make sure the accommodation is implemented.

Not every student with a disability will require accommodations, and not every student with a disability requires the same accommodation all the time.

Think of the student described above. The limited mobility in Jim's hands presents a barrier in a class that requires rapid note taking or the writing of long essays in class. There are several accommodations that can result in equal access. Jim might tape the lesson and take notes later. These notes could be written or dictated into a computer. Essays could be composed verbally at a computer workstation or dictated into a tape recorder or to a scribe. A computer might be adapted so typing becomes an effective way to record information on paper. In yet another type of accommodation, essays could be replaced by oral reports.

Are there some accommodations that should not be used?

Like many difficult questions, the answer depends on the context. An accommodation should not alter the essential purpose of the assignment. If the skill you want to measure is the ability to make multiple rapid hand movements, then there is probably no accommodation that is appropriate. Jim will not do well because of his disability. Alternately, if the purpose of a task is to see if someone has perfect vision without glasses, using those glasses is not an appropriate accommodation. If the purpose is to see if you can read, the glasses become a reasonable accommodation.

Who decides about accommodations?

The team that writes IEPs and 504 Plans reviews the disability and determines what accommodations, if any, are necessary. These are then written into the EIP or 504 Plan.

Once more, return to Jim. As you consider the requirements of your class, think of the most appropriate way to remove the barrier that is presented by the limited mobility Jim has in his hands.

If we use accommodations, how will the student ever be prepared for independent life in college or the world of work?

Some people are concerned that the supports provided in school will result in the student being unable to work productively when he or she leaves school. As a matter of fact, Section 504 applies to colleges and employers as well. Colleges offer support centers and provide accommodations upon documentation that a disability exists. Employers are required to provide reasonable accommodations to any person who is otherwise qualified to fulfill the elements of the job.

If companies remove barriers at the workplace, educators should be willing and able to take barriers out of the school activities that prepare a student for the workplace. Teachers can help a student identify the type of accommodation that will be the least cumbersome for everyone, and those that will permit the student to be most independent.

Don't accommodations just make school easier?

That depends on how you view the world. Does wearing glasses make driving easier? Not really—for a person with limited vision, wearing glasses makes driving *possible*. With or without glasses, you need to be able to drive to pass the test. The same is true of an academic accommodation; whether or not the accommodation is provided, the students still must demonstrate that they know required material.

An accommodation should not alter the essential purpose of the assignment.

Think about the important elements of your class: Is it more important that Jim take notes in class or understand the material? Is it more important that Jim demonstrate good handwriting or the ability to communicate thoughts in print? Often, when you identify the main purpose of your assignments and consider the skills and abilities of a student, you will see that an accommodation lets you determine more clearly what a student knows, understands, and can do.

Does a student need to follow the IEP accommodations in all classes?

The IEP or 504 Plan needs to address any area in which the student's disability affects life in school. Sometimes this means in all classes, but not always. For example, a student who was blind would need to use Braille in all classes dealing with written material. Jim, our student with limited mobility in his hands, might not require accommodations in world languages or physical education.

Can we make accommodations without having students on an IEP?

Many accommodations are just different ways of teaching or testing. You should be able to have this freedom in your classes. In some cases, the way in which a class is taught makes accommodations unnecessary. Accommodations change the situation, not the content of the instruction. However, accommodations on standardized tests must be connected to IEP's or 504 Plans.

May teachers give different assignments on the same content as a way to meet the needs of different learning styles without lowering standards?

Absolutely. The point is to remove the barrier of the disability; this is one way to accomplish that. Some teachers find they tap student knowledge best in active projects; others find that written work is best. Many secondary schools are using portfolios or performance activities to document student learning.

These assessment activities can be very compelling and they do tap different methods of expression. A student like Jim, for example, might communicate depth of understanding and analysis to a social studies debate with a disability in the area of speech or language might find barriers in the performance activities that do not exist on a paper-and-pencil task.

. . . educators should be willing and able to take barriers out of the school activities that prepare a student for the workplace.

What if accommodations are not implemented?

Since accommodations allow equal access, refusing to provide them can be viewed as discrimination. Individuals who knowingly refuse to implement accommodations make themselves personally liable for legal suit.

This sounds serious, and it is serious. Once the accommodations are found to be necessary, everyone must implement them in situations where the student's disability poses a barrier that prevents equal access.

If no barrier exists in your class, the accommodation is not necessary. No one has the option, however, of deciding not to implement a necessary accommodation. Telling students they could not wear glasses or use a hearing aid is unthinkable. Just as inappropriate is a decision not to allow Jim to use accommodations to remove the barrier posed by his disability, even though it means making some changes to your own work.

Questions About Specific Accommodations

Now that the issues underlying accommodations have been addressed, it is time to talk about frequently-encountered accommodations that raise questions and concern. All these questions have come from secondary school faculty members in a variety of school systems.

Why is it fair to read material aloud to some students?

Some students have a learning disability that makes it difficult for them to decode print. They can understand the concepts; they can comprehend the material when they hear it; they can reason through the material. They just can't turn print into meaning. If the task is to determine if the student can read, you already know they will have difficulty. If the task is to determine if the student has content knowledge, reading material aloud removes the barrier of the learning disability. Reading material aloud to a student who does not understand the material will not result in a higher grade.

Why is it fair to give some students extra time on tests?

Some students have motor difficulties that make writing an enormous challenge. They may not be able to form the letters correctly. They may not be able to monitor their thoughts while they work on the physical act of writing. They understand the material, and they know what they want to respond; it just takes longer to write the answer. If the task is to determine how quickly the student can respond, you already know they will have difficulty. If the task is to determine if the student has the knowledge, providing extra time removes the

barrier of the motor disability. Providing extra time to a student who does not understand the material will not result in a higher grade.

Why is it fair to permit some students to respond orally to tests?

Think about the example above. For some students, responding orally would be a comparable accommodation. In this case, allowing an oral response will not result in a higher grade if the student does not know the material.

A student with a disability in the area of speech or language might find barriers in the performance activities that do not exist on a paper-and-pencil task.

The Bottom Line

It all comes down to deciding what is important. Think about your assignment and expectations. Think about the disability. If the disability provides a barrier, the accommodation removes it. The accommodation does not release a student from participating or demonstrating knowledge—it allows the student to be able to participate and demonstrate knowledge. And isn't that what school is all about?

References

Americans with Disabilities Act of 1990, P.L. 101–336, 2, 104 Stat. 328.1991.

Individuals with Disabilities Education Act Amendments of 1997, P.L. 105–17, 20 U.S. Code Sections 1401–1486.

Livovich, Michael P. *Section 504 of the Rehabilitation Act of 1973 and the Americans with Disabilities Act. Providing access to a free appropriate public education: a public school manual.* Indianapolis, Ind.: 1996.

Vocational Rehabilitation Act of 1973, 29 U.S.C. 794.

MaryAnn Byrnes (byrnes@mediaone.net) is assistant professor at the Graduate College of Education, University of Massachusetts-Boston.

Trick Question

A liberal 'hoax' turns out to be true.

By MICHAEL FUMENTO

IT'S BOTH RIGHT-WING and vast, but it's not a conspiracy. Actually, it's more of an anti-conspiracy. The subject is Attention Deficit Disorder (ADD) and Attention Deficit Hyperactivity Disorder (ADHD), closely related ailments (henceforth referred to in this article simply as ADHD). Rush Limbaugh declares it "may all be a hoax." Francis Fukuyama devotes much of one chapter in his latest book, *Our Posthuman Future*, to attacking Ritalin, the top-selling drug used to treat ADHD. Columnist Thomas Sowell writes, "The motto used to be: 'Boys will be boys.' Today, the motto seems to be: 'Boys will be medicated.'" And Phyllis Schlafly explains, "The old excuse of 'my dog ate my homework' has been replaced by 'I got an ADHD diagnosis.'" A March 2002 article in *The Weekly Standard* summed up the conservative line on ADHD with this rhetorical question: "Are we really prepared to redefine childhood as an ailment, and medicate it until it goes away?"

Many conservative writers, myself included, have criticized the growing tendency to pathologize every undesirable behavior—especially where children are concerned. But, when it comes to ADHD, this skepticism is misplaced. As even a cursory examination of the existing literature or, for that matter, simply talking to the parents and teachers of children with ADHD reveals, the condition is real, and it is treatable. And, if you don't believe me, you can ask conservatives who've come face to face with it themselves.

MYTH: ADHD ISN'T A REAL DISORDER.

The most common argument against ADHD on the right is also the simplest: It doesn't exist. Conservative columnist Jonah Goldberg thus reduces ADHD to "ants in the pants." Sowell equates it with "being bored and restless." Fukuyama protests,

"No one has been able to identify a cause of ADD/ADHD. It is a pathology recognized only by its symptoms." And a conservative columnist approvingly quotes Thomas Armstrong, Ritalin opponent and author, when he declares, "ADD is a disorder that cannot be authoritatively identified in the same way as polio, heart disease or other legitimate illnesses."

The Armstrong and Fukuyama observations are as correct as they are worthless. "Half of all medical disorders are diagnosed without benefit of a lab procedure," notes Dr. Russell Barkley, professor of psychology at the College of Health Professionals at the Medical University of South Carolina. "Where are the lab tests for headaches and multiple sclerosis and Alzheimer's?" he asks. "Such a standard would virtually eliminate all mental disorders."

Often the best diagnostic test for an ailment is how it responds to treatment. And, by that standard, it doesn't get much more real than ADHD. The beneficial effects of administering stimulants to treat the disorder were first reported in 1937. And today medication for the disorder is reported to be 75 to 90 percent successful. "In our trials it was close to ninety percent," says Dr. Judith Rapoport, director of the National Institute of Mental Health's Child Psychiatry Branch, who has published about 100 papers on ADHD. "This means there was a significant difference in the children's ability to function in the classroom or at home."

Additionally, epidemiological evidence indicates that ADHD has a powerful genetic component. University of Colorado researchers have found that a child whose identical twin has the disorder is between eleven and 18 times more likely to also have it than is a non-twin sibling. For these reasons, the American Psychiatric Association (APA), American Medical Association, American Academy of Pediatrics, American Academy of Child

Adolescent Psychiatry, the surgeon general's office, and other major medical bodies all acknowledge ADHD as both real and treatable.

MYTH: ADHD IS PART OF A FEMINIST CONSPIRACY TO MAKE LITTLE BOYS MORE LIKE LITTLE GIRLS.

Many conservatives observe that boys receive ADHD diagnoses in much higher numbers than girls and find in this evidence of a feminist conspiracy. (This, despite the fact that genetic diseases are often heavily weighted more toward one gender or the other.) Sowell refers to "a growing tendency to treat boyhood as a pathological condition that requires a new three R's—repression, re-education and Ritalin." Fukuyama claims Prozac is being used to give women "more of the alpha-male feeling," while Ritalin is making boys act more like girls. "Together, the two sexes are gently nudged toward that androgynous median personality… that is the current politically correct outcome in American society." George Will, while acknowledging that Ritalin can be helpful, nonetheless writes of the "androgyny agenda" of "drugging children because they are behaving like children, especially boy children." Anti-Ritalin conservatives frequently invoke Christina Hoff Sommers's best-selling 2000 book, *The War Against Boys*. You'd never know that the drug isn't mentioned in her book—or why.

"Originally I was going to have a chapter on it," Sommers tells me. "It seemed to fit the thesis." What stopped her was both her survey of the medical literature and her own empirical findings. Of one child she personally came to know she says, "He was utterly miserable, as was everybody around him. The drugs saved his life."

MYTH: ADHD IS PART OF THE PUBLIC SCHOOL SYSTEM'S EFFORTS TO WAREHOUSE KIDS RATHER THAN TO DISCIPLINE AND TEACH THEM.

"No doubt life is easier for teachers when everyone sits around quietly," writes Sowell. Use of ADHD drugs is "in the school's interest to deal with behavioral and discipline problems [because] it's so easy to use Ritalin to make kids compliant: to get them to sit down, shut up, and do what they're told," declares Schlafly. The word "zombies" to describe children under the effects of Ritalin is tossed around more than in a B-grade voodoo movie.

Kerri Houston, national field director for the American Conservative Union and the mother of two ADHD children on medication, agrees with much of the criticism of public schools. "But don't blame ADHD on crummy curricula and lazy teachers," she says. "If you've worked with these children, you know they have a serious neurological problem." In any case, Ritalin, when taken as prescribed, hardly stupefies children. To the extent the medicine works, it simply turns ADHD children into normal children. "ADHD is like having thirty televisions on at one time, and the medicine turns off twenty-nine so you can

concentrate on the one," Houston describes. "This zombie stuff drives me nuts! My kids are both as lively and as fun as can be."

MYTH: PARENTS WHO GIVE THEIR KIDS ANTI-ADHD DRUGS ARE MERELY DOPING UP PROBLEM CHILDREN.

Limbaugh calls ADHD "the perfect way to explain the inattention, incompetence, and inability of adults to control their kids." Addressing parents directly, he lectures, "It helped you mask your own failings by doping up your children to calm them down."

Such charges blast the parents of ADHD kids into high orbit. That includes my Hudson Institute colleague (and fellow conservative) Mona Charen, the mother of an eleven-year-old with the disorder. "I have two non-ADHD children, so it's not a matter of parenting technique," says Charen. "People without such children have no idea what it's like. I can tell the difference between boyish high spirits and pathological hyperactivity…. These kids bounce off the walls. Their lives are chaos; their rooms are chaos. And nothing replaces the drugs."

Barkley and Rapoport say research backs her up. Randomized, controlled studies in both the United States and Sweden have tried combining medication with behavioral interventions and then dropped either one or the other. For those trying to go on without medicine, "the behavioral interventions maintained nothing," Barkley says. Rapoport concurs: "Unfortunately, behavior modification doesn't seem to help with ADHD." (Both doctors are quick to add that ADHD is often accompanied by other disorders that are treatable through behavior modification in tandem with medicine.)

MYTH: RITALIN IS "KIDDIE COCAINE."

One of the paradoxes of conservative attacks on Ritalin is that the drug is alternately accused of turning children into brain-dead zombies and of making them Mach-speed cocaine junkies. Indeed, Ritalin is widely disparaged as "kiddie cocaine." Writers who have sought to lump the two drugs together include Schlafly, talk-show host and columnist Armstrong Williams, and others whom I hesitate to name because of my longstanding personal relationships with them.

Mary Eberstadt wrote the "authoritative" Ritalin-cocaine piece for the April 1999 issue of *Policy Review*, then owned by the Heritage Foundation. The article, "Why Ritalin Rules," employs the word "cocaine" no fewer than twelve times. Eberstadt quotes from a 1995 Drug Enforcement Agency (DEA) background paper declaring methylphenidate, the active ingredient in Ritalin, "a central nervous system (CNS) stimulant [that] shares many of the pharmacological effects of amphetamine, methamphetamine, and cocaine." Further, it "produces behavioral, psychological, subjective, and reinforcing effects similar to those of d-amphetamine including increases in rating of euphoria, drug liking and activity, and decreases in sedation." Add to this the fact that the Controlled Substances Act lists it as a

Schedule II drug, imposing on it the same tight prescription controls as morphine, and Ritalin starts to sound spooky indeed.

What Eberstadt fails to tell readers is that the DEA description concerns methylphenidate *abuse*. It's tautological to say abuse is harmful. According to the DEA, the drugs in question are comparable when "administered the same way at comparable doses." But ADHD stimulants, when taken as prescribed, are neither administered in the same way as cocaine nor at comparable doses. "What really counts," says Barkley, "is the speed with which the drugs enter and clear the brain. With cocaine, because it's snorted, this happens tremendously quickly, giving users the characteristic addictive high." (Ever seen anyone pop a cocaine tablet?) Further, he says, "There's no evidence anywhere in literature of [Ritalin's] addictiveness when taken as prescribed." As to the Schedule II listing, again this is because of the potential for it to fall into the hands of abusers, not because of its effects on persons for whom it is prescribed. Ritalin and the other anti-ADHD drugs, says Barkley, "are the safest drugs in all of psychiatry." (And they may be getting even safer: A new medicine just released called Strattera represents the first true non-stimulant ADHD treatment.)

Indeed, a study just released in the journal *Pediatrics* found that children who take Ritalin or other stimulants to control ADHD cut their risk of future substance abuse by 50 percent compared with untreated ADHD children. The lead author speculated that "by treating ADHD you're reducing the demoralization that accompanies this disorder, and you're improving the academic functioning and well-being of adolescents and young adults during the critical times when substance abuse starts."

MYTH: RITALIN IS OVERPRESCRIBED ACROSS THE COUNTRY.

Some call it "the Ritalin craze." In *The Weekly Standard*, Melana Zyla Vickers informs us that "Ritalin use has exploded," while Eberstadt writes that "Ritalin use more than doubled in the first half of the decade alone, [and] the number of schoolchildren taking the drug may now, by some estimates, be approaching the *4 million mark*."

A report in the January 2003 issue of *Archives of Pediatrics and Adolescent Medicine* did find a large increase in the use of ADHD medicines from 1987 to 1996, an increase that doesn't appear to be slowing. Yet nobody thinks it's a problem that routine screening for high blood pressure has produced a big increase in the use of hypertension medicine. "Today, children suffering from ADHD are simply less likely to slip through the cracks," says Dr. Sally Satel, a psychiatrist, AEI fellow, and author of *PC, M.D.: How Political Correctness Is Corrupting Medicine*.

Satel agrees that some community studies, by the standards laid down in the APA's *Diagnostic and Statistical Manual of Mental Disorders (DSM)*, indicate that ADHD may often be over-diagnosed. On the other hand, she says, additional evidence shows that in some communities ADHD is *under*-diagnosed and *under*-treated. "I'm quite concerned with children who need the medication and aren't getting it," she says.

There *are* tremendous disparities in the percentage of children taking ADHD drugs when comparing small geographical areas. Psychologist Gretchen LeFever, for example, has compared the number of prescriptions in mostly white Virginia Beach, Virginia, with other, more heavily African American areas in the southeastern part of the state. Conservatives have latched onto her higher numbers—20 percent of white fifth-grade boys in Virginia Beach are being treated for ADHD—as evidence that something is horribly wrong. But others, such as Barkley, worry about the lower numbers. According to LeFever's study, black children are only half as likely to get medication as white children. "Black people don't get the care of white people; children of well-off parents get far better care than those of poorer parents," says Barkley.

MYTH: STATES SHOULD PASS LAWS THAT RESTRICT SCHOOLS FROM RECOMMENDING RITALIN.

Conservative writers have expressed delight that several states, led by Connecticut, have passed or are considering laws ostensibly protecting students from schools that allegedly pass out Ritalin like candy. Representative Lenny Winkler, lead sponsor of the Connecticut measure, told *Reuters Health*, "If the diagnosis is made, and it's an appropriate diagnosis that Ritalin be used, that's fine. But I have also heard of many families approached by the school system [who are told] that their child cannot attend school if they're not put on Ritalin."

Two attorneys I interviewed who specialize in child-disability issues, including one from the liberal Bazelon Center for Mental Health Law in Washington, D.C., acknowledge that school personnel have in some cases stepped over the line. But legislation can go too far in the other direction by declaring, as Connecticut's law does, that "any school personnel [shall be prohibited] from recommending the use of psychotropic drugs for any child." The law appears to offer an exemption by declaring, "The provisions of this section shall not prohibit *school medical staff* from recommending that a child be evaluated by an appropriate medical practitioner, or prohibit school personnel from consulting with such practitioner, with the consent of the parent or guardian of such child." [Emphasis added.] But of course many, if not most, schools have perhaps one nurse on regular "staff." That nurse will have limited contact with children in the classroom situations where ADHD is likely to be most evident. And, given the wording of the statute, a teacher who believed a student was suffering from ADHD would arguably be prohibited from referring that student to the nurse. Such ambiguity is sure to have a chilling effect on any form of intervention or recommendation by school personnel. Moreover, 20- year special-education veteran Sandra Rief said in an interview with the National Education Association that "recommending medical intervention for a student's behavior could lead to personal liability issues." Teachers, in other words, could be forced to choose between what they think is best for the health of their students and the possible risk of losing not only their jobs but their personal assets as well.

"Certainly it's not within the purview of a school to say kids can't attend if they don't take drugs," says Houston. "On the other hand, certainly teachers should be able to advise parents as to problems and potential solutions.... [T]hey may see things parents don't. My own son is an angel at home but was a demon at school."

If the real worry is "take the medicine or take a hike" ultimatums, legislation can be narrowly tailored to prevent them; broad-based gag orders, such as Connecticut's, are a solution that's worse than the problem.

THE CONSERVATIVE CASE FOR ADHD DRUGS.

There are kernels of truth to every conservative suspicion about ADHD. Who among us has not had lapses of attention? And isn't hyperactivity a normal condition of childhood when compared with deskbound adults? Certainly there are lazy teachers, warehousing schools, androgyny-pushing feminists, and far too many parents unwilling or unable to expend the time and effort to raise their children properly, even by their own standards. Where conservatives go wrong is in making ADHD a scapegoat for frustration over what we perceive as a breakdown in the order of society and family. In a column in *The Boston Herald*, Boston University Chancellor John Silber rails that Ritalin is "a classic example of a cheap fix: low-cost, simple and purely superficial."

Exactly. Like most headaches, ADHD is a neurological problem that can usually be successfully treated with a chemical. Those who recommend or prescribe ADHD medicines do not, as *The Weekly Standard* put it, see them as "discipline in pill-form." They see them as pills.

In fact, it can be argued that the use of those pills, far from being liable for or symptomatic of the Decline of the West, reflects and reinforces conservative values. For one thing, they increase personal responsibility by removing an excuse that children (and their parents) can fall back on to explain misbehavior and poor performance. "Too many psychologists and psychiatrists focus on allowing patients to justify to themselves their troubling behavior," says Satel. "But something like Ritalin actually encourages greater autonomy because you're treating a compulsion to behave in a certain way. Also, by treating ADHD, you remove an opportunity to explain away bad behavior."

Moreover, unlike liberals, who tend to downplay differences between the sexes, conservatives are inclined to believe that there are substantial physiological differences— differences such as boys' greater tendency to suffer ADHD. "Conservatives celebrate the physiological differences between boys and girls and eschew the radical-feminist notion that gender differences are created by societal pressures," says Houston regarding the fuss over the boy-girl disparity among ADHD diagnoses. "ADHD is no exception."

But, however compatible conservatism may be with taking ADHD seriously, the truth is that most conservatives remain skeptics. "I'm sure I would have been one of those smug conservatives saying it's a made-up disease," admits Charen, "if I hadn't found out the hard way." Here's hoping other conservatives find an easier route to accepting the truth.

MICHAEL FUMENTO is a senior fellow at the Hudson Institute in Washington, D.C., where he is completing his latest book, tentatively titled *Bioevolution: How Biotechnology Is Changing our World*, due this spring from Encounter Books.

Finding What Works

[Medication helps many kids. But it's hard to know which drugs for which kids.]

Peg Tyre

HUNTER WALRATH'S PARENTS were hopeful when a child psychiatrist prescribed Concerta for their 9-year-old son. A bright, highly verbal boy, Hunter has a laundry list of disabilities: he suffers from ADHD, faulty executive functioning, dyslexia and emotional problems that suggest Asperger's syndrome. His limited attention span and poor impulse control made him an outcast at school. But the Concerta, his parents say, had little effect. His doctor upped the dose, but still, Hunter struggled. A few months later, when the doctor switched Hunter to a cocktail of Ritalin and Strattera, their boy's behavior changed—but not for the better. He gained 25 pounds and his outbursts in class grew more intense. Back on Concerta, Hunter has improved and is starting a new school, but the Walraths are shaken. "Sometimes we wondered," says John Walrath. "Are the doctors making this up as they go along?"

The Walrath's aren't alone on the medication merry-go-round. In the last decade, the number of psychoactive medications available to children has more than tripled. And increasing numbers of children are taking the drugs, too. In a national study completed this February, the New York University's Child Study Center found that 15 percent of parents with children between the ages of 5 and 18 reported giving their kids psychoactive medication daily.

When they work, psychoactive medications can be a godsend. But John Walrath wonders if Hunter's medical team "had a solid understanding" of his son's complex interplay of issues. "Those doctors' visits are fleeting," he says. Experts share the concern. In the Child Study Center survey, about 28 percent of parents who gave their kids drugs deemed the treatment "somewhat unhelpful" or "extremely unhelpful." "We find this worrisome," says Dr. Harold S. Koplewicz, director of the center, because it suggests that many kids may be on the wrong meds. With only 7,000 child psychiatrists practicing in the United States and a growing wave of kids seeking treatment, "you have to wonder who is making the diagnosis," says Koplewicz. Most prescribing is done by a general practitioner or pediatrician, who may not have the time or expertise to do a thorough analysis.

The children who respond best to medication, experts say, are often the ones who fit snugly into widely recognized diagnostic categories like attention deficit or obsessive-compulsive disorders. For quirkier kids, whose symptoms are hard to classify or who seem to have several disorders at once, pinpointing the right treatment can depend more on clinical judgment than on hard science. For those kids, says Dr. Richard Gorman, chairman of the American Academy of Pediatrics' Committee on Drugs, "there is a lot more ambiguity and a lot less data about what works." Medicine aimed at one set of symptoms can exacerbate other symptoms. Susannah Budington says that by the time her daughter Allison Stoll was 5, she'd already been diagnosed with ADHD but was prescribed Prozac to help manage her hypersensitivity, anxiety and an extreme phobia about bugs. In first grade, though, Allison's teacher complained that while Allison was bright and kind, she was disruptive: she couldn't sit still and blurted out answers. So Stoll's psychiatrist added dexadrine to Allison's menu of meds. The next day, her mother noticed Allison was pulling out her eyebrows and her eyelashes. "The dexadrine overrode the Prozac," says Budington, who discontinued the dexadrine.

Even with the right drugs, determining the right dosage isn't easy. Children metabolize some drugs faster than adults—so pound for pound, they often require more. But too much medication has dangers, of course. Dr. Anne McBride, a pediatric psychopharmacologist at the

Payne Whitney clinic in New York, has seen young patients suffering from agitation, sedation, cognitive dulling, abnormal liver and kidney function, and an impaired immune system. "They're toxic from too many drugs," she says. In those cases, McBride retains the medications that are appropriately prescribed and withdraws the questionable drugs one at a time. Another challenge: children can "outgrow" a drug's benefits. From third to sixth grade, Khristopher Royal used Ritalin to help him stay focused in class. But in sixth grade, it simply stopped working.

His doctor tried Aderall, dexadrine and Wellbutrin. "Nothing worked," says his mother, Karran Harper Royal. "It was frustrating."

Prescribing drugs for kids can be an art and a science.

To help children get the most effective treatment, experts say that front-line physicians need better support. Pediatricians should be trained to treat simple cases and refer trickier kids to the specialists—child psychiatrists. Parents need to make sure that information flows between the child's prescribing physician and his teachers and therapist. And with a well-integrated program of behavioral therapy, says Dr. L. Eugene Arnold, an ADHD specialist at the Ohio State University Nisonger Center, "doctors can often reduce dosages of medication." Some can eliminate them altogether—giving parents and their quirky kids something to cheer about.

UNIT 10
Giftedness

Unit Selections

30. **Understanding the Young Gifted Child: Guidelines for Parents, Families, and Educators**, Jennifer V. Rotigel
31. **Read All About It**, Bruce Bower
32. **Teaching Strategies for Twice-Exceptional Students**, Susan Winebrenner

Key Points to Consider

- How can significant adults identify children with exceptional gifts and talents? What types of assessment are valid and reliable? What guidelines are important for their individualized education programs?

- What is hyperlexia? How can it be assessed and enriched?

- What types of instruction are effective for students who have both giftedness and learning disabilities?

Student Website

www.mhcls.com/online

Internet References

Further information regarding these websites may be found in this book's preface or online.

The Council for Exceptional Children
http://www.cec.sped.org/index.html

The individuals with Disabilities Education Act (IDEA) mandates special services for children with disabilities, but not for children with exceptional gifts or talents. The monies spent to provide special services for three children with high-cost disabilities could pay for accelerated lessons for a classroom full of college-bound students with intellectual giftedness. Should schools in the twenty-first century be more egalitarian? IDEA mandates appropriate education but not sameness of quantity or degree of knowledge for every child. Are we inclined to push compensatory education of students with shortcomings in learning, while leaving students with a gift for learning to cope for themselves to counterbalance the equation? Do we want educational parity?

Since many textbooks on exceptional children include children with special gifts and talents, and since these children are exceptional, they will be included in this volume. Instructors who deal only with the categories of disabilities covered by IDEA may simply omit coverage of this unit.

The Omnibus Education Bill of 1987 provided modest support for gifted and talented identification and the education of students with giftedness in the United States. It required, however, that each state foot the bill for the development of special programs for children with exceptional gifts and talents. Some states have implemented accelerated or supplemental education for the gifted. Most states have not.

Giftedness can be viewed as both a blessing and a curse. Problems of jealousy, misunderstanding, indignation, exasperation, and even fear are often engendered in people who live with, work with, or get close to a child with superior intelligence. Are children with giftedness at a disadvantage in our society? Do their powerful abilities and potentialities in some area (or areas) leave them ridiculed or bored in a regular classroom?

Children with special gifts and talents may be deprived of some of the opportunities with which less exceptional children are routinely provided.

Students who are gifted tend to ask a lot of questions and pursue answers with still more questions. They can be incredibly persistent about gathering information about topics that engage them. They may, however, show no interest at all in learning about topics that do not. They may be very competitive in areas where they are especially skilled, competing even with teachers and other adults. They may seem arrogant about their skills, when, in their minds, they are only being honest.

Many children and youth with special gifts and talents have extraordinary sensitivity to how other people are reacting to them. As they are promoted through elementary school into middle school and high school, many such children learn to hide their accomplishments for the secondary gain of being more socially acceptable or more popular. Because they have not been challenged or have been discouraged from achieving at their highest potentialities, under achievement becomes a problem. They have poor study habits as a result of not needing to study. They may be unmotivated, intensely bored, and discouraged by the educational programs available to them.

Researchers who have studied creative genius have found that most accomplished high achievers share one childhood similarity. Their parents recognized their special abilities early and found tutors or mentors who would help them develop their skills. This is true not only of mathematicians and scientists but also of world-class sports players, musicians, artists, performers, writers, and other producers of note.

Educational programs that refuse to find tutors or mentors, to encourage original work, or to provide special education in the skill areas of students with gifts are depriving the future of potential producers.

The earlier that children with special gifts and talents are recognized, the better. The sooner they are provided with enriched education, the more valuable their future contributions will become. Children from all ethnic backgrounds, from all socioeconomic levels, and from both sexes can have exceptional gifts and talents. Researchers have reported that parents of gifted persons seldom have any special creative skills or talents of their own.

The assessment of children with special gifts and talents, especially in the early childhood years, is fraught with difficulties. Should parents nominate their own children when they see extraordinary skills developing? How objective can parents be about their child's ability as it compares to the abilities of other same-aged children? Should measures of achievement be used (recitals, performances, art, reading levels, writings)? Many parents are embarrassed by their child's extraordinary aptitudes. They would rather have a popular child or a child more like his or her peers.

The first article in this unit suggests resources for parents and teachers of young gifted children. Guidelines are given for understanding the uniqueness of each preschooler with special gifts and talents. They are often described as "4 going on 40." In fact, each one has different areas of acceleration. Helping them understand themselves and their environments can be a challenging task. Many persons, unaccustomed to working with children with advanced talents, may misinterpret their unique behaviors. If unattended, they may learn to camouflage their giftedness in order to "fit in" with their peers. While peer tutoring can make children with advanced abilities feel needed, if used excessively it can lead to problems. Finding and reinforcing areas of giftedness, while attending to their social needs, and their self-esteem, are areas addressed in this article.

The second article, "Read All About It" discusses the unique gift of hyperlexia. Children with hyperlexia are very early readers. Using functional magnetic resonance imaging, scientists have discovered extraordinary temporal lobe activity in hyperlexics. How should these talented preschoolers be challenged to maximize their giftedness?

In the last article Susan Winebrenner describes students who are twice-exceptional: both exceptionally gifted and learning-disabled or ADHD, a not uncommon phenomenon. They usually do not receive gifted education. Their school work may be patronizingly simple. Ms. Winebrenner cautions us not to take time away from their strengths to focus on their weaknesses. She gives 9 suggestions for educating them more appropriately.

Understanding the Young Gifted Child:
Guidelines for Parents, Families, and Educators

Young children who are gifted or talented share special characteristics that impact on the way they learn and develop. Teachers and parents need to consider the unique needs of each child as they plan ways to nurture and educate these youngsters. Concerns such as uneven development, the need for acceleration and/or enrichment, appropriate socialization and peer interactions, and modification of the curriculum are some of the topics discussed. Suggestions for teachers and parents are included along with a variety of resources.

KEY WORDS: gifted; talented; acceleration; enrichment; socialization.

Jennifer V. Rotigel

INTRODUCTION

Much has been written about the development of children, and it is generally agreed that early development has profound consequences for later development. However, the social, emotional, and intellectual development of young *gifted* children has received little attention outside of the journals that deal specifically with gifted and talented children. The net result is that teachers and parents are often uninformed or misinformed regarding the social and emotional development of young gifted children, particularly in relation to intellectual development and schooling. This article describes characteristics of young gifted children, focuses on typical concerns voiced by parents and teachers, and provides suggestions for appropriately meeting the needs of the young gifted child through curricular modification and enhanced understanding.

WHAT DOES IT MEAN TO BE GIFTED AND TALENTED?

Gifted and talented children are usually identified by schools in the early grades when they are referred for evaluation by either the teacher or the parents. The child may be evaluated through the consideration of a constellation of factors, such as scores on an intelligence test, grades in school, classroom achievement, and teacher and parent input. For example, some schools require that the child demonstrate achievement of at least two grade levels above their current grade placement in reading or mathematics. The identification process varies from district to district and state to state, but the outcome should be that the gifted child receives necessary modifications to the school's curriculum so that she can be appropriately challenged in school.

It is important to realize that when a child is gifted and talented, all aspects of the child's experience are affected. Young gifted children are gifted all day, not just when they are in school or in a "pull-out" program. The cluster of traits that are characteristic of gifted and talented individuals encompasses intellectual, social, emotional, and physical aspects of the child's life. Not all gifted children demonstrate all traits, of course, but there is a commonality that allows for some description of the gifted individual. For example, gifted children often become deeply absorbed in a topic and need to know all there is to know about it, while high achieving children may be satisfied with a more superficial understanding and are then ready to move on. Gifted individuals are often perfectionists, and they grasp new information with little or no repetition. Many gifted children have advanced vocabularies and seek to understand and be involved in world events, even at a young age.

Research in the area of emotional and social adjustment of gifted children has produced overwhelmingly positive results. Children who are gifted are, in general, as well adjusted and emotionally mature as other students (Howley, Howley, & Pendarvis, 1995). As noted by Clark (1997), gifted children need to be given the opportunity to understand themselves and experience positive educational opportunities.

Helping young gifted children understand themselves and their world can be a challenging task for teachers and parents. Many gifted children strive to understand at an early age why they do not seem to fit in with their peers, and it is important that their questions be answered truthfully and carefully. Too many children misunderstand the interactions that they experience and draw conclusions that may be harmful to their development. For example, a young gifted child may be frustrated by his inability to guess the "right" answer that the kindergarten teacher is looking for. Often this is because he is thinking more deeply about a topic than the other children or than the teacher expects and therefore does not supply the simple answer to a simple question. Since he fails to have the answer that the teacher rewards, he may conclude that he is stupid or inadequate.

WHAT ARE TYPICAL CONCERNS REGARDING GIFTED YOUNG CHILDREN?

The information that a child has been identified as being gifted is not always welcomed by adults or even by the child. Teachers are sometimes intimidated by the news and fearful of the demands that may be made of them in terms of providing an appropriate education for the child. Teachers may lack specific information that would assist them in meeting the child's educational needs, and they may be uninformed regarding the social and emotional factors that must be considered in planning for the child. Teachers with little experience in educating gifted children may misinterpret a child's behavior. For example, at a meeting between the parents and the first-grade teacher of a gifted child, the teacher assured the parents that the child was being appropriately challenged in school. The parents reported that their daughter often complained that she was bored in school. The teacher countered with her observation that the child seldom participated in class, so she must not really know the material. When they got home, the parents asked their daughter about her reported lack of participation in class. She responded, "Well, I don't want the other kids to know that I know all of the answers. I do put up my hand when the teacher is really stuck, because I feel like I should help her out when no one else has the answer."

Schools that are already under fire for low performance in academic areas may not have the resources to devote to children who are already able to perform well on required state assessment tests. As school funding becomes increasingly problematic, programs for gifted children are among the first to go, thereby placing an increased burden on the classroom teacher.

Parents sometimes greet a diagnosis of giftedness with relief, as they may feel that there should be some explanation of their child's differences. Along with the information that the child is gifted, however, comes the expectation that somehow the child's educational experiences will improve. Unfortunately, this is not always the case, as school districts vary widely in their provisions for gifted children. This can lead to struggles between the school and the parents who advocate for their children. In many cases, the teachers and parents are in agreement regarding what would be best for the child, but the school administrators are unable to commit financial resources or are fearful of setting a precedent of service that they may not be able to provide for other gifted children.

Some parents, however, are upset by the news that their child is gifted, as they feel overwhelmed by the responsibility of raising a child who seems to be so different from anyone that they know. Many parents have little understanding of what giftedness really means and have heard some of the myths that surround giftedness. For example, on receiving the news of her 3-year-old child's high score on a screening test, a mother burst into tears because she believed that her child would grow up to be "weird" or "like Einstein." If parents are told that their child scored in the top 2% of the population, they may fear that they will need to send the child to a boarding school for very bright children.

Although to the uninitiated it might seem to be a blessing to be a gifted child, many children do not view their life experience as particularly lucky. Many will go to great lengths to camouflage their giftedness in order to "fit in" with their peers (Roedell, 1988). For example, one young gifted child who learned to read at an early age tried to hide this newfound skill from everyone. His mother overheard him confiding to his younger brother, saying, "It's not my fault that I can read, the words just keep jumping out at me!" This same child tried to conceal his reading abilities from his mother because he was afraid that she would stop reading aloud to him. He was, emotionally speaking, a young child who really enjoyed the closeness of the time that he spent each day sitting in his mother's lap as they shared books together.

HOW DO YOUNG GIFTED CHILDREN DEVELOP?

Gifted children sometimes demonstrate uneven development that can be problematic (Tolan, 1989). For example, gifted children often have interests that are unusual for their age. A 4-year-old who is interested in the Civil War is unlikely to find someone among his age mates who is interested in exploring this topic with him. Unfortunately, it is sometimes difficult to find reading material that is suitable for such a child and similarly difficult to find an adult who wants to discuss Civil War events with a young child.

Because of their advanced vocabulary skills and unusual interests, gifted children sometimes seem to be more mature than their age mates. In fact, since they spend so much time conversing with adults about their shared interests, these young gifted children may seem to be 4 years old, going on 40. This can lead to difficulties, as often there is a gap between their emotional development and their intellectual development that is not as obvious as is the difference between their physical and intellectual development.

There are many ways to describe the differential that may occur between the physical, intellectual, social, and emotional development of gifted children. Researchers have called this differential "internal dyssynchrony" and use the term to describe areas of development that are not "in sync" with other areas within a particular child (Callahan, 1997; Roedell, 1988). Internal dyssynchrony may be a significant problem for some gifted children, yet it is poorly understood and seldom addressed by parents or teachers. A young gifted child may be able to function intellectually at a much higher level than her age mates and thus finds that sometimes she needs to discuss ideas with older children or adults who share her interests. But if a 6-year-old child is able to read at the fourth grade level, it may be very inappropriate to place her in a fourth-grade class because of physical, social, and emotional factors.

The level of dyssynchrony varies with each individual and is felt more severely by highly gifted children. For example, the 7-year-old child who is interested in the war on terrorism and how it relates to his understanding of religion is likely to have difficulty engaging a classmate in a conversation of this type. On the other hand, he may not have the emotional development that would allow him to participate in viewing the CNN reports on this subject, so his information must come from secondary sources. This child may be very concerned about what he hears adults discussing but lack the social development to understand that this is not a topic that can be adequately addressed in school. With no one to help him make sense of this, the child may become frightened and withdrawn, unable to explore ideas that have captured his imagination.

One of the most important aspects of socialization for gifted children is having peers who share similar interests. Because of the dyssynchrony they experience, many gifted children will need several different peer groups. One group may satisfy their intellectual needs and be able to discuss topics of mutual interest. Another group may fit better emotionally, and yet a third group may be the social solution that the child needs. The gifted child may have to hide her intellectual ability from the social group and her emotional development from the intellectual group. This role-playing can be difficult for the young child to understand, and she will need to talk with understanding adults who can help her to cope.

Gifted children are sometimes teased about their abilities and interests. One of the most common strategies is for someone to ask a very difficult question of the child. If the gifted child admits that they do not know the answer, the person may respond, "What's the matter, you should know since you are so smart!" Such exchanges are bound to cause the gifted child to resolve that they will no longer appear to know the answers to anything, if that would be the way to avoid such cruel teasing. In this way, abilities that cause very bright children to be so out of step with their classmates can come to be regarded by the child a poor gift, indeed.

WHAT ARE THE IMPLICATIONS FOR TEACHING AND CURRICULUM?

Many people have criticized programs for gifted children on the grounds that providing programs for them is elitist, since the gifted and talented child already seems to have so much. Although it is certainly true that enrichment programs such as trips to the museum or the opera can and should be provided to all children who are interested in them and can benefit from them, it is equally true that gifted children deserve to learn something of value in school each and every day, just as we think all children should.

Gifted children are as different from the norm as are children with other special needs, and the range of abilities covered by the gifted label is wide. Gifted children are not necessarily gifted in all academic areas, either. The child who may absolutely zoom in math may be an average reader. Unfortunately, schools often attempt to treat gifted children as though they all possess the same strengths and weaknesses (Fiedler, 1993).

The curriculum in most schools is designed to meet the needs of the "average" student, so the assumption is made that most children benefit from that curriculum. However, many gifted children begin a school year having mastered most of the content that will be presented that year. Few schools provide routine pretesting of content mastery, so gifted children are expected to march in place for a large portion of their days, waiting for their classmates to grasp the material. This situation causes gifted children to waste much of their instructional time, unless their educational programs are modified to better meet their needs. Gifted children who are forced to waste much of their time in school sometimes resort to misbehavior in order to combat boredom. In addition, when schoolwork is always too easy, children do not learn how to study and are robbed of the opportunity to feel satisfaction in the accomplishment of a project that challenged them intellectually. Researchers have pointed out that when we reward children for doing tasks that are too easy, their self-esteem is not enhanced (Tomlinson, 1994).

For highly gifted children, the question of whether to provide acceleration or enrichment programs may come up very early in their schooling. Of course, the answer to this question is that both acceleration and enrichment should be provided as needed. According to Boatman, Davis, and Benbow, "the goal of acceleration is curricular flexibility or curricular access without regard to age" (1995, p. 1085). An appropriate education for gifted children is one that allows the learners to make progress at their own pace. Since one of the hallmarks of giftedness is an increased rate of acquisition, this means that children who are gifted and talented naturally accelerate themselves. Allowing a kindergarten child to have access to third-grade materials is appropriate if he is reading on the third-grade level and comprehending the content well.

If a young gifted child needs to receive modifications in the school program, it is important to explain to the child why this is being done. One young 6-year-old whom I met was upset when he was told that he had been chosen to attend the special class. He concluded that he must have fallen far behind his classmates if he needed so much special help.

One of the surest ways to foster an unrealistic view of the world is to isolate a gifted child in a classroom where he has no intellectual peers. It is very important for gifted children to interact with each other so they can see that they are not the only ones with lots of answers, lots of questions, and perhaps some unusual hobbies and interests.

One difficulty that is sometimes ignored is the problem of providing reading material of an appropriate social and emotional level for a precocious reader (Halstead, 1990). For example, a third grader who reads on the college level cannot be expected to read only the third-grade text and elementary level chapter books. But finding college-level novels that have an appropriate theme and content for a young child can be a challenge to teachers and parents. Young children should not be exposed to the inappropriate language and adult content that are so often found in popular literature. It is also essential that the child have someone with whom to discuss his reading, and this can be problematic. Gifted children have lots of time to read and often can read faster than the adults who are trying to keep up. Local reading groups seldom welcome a young gifted child since they may indulge in gossip or adult conversation along with their discussion of the book of the week. If a child has no one to share his reading with, it can reinforce his feelings of isolation and limit his understanding of the content.

One of the inappropriate solutions that are sometimes employed is giving children three books to read while the other students are only expected to read one. This is referred to as "more of the same, piled higher" and often serves to make gifted children feel that they are being punished for their ability, especially if all of the books are at an inappropriately low level. The curriculum needs to be modified to meet a gifted child's needs, and this can only be done by assessing the child's needs and carefully planning strategies and content that will allow her to interact with challenging and appropriately difficult materials.

In school, group work may be assigned with a mixed-ability group. Unfortunately, the gifted child sometimes ends up "carrying" the group. Even when gifted children resent this, they are often trapped because they do not want to receive a bad grade or disappoint the teacher or the other group members. Gifted children are often asked to teach other children. Within reason, this can be beneficial to both parties, but if the strategy is used excessively, it can lead to problems. For example, when does the gifted child get a chance to learn something new if his time is spent tutoring his classmates? Additionally, simply because someone has ability in a particular area or understands a concept does not mean that he will be able to teach it to classmates. Some children do not want to be viewed as the teacher's aide, or worse, the teacher's pet. The child is often asked to tutor others in an area of content in which he excels. If the gifted child's progress is hampered by too much time spent tutoring others, he may lose interest in the subject completely.

CONCLUSION

Parents and teachers need to develop a more complete understanding of the gifted child so that they can truly be helpful (Table I). Nurturing young gifted children requires sensitivity to the special challenges that gifted children face and a willingness to work together with other adults who are involved with the child. Adults must clearly define giftedness, understand how it develops in children, and recognize the impact that it has on curriculum and instruction. When all of this is in place, a gifted and talented child is not likely to say, as one 8-year-old did, "school must be made for someone else, because it just doesn't work for me."

Table I. How Can Teachers and Parents Help?

- View each gifted child as an individual. Make clear assessments of the child's social, emotional, physical, and educational needs.
- Group children according to ability, achievement, or interest. Flexible group strategies can be powerful tools in assisting children to find appropriate intellectual, social, and emotional peer groups.
- Guard against unrealistic and unfair expectations. Do not ignore the social and emotional development of the child when setting goals.
- Talk with children to discover their level of understanding regarding their giftedness. Children are not always able to articulate the reasons they do certain things.
- Ensure that the gifted child has intellectual peers who are also age mates.
- Encourage hobbies and interest. Mentors can be a wonderful help, as they can share their expertise in the area of interest.
- Remember that although children may interact with adults in a seemingly mature way, their emotional development may be more closely matched with that of their age mates.
- Make sure that the educational program is appropriate. Each gifted child needs to have an individual assessment and the curriculum needs to be modified in order to meet the child's needs.
- Do not expect the gifted child to spend too much time tutoring his classmates. All children need to be able to learn new things every day, not just repeat lessons already learned.
- Search out reading materials that are age appropriate as well as challenging, and make sure that the child has someone with whom to discuss his reading.

APPENDIX: RESOURCES FOR TEACHERS AND PARENTS

National Association for Gifted Children
http://www.nagc.org

American Association for Gifted Children
http://www.aagc.org/index.html

Hoagies Gifted Education Page
http://www.hoagiesgifted.org/

National Research Center on Gifted and Talented, University of Connecticut
http://www.gifted.uconn.edu

Gifted Development Center
http://www.gifteddevelopment.com

Gifted and Talented Resources
http://www.Gtworld.org/links.html

Center for Talent Development
Northwestern University
617 Dartmouth Place
Evanston, IL 60208
(847) 491-3782

The Council for Exceptional Children
1920 Association Drive
Reston, VA 22091-1589
(703) 620-3660

Gifted Child Society, Inc.
Ms. Gina Ginsberg Riggs, Ex. Dir.
190 Rock Rd.
Glen Rock, NJ 07452
(201) 444-6530

Institute for the Academic Advancement of Youth (IAAY)
Johns Hopkins University–IAAY
Office of Public Information
3400 N. Charles Street
Baltimore, MD 21218
(410) 516-0245

National Association for Gifted Children
Suite 550
1707 L Street, NW
Washington, DC 20036
(202) 785-4268

National Research Center on the Gifted and Talented
The University of Connecticut
2131 Hillside Road, Unit 3007
Storrs CT 06269-3007
(860) 486-4676

REFERENCES

Boatman, T. A., Davis, K. G., & Benbow, C. P. (1995). Best practices in gifted education. In A. Thomas & J. Grimes (Eds.), *Best practices in school psychology-III* (pp. 1083–1095). Washington, DC: The National Association of School Psychologists.

Callahan, C. M. (1997). Giftedness. In G. Bear, K. Minke, & A. Thomas (Eds.), *Children's needs II* (pp. 431–448). Bethesda, MD: National Association of School Psychologists.

Clark, B. (1997). *Growing up gifted* (5th edition). Upper Saddle River, NJ: Merrill.

Fiedler, E. (1993). Square pegs in round holes: Gifted kids who don't fit in. *Understanding Our Gifted, 5*(5A), 1, 11–14.

Halstead, J. W. (1990). *Guiding the gifted reader.* Reston, VA: ERIC Clearinghouse on Handicapped and Gifted Children.

Howley, C. B., Howley, A., & Pendarvis, E. D. (1995). *Out of our minds: Anti-intellectualism and talent development in American schooling.* New York: Teachers College Press.

Roedell, W. C. (1988). "I just want my child to be happy." Social development and young gifted children. *Understanding Our Gifted, 1*(1), 1, 7–11.

Tolan, S. S. (1989). Helping your highly gifted child (ERIC Digest #477). Reston, VA: ERIC Clearinghouse on Handicapped and Gifted Children. (ERIC Document Reproduction Service No. ED321482 90)

Tomlinson, C. A. (1994). The easy lie and the role of gifted education in school excellence. *Roeper Review, 16*(4), 258–259.

Jennifer V. Rotigel, Department of Professional Studies in Education, Indiana University of Pennsylvania.

Correspondence should be directed to Jennifer V. Rotigel, D.Ed., Professional Studies in Education, 312 Davis Hall, Indiana University of Pennsylvania, Indiana, PA 15705; e-mail: jrotigel@iup.edu.

From *Early Childhood Education Journal,* Summer 2003, pp. 209-214. © 2003 by Human Sciences Press.

READ ALL ABOUT IT

Kids take different neural paths to reach print mastery.

Bruce Bower

Ethan refused to play with the children who attended his first-birthday party. He ignored the presents that they brought for him. When Ethan's father tried to hold him in his lap, the boy wriggled free and returned to his true passion—scanning printed material. On this special day, Ethan plopped on the floor by his father's chair and intensely perused a pile of magazines. Although Ethan couldn't read, print riveted his attention with a power that neither brand-new toys nor gooey birthday cake could approach.

Ethan's romance with print blossomed with time. At age 1, he scrutinized each license plate in the supermarket parking lot. At 2½, he placed letter-emblazoned blocks in alphabetic order and corrected his mother, by moving her hand, when she pointed to the wrong line of text while reading to him. However, the boy was 3 before he uttered his first spoken word.

Now nearly 11 years old and attending fourth grade in a public school, Ethan reads words and spells as well as most high school seniors do, although his comprehension of written passages is only average for his age. He's also learning to read Hebrew. Ethan talks to other children awkwardly and has difficulty, maintaining conversations.

Scientists refer to Ethan's unusual condition, which afflicts roughly 1 in 5,000 people, as hyperlexia. Initially described in 1967, hyperlexia combines autismlike speech and social problems with a jump-start on reading. As the first precocious reader of this kind to submit to a brain-imaging analysis, Ethan stands at the forefront of scientific efforts to understand how the brain underwrites reading. In a report last year, a team at Georgetown University Medical Center in Washington, D.C., outlined the neural structures that foster Ethan's advanced grasp of printed words.

Since then, these and other researchers have accumulated evidence on neural regions that contribute to skilled reading of both Western-style alphabetic text and non-alphabetic systems, such as Chinese writing. These findings are beginning to show how learning to read triggers certain universal brain accommo-dations, no matter what the language. At the same time, other brain responses critical for effective reading vary with the nature of one's writing system.

Increased understanding of the neural building blocks of successful reading may inspire improved forms of reading instruction. For now, brain research on Ethan and normal readers underscores the resilience and adaptability of each person's brain, so that there's more than one way to become a good reader, says G. Reid Lyon of the National Institute of Child Health and Human Development in Bethesda, Md.

SKILLED BRAINS When Ethan piqued the interest of Georgetown's Guinevere Eden, her team had already made headway in identifying how the brain develops in healthy kids who read well. Like professional musicians, Eden says, good readers learn a complex skill through nearly lifelong practice. At some point, playing musical notes or reading script becomes effortless, injecting newfound joy into the enterprise.

The brain makes accommodations to achieve such expertise. For instance, one research team has reported that in brain areas devoted to seeing, hearing, and coordinating muscle movements, professional musicians possess more neurons than either amateur musicians or nonmusicians do.

Reading invokes activity in a unique set of brain regions, according to Eden's group. The team used functional magnetic resonance imaging (fMRI) to measure the rate of blood flow, a marker of cell activity, in the brains of 41 young people, ages 6 to 22, who read well for their ages.

"One could envision this area as a dial that predicts a child's aptitude for reading."

—Guinevere Eden, Georgetown University

Reading skill in these people displayed a critical link to activity in a brain region known as the superior temporal cortex, which is located above the left ear. Rapid word reading ignited neural responses in this area for study participants of all ages.

In the fMRI test, each participant used handheld buttons to indicate whether a word briefly flashed on a computer screen contained a tall letter or not. The word *sauce*, for instance, contains no tall letter, but *alarm* has the tall letter *l*. Earlier studies had indicated that volunteers automatically read each word as they searched for tall letters.

The superior temporal cortex brokers an essential element of reading alphabetic text, Eden proposes. It assists in matching appropriate sounds to printed letters, so that words can be sounded out. "One could envision this area as a dial that predicts a child's aptitude for reading," she remarks.

At 9 years old, Ethan exhibited unusually intense activity in this brain region, even when compared with older children who read as well as he did.

Word reading also galvanizes two related parts of the frontal left brain, but only in experienced readers, Eden's team finds. Adults who performed particularly well on two phonies-related tests—using different-colored blocks to represent specific speech sounds and naming printed letters as fast as possible—exhibited the most activity in these neural locales while reading words.

In these frontal regions, Ethan displayed activity similar to that of adults. Eden suggests that these frontal-brain responses reflect an experienced reader's accumulated knowledge of spelling regularities and of the many exceptions to those rules.

Conversely, in budding readers, word reading evokes strong activity in right brain areas, at least for a few years. These regions, which exhibit much weaker activity in adult readers, were previously implicated in identifying objects by sight. Children often use visual patterns and cues in the early stages of learning to read, as in recognizing *dog* as a small word with a tail on its last letter, just as a real-life dog sports a tail on its end.

Intriguingly, Ethan displayed more such right brain activity than did the older volunteers who read at his level or children of his age who read at their age-appropriate levels. Right brain mechanisms may contribute to Ethan's intense focus on words, Eden says.

WORD HUB Neither Ethan nor the other good readers studied by Eden's team exhibited much activity in a brain area that receives considerable attention from other neuroseientists who study reading. Some argue that this small structure, situated at the back and bottom of the left brain, gradually specializes to recognize words instantly. Others suspect that this clump of tissue aids recognition of all sorts of objects, not just printed words.

Activity rises in this brain structure, called the left fusiform gyrus, as children become better readers, according to a group led by Sally Shaywitz and Bennett Shaywitz, both of Yale University School of Medicine. The team's findings suggest that the area specializes in identifying frequently encountered printed words, proposes Bruce D. McCandliss of Weill Medical College of Cornell University in New York City.

Cathy J. Price of University College London disagrees. People who suffer damage to the left fusiform gyrus experience difficulties in naming pictures of objects as well as in reading, she argues. Recent evidence suggests that this brain structure contributes to the identification of any item in the center of one's visual field, which includes a word being read, Price says.

This area was inactive in Eden's fMRI studies of young readers. However, her simple tests may not have called upon it. Conscious consideration of a word's spelling or pronunciation may rev up the left fusiform gyrus.

That and several other left brain areas respond to spelling and rhyming tasks with increasing vigor as good readers get older, according to James R. Booth of Northwestern University in Evanston, Ill. In the August 2004 *Journal of Cognitive Neuroscience*, he and his coworkers reported results of an fMRI study of 15 kids, ages 9 to 12, and 15 adults, ages 20 to 35.

In one series of trials, volunteers alternately read or listened to two words, such as *hold* and *plant*, and then indicated which word resembled the spelling of a third word, such as cold. In other tasks, participants read or heard two words, such as *myth* and *home*, and determined which one rhymed with a third word, such as *foam*.

Both the spelling task and the rhyming task evoked left fusiform gyrus activity in adults and children, Booth says. However, only adults exhibited strong responses in another left-brain structure, the angular gyrus. This tissue may foster experienced readers' ability to ladle out a stream of words from a stew of spelling regularities and exceptions, Booth proposes.

CHINESE UNIVERSALS Just as the precocious Ethan offers an intriguing perspective on the brain's role in reading, so does a huge group of print consumers that has received surprisingly little scientific attention—the Chinese.

Recent investigations of Chinese readers suggest that people everywhere invoke core neural responses in order to read, but other types of brain activity are necessary to attain mastery of alphabetic or non-alphabetic writing systems, psycholinguist Charles A. Perfetti of the University of Pittsburgh explained last February in Washington, D.C., at the annual meeting of the American Association for the Advancement of Science.

Many investigators have assumed that, unlike alphabetic systems, written Chinese employs drawings that symbolize whole words.

Even if that were the ease with ancient Chinese pictographic symbols, those characters have transformed into much more abstract shapes that induce sounds of spoken syllables in modern readers' minds, Perfetti says. Chinese characters thus represent bigger chunks of spoken words than alphabetic letters do.

"All writing systems represent spoken language, but they have different design principles," Perfetti asserts.

Consider Mandarin Chinese. It currently includes 420 syllables. These syllables correspond to nearly 4,600 written characters, so an average of about 11 characters share a single pronunciation, which can be modified by using any of four tones.

In spoken Chinese, the meaning of the many different words that sound alike becomes apparent only in the context of conversation. People listening to English sometimes discern word meanings in this way—consider the words *guise* and *guys*—but need to do so much less often than Chinese listeners do.

Many Mandarin Chinese words consist of only one syllable, Perfetti adds. That has encouraged the false impression, at least among Westerners, that the language's written characters represent only words, he says.

Experiments show that Mandarin Chinese characters correspond to spoken Chinese rather than to the idea that the word represents, Perfetti says. For instance, if shown the written character for the word *red* printed in blue ink, volunteers name the ink color more slowly than if the same character is printed in red ink. Analogous results have been noted among English readers, whose writing system inarguably represents spoken sounds.

Response times for Chinese readers turn almost as sluggish if a different character with same pronunciation and tone as *red*, such as the character for *flood*, appears in blue ink. This effect indicates that written characters correspond to sounds in spoken Chinese, not to specific words. The pronunciation of *flood* calls to mind *red* and slows naming of the clashing ink color, Perfetti

says. If the characters represented specific words, instead of sounds, this delay would not occur.

A smaller but still notable slowdown occurs when a character with the same pronunciation as *red* but a different vocal tone, such as character for *boom*, appears in blue ink. Again, the common pronunciation calls to mind *red*, causing readers to take a little longer to identify the different ink color.

Studies of blood flow and electric responses indicate that Chinese readers activate many of the same left brain areas that English readers do, Perfetti adds. Right brain regions involved in vision also contribute to reading Chinese but not to reading English. This finding is consistent with the possibility that learning to read Chinese stimulates spatial perception (*SN: 2/12/05, p. 99*).

Such results suggest that different neural disruptions may underlie severe problems in reading, depending on the writing system. For example, despite sharing some facets of disturbed brain function, kids with dyslexia in China and the United States display low activity in different parts of the frontal brain (*SN: 9/4/04, p. 148*). "The brain basis of dyslexia might not be universal," Perfetti says.

The neural roots of hyperlexia may also vary from one writing system to another. Someday, Ethan may pick up a magazine and read about how his brain compares with that of a precocious reader living halfway around the world.

Teaching Strategies for Twice-Exceptional Students

For many years, parents and teachers have been perplexed about youngsters who have dramatic learning strengths in some areas and equally dramatic learning weaknesses in others. These students appear to defy accurate labeling: Are they gifted or learning disabled? Finally, the debate has stopped, and educators are now recognizing these students as "twice-exceptional." Rather than trying to use evidence from their weak learning areas to prove they are not "truly gifted," savvy teachers are now learning how to allow these students to experience the same opportunities available for gifted students when they are learning in their strength areas. When students are learning in their areas of weakness, teachers are learning to provide the same compensation strategies used by other students with learning disabilities. This article offers specific instruction to empower teachers to effectively teach twice-exceptional students.

SUSAN WINEBRENNER

Can you visualize the well-known Far Side (Larson, 2000) cartoon that depicts a boy pushing a door with all his might to get into a school for gifted? The problem is, the door is clearly marked "PULL." Many in my audience laugh when I show this picture. Some nod ruefully, recognizing themselves or a child they know. In gifted education over the years, students like this have caused great frustration for their teachers and parents because their obvious exceptional abilities in some areas of learning seem overshadowed by their painfully apparent weaknesses, particularly in the areas of organizational or social skills and just plain common sense.

At the workshops I present for teachers, I often hear statements of extreme frustration with students who seem to defy accurate description. In some ways, their clearly exceptional abilities are apparent. But in many other ways, their learning deficiencies seem to make it nearly impossible for learning success to occur, even in their areas of greatest strength, because they often skip important steps as they make intuitive leaps toward answers or problem solutions. Sometimes, these students impress their teachers and peers with highly creative stories and scenarios, but when their teachers ask them to write their great ideas, the students contend, "I can't write!" Teachers are caught between belief and disbelief, as they wonder if the student actually cannot do a task or simply is "too lazy" to exert the required effort. Teachers have often used evidence of the student's learning weaknesses to prove to a parent or administrator that the child is not "truly gifted," by which they usually mean gifted in all learning areas. Sometimes, students' learning difficulties depress their gifted potential into very average performance. Teachers may wonder how the parents of such kids could claim their children are exceptionally capable when their perfectly average performance should satisfy.

When we add to these facts the reality that some gifted students are extremely active and nonconforming, we can predict that many of them have been or will be diagnosed as having an attention-deficit/hyperactivity disorder (ADHD) or a learning disability (LD), and they probably will not receive services in gifted education during their years in public school (Webb & Latimer, 1993).

Slowly but surely, educators have come to acknowledge the dichotomy of abilities that characterize students we now refer to as *twice exceptional:* youngsters who have clearly exceptional abilities in some areas and weaknesses in others. Sadly, most classroom time and attention is focused on student weaknesses, with little or no attention to their remarkable strengths. Are these kids gifted? Do they have learning disabilities? Yes … and yes!

Working together, educators in gifted and special education are discovering ways to create and maintain optimum learning conditions for twice-exceptional students. More important than understanding how each specific learning challenge manifests itself is that educators encourage twice-exceptional students to use proven strategies that will allow them to compensate for their areas of weakness while simultaneously experiencing opportunities gifted students appreciate in their areas of learning strength. Twice-exceptional students cannot improve by simply "trying harder." Their learning challenges often emanate from a series of neurological twists and turns as messages try to make their way to the brain from the original stimulus. By the same token, many students already labeled as having LD do not actually have neurological implications. Such students would better be labeled as "learning strategy disabled" because their academic outcomes can improve dramatically when they learn to use appropriate compensation techniques. This article describes specific teaching and learning methods that teachers and parents can use to facilitate significant learning progress for twice-exceptional students in areas of both strengths and weaknesses.

Teach Them the Way They Learn

While planning and teaching compensation strategies, educators must acknowledge the need for teaching the same concepts in many different ways: If students are not learning the way we teach them, teach them the way they learn. When we keep trying to teach something to a child in a way in which he or she has repeatedly failed, discouragement and self-blame quickly become a self-fulfilling prophecy. If learners assume that their failures to learn are caused by stupidity or laziness, their primary purpose in the classroom is to hide their ineptness from peers and teachers. Clowning and other misbehaviors, they believe, can obfuscate their perceived lack of ability. When they are in the classes of teachers who can "teach them the way they learn," they can begin to gather evidence that learning success is probable when they can use methods that

capitalize on their strengths and compensate for their weaknesses.

Beware of creating a situation that Landfried (1989) has designated as "educational enabling." His work documented that our tendency is often to make learning tasks as easy as possible so students can feel successful. However, the more evidence students get that their teachers do not expect them to handle grade-level work, the more convinced these students become that no one believes they can handle more challenging content. Instead of implying there is something wrong with the students themselves because of their repeated failures, we can demonstrate that we will help students try as many different methods as necessary until we find the "fit" that allows the students to experience learning success with material that is close to grade-level standards.

Recently, I was in a conversation with a friend whose learning challenges sometimes interfere with his speech fluency. As hesitations, repetitions, backtracking, and loss of memory about what he was trying to say became ever more frustrating, I offered a suggestion. I asked him to straighten his arm, use his hand to trace an imaginary infinity sign lying on its side, and allow his eyes to follow his hand as it traced that sign in large arches that crossed the center of his body. After a few moments of this exercise, he resumed his story with remarkable fluency. The method comes from a program called Brain Gym, which was created by Dennison (1989). It is based on the concept that specific kinesiology exercises can facilitate cross-over between brain hemispheres and improve fluency and competence in learning tasks. It is just one dramatic example of ways in which simple compensation strategies may facilitate learning for persons with learning difficulties, including those who fit the profile of the twice-exceptional learner.

The rule to follow when teaching twice-exceptional students is simple. When teaching these students in their areas of strength, offer them the same compacting and differentiation opportunities available to other gifted students. When teaching in their areas of challenge, teach them directly whatever strategies they need to increase their learning success. *Never* take time away from their strength areas to create more time to work on their deficiencies.

Are these kids gifted? Do they have learning disabilities? Yes . . . and yes!

The first twice-exceptional student I recall having in my class was a fifth grader named Eric. He had serious difficulty with any written task, which was compounded by almost illegible handwriting. His math skills were weak; he had great trouble writing coherent sentences and appeared to be very frustrated when asked to recall skill work he had "mastered" a short time ago. When we started a unit on maps, Eric really shined. He had always been in charge of mapping his family's summer auto trips and could remember in incredible detail the routes of trips they had taken since he was 7 years old. He also had an almost photographic memory of information about national parks and monuments. Eric asked if he could demonstrate what he knew about these subjects in order to be excused from "learning" it all over again. I agreed and simply offered the end of the unit test to anyone who wanted to take it, explaining that anyone who earned an *A* would be allowed to work on extension activities instead of the regular content.

Eric and several other students met the required criteria, but I then faced a serious dilemma. I was sorely tempted to use some of Eric's social studies time to remediate his glaring weaknesses. However, the truth was that he was exceptionally capable in the content his classmates were just beginning to learn. Therefore, I decided that he was as entitled as anyone else to engage in differentiated learning during the length of this map unit. Remediation could wait for the appropriate class period.

From a menu of activities, Eric chose to create a country from papier mâché and was expected to demonstrate the placement in his imaginary country of the same geographic features the class was studying. He was also expected to explain why he placed elements where he did as well as the relationships between elements. The other students did not resent Eric's freedom to work in this manner because everyone in the class had a similar opportunity to take the pretest. Watching Eric work sparked interest from other students to create a country also. Creating group countries became the culminating activity for all students. During their work on this project, Eric became the "create a country consultant." The status he earned from this experience significantly improved classmates' perception of Eric's ability, and he felt good about the experience as well. So remember the rule: Never remediate students' weaknesses until you first teach to their strengths!

Tips for Teachers When Addressing Students' Learning Challenges

The following strategies provide a framework for addressing the specific learning needs of children who are twice exceptional.

1. Teach students to appreciate individual differences. For all students in a class to accept the presence of differentiation opportunities, teachers need to be willing to spend time helping all students understand and appreciate individual differences. This is an area in which I think our schools fall short. Schools support programs of multicultural diversity appreciation yet fail to understand how short-sighted it is to limit teachers' efforts for

the benefit of children from other cultures. Why not use the same type of techniques to help students become more accepting of all individual differences?

Take time at the beginning of every school year to help all your students appreciate, respect, and support individual differences in everything from observable physical differences to apparent differences in learning abilities. When teachers can consistently demonstrate that diversity is a positive and desirable condition, students will follow their lead, and acceptance of individual differences becomes the modus operandi. Many students who have committed violence in schools have a history of being teased mercilessly for their noticeable differences. Efforts to facilitate respect for learning differences should continue throughout the school year and should become a schoolwide initiative. Teachers and schools must enforce policies that simply do not allow teasing, name calling, or other harassment practices that demonstrate rejection of kids for any reason.

This is a very tall order, given the assumption that "kids will be kids." Is it possible that students can learn to be more tolerant instead of so demanding of conformity? I believe it is, in much the same way as U.S. citizens have changed their attitudes about the acceptability of driving while under the influence of addictive substances. Twenty years ago, jokes about drunken behavior were ubiquitous. Now, the humor seems less politically correct than a national effort to save lives that may be lost to drunk drivers on our highways. If a nation can change its culture in a positive way, so can schools. If students could learn to cheer when someone learns something a different way, soon they would become conditioned to celebrate diversity.

I further believe this can be accomplished even without apparent support from parents. Although it is best to have parental support, it is not always possible. The mores of classrooms reflect wide discrepancies compared with what is found in some students' homes. This respect for diversity could simply be one more area in which students understand that "We do things differently at school, and that's the way it is." The only arena in which teachers can have real influence is at school. If teachers believe they must wait for families to communicate only helpful values to their children, they will be waiting a long time in some cases. Let's consider the classroom as the place for these reforms to begin.

2. Be aware that many students who have learning difficulties are global learners who prefer visual and tactile-kinesthetic formats for learning success. Some students with learning problems may have sensory challenges. They may be uncomfortable in absolutely quiet places, prefer soft light to brightly lighted areas, appreciate multiple opportunities for movement, or prefer relaxed postures (Carbo, Dunn, & Dunn, 1986). Teachers should offer these students choices of different work areas. They should be free to choose the place in which they will do their work as long as they follow three simple rules:

- Do not bother anyone while you are working, including the teacher.
- Do not call attention to yourself or the fact you are doing something different than other students.
- Do the work you are supposed to do.

Students who follow these expectations are allowed to choose where they will work. Students who do not follow these guidelines will have their working area chosen by the teacher, one day at a time (Winebrenner, 1996).

3. Always teach content by teaching concepts first and details second. Make sure students see the big picture before they try to learn its pieces. Strategies that are helpful include the Survey and Question strategies from SQ3R (Robinson, 1970), watching a video before and after studying a novel or other unit of work, hearing a story read aloud before reading it individually, and working from graphic organizers that fit on one page so that students can see the entire unit content. All skills should be integrated into meaningful content rather than taught as separate learning activities.

4. Teach students how to set realistic short-term goals and to take credit for reaching those goals, even if they represent only a partial amount of the entire task. This technique is highly effective in helping discouraged learners become positively motivated to put more effort into their work because it makes larger assignments feel more manageable. Both in-class assignments and homework should be designated in terms of the amount of time these students are expected to work rather than as a prescribed number of problems or specific amount of work to be completed. Parents can help by monitoring that the designated time was spent. This is preferable to having students spend several painful hours trying to complete an arbitrary amount of work. When teachers feel frustrated by students who do not do their homework, the issue of whether students *can* do the work must be taken into consideration. This means that teachers must be sure students have learned enough during class time to have the skills to complete their assignments at home. It also means that parents or caretakers need to provide an appropriate place at home to work on school assignments.

5. Teach in a way that ties past learning to new content. In order for students to learn and generalize new skills, they must be able to connect the new learning to something they already know. Many students with learning difficulties prefer making everything visual so they can see the patterns and connections they need to assimilate new learning. Use graphic organizers, charts, graphs, timelines, semantic maps, vocabulary maps, and similar tools that condense words into pictures or graphics. If you lecture, supplement your words with visual organizers as you talk. Stop frequently to check for understanding with group signals and other group response methods rather than simply accepting one or two verbal responses from volunteers as evidence that all students have learned the content.

6. Immerse all the senses in learning activities. Use musical chants, raps, rhymes, or rhythms for students who respond to those methods. Companies that stock teaching and learning aids will often carry such products. For many students, the simple act of singing or chanting the content makes mastery much easier to achieve.

Build movement into learning tasks. Recognize the validity of needing to move as an actual learning style, and observe how movement helps some students learn specific content. Ask students to stand or jump to indicate their responses to questions. Use team games where students can walk to different areas of the room to indicate a response. Allow them to hold squeezeable objects, such as Kush Balls®, that enable them to keep moving their hands. Guard against the impulse to automatically label highly kinesthetic learners as having ADHD.

Understand that twice-exceptional students often prefer hands-on and experiential learning situations. Such opportunities meet students' needs to learn from the concrete to the abstract. Actual manipulation of objects often helps these students better understand concepts when they are transferred to more abstract applications within content areas. Include projects, models, and visual representations as assignments because students can often understand concepts better when they are encouraged to "do" rather than to hear or see. Unfortunately, teachers sometimes prevent this type of learning activity because it is thought to be more difficult to manage classroom behavior. The irony is that acceptable behavior is much more likely to occur when students are vitally interested and involved in what they are learning.

Allow struggling readers to listen to the books on tape before the class reads a designated story or novel. Listening to one chapter at a time allows many students to become more active participants in class discussions and activities. An agency called Recording for the Blind and Dyslexic (see Resources) has recordings of almost every book used in U.S. classrooms and allows schools or individual families to borrow taped books for a nominal fee. All that is required is a letter from a medical or educational professional indicating that the child has some learning difficulty.

7. Provide specific instruction in organizational techniques. Provide color-coded notebooks by subject areas and two sets of texts, one that can be kept at home. Teach students to organize their lockers, desks, and supplies. Help students learn to use an assignment notebook or personal desk assistant to keep track of assignments and long-term projects. Use any other methods that work.

8. Find and use any available technology that will improve a student's productivity. Students are not "cheating" by using calculators, tape recorders, word processors, and spell-check programs if not using such aids would contribute to the continuation of the learning weaknesses. These aids help students concentrate on conceptual content instead of forcing them to focus on less important details such as spelling. In addition, teaching students to use technology provides them with a useful life skill.

9. Allow students to take tests in separate, supervised environments so they can either read the test aloud to themselves or have someone else read it to them. Some students have difficulty concentrating on tests when typical classroom noise occurs. A quiet place allows a student to focus. Furthermore, listening to a voice read the questions aloud helps the student better understand the questions.

Tips for Teachers to Accommodate Gifted Abilities in Students Who Are Twice Exceptional

It is often difficult for teachers to understand that students with learning difficulties might also be gifted in some areas of learning. However, if we remember that the essential definition of twice exceptional is exactly that, we can see such learners from a different perspective. Allow these students to experience the same compacting and differentiation opportunities available to other students. Offer pretests to allow them to document previous mastery of upcoming content. Allow opportunities for students to move through new content at a faster pace and to use allocated worktime on projects related to topics in which they have a particular interest (Winebrenner, 2000).

Compacting is the process of allowing highly capable students to demonstrate their previous mastery of some of the required curriculum. Compacting also occurs when students are allowed to demonstrate that they need less time than their peers to learn new material (Renzulli, 1977). When the evidence of the need for compacting is present, differentiation follows. Thus, when students demonstrate that the general curriculum or pacing does not provide an appropriate challenge, they can gain access to more challenging topics or activities. Gifted students deserve these opportunities, not simply because they are gifted but because all students are entitled to experience the promises of the school's mission statement. If it promises that students are supposed to be able to achieve learning to the highest levels of their potential, gifted students must be allowed access to activities that are personally challenging. If giftedness implies a learning ability that exceeds expectations for same-age peers, it is natural to understand the need for differentiated curriculum.

> # The most serious challenge is that the giftedness will go unnoticed and unaccommodated in favor of attending to learning deficits.

Teachers often cannot be convinced of the real need for differentiation until they know the value of challenging all students to move into uncharted waters. Gifted students often do not come close to their learning potential, especially when they are "given" high grades for work they know took little to no effort. Although most teachers believe that all students should have their self-esteem needs met as part of their learning experience, few realize that self-esteem actually is enhanced when success is attained through tasks an individual considers challenging (Rimm, 1986). Development of high self-esteem requires that students be allowed to challenge themselves in an environment in which their mistakes and struggles, as well as their successes, will be allowed and appreciated.

When students receive high grades and other acknowledgements for assignments or projects they know required little or no effort, their self-confidence may be undermined. These students may learn to always find the easiest way out or creatively postpone their exposure to challenges. Others students fear that if they try something challenging and do not instantly master content with little or no effort, others might conclude that they are not really very smart after all.

To assume that gifted students are learning by virtue of the fact that they demonstrate minimum standards on state assessments is ludicrous. When appropriate compacting and differentiation opportunities are regularly available, gifted students can spend considerable class time working on differentiated activities while their classmates are preparing for these high-stakes assessments.

Compacting and differentiation efforts should revolve around the following guidelines. Many children who are twice exceptional have very uneven standardized test scores. This profile paints an accurate picture of the very definition of this condition—strong highs and significant lows. Often, the learning disability depresses the gifted ability so the child scores in the average range.

All learning activities, including thematic, interdisciplinary units, should have preassessment opportunities available for students who volunteer to demonstrate prior knowledge and mastery of concepts, ideas, and skills. Whatever method has been planned for assessing student progress during or at the end of a particular unit of study is the same method that can be used for the preassessment.

Whether the preassessment takes the form of a written test, measuring student response as the class brainstorms all they know about an upcoming topic, or performance on a designated task, any student who chooses to participate in the designated task should be encouraged to do so. When the preassessment tasks are available to all who think they could demonstrate the required degree of mastery, there should be little resentment from students who are unable to do so, particularly if the "regular" activities are interesting and challenging.

Students who qualify for differentiation after the preassessment spend much of their class time working on extension activities, some designed by the teacher and some reflecting student choice. These students are required to pay attention to direct instruction only when the teacher is presenting material the students have not mastered.

In subjects where pretesting is not feasible because the content is new for all students, teachers compact the amount of time students have to spend learning the designated content. Students who can and want to are allowed to work with study guides to learn the designated content at their own pace without actually being required to do the actual activities other students are doing. Their class time is spent instead on becoming resident experts on a topic related to the unit content. When they share what they have learned with the class, the unit content is enriched for everyone. During the duration of the unit, students take the same assessments at the same time as others in the class, which helps the teacher document that they are learning the required material. When students can do this, they are allowed to continue work on their projects. If the students indicated through the assessments that they are not keeping up with the required content, they must rejoin their classmates for the duration of the unit and do the required activities from that point on.

When students need acceleration of content in addition to or in place of extensions, such as in subjects that are very sequential like reading or math, acceleration opportunities should be made available, even if the student is working below grade level in other subjects. Students might be allowed to work with a group of students from a higher grade for the subject areas in which they are significantly advanced. In rare cases, where a youngster's entire learning level is significantly advanced from that of same-age peers, radical acceleration or double promotion is another option.

Don't worry about the fairness issue. If you are concerned that other students will resent the options available for your gifted students or students with learning challenges, simply allow any students who are interested to participate for a short period of time. When assessments are required at regular intervals, it is easy to identify students who should not continue with the compacting and who need to return to direct instruction. It is also a good idea to allow all class members to choose extension activities from time to time, even though they would spend less time on these activities than time spent by the "resident expert."

Summary

Teaching children who are twice exceptional is very challenging. The most serious challenge is that the giftedness will go unnoticed and unaccommodated in favor of attending to learning deficits. Any efforts teachers can direct toward understanding and teaching the whole child will go a long way toward creating optimum learning conditions for these very interesting and challenging youngsters. Happily, there are many more resources available now than at any time in the past to aid teachers in their quest for making educational plans that will challenge and enrich students' school experiences.

ABOUT THE AUTHOR

Susan Winebrenner, MS, is the author of two books: *Teaching Gifted Kids in the Regular Classroom* and *Teaching Kids with Learning Difficulties in the Regular Classroom.* She has consulted with school districts in more than 40 states and in several foreign countries, helping teachers learn how to meet the needs of twice-exceptional students in heterogeneous classes. Address: Susan Winebrenner, PO Box 667, San Marcos, CA 92069.

REFERENCES

Carbo, M., Dunn, R., & Dunn, K. (1986). *Teaching students to read through their individual learning styles.* Englewood Cliffs, NJ: Prentice Hall.

Dennison, P. (1989). *Brain gym.* Ventura, CA: Edu-Kinesthetic. (Web site: www.braingym.org)

Landfried, S. E. (1989, November). "Enabling" undermines responsibility in students. *Educational Leadership, 47*(3), 79-83.

Larson, G. (2000). *The far side.* Seattle: Farworks.

Renzulli, J. (1977). *The enrichment triad model.* Mansfield Center, CT: Creative Learning Press.

Rimm, S. (1986). From a class at the University of Wisconsin.

Robinson, F. (1970). *Effective study* (4th ed.). New York: Harper & Row.

Webb, J., & Latimer, D. (1993). *ADHD and children who are gifted.* Reston, VA: Clearinghouse on Disabilities and Gifted Education.

Winebrenner, S. (1996). *Teaching kids with learning difficulties in the regular classroom.* Minneapolis: Free Spirit.

Winebrenner, S. (2000). *Teaching gifted kids in the regular classroom* (2nd ed.). Minneapolis: Free Spirit.

Winebrenner, S. (2002). Strategies for teaching twice exceptional students. *Understanding Our Gifted, 14*(2), 3-6.

RESOURCES

Freed, J. (1998). *Right brained children in a left brained world: Unlocking the potential of your ADD child.* New York: Simon & Schuster.

Hoagies Gifted Education: An excellent resource for information about gifted education and twice-exceptional issues. Web site: www. hoagiesgifted.com

Kay, K. (Ed.). (2000). *Uniquely gifted: Identifying and meeting the needs of the twice-exceptional student.* Gilsum, NH: Avocus Publishing.

LaVoie, R. *How Difficult Can This Be?* and *Last One Picked—First One Picked On.* PBS Video (800/344-3337).

LD Online: An excellent resource for information about all types of learning disabilities. Web site: www.ldonline.com

Levine, M. (1990). *Keeping a head in school: A student's book about learning abilities and learning disorders.* Toronto: Educator's Publishing Service.

Recording for the Blind and Dyslexic. (800/221-4792); Web site: www.rfbd.org

Willard-Holt, C. (1999). *Dual exceptionalities.* Reston, VA: Clearinghouse on Disabilities and Gifted Education.

UNIT 11
Transition

Unit Selections

33. **Moving From Elementary to Middle School: Supporting a Smooth Transition for Students With Severe Disabilities**, Erik W. Carter, et al.
34. **The Transition from Middle School to High School**, Theresa M. Letrello and Dorothy D. Miles
35. **Navigating the College Transition Maze: A Guide for Students with Learning Disabilities**, Joseph W. Madaus

Key Points to Consider

- Is there a timeline for assisting students with disabilities to make the transition from elementary to middle school? What does it entail?

- What services are needed to make the transition smoother from middle school to high school for students with disabilities?

- What does U.S. law require of college, and students with disabilities who pursue college degrees?

Student Website

www.mhcls.com/online

Internet References

Further information regarding these websites may be found in this book's preface or online.

National Center on Secondary Education and Transition
http://www.ncset.org

Transitional services help young children with disabilities who have been served by Individualized Family Service Programs (IFSPs) before school, make a smooth passage into the public school system. Transitional programs help modulate the next stages when students with special needs transfer from elementary to middle school, from middle school to high school, from special classes into inclusionary classes, or from one school district to another. The special services link the educational changes which take place.

Special educational services are also required by law for students from the completion of their public school education through age 21 if they have a diagnosed condition of disability. The U.S. Individuals with Disabilities Education Act (IDEA), when it was reauthorized in 1997, made terminal transitional services mandatory. Services are to help them transfer from their relatively protected life as students into the more aggressive world of work, driven by forces such as money and power.

The terminal services that the educational system needs to give to students with disabilities to help them prepare for the world of work start with an assessment of their interests, abilities, and aptitudes for different types of work. Career counseling about what they need to do to prepare for such employment, and its feasibility, comes next. Counselors must remember to allow students to dream, to think big, and to have optimistic visions of themselves. They also need to inculcate the idea that persistence pays: It takes a lot of little steps to achieve a goal.

The implementation of transitional services has been slow. The U.S. government defined transitional services as outcome-oriented, coordinated activities designed to move students with disabilities from school to activities such as college, vocational training, integrated employment, supported employment, adult education, adult services, independent living, and community participation. Choices are not either/or but rather multiple: to help students with disabilities move from school to successful adulthood. While some students may only be able to achieve partial independence and supported employment, others may achieve professional degrees and complete self-sufficiency.

Every student with a disability should have an Individualized Transition Plan (ITP) added to his or her Individualized Education Plan (IEP) by age 16, the upper limit for beginning transition planning. Transitional services are more difficult to design than educational plans because of the nearly unlimited possibilities for the rest of one's life compared to the defined academic subjects it is possible to learn while in school.

The first step is to determine an appropriate Individualized Transition Plan (ITP) for each unique student. Many teachers, special educators, vocational counselors, and employment mentors (job coaches) are not sure what kind of vocational preparation should be given in the public schools or when. Should children with disabilities start planning for their futures in elementary school, in middle school, in high school, throughout their education, or just before they finish school? Should there be a trade-off between academic education and vocational education for these students? Should each student's vocational preparation be planned to meet the kind of needs and abilities of the individual, with no general rules about the wheres and whens

of transitional services? Should students with disabilities be encouraged to seek out post-secondary education? The choices are legion. The need to rule out some possibilities and select others is frightening. Nobody on a team wants to make a mistake. Often the preferences of the student are quite different from the goals of parents, teachers, counselors, or significant others. Compromises are necessary but may not please everyone, or anyone.

The transition to the world of work may take the form of supported employment (mobile work crew, clustered or enclave placement, on-site training and supervision by a job coach, group providing a specific service product) or sheltered employment (in a workshop). Many students with disabilities can make a transition from school to competitive employment. If they will eventually work side-by-side with nondisabled coworkers, they may need transitional services such as assertiveness training, conflict resolution, negotiating skills, and personal empowerment counseling.

Just a few years ago, adults with disabilities were expected to live in institutions or with parents, siblings, or extended family members. This is no longer considered appropriate. Each individual with a disability should be encouraged to be as autonomous as possible in adulthood. Self-sufficiency is enhanced by providing education in life skills such as meal preparation and cleanup, home deliveries (for example, mail) and delivery pickups (for example, trash), using money and paying bills, making household repairs, and following home safety precautions.

The transition from a noncommunity participant to a fully participating member of society requires ITP modifications quite different from IEP academic goals. Students with exceptional conditions may need more than the usual amount of assistance in learning to drive a car or to use public transportation. They need to know how to read maps and schedules. They must be able to assert their right to vote in secret (for instance, ballot in braille or computerized for their software) and to marry, divorce, reproduce, sue, defend themselves, or even run for public office. They should know social conventions (greetings, conversation skills, manners), grooming fashions, and clothing styles. They deserve to have the same access to health settings, religious locales, social activities, and information services (telephone, television, computer networks) as do persons without disabilities.

The first article in this unit gives insights into the transition from smaller, more personalized elementary schools into larger, less individualized middle schools. This is a difficult transition for all students, but especially for students with disabilities or special abilities and unique needs. The authors make suggestions for easing this transition.

In the second article, Theresa Letrello and Dorothy Miles address the problems which occur when students with disabilities change school programs and schools, while also undergoing the vast physical transitions of puberty. The article gives suggestions for making this period of time less traumatic.

The last article in this transition unit deals with "Navigating the College Transition Maze." It gives important information about the civil rights bills in the United States (Americans With Disabilities Act and Section 504 of the Rehabilitation Act). It also discusses how IDEA (Individuals With Disabilities Education Act) and No Child Left Behind (NCLB) impact on post-secondary education for students with disabilities.

Moving From Elementary to Middle School:

Supporting a Smooth Transition for Students With Severe Disabilities

Erik W. Carter • Nitasha M. Clark • Lisa S. Cushing • Craig H. Kennedy

Excitement, apprehension, curiosity, and concern—the transition to middle school is often accompanied by a mix of such emotions. For some students, middle school represents a new milestone—an indicator that they are approaching young adulthood. Simultaneously, it can be a time that evokes anxiety, uneasiness, and worry (Akos, 2002; Mullins & Irvin, 2000). Parents wonder what middle school will be like for their children:

- How will they adjust to social pressures?
- Will they be able to keep up academically?
- Will they make friends?
- Will they be excited about going to school each day?

For students with severe disabilities, adjusting to a new school environment can be particularly stressful and even more challenging. In this article, we draw from the research literature to illustrate how educators can support students with severe disabilities and their families as they make the transition from elementary to middle school.

Changes in Middle School

The middle school years are accompanied by a number of changes for students and their families (Chung, Elias, & Schneider, 1998; Schumacher, 1998). What makes middle school so different from elementary school? What changes might students and their families expect?

> The transition to middle school often is accompanied by a mix of emotions: excitement, apprehension, curiosity, and concern.

Although variations exist across schools and districts, the transition from elementary to middle school typically involves moving from a smaller, tight-knit school community to one that is substantially larger and sometimes less personal (Irvin, 1997). In many elementary schools, students spend the majority of their school day with just one or two educators and a familiar cohort of peers. Upon entering middle school, however, students experience rotating classes, during which they may encounter different classmates and teachers each class period. Moreover, teachers' expectations and rules sometimes fluctuate from one class period to the next, requiring students to adjust their behavior to changing expectations.

The instructional context changes in middle school as well (Clements & Seidman, 2002; Midgley, Middleton, Gheen, & Kumar, 2002). Classes become more demanding, requiring coverage of more course content, a heavier emphasis on grades, and, of course, more homework. Educators expect students to assume increased responsibility for their own academic and behavioral performance while providing less individualized attention than students received during the elementary years. At the same time, the gap between the academic performance of students with severe disabilities and their classmates without disabilities widens, increasing the challenges associated with ensuring that all students are accessing the general curriculum.

As adolescence approaches, students also experience rapid social, emotional, cognitive, and physical growth. These developmental changes make the middle school years an especially awkward and complicated time for students. For exam-ple, relationships with peers take on increasing importance during adolescence, and students experience growing concerns about making friends, fitting in, and avoiding teasing (Pelligrini & Long, 2002). For students with severe disabilities, who characteristically exhibit social skills deficits compared with their peers (Downing, 1999), any sense of belonging enjoyed during elementary school may give way to feelings of isolation. Moreover, as general education students become more preoccupied with fitting in among peer groups, they may be less inclined to maintain or develop friendships with students with disabilities (e.g., Kishi & Meyer, 1994)

Importance of Addressing the Middle School Transition

Although the transition to middle school can pose a challenge for any student (Chung et al., 1998), children with disabilities are at particular risk for difficulties (Weldy, 1995). Elementary and middle school educators must find effective and meaningful ways of supporting these students' transitions to ensure that all students are confident, knowledgeable, and well prepared as they begin their new school experience. Moreover, schools should develop thoughtful plans for supporting both students with severe disabilities and their families (National Middle School Association and National Association of Elementary School Principals, 2002). Unfortunately, the transition to middle school for students with disabilities often is not addressed deliberately and comprehensively (Repetto & Correa, 1996).

Strategies for Supporting Students and Their Families

What practical steps can educators take to ensure a smooth transition from elementary to middle school? In the remainder of this article, we offer nine strategies that educators and parents can implement to prepare students with severe disabilities for middle school and support a successful adjustment. These ideas should be tailored to meet the specific needs of your students and the local realities of your school (see box, "Anna: Case Study").

1. Start Planning Early

Preparation for middle school should be addressed long before the arrival of the first day of classes (Akos & Martin, 2003). Together with parents and other team members, educators should reflect on the child's elementary school experiences. Which supports (e.g., assistive technology, adaptive equipment) have been successful during the elementary school years, and which have not? Which instructional strategies (e.g., cooperative learning, peer supports, academic modifications) have been particularly effective, and which should be adapted? What has the team learned about the student (e.g., learning style, interests, preferences, dislikes) that should be passed on or incorporated into the child's middle school educational plan? At the same time, planning teams should

keep an eye on the future. Speak with administrators, counselors, educators, and parents of middle school students to identify those skills and supports that the child will need to be successful in middle school. During planning meetings, prioritize and incorporate these instructional needs into the student's individualized education program (IEP) as early as the fourth or fifth grade so that the child has frequent opportunities to work on these goals early on. Students with severe disabilities will benefit from additional time to learn the skills that will help them be successful in middle school.

2. Collaborate Across Schools

Elementary and middle school staff should view preparing students for the transition to middle school as a shared responsibility. Educators, administrators, and counselors from adjoining elementary and middle schools must create opportunities to learn about one another's curricular requirements, program offerings, and expectations for students. Schools should consider establishing a joint transition planning team as a starting point for collaboration (see box, "Case Study"). When elementary and middle school staff come to consensus on each other's roles and responsibilities in the middle school transition, they can design educational programs that ensure consistency in focus and preparation across grade levels. Such collaboration increases the likelihood that elementary school special educators are equipped to convey accurate and useful information to parents about their child's upcoming transition.

> Although the transition to middle school can pose a challenge for any student, children with disabilities are at particular risk.

3. Prepare Students Early

Students with severe disabilities may experience considerable anxiety about what the first days and weeks at a new school might hold. The changes associated with middle school may feel overwhelming, particularly among students with disabilities (e.g., autism), for whom predictable routines are

important. They may be beset with a bewildering array of questions and concerns:

- Who will be my teachers?
- Will I get lost?
- How do I open my locker?
- Where do I go for lunch?
- Are the rules the same as at my old school?
- Will I fit in?

Fortunately, many of these concerns can be readily addressed with advance planning. The more familiar students are with their new school environment, the more excited about, and comfortable with, the change they are likely to be.

A variety of strategies may serve to ease students' (and their families') concerns about middle school life (National Middle School Association & National Association of Elementary School Principals, 2002):

1. First, schools should offer orientation activities and open houses designed to provide information about, and demonstrations of, the many curricular and extracurricular activities that take place in middle schools. For example, schools can invite transitioning fifth graders and their families to join middle schoolers at a joint spaghetti dinner, home basketball game, school breakfast, or other school activity. These events can be followed by a question-and-answer session in which information can be shared about the activities that middle school life comprises.

2. Second, schools can send "middle school ambassadors" in the form of administrators and educators to speak with elementary school students attending feeder schools. Including middle school students in these visits may be especially beneficial, in that experienced students can offer firsthand confirmation of the excitement of middle school life.

3. Third, multiple opportunities can be provided for students to visit their future school. Offer incoming students with disabilities opportunities to shadow an older middle school student for a day or several days. This experience allows students to visit the school, follow a daily schedule, visit classrooms, meet future educators and staff, and walk through the cafeteria line.

Anna: Case Study

Predictable routines are incredibly important for Anna, a fifth grader with autism and intellectual disabilities. When encountering new or unfamiliar events, Anna becomes agitated and, often, her anxiety manifests itself in severe behavioral challenges. Last year Anna required many months to settle into a routine after suddenly moving to her current school from another city. With her move to Riverdale Middle School approaching at the end of this school year, her parents and teachers are extremely concerned. What can they do to make this upcoming transition a successful one for Anna? How can they ensure that Anna feels at home at her new school and develops friendships?

Case Study

Ms. Randall, a special education teacher at Riverdale Middle School, received a worried call from Mr. Tarver, Anna's elementary school teacher, to discuss concerns he had about Anna's upcoming transition. Ms. Randall had observed that many students with severe disabilities (and students without disabilities) had a difficult time adjusting to middle school life. In fact, she often found herself frustrated by the amount of time that had to be devoted to addressing behavioral issues related to this adjustment—time that she believed would be better spent on instruction. Perhaps the two educators could take some joint steps to begin addressing this issue? Ms. Randall and Mr. Tarver decided to get together with several other teachers, guidance counselors, and administrators from both schools to develop a plan to help students like Anna transition smoothly to Riverdale.

The group began by surveying parents and students regarding their areas of greatest concern and soliciting recommendations for addressing those concerns. They asked teachers in their schools to brainstorm practical steps that they might take to be responsive to students' transition needs. Finally, they read through literature describing effective transition practices for elementary and middle school students. After sorting through their findings, the group outlined a series of steps that school staff could take to support successful transitions for students (see Figure 1). The group decided to organize the steps into a timeline so that it was easier for teachers, parents, and other members of the students' planning team to follow. This template for planning could then be individualized for each student on the basis of her or his needs and the recommendations of the IEP team.

Anna's IEP team, which included her parents and educators from both her current and future school, met to identify potential challenges that Anna might face as she moves to a new school, and to discuss the educational and behavioral strategies that had worked well for Anna in the past. Using the timeline as a guide, the team crafted an individualized transition plan for Anna. Her teachers began focusing extra attention on teaching Anna skills that would benefit her in middle school, such as utilizing a picture calendar, keeping a planner, and using self-management strategies. Anna visited Riverdale several times during her fifth-grade year, meeting her future teachers and familiarizing herself with the school facilities and routines. Because Anna had developed several close friendships at her elementary school, the team designed a class schedule that would include some of those familiar students in her classes. Teachers also identified a small group of older peers who volunteered to provide social support to Anna once she arrived at Riverdale by joining her at lunch and accompanying her to photography club and service-learning activities. Anna's parents, along with other family members of students with severe disabilities, met with the middle school teachers to share additional information about Anna and to find out more about Riverdale and how they might assist in preparing her for a new school.

Anna benefited greatly from the transition plan developed and implemented by her teachers and parents. The first few weeks of school at Riverdale were still tough for Anna, but by anticipating and preparing for her needs in advance, many of the difficulties she might have experienced were circumvented or minimized. Anna's team, now comprised of just middle school staff, continued to meet formally and informally to make sure that Anna was successful throughout her time at Riverdale.

Families should also be encouraged to be involved in preparing their children for the transition to middle school:

1. Encourage family members to talk with their children about what they can expect during the first days and weeks of school.

2. Provide parents with pictures of the middle school and its educators and staff so that parents can use to familiarize their children with the people and places the student will encounter.

3. Remind parents to begin establishing middle school routines prior to the first day of school. For example, middle school may start at an earlier hour and additional time for completing homework may need to be set aside in the afternoons. Helping students with severe disabilities develop these habits early may circumvent obstacles later and add to the repertoire of skills that students will need in middle and later in high school.

4. Encourage and Support Family Involvement

Research findings indicate that family involvement often decreases as students progress through the school years—that is, unless schools take deliberate steps to encourage and support their involvement (Barber & Patin, 1997). Yet, the link between parent involvement and student achievement is strong (Kettler & Valentine, 2000). Despite the continued importance of ongoing communication with families during the pivotal middle school years, maintaining communication becomes increasingly difficult. Instead of having one educator to communicate with during elementary school, families may now have six or more, each of whom has more than 100 students and families that they are expected to communicate with. Therefore, efforts to maintain communication must be much more deliberate than before.

> Educators can take nine practical steps to ensure a smooth transition from elementary to middle school.

Connections with parents should be established and maintained by educators as early as possible (Shoffner & Williamson, 2000). In part, this communication involves making certain that parents have available all the information that they need (see Figure 2, "Recommended Resources for Educators and Parents"). Most parents want to know about middle school programs, procedures, and expectations. Establish a mutually acceptable vehicle for communicating regularly with family members, such as through communication books, school visits, notes to family members, telephone calls, and e-mail messages. Moreover, make sure that the family is assigned at least one educator who knows their child

Figure 1. Transition Timeline for Students With Severe Disabilities

During the final elementary school years:

- Begin incorporating goals into students' IEPs that address skills and supports needed during middle school.
- Involve future middle school educators in elementary students' IEP meetings.
- Have students' current educators begin communicating with students' future educators.
- Begin teaching basic self-management strategies to students and assist students in applying those strategies in various school settings.
- Arrange for middle school students to begin writing letters/e-mail to future incoming students.
- Have middle school administrators, educators, and students visit feeder schools to build enthusiasm and confidence among elementary students with disabilities.
- Survey the concerns of elementary students and their families in order to focus information directly to those concerns.
- Develop a written plan for transitioning students with severe disabilities.
- Begin mailing copies of middle school parent newsletters to parents of elementary students.
- Develop and distribute a parent handbook that provides a checklist of transition activities and middle school contacts.

During the months prior to entering middle school:

- Provide opportunities for students to visit and become acquainted with the middle school (e.g., walk through a typical school day, practice important routines, introduce students to educators).
- Encourage families to begin establishing middle school routines.
- Role play scenarios that are expected to be most challenging for the student.
- Identify an educator, counselor, or administrator who can serve as primary point of contact for the family.
- Deliver any additional training needed for educators who will be working with the student.
- Offer middle school orientation activities to students and parents.
- Provide families with information about course offerings, rules and regulations, and the school mission/philosophy.

During the first few weeks of middle school:

- Assign students to classes with at least one student with whom they are familiar from elementary school.
- Ensure that appropriate modifications and adaptations are implemented meaningfully.
- Arrange peer support systems for students in general education classrooms.
- Identify opportunities for students to become actively involved in everyday school activities.
- Continue to familiarize students with middle school routines.

Throughout middle school:

- Stay attuned to students' social, academic, and behavioral adjustment on a regular basis.
- Maintain regular contact with family members.
- Arrange for support for students to participate in school clubs and organizations.
- Provide forums for family members to meet to share strategies, discuss issues, and provide answers to common questions.
- Survey students and parents about their recent transition experiences and, based on their responses, adjust future transition planning for incoming students.

well and who is willing to maintain an open line of communication. In addition to providing information, educators should identify strategies for encouraging active involvement—not only prior to beginning middle school but also throughout the middle school years. Invite parents to visit the middle school, meet with prospective educators, and ask questions. Informational meetings can be conducted with small groups of parents rather than individually, to offer op-

portunities to ask shared questions. Most important, demonstrate clearly to families that their involvement really does make a difference in their children's success in school.

5. Encourage Ongoing Communication

Prior to, and throughout the transition to middle school, educators and family members should strive to maintain open and ongoing communication with stu-

dents with severe disabilities about their school experiences. Indeed, parents and educators should talk often with students to identify potential problems early on and to circumvent difficulties before they become too overwhelming. The fact that a student is having a difficult time adjusting to middle school life is often not readily apparent. Children are often reluctant to talk about such issues as bullying, loneliness, peer pressure, or other struggles, so it is important to initiate conversations

Figure 2. Recommended Resources for Educators and Family Members

Many middle schools provide basic orientation information to families about programs, expectations, and opportunities specific to their school. In addition to this school-specific information, the following readily available resources addressing the transition to middle school may be useful to share with parents.

Adreon, D., & Stella, J. (2001). Transition to middle and high school: Increasing the success of students with Asperger Syndrome. *Intervention in School and Clinic, 36*, 266-271.

Alper, S., Schloss, P. J., & Schloss, C. N, (1995). Families of children with disabilities in elementary and middle school: Advocacy models and strategies. *Exceptional Children, 62*, 261-270.

Bernstein, E. (2002). *Middle school and the age of adjustment: A guide for parents.* Westport, CT: Bergin & Garvey.

Demchak, M. A., & Greenfield, R. G. (2002). *Transition portfolios for students with disabilities: How to help students, teachers, and families handle new settings.* Thousand Oaks, CA: Corwin.

Giannetti, C. C. & Sagarese, M. (1997). The roller-coaster years: *Raising your child through the maddening yet magical middle school years.* New York: Broadway Books.

Kaiser, J. S. (1997). Advocate for your adolescent: Encouraging special needs parents to get involved. *Schools in the Middle, 7*(1), 33-34, 52.

Kennedy, C. H., & Fisher, D. (2001). *Inclusive middle schools.* Baltimore: Paul H. Brookes.

Myles, B. S., & Adreon, D. (2001). *Asperger syndrome and adolescence: Practical solutions for school success.* Shawnee Mission, KS: Autism Asperger.

Simonelli, S. (2002). *Creating successful transitions for your child: Helpful tips for parents.* Manoa, HI: Center for Disability Studies, University of Hawaii at Manoa. Available at http://www.sig.hawaii.edu/final_products/final.htm.

with children rather than wait for them to approach you. Moreover, many students with severe disabilities are challenged by limited communication skills. Therefore, adults should remain alert for external indicators that a child is struggling with the adjustment to middle school. The development of physical problems, behavioral challenges, poor academic performance, indices of unhappiness, or limited social relationships can be signs that a child is struggling to adjust to a new school.

Parents need to know that they are not alone in dealing with issues associated with their children's transition to middle school. Educators can go a long way toward easing parents' concerns by providing opportunities for parents to network and communicate with other parents of students undertaking the same transition. Schools might offer parent information meetings facilitated by a school counselor or administrator on topics ranging from the needs of middle school students to strategies for supporting children's general education participation. These meetings can provide a forum for parents to discuss important issues and establish connections and support systems with other parents. Including parents of both elementary and middle school students in these meetings may be especially beneficial.

6. Address Organizational Issues

For many children entering middle school, the organizational and logistical issues associated with a new school present the most anxiety (Akos, 2002). Such tasks as

learning to open a locker, finding classrooms, locating the restroom, and keeping track of assignments and books can be overwhelming for students. By talking about these events ahead of time, designing meaningful accommodations, and role-playing their use, educators may help ease these areas of worry for students. A number of adaptations can assist students with severe disabilities in navigating these organizational challenges. Examples of helpful adaptations might include providing an extra set of textbooks to be kept at home; teaching the student to use assignment calendars, electronic organizers (e.g., PDAs), visual class schedules, or color-coded notebooks; providing the student with an adapted locker; and partnering the student with a peer support who can provide any needed assistance.

7. Develop Peer Support Programs

As students approach and progress through middle school, the importance of peer relationships grows and the pressure to "fit in" intensifies (Hardy, Bukowski, & Sippola, 2002). Students become increasingly concerned about whether and how they will make friends and, often, students with severe disabilities remain socially isolated from their peers (Carter & Hughes, 2004). Therefore, educators should intentionally create opportunities for students with severe disabilities to interact with their general education peers.

Peer support programs can address these social needs by providing much needed social and academic support to students with

disabilities throughout their time in middle school (Kennedy, 2004). Within the general education classroom, peer supports sit next to their classmates with disabilities and assist in adapting materials, encouraging social interaction with classmates, and facilitating participation in class activities. Peer support programs should also be designed to extend beyond the classroom setting to include unstructured times, such as during lunch, in the hallways, before and after school, and on the bus, when students with disabilities often are most isolated. For example, some middle schools have instituted programs whereby older students serve as mentors to younger, new students. Indeed, peer support arrangements are mutually beneficial for all students involved, as peer supports typically take pride in their support role and new responsibilities and students with disabilities acquire beneficial support and develop friendships (e.g., Copeland et al., 2004; Kamps et al., 1998).

8. Support School Involvement

Many students with disabilities miss out on the numerous opportunities to become involved in an exciting array of curricular and extracurricular activities that become available in the middle school years (Simeonsson, Carlson, Huntington, McMillen, & Brent, 2001). School clubs, programs, organizations, and athletic teams provide valuable opportunities for students to explore their interests, develop important skills, establish new friendships, and participate in experiences that will contribute to a smooth transition to life after high school. Moreover, such involvement promotes a sense of belonging and connection with the wider school community (Mahoney & Cairns, 1997). Therefore, these opportunities, and the supports necessary to make such opportunities a reality, should be incorporated into students' IEPs. Peer support programs are an effective vehicle for supporting the participation of students with severe disabilities in school activities.

9. Foster Independence

Middle school environments require students to demonstrate a greater degree of independence than do elementary school environments (Midgley et al, 2002). Although middle school educators generally have higher expectations regarding students' academic and social performance, students with disabilities may remain unequipped for these new expectations. Many students with severe disabilities remain highly dependent on adults for assistance. Educators should teach students with disabilities to use self-management strategies to enable them to take increased responsibility for managing their own academic and social behavior (Agran, King-Sears, Wehmeyer, & Copeland, 2003). For example, students can be taught to manage their time using a picture calendar, evaluate their school work using a rubric, monitor their progress on academic goals using checklists, or initiate interactions with others using a communication book. Moreover, students should also be taught how to advocate for accommodations, support, inclusion, and for other educational rights. Such skills will be indispensable as students encounter future transitions. Promoting students' independence does not mean others should remain uninvolved. Rather, educators, peers, and family members should be active in designing educational environments that provide students with severe disabilities with supported opportunities to assume increased responsibility for their own behavior.

Final Thoughts

The strategies described in this article are not only relevant to students with severe disabilities but also constitute effective approaches for addressing the needs of all students making the transition to middle school. Administrators, general and special educators, and families should partner to ensure that the transition to middle school is a smooth and successful endeavor for every student.

How will you know whether students' transitions are effective? The school must monitor the degree to which participants' efforts are contributing to a successful transition for students and their families (Mullins & Irvin. 2000). Transition planning is never a one-time endeavor—educators must make certain to maintain an ongoing conversation with students and their family members about their expectations, concerns, and questions. Although the strategies we describe here clearly are not exhaustive, they provide a promising framework for supporting a smooth transition to middle school for students with disabilities.

References

Agran, M., King-Sears, M., Wehmeyer, M. L., & Copeland, S. R. (2003). *Self-directed learning strategies*. Baltimore: Paul H. Brookes.

Akos, P. (2002). Student perceptions of the transition from elementary to middle school. *Professional School Counseling, 5*, 339-345.

Akos, P., & Martin, M. (2003). Transition groups for preparing students for middle school. *Journal for Specialists in Group Work, 28*, 139-154.

Barber, R. J., & Patin, D. (1997). Parent involvement: A two-way street. *Schools in the Middle, 6*(4). 31-33.

Carter, E. W, & Hughes, C. (2004). Social interaction interventions in secondary school settings: Effective practices. Manuscript in preparation.

Chung, H., Elias, M., & Schneider, K. (1998). Patterns of individual adjustment changes during middle school transition. *Journal of School Psychology, 36*, 83-101.

Clements, P., & Seidman, E. (2002). The ecology of middle grades schools and possible selves: Theory, research, and action. In T. M. Brinthaupt (Ed.), *Understanding early adolescent self and identity: Applications and interventions* (pp. 133-164). Albany: State University of New York Press.

Copeland, S. R., Hughes, C., Carter, E. W., Guth, C., Presley, J., Williams, C. R., & Fowler, S. E. (2004). Increasing access to general education: Perspectives of participants in a high school peer support program. *Remedial and Special Education, 26*, 342-352.

Downing, J. E. (1999). *Teaching communication skills to students with severe disabilities*. Baltimore: Paul H. Brookes.

Hardy, C. L., Bukowski, W. M., & Sippola, L. K. (2002). Stability and change in peer relationships during the transition to middle-level school. *Journal of Early Adolescence, 22*, 117-142.

Irvin, J. L. (1997). *What current research says to the middle level practitioner*. Columbus, OH: National Middle School Association.

Kamps, D. M., Kravits, T., Lopez, A. G., Kemmerer, K., Potucek, J., & Harrell. L. G. (1998). What do peers think? Social validity of peer-mediated programs. *Education and Treatment of Children, 21*, 107-134.

Kennedy, C. H. (2004). Social relationships. In C. H. Kennedy & E. M. Horn (Eds.), *Including students with severe disabilities* (pp. 100-119). Boston: Allyn & Bacon.

Kettler, R., & Valentine, J. (2000). *Parent involvement and student achievement at the middle school* (NMSA research summary #18). Westerville, OH: National Middle School Association.

Kishi, G. S., & Meyer, L. H. (1994). What children report and remember: A six-year follow-up of the effects of social contact between peers with and without severe disabilities. *Journal of the Association for Persons With Severe Handicaps, 19*, 277-289.

Mahoney, J. L., & Cairns, R. B. (1997). Do extracurricular activities protect against early school dropout? *Developmental Psychology, 33*, 241-253.

Midgley, C., Middleton, M. J., Gheen, M. H., & Kumar, R. (2002). Stage-environment fit revisited: A goal theory approach to examining school transitions. In C. Midgley (Ed.), *Goals, goal structures, and patterns of adaptive learning* (pp. 109–142). Mahwah, NJ: Lawrence Erlbaum.

Mullins, E. R., & Irvin, J. L. (2000). What research says: Transition into middle school. *Middle School Journal, 31*(3), 57-60.

National Middle School Association and National Association of Elementary School Principals, (2002). *Supporting students in their transition to middle school*. Westerville, OH: Author.

Pelligrini, A. D., & Long, J. D. (2002). A longitudinal study of bullying, dominance, and victimization during the transition from primary school through secondary school. *British Journal of Developmental Psychology, 20*, 259-280.

Repetto, J. B., & Correa, V. I. (1996). Expanding views on transition. *Exceptional Children, 62*, 551-563.

Schumacher, D. (1998). *The transition to middle school*. Champaign, IL: ERIC Clearinghouse on Elementary and Early Childhood Education.

Shoffner, M. R., & Williamson, R. D. (2000). Facilitating student transitions into middle school. *Middle School Journal, 31*(4), 47-52.

Simeonsson, R. J., Carlson, D., Huntington, G. S., McMillen, J. S., & Brent, J. L. (2001). Students with disabilities: A national survey of participation in school activities. *Disability and Rehabilitation, 23*, 49-63.

Weldy, G. R. (1995). Critical transitions. *Schools in the Middle, 4*(3), 4-7.

Erik W. Carter (CEC Chapter #832), Assistant Professor, Department of Special Education, University of Wisconsin-Madison.

Nitasha M. Clark (CEC TN Federation), Doctoral Student. Lisa S. Cushing, (CEC Chapter #98). Assistant Research Professor, and Craig H. Kennedy (CEC TN Federation), Professor, Special Education and Pediatrics, and Director, Vanderbilt Kennedy Center Behavior Analysis Clinic, Vanderbilt University, Nashville, Tennessee.

Address correspondence to Craig H. Kennedy, Special Education and Pediatrics, Box 328. Peabody College. Vanderbilt University, Nashville, TN 37203 (e-mail: craig.kennedy @vanderbilt.edu)

From *Teaching Exceptional Children*, Vol. 37, No. 3, January/February 2005, pp. 8-14. Copyright © 2005 by Council for Exceptional Children. Reprinted by permission.

The Transition from Middle School to High School

Students with and without Learning Disabilities Share Their Perceptions

By THERESA M. LETRELLO and DOROTHY D. MILES

The move to high school by eighth grade students can be a traumatic experience, especially for students with learning disabilities. Because this transition can have an impact on students' success in high school, we felt that it was an important subject to investigate. We explored how students perceived this transition period and whether there was a difference in the perceptions of students with learning disabilities and those without.

As students in eighth grade prepare to enter ninth grade, they are experiencing significant physical growth and change. Wiles and Bondi (2001) said that the middle school years for ten to fourteen-year-olds are characterized by emotional instability. Erratic and inconsistent behavior is present; anxiety and fear are also common and contrast with reassuring false security. Dealing with physical changes, striving for independence from family, and acquiring new methods of intellectual functioning are all emotional issues for emerging adolescents. "Students have many fears real and imagined. At no other time in development is a student likely to encounter such a diverse number of problems simultaneously" (Wiles and Bondi 2001, 35). Students experience a transition in their physical environment in the move from one school to another, as well as different academic requirements, larger school size, and new social interactions.

Although for some the transition from middle school to high school can be easy, many young adolescents experience a decline in grades and attendance (Barone, Aguirre-Deandreis, and Trickett 1991); they begin to view themselves more negatively and experience an increased need for friendships (Hertzog et al. 1996). The change can overwhelm the coping skills of some students, lower self-esteem, and decrease motivation to learn (Mac Iver 1990). For some students, the singular and unsettling act of changing from one school in eighth grade to a new school in high school may be a precipitating factor in dropping out (Roderick 1993).

Students with learning disabilities making the move to high school face even more challenges (Smith and Diller 1999). A crisis often develops when the student enters high school because the students' compensating efforts are no longer adequate (Smith and Diller 1999). Wagner (1993), in a report from the National Longitudinal Transition Study of Special Education Students (NLTS) (which studied a nationally representative sample of 8,000 students aged 15 to 23 in secondary special education classes), found that the school programs for students with disabilities in the ninth and tenth grades were strenuous. Because of the heavy load of academic requirements, students with disabilities were more likely to experience problems in these years.

With the heavy academic focus in high school, the predominance of regular education placements, and the lower level of support services provided, it is not surprising that ninth and tenth grade students were more likely to receive failing grades than were students in the upper grades. By failing classes, students with disabilities may fall behind their peers in progress toward graduation. Marder (1992) reported that students with learning disabilities had a dropout rate of 30 percent, one of the highest for students with disabilities.

Students in eighth grade usually begin to prepare for the move to the high school during their last semester. To do so, most students experience transition activities that acquaint them with the high school. Transition programs should address all aspects of the transition—academic and social—so that the students have the greatest opportunity to succeed (Hertzog and Morgan 1998). Typical transition activities consist of registration, high school principal talks, peer panels, high school visits, and pairing with upperclassmen. Students with learning disabilities experience these activities also, but often more is involved in their transition process. According to their Individual Education Programs (IEPs), learning-disabled students are usually followed more closely by parents and special educators. These special educators track the progress of learning disabled students and make sure they are placed in classes where they will receive needed assistance.

Interviews

The first researcher did individual interviews of twelve ninth grade students—six with learning disabilities and six without learning disabilities—about their transition to high school. All students attended the same Midwestern high school at the time of the interviews. The school, located in a suburban district, had a total of 1,200 students in grades 9-12. In the eighth grade, all students had attended the local middle school with a total population of 1,150 students in grades 6-8. All interviews took place at the high school in a private room. To assure confidentiality, all participating students were identified by codes and not names. After all interviews were completed, we divided the interview data into two groups for study: students with learning disabilities and students without learning disabilities. We then analyzed the data for emerging themes or concepts.

The major research question was, "What transition activities did the students find helpful, and were there differences between the experiences of those with learning disabilities and those without?" We used the following interview questions:

1. What were some of your fears about going to high school when you were in eighth grade?

2. As an eighth grader, what were some of your expectations of high school?

3. What major differences between middle school and high school have you observed?

4. What do you feel was the most difficult aspect of moving to high school?

5. What do you feel was the easiest aspect of moving to high school?

6. What activities have you been involved in at high school?

7. While in eighth grade, you were introduced to the high school with various activities, such as counselor and principal visits. What activities helped you get acquainted with the high school?

8. If you had a chance to talk to current eighth graders, what advice would you give them as they prepare for the move to ninth grade?

Results

When we analyzed the interviews, it was apparent that both groups gave extremely similar responses to the questions. Both groups expressed that as eighth graders they were fearful of high school, especially of the size of the school, of older students, of not having enough friends, and of not being able to find all their classes. Students in both groups expected that high school would be "hard," that they wouldn't see their friends, that they would have difficult classes and difficult and demanding teachers, and that high school students would be more mature than those in middle school.

Major differences that students in both groups described were that the high school was bigger, that they had more freedom in high school, that they participated in more extracurricular activities, and that high school students were more accepting of student differences. The students said that the most difficult aspects of moving to high school included getting accustomed to the block schedule, high expectations of the teachers, managing time, and lack of time for social activities because of the demands of homework. Students with learning disabilities indicated that they relied more heavily on help from peers and teachers to be successful in the ninth grade year than did students without learning disabilities.

The easiest aspect of moving to the high school, expressed by students in both groups, included making friends, getting involved in extracurricular activities, and having more fun and freedom. All of the students were involved in extracurricular activities such as sports, band, drama productions, and student council, but students with learning disabilities were involved in fewer such activities than students without. Activities that helped both groups get acquainted with the high school as eighth graders included talking to their academic counselors and friends. Many students in both groups felt that just talking to older friends and siblings helped them understand life in high school. Some students in both groups also said they learned about the high school by visiting the school on their own and attending athletic events. Students in both groups said they would advise future ninth graders to use good study habits, to get involved in extracurricular activities, complete homework, and be prepared to meet new and different people.

The interview data revealed two major recurring themes—social interaction and activity involvement. Students in both groups talked frequently about interaction with friends and other students. This demonstrates that social interaction, particularly with peers, was important for them in their transition to high school. Moreover, even though students with learning disabilities engaged in fewer activities, participation was important for students in both groups during the transition.

Recommendations

From this study, we have produced the following recommendations to enhance the transition from eighth grade to ninth grade:

1. Middle schools should have as many activities as possible to prepare students for the change to high school. These activities should include high school visits and explanation of activities as well as curricula.

2. Transition teams should be formed at the middle school and the high school to plan activities for the transition to ninth grade. These teams should work together with planned activities starting in eighth grade.

3. Students' needs and fears regarding the move to high school should be assessed and addressed in eighth grade.

4. Because social interaction proved to be an important facet of satisfaction with high school, high school students should be trained to facilitate groups at the middle school to discuss concerns with eighth graders and should also become peer mentors to the students when they move to the high school.

5. Students with learning disabilities should have continuous support from teachers and staff during the transition and after they have entered high school.

6. Students entering ninth grade should be encouraged to get involved in extracurricular activities.

Key words: learning disabled, transition activities, middle school, high school

References

Barone, C., A. J. Aguirre-Deandreis, and E. J. Trickett. 1991. Means - end problem solving—solving skills, life stress, and social support as mediators of adjustment in the normative transition to high school. *American Journal of Community Psychology* 19:207-25.

Hertzog, C. J., and P. L. Morgan. 1998. Breaking the barriers between middle school and high school: Developing a transition team for student success. *National Association of Secondary School Principals Bulletin* 82:94-98.

Hertzog, C., P. L. Morgan, P. A. Diamond, and M. J Walker. 1996. Making the transition from middle level to high school. *The High School Magazine* 3(1): 28-30.

Mac Iver, D. J 1990. Meeting the needs of young adolescents: Advisory groups, interdisciplinary teaching teams, and school transition programs. *Phi Delta Kappan* 71:458-64.

Marder, C. 1992. Education after secondary school. In Wagner, M., *next? Trends in post school outcomes of youth with disabilities. The second comprehensive report from the National Longitudinal Transition Study of Special Education Students.* Menlo Park, CA: SRI International

Milligan, P. 1995. The fast lane to high school: Transitions from middle school/ junior high school to high school. Salt Lake City, UT: *Systematic transition of Utah's disabled youth.* ERIC, ED 389105.

Roderick, M. 1993. *The path to dropping out. Evidence for intervention.* Westport, CT: Auburn House.

Smith, J. and H. Diller. 1999. *Unmotivated adolescents.* Dallas, TX: Apodixis Press.

Wagner, M. (Ed) 1993. *The secondary school programs of students with learning disabilities: A report from the National Longitudinal Transition Study of Special Education Students.* Menlo Park, CA: SRI International.

Wiles, J., and J. Bondi 2001.*The new American middle school: Educating preadolescents in an era of change* (3rd ed.). Upper Saddle River, NJ: Prentice-Hall, Inc.

Theresa M. Letrello is a language arts and history teacher at Parkway West Middle School, in Chesterfield, Missouri. Dorothy D. Miles is an associate professor of educational psychology, disabilities studies, and research and statistics at Saint Louis University, in Missouri.

Navigating the College Transition Maze: A Guide for Students With Learning Disabilities

Joseph W. Madaus

The transition from high school to college can be a confusing and overwhelming time for students with learning disabilities (LD), their families, and the secondary-level professionals who assist them. In addition to the challenges that all students face when transitioning to college, additional obstacles confront students with LD. Chief among them is the move from the familiar model of special education services at the high school level to very different services at the college level. Not only does the scope of these services change considerably from high school to college, but there can also be a great deal of institutional variation in the way that these services are provided. Additionally, at the college level, significant changes occur in the legal rights of students, and there is a sharp reversal of parental and student responsibility.

As the former director of a university LD program, I frequently worked with students and their families during this transition. The students included high school students who were searching for a college, students who were accepted into the university and were preparing to enroll, and students who bad matriculated and were trying to negotiate the first semester of college as a student with LD.

Questions and misconceptions about postsecondary disability services commonly arise during these interactions. At minimum, these misconceptions simply add to the confusion surrounding the college transition process and can be overcome with time and experience in the college setting. At worst, the misconceptions can create false expectations for families and students in transition, which may ultimately lead to a college experience that is less successful than it might otherwise be. This article presents sev-

eral of the most common questions and misconceptions related to transition and LD services and is intended to furnish useful information about the process to students with LD, their parents, and the professionals who assist them in the transition process.

"Are you the special education department? Can you tell me about your special education services?"

These questions go directly to the heart of the primary difference between high school and college services for students with LD. The Individuals with Disabilities Education Act (IDEA, Public Law 105-17, 1997) is the law that addresses the education of students with LD at the secondary level. It states that special education services are required for students who are not making satisfactory academic progress because of a disability. Students who meet this criterion are entitled to these services, which must be free and individually appropriate for the student and must be based on data from a comprehensive evaluation that is conducted and paid for by the school. The school must develop an individualized education program (IEP) for each student. This document must contain educational goals for the student, objectives for achieving these goals, and specific modifications that must be used to assist the student in reaching these goals. A team consisting of professionals and parents makes the significant decisions related to creating and implementing this document, and the school must ensure that the student is making satisfactory progress.

In stark contrast, no similar special education system exists at the postsecondary level. Rather, at the postsecond-

ary level, disability services are provided. These services are based on two civil rights mandates, Section 504 (P.L. 93-112) of the Rehabilitation Act of 1973 and the Americans with Disabilities Act of 1990 (ADA; P.L. 101-336). Both statutes prohibit discrimination on the basis of disability and require that postsecondary institutions ensure equal access for otherwise qualified students with disabilities. Equal access includes providing students with reasonable academic adjustments (also called accommodations) and auxiliary aids.

At a minimum, postsecondary institutions are required to offer disability services. Such services are sometimes called *generic* (Brinckerhoff, McGuire, & Shaw, 2002) and are made available to all students with disabilities. Section 504 requires that the institution designate an institutional contact person, or "a responsible employee" (104.7(a)), who ensures that qualified students with disabilities receive individually appropriate accommodations (e.g., extended test time, separate exam locations) and auxiliary aids (e.g., access to assistive technology). This person is not required to have training in special education or disabilities and may have other responsibilities on the campus. Institutions may not charge additional fees to students for providing such accommodations.

Institutions can go beyond this minimum level of services and offer a disability program, in these programs, a full-time disability program coordinator or director administers services that exceed the reasonable accommodations discussed previously. Although the exact nature of these programs differs from college to college, they may include varying levels of individualized contacts for students, such as work in learning skills and strategies, instruction in writing strategies, or individualized tutoring (Brinckerhoff et al., 2002). The institution may require that students pay a fee for these more comprehensive programs (although not for reasonable accommodations, as previously noted). Table 1 indicates the range of LD support services that may be available. The disability contact person at each school of interest can offer advice about the exact nature of services available at that school.

Institutions are not required to modify admissions standards, course content, or programs of study for a student because of his or her disability.

Regardless of the model used, institutions are not required to modify admissions standards, course content, or programs of study for a student because of his or her disability. Section 504 and the ADA are civil rights mandates designed to ensure access; they are not special education laws. Any special education services, as well as the modifications outlined in a student's IEP, end when the student graduates from high school. The student is responsible for self-identifying to the college and for providing appropriate documentation of his or her disability. If the student does not self-disclose, accommodations need not be provided, nor must they be provided retroactively to a student who did not self-identify and who then struggled. Grades earned in courses taken before the student's self-disclosure do not need to be deleted or modified (Madaus & Shaw, 2004). Additionally, a student is only eligible for protections and services if he or she maintains a grade point average (GPA) that the institution or a program within the institution has set and that applies to all students (Heyward, Lawton, & Associates, 1990).

"My daughter is on a Section 504 plan in high school. We were told that her plan would automatically transfer to your college since you are also covered under Section 504. Is this true?"

High school students with LD who do not require intensive special education services but who still need reasonable accommodations (such as extended test

time) may be placed on a Section 504 plan at the high school level. These plans outline the specific accommodations that must be provided to the student and the personnel responsible for ensuring that the accommodations are provided. Although colleges and universities are obligated by the mandates of Section 504, they are bound to Subpart E of the law, whereas Subpart D covers secondary schools. These subparts place significantly different requirements on secondary schools and postsecondary institutions. Thus, as with an IEP, the services outlined in a secondary-level Section 504 plan end at graduation from high school. Although colleges may use these plans in decision making, they are not obligated to follow the requirements of these plans. Madaus and Shaw (2004) presents a detailed examination of the differences between Subparts D and E and the implications for students in transition.

A newer, but increasingly common, problem at the postsecondary level relates to two groups of students in transition. One group consists of students who were not diagnosed with LD but who exhibited difficulty at the secondary level in a specific area, such as test taking. The second group consists of students who no longer meet the diagnostic criteria for a learning disability but who are provided with a monitoring plan. Instead of using special education services, secondary teams may create Section 504 plans for these students. Sympathetic teachers may give the student informal accommodations, such as extended time to complete a test or a quiz. Students may become reliant on these accommodations and may expect these services to continue at the college level. Without documentation that verifies the existence of a learning disability and a subsequent substantial limitation to learning, postsecondary institutions may deny the student's accommodation request. Thus, regardless of how well-intended such informal accommodations may be, secondary school personnel and parents should carefully consider the long-term impact of these accommodations and their ramifications for the student.

"Can you tell me about the admissions process for students with special needs?"

As noted previously, postsecondary institutions are not required to modify admission requirements for applicants with disabilities. For an applicant to be admitted, the institution must consider him or her "otherwise qualified" despite the existence of a disability. According to Section 504, a qualified person at the postsecondary level is one "who meets the academic and technical standards requisite to admission or participation in the recipient's education program or activity" (104.3 (k)(3)). In other words, the student must participate in the standard admissions process and must have academic credentials that are equivalent to those of his or her peers without disabilities. The institution may consider the impact of the disability when making the admission decision, but doing so is not required.

If a particular college does not allow for formal self-disclosure on the application or if it does not consider specific documentation during the admissions process, applicants might consider including information about the LD in their personal statement or in a supplemental personal statement. Students might describe how the LD affected a particular area of coursework, why no foreign language courses appear on the student's transcript, how the LD contributed to lower standardized test scores, or what methods or techniques were developed to compensate for the LD. Although this disclosure will not guarantee the student admission, it may give an admissions committee supplemental information that might help explain inconsistencies in the application (e.g., between grades and standardized test scores) and help the committee make decisions about students who are marginal for admission to a particular institution. Of course, it is critical that the student be comfortable with this self-disclosure and that the statement be carefully and thoughtfully prepared.

Focusing almost solely on the admissions requirements of an institution— such as required high school GPA, SAT, or ACT scores and number of years of foreign language study is natural. How-

Index

A

ABCs of misbehavior, 113
acceleration: gifted students and, 171–172; twice-exceptional students and, 182
accommodations: requests for, 196; for students with disabilities, 156–159
administrators. *See* principals
adolescence, social skills and, 53–57
advocacy, and the deaf, 121–122
American Sign Language (ASL), 119–120
Americans with Disabilities Act of 1990 (ADA), 122, 156–157; postsecondary LD students and, 195–199
angular gyrus, 175
antidepressants, 98, 100
anxiety disorders, 99–100
Asperger's syndrome, 77–79, 101
assessment, 14–16, 46; alternate, and service-learning activities, 84–85; alternative, for second-language students, 64–65. *See also* testing
ataxia-telangiectasia, 154
attention, teachers paying, 107–108
attention deficit disorder (ADD), 96–98; politics and, 160–163
attention deficit hyperactivity disorder (ADHD), 96–98
attention seeking, classroom management and, 114
audiology, deaf individuals and, 120–121
autism, 29, 77–79, 87–91, 101
Autism Treatment Network, 79
autistic spectrum disorders (ASD), 77–79, 101

B

barriers, removing, for disabled students, 156–159
behavior, unintentional, of inarticulate students, 90–91
behavior assessment, with a T-chart, 16
behavioral disorders. *See* emotional and behavioral disorders
behavioral intervention, for autism, 78–79

behavioral therapy, psychiatric disorders and, 96, 97–98, 99, 100
bipolar disorder, 98–99
blind students. *See* visually impaired students
Block, M. E., four standards of, 17–21
bonding, intervention programs and, 34–35
brain development, 77–79, 174–176
Brain Gym, twice-exceptional students and, 178
breaks, classroom management and, 114
burnout, teacher, 108–109

C

careers, for deaf individuals, 119
Cascade of Integration Options, for severely disabled students, 131–136
challenging standard, 17–18
checklist, for assessment, 16
chelation, for autism, 79
Chinese pictographic symbols, the brain and, 175
choice-making ability, 137–143
chromosomal abnormalities, 153–155
civil rights mandates, postsecondary LD students and, 195–199
classroom management, 106–108, 112–115
cochlear implants, 121
cognitive behavioral therapy, psychiatric disorders and, 99, 100
cognitive realm, 55
collaboration, 3–6; inclusion of severely disabled students and, 132–133
college, transition to, 195–199
communication development: classroom management and, 114–115; understanding inarticulate students and, 87–91
communication skills, of the severely disabled, 144–149
communities: SAM and, 10–11; service-learning activities and, 80–81
compacting, twice-exceptional students and, 181
competence-oriented teachers, 87–91
compulsions, 99

conduct disorders, 96. *See also* emotional and behavioral disorders
conflict resolution, 33–35, 53–57, 106–111, 112–115
constant time delay, 138, 139
cultural diversity, 61–68
curriculum: for the gifted, 171–172; reexamining, 46–47

D

deaf children, 119–122
deficit-oriented teachers, 87–91
delay cues, classroom management and, 113
depression, 98–99
developmental disabilities, 80–91
diagnosis, early, of autism, 77–79; of learning disabilities, 25–28
Diagnostic and Statistical Manual (DSM IV) (American Psychiatric Association), 95, 96, 97, 98, 99–100
differences, learning, 45–49
differentiation: paradox of, and integration, 7–13; twice-exceptional students and, 181–182
disabilities, severe: communications kills and, 144–149; making choices and, 137–143. *See also* individual disabilties
disability services, for postsecondary students, 195–199
discipline, classroom, 106–111, 112–115
discrepancy, determining a, 26
disruptive student behavior, 106–111
district leadership team, 11–12
district resource team, 12
drug therapy, 164–165; for autism, 78; for psychiatric disorders, 95–103
dyssynchrony, giftedness and, 171
dysthymia, 98

E

education, of the deaf, changes in, 120
effort conversion strategy, 18–21
18th chromosome, 153
elementary school, transition from, to middle school, 187–192

Because special education services and IEP mandates end at high school graduation, some requested services and accommodations might be available at the college level whereas others may not. These decisions are based on the intersection of the student's disability and the essential requirements of a course or a program of study, and they do not consider whether the student will be successful. For example, parents and students may request a tutor or a teacher to reteach or explain course material in a different way. Some high school students may have exam questions rephrased or modified. Although high schools might furnish these services, they are not likely to be considered reasonable at the postsecondary level under Section 504 or the ADA.

An additional area of confusion often arises in relation to course substitutions. Students who receive waivers of secondary graduation requirements in such areas as mathematics or foreign languages may expect that such waivers will automatically carry over to the postsecondary level. However, these waivers may not carry over; and in fact, if the student's program of study is such that mathematics or foreign language study is an essential requirement (e.g., mathematics for a nursing major, foreign language for an international business major), the school does not need to allow that the requirement be substituted. Fur-

thermore, providing such modifications at the high school level may actually restrict the admissions eligibility of a student to some institutions. Madaus (2003) explores in greater detail issues related to course substitutions.

Attending college is an important and attainable goal for many students with disabilities

---

Final Thoughts

Attending college is an important and attainable goal for many students with disabilities. However, significant differences occur in the ways that services are furnished at the secondary and postsecondary levels. The information in this article is intended to provide students and families in the transition process—as well as the secondary school professionals who work with them—important and useful information. Additional resources regarding the transition process appear in the box entitled "Useful Transition Resources." Understanding these differences and allowing the student to be an active participant in the decision-making process are vital to promoting successful transition.

References

Americans with Disabilities Act of 1990, 42 U.S.C, § 12101 *et seq.*

Brinckerhoff, L. C., McGuire, J. M., & Shaw, S. F. (2002), *Postsecondary education and transition for students with learning disabilities* (2nd ed.). Austin, TX: PRO-ED.

Heyward, Lawton, & Associates, (1990). *Access to 504: A complete reference guide to Section 504*. Atlanta, GA: Author.

Individuals with Disabilities Education Act Amendments of 1997, 20 U.S.C. § 1400 *et seq.*

Madaus, J. W. (2003), What high school students with learning disabilities need to know about college foreign language requirements: *TEACHING Exceptional Children, 36*(2), 62–67,

Madaus, J. W., & Shaw, S. F. (2004). Section 504: The differences in the regulations regarding secondary and postsecondary education. *Intervention in School and Clinic, 40*(2), 81–87.

McGuire, J. M., & Shaw, S. F. (1989), *Resource guide of support services for students with learning disabilities in Connecticut colleges and universities* (Rev. ed.) Storrs, CT: A. J. Pappanikou Center on Special Education and Rehabilitation: A University Affiliated Program, University of Connecticut. (Revised, 1996)

Rehabilitation Act of 1973, Section 504, Pub. L. 93-112, 29 U.S.C. 794 (1977).

Joseph W. Madaus (*CEC CT Federation), Director. University Program for Students With Learning Disabilities, Neag School of Education, University of Connecticut, Storrs.*

Address correspondence to the author at Department of Educational Psychology, University of Connecticut, 249 Glenbrook Road, Unit 2064, Storrs, CT 06269 (e-mail: joseph.madaus@uconn.edu).

From *Teaching Exceptional Children,* Vol. 37, No. 3, January/February 2005, pp. 32-37. Copyright © 2005 by Council for Exceptional Children. Reprinted by permission.

emergent literacy skills, speech-language approach to, 69–73
emotional and behavioral disorders (EBD), 95–115; teacher self-awareness and students with, 106–111
emotional realm, 54
emotional triggers, teachers and, 106–107
English as a Second Language (ESL) students, 61–68
enrichment programs, gifted students and, 171–172
"essential" standard, 18–21
executive realm, 55

F

failure cycle, 39
family involvement: in transition to middle school, 189; with postsecondary institution, 198; SAM and, 10–11
Far Side cartoon, 177
Friend, Marilyn, interview with, 3–6
friendship groups, for improving social skills, 53–57
friendships: group counseling to improve, 55–56; transition from middle school to high school and, 194
frustration, of students and classroom management, 114
Fukuyama, Francis, 160, 161
fusiform face area, 78
fusiform gyrus, left, 175

G

Gallaudet University, 120
GED teacher, 104–105
general education, student learning and, 8–12
genetic disease, 153–155
gentle intervention, 34
gifted students: guidelines for parents and educators of, 169–173; reading and, 174–176; twice-exceptional students and, 177–183
Grandma's Rule, of classroom management, 113
group counseling, for improving social skills, 53–57

H

head size, autism and, 78

hearing-impaired children. *See* deaf children
high school: transition from, to college, 195–199; transition from middle schools to, 193–194
high-probability request sequences, classroom management and, 113
humor: inarticulate students and, 89; students with emotional and behavioral disorders and, 109–110
hyperlexia, 174–176
hyperresponsivity, tactile strategies and, 125–126

I

IDEA. *See* Individuals with Disabilities Education Act
identification, early: of autism, 77–79; of learning disabilities, 25–28
IEP (Individualized Education Program), 14–16, 131, 132, 133, 156, 157, 158; goals of, 17–21; service-learning and, 81
implementation standard, 17–18
inarticulate students, 87–91
Incarcerated Education Program, 104–105
inclusion, 3–6, 7–13, 14–16; music and, 29–32; service-learning activities and, 80–86; of severely disabled students, 131–136
independence: in middle school, 192; scaffolding and, 39–44
Individualized Education Plans. *See* IEP
Individuals with Disabilities Education Act (IDEA), 3–4, 8–9, 14, 157; alternate assessment, 84–85; on language differences, 61–68
instruction, choice, 141–142
instructional decision making, assessment and, 14–16
integration, paradox of differentiation and, 7–13
integration options, for the severely disabled, 131–136
integrity standard, 17–18
internal dyssynchrony, giftedness and, 171
Internet, sharing information on genetic diseases and, 154–155
interpersonal realm, 55–56
interventions: for learning disabilities, 26–28; relationship building and, 33–35

J

jail, teaching in, 104–105

K

kinesthetic formats, twice-exceptional students and, 178, 179–180

L

labeling, learning disabilities and, 25
language: differences in processing, 88–89; music and, 29, 30; LD identification and, 26; severely disabled and, 144–149
language differences, in second-language students, 61–68
language impairment: in second-language students, 61–68; inarticulate students and, impairment, 87–91
learning differences, 45–49
learning disabilities, 39–57, 157, 159; transition to college and, 195–199; transition to high school and, 193–194; early identification of, 25–28; versus language differences, 61–68
least restrictive environment (LRE), 131
legislation, progress for deaf individuals and, 121–122
lexicon, noncategorical, 10
life experience differences, second-language students and, 65–68
Life Skills Program, 54
loneliness, social skills and, 55–56

M

mainstreaming. *See* inclusion
manic depression, 98–99
measurement strategies, 11
medication, 164–165
mental health: deaf individuals and, 121; psychiatric disorders and 95–103; emotional and behavioral disorders and, 108–109
mental retardation, communication and children with, 144–149
middle school: transition from elementary to, 187–192; transition from, to high school, 193–194
modifications, of games, 17–21
mood disorders, 98–99

Index

movement: inarticulate students and, 88, 89; twice-exceptional students and, 180

multidisciplinary teams, second-language students and, 61–68

music, in inclusive environment, 29–32

N

No Child Left Behind (NCLB), integration and, 8, 9, 85

O

observation, for LD identification, 26

obsessions, 99

obsessive-compulsive disorder, 99, 100

oppositional defiant disorder, 96. *See also* emotional and behavioral disorders

organizational techniques, twice-exceptional students and, 181–182

P

parental advocacy, 153–155

parents, and a gifted child, 170

pay-off, of misbehaving, 113, 114

peer support programs, for transition to middle school, 191

peer tutoring, service-learning activities, and 80–86

Penny Transfer Technique, 108

performance, disappointing school, 45–49

pervasive developmental disorder, 101

phonemic awareness, 69–73

phonological decoding, reading and, 69–73

Player's Choice, 113

politics, attention deficit disorder and, 160–163

positive behavior support (PBS), 10

positive reinforcement, classroom management and, 107–108, 113

posttraumatic stress disorder, 99–100

preference assessment, for choice-making, 138–139

Premack Principle, 113

prevention strategies, for difficult behaviors, 113–114

principals, collaboration and, 4, 5, 6

processing language, differences in, 88–89

professional development, 47–49

progeria, 154

psychiatric disorders, 95–103

psychoactive medications, 164–165

psychopharmacology, child, 95–103

psychotic disorders, 100–101

Public Law 107-110 (NCLB), 8, 9, 85

punishment, relationship building and, 34

R

reading, 174–176; speech-language approach to, 69–73

reading deficits, early intervention and, 25

refusals, inarticulate students and, 89–90

Regular Education Initiative, 7–8

Rehabilitation Act of 1974, 156, 157, 158, 195–199

Relationship Development Intervention (RDI), 79

relationships, building, 33–35

resistance, inarticulate students and, 89–90

Ritalin, 97, 160–163

rubric: for assessment, 14–15; spelling, 50–52

S

safety standard, 17–18

SAMAN (Schoolwide Applications Model Analysis System), 9, 11

scaffolded instruction, 39–44; guidelines for, 42; resources for, 44

schizophrenia, 100–101

school-centered planning, 10, 11

Schools Attuned, 48–49

Schoolwide Applications Model (SAM), 9–13

schoolwide approach, to inclusion, 8–9

second-language acquisition, , 61–68; stages of, 64

Section 504, of Rehabilitation Act, 156, 157, 158, 195–199

selective serotonin reuptake inhibitors (SSRIs), 98

self-awareness, teacher, and students with emotional and behavioral disorders, 106–111

self-disclosure, of LDs to postsecondary schools, 196–197

self-esteem, low, and poor social skills, 53–57

self-management strategies, classroom management and, 112

separation anxiety disorder, 99

service-learning opportunities, 80–86

severe disabilities: inclusion of students with, 131–136; transition to middle school of students with, 187–192

site leadership team, 10, 11

skill actualization, 145–149

social interaction, transition from middle school to high school and, 194

social skills: improving, 10, 53–57, 112–115; music and, 30–31

socialization: autism and, 78; gifted child and, 171; team sports and, 18; transition to high school and, 193–194

special education, reform of, 7–8

speech-language, atypical, 87–91

speech-language approach to reading, 69–73

speech-language pathologist, severely disabled and the, 144–149

spelling assessment, 50–52

sports, inclusion in, 17–21

stigma, learning disabilities and, 25

superior temporal cortex, 175

supportive environment, for the learning disabled, 39–44

T

tactile defensiveness, 125–126

tactile modeling, 123

tactile mutual attention, 124

tactile strategies: for blind and severely disabled students, 123–127; twice-exceptional students and, 179–180

talented students. *See* gifted students

T-chart, for assessment, 16

teachers: burnout, 108–109; and a gifted child, 170, 179–182; improving students' social skills, 56–57; inarticulate students and, 87; self-awareness of, and students with emotional and behavioral disorders, 106–111

team sports. *See* sports

technology, and the deaf, 119, 121

Telecommunications Act, 122

testing: learning disabilities and, 25–26; ESL students, 64–65. *See also* assessment

titration, 97

touch. *See* tactile strategies

Tourettes disorder, 101

transition: to high school, 193–194; to middle school, 187–192; to college, 195–199

treatment, for psychiatric disorders, 95–103twice-exceptional students, 177–183

U

uneven development, and the gifted child, 1790–171

unintentional behaviors, inarticulate students and, 90, 91

V

venting, students with emotional and behavioral disorders and, 108–109

verbal and nonverbal disabilities, social skills and, 56–57

visually impaired students, tactile strategies for, 123–127

vocational rehabilitation, for deaf individuals, 119

W

War Against Boys, The (Sommers), 161

Test Your Knowledge Form

We encourage you to photocopy and use this page as a tool to assess how the articles in *Annual Editions* expand on the information in your textbook. By reflecting on the articles you will gain enhanced text information. You can also access this useful form on a product's book support Web site at *http://www.mhcls.com/online/*.

NAME: _____ DATE: _____

_____

TITLE AND NUMBER OF ARTICLE:

_____

BRIEFLY STATE THE MAIN IDEA OF THIS ARTICLE:

_____

_____

LIST THREE IMPORTANT FACTS THAT THE AUTHOR USES TO SUPPORT THE MAIN IDEA:

_____

_____

WHAT INFORMATION OR IDEAS DISCUSSED IN THIS ARTICLE ARE ALSO DISCUSSED IN YOUR TEXTBOOK OR OTHER READINGS THAT YOU HAVE DONE? LIST THE TEXTBOOK CHAPTERS AND PAGE NUMBERS:

_____

_____

LIST ANY EXAMPLES OF BIAS OR FAULTY REASONING THAT YOU FOUND IN THE ARTICLE:

_____

_____

LIST ANY NEW TERMS/CONCEPTS THAT WERE DISCUSSED IN THE ARTICLE, AND WRITE A SHORT DEFINITION:

We Want Your Advice

ANNUAL EDITIONS revisions depend on two major opinion sources: one is our Advisory Board, listed in the front of this volume, which works with us in scanning the thousands of articles published in the public press each year; the other is you—the person actually using the book. Please help us and the users of the next edition by completing the prepaid article rating form on this page and returning it to us. Thank you for your help!

ANNUAL EDITIONS: Educating Exceptional Children 06/07

ARTICLE RATING FORM

Here is an opportunity for you to have direct input into the next revision of this volume.
We would like you to rate each of the articles listed below, using the following scale:

1. **Excellent: should definitely be retained**
2. **Above average: should probably be retained**
3. **Below average: should probably be deleted**
4. **Poor: should definitely be deleted**

Your ratings will play a vital part in the next revision.
Please mail this prepaid form to us as soon as possible.
Thanks for your help!

RATING	ARTICLE
	1. An Interview With Dr. Marilyn Friend
	2. Rethinking Inclusion: Schoolwide Applications
	3. Assessment That Drives Instruction
	4. Meaningful Inclusion of All Students in Team Sports
	5. Making the Case for Early Identification and Intervention for Young Children at Risk for Learning Disabilities
	6. Music in the Inclusive Environment
	7. Building Relationships With Challenging Children
	8. Providing Support for Student Independence Through Scaffolded Instruction
	9. Celebrating Diverse Minds
	10. No More Friday Spelling Tests? An Alternative Spelling Assessment for Students With Learning Disabilities
	11. Group Intervention: Improving Social Skills of Adolescents with Learning Disabilities
	12. Language Differences or Learning Difficulties
	13. A Speech-Language Approach to Early Reading Success
	14. When Does Autism Start?
	15. Service-Learning Opportunities That Include Students With Moderate and Severe Disabilities
	16. Inscrutable or Meaningful? Understanding and Supporting Your Inarticulate Students
	17. Psychiatric Disorders and Treatments: A Primer for Teachers
	18. I Want to Go Back to Jail
	19. The Importance of Teacher Self-Awareness in Working With Students With Emotional and Behavioral Disorders
	20. Classroom Problems That Don't Go Away
	21. A Half-Century of Progress for Deaf Individuals
	22. Using Tactile Strategies With Students Who Are Blind and Have Severe Disabilities
	23. Making Inclusion a Reality for Students With Severe Disabilities
	24. Choice Making: A Strategy for Students With Severe Disabilities

RATING	ARTICLE
	25. Empowering Students With Severe Disabilities to Actualize Communication Skills
	26. Savior Parents
	27. Accommodations for Students With Disabilities: Removing Barriers to Learning
	28. Trick Question
	29. Finding What Works
	30. Understanding the Young Gifted Child: Guidelines for Parents, Families, and Educators
	31. Read All About It
	32. Teaching Strategies for Twice-Exceptional Students
	33. Moving From Elementary to Middle School: Supporting a Smooth Transition for Students With Severe Disabilities
	34. The Transition from Middle School to High School
	35. Navigating the College Transition Maze: A Guide for Students with Learning Disabilities

(Continued on next page)

BUSINESS REPLY MAIL
FIRST CLASS MAIL PERMIT NO. 551 DUBUQUE IA

POSTAGE WILL BE PAID BY ADDRESEE

McGraw-Hill Contemporary Learning Series
2460 KERPER BLVD
DUBUQUE, IA 52001-9902

ABOUT YOU

Name _____   Date _____

Are you a teacher? ☐   A student? ☐
Your school's name _____

Department _____

Address _____   City _____   State _____   Zip _____

School telephone # _____

YOUR COMMENTS ARE IMPORTANT TO US!

Please fill in the following information:
For which course did you use this book?
_____

Did you use a text with this ANNUAL EDITION? ☐ yes ☐ no
What was the title of the text?
_____

What are your general reactions to the *Annual Editions* concept?
_____

Have you read any pertinent articles recently that you think should be included in the next edition? Explain.
_____

Are there any articles that you feel should be replaced in the next edition? Why?
_____

Are there any World Wide Web sites that you feel should be included in the next edition? Please annotate.
_____

May we contact you for editorial input? ☐ yes ☐ no
May we quote your comments? ☐ yes ☐ no

3/07

ML